TRADE MARKS
THE NEW LAW

TRADE MARKS
THE NEW LAW

Alison Firth, MA, MSc, *Barrister*
Senior Lecturer, Intellectual Property Law Unit,
Centre for Commercial Law Studies
Queen Mary and Westfield College
University of London

JORDANS
1995

Published by
Jordan Publishing Limited
21 St Thomas Street
Bristol BS1 6JS

© Jordan Publishing Limited 1995

British Library Cataloguing-in-Publication Data
A catalogue record for this book is available from the British Library.

ISBN 0 85308 236 7

Typeset by Create Publishing Services Limited, Bath
Printed by Henry Ling Ltd, The Dorset Press, Dorchester

PREFACE

31 October 1994 was a watershed in trade mark law. On that day the Trade Marks Act 1994 came into effect. The effects of previous legislation will be felt for a while. The complexion of the register will continue to reflect the former regime, but a wider range of registrations will be made under the new law. Registry practice has had to change to accommodate this, but where old practice is not clearly displaced, it will continue. New tests for infringement will apply from commencement, and decisions are already being handed down, but prior actions will be governed by the Trade Marks Act 1938. Trade may be continued where this previously did not infringe. The old landscape is present, but UK law is flowing in a new direction, under the influence of European harmonisation. The Community Trade Mark and Madrid Protocol for the international registration of marks have yet to take effect, but the Trade Marks Act is ready for them.

This book attempts to place the Act in its legal and commercial context. I hope that it will be useful to specialist and non-specialist lawyers, company officers, trade mark professionals and those responsible for trading standards, and that students and academic colleagues will find it helpful reading.

I would like to thank colleagues, former colleagues, students and researchers at Queen Mary and Westfield College for support and for helpful discussion. I have benefited enormously from QMW's seat on the Standing Advisory Committee on Industrial Property. Special thanks go to Dr Herchel Smith, whose generosity led to the founding of the Intellectual Property Law Unit at QMW; to Ellen Gredley and to Shelley Lane; and thanks to Julian Hickey for help with proof-reading. I would also like to thank my chambers. My son, William Thompson, has encouraged me by his cheerful presence and his computer expertise. He and his father Stephen helped save the day after my portable computer was damaged. Warm thanks to them. I am also very appreciative of the efforts of David Chaplin, Mollie Dickenson and their colleagues at Jordans. Any errors, of course, remain my own.

The law is stated as at March 1995.

Alison Firth
March 1995

CONTENTS

Preface   v
Table of Cases   xi
Table of Statutes   xxi
Table of Statutory Instruments   xxv
Table of European Legislation and International Treaties   xxvii

Chapter 1   THE COMMERCIAL FUNCTIONS OF A TRADE MARK   1
            Introduction   1
            Competitors and Consumers   3
            Goods and Services   6
            Products and Businesses   8
            Guarantees of Origin   9
            Indications of Quality   10
            Vehicles for Advertising   11
            Special Category Marks   12
            Other Uses of Marks   13

Chapter 2   THE MARK ITSELF   15
            Impact Upon the Senses   15
            Suitability for Marking and the 'Integral Mark' Problem   17
            Shapes of Goods or their Packaging – Functionality and
                Substantial Value   17
            Compound Marks   19
            'Substantial Value' Generally   19
            Suitability for Advertising; Slogans   20
            Entering on the Register   20
            Ability to Distinguish   21
            Non-distinctive Signs   22
            Inappropriate Signs   25
            Choosing a Mark   26

Chapter 3   LEGAL MODES OF PROTECTION   27
            Historical Background   27
            Passing off and other Torts   29
            Registration   36
            Civil Proceedings for Infringement   37
            Criminal Sanctions   37
            Personnel of Trade Mark Law   37

Chapter 4   LIMITS TO TRADE MARK PROTECTION   39
            Introduction   39
            Intrinsic Limits   39

Territorial Limits	41
Extrinsic Limits	43

Chapter 5   REGISTRATION   46
The Criteria   46
The Process   48
The Obstacles   50
Overcoming the Obstacles   50
Conflict with Earlier Marks   55
Oppositions and Observations   60
Appeals and Stays   61
Duration and Renewals   61
Transitional Provisions   61
Special Category Marks   63

Chapter 6   USING THE MARK   64
Introduction   64
The Significance of Use   64
Manner of Use   64
Problems of Use   66
Educating Customers and Consumers   67

Chapter 7   PURSUING INFRINGEMENTS   69
Introduction, Routes and Remedies   69
The Exclusive Rights of the Proprietor under the 1938 and
    1994 Acts   69
Comparative Advertising   72
Non Trade Mark Use   73
Comparison of Marks and Products under the 1994 Act   74
Marks with a Reputation   77
Well-known Marks   79
Manner of Infringing Use   79
Use in Relation to the Proprietor's Goods or Services   80
Other Causes of Action   81
Remedies and Seizure Provisions   82
Criminal Provisions   83
Infringement – Transitional Provisions   85

Chapter 8   DEFENDING INFRINGEMENT PROCEEDINGS   86
Prior Considerations; Threats   86
Challenging the Claims   87
Interlocutory Tactics   87
Justifying Use – Substantive Defences   88
Attacking the Mark   90
Settlement   90

Chapter 9   CANCELLATION OF REGISTRATION   91
             Introduction   91
             Grounds – Invalidity   92
             Grounds – Revocation   94
             Procedures   96

Chapter 10   LICENSING OTHERS TO USE THE MARK   98
             Introduction   98
             The Licensee   99
             General and Limited Licences   101
             Quality Control   101
             Other Terms   102
             Impact of Competition Laws   102

Chapter 11   ASSIGNMENT OF MARKS   104
             Marks and Goodwill   104
             Assignment with Business Goodwill   105
             Assignment without Business Goodwill   106
             Formalities and Pitfalls   107
             Specific Cases and Transactions   108
             Transitional Provisions   110

Chapter 12   SPECIAL CATEGORY MARKS   111
             Introduction   111
             Certification Marks   113
             Collective Marks   117
             Well-known Marks   119

Chapter 13   TRADE MARKS IN EUROPE   122
             Introduction   122
             Implementation of the Directive and Enforcement of Trade
                 Mark Rights in Other European Union Member States   122
             The Community Trade Mark   123
             Free Movement and Competition Rules   129
             Anti-counterfeiting Measures   132

Chapter 14   TRADE MARKS WORLDWIDE   133
             Varieties of System   133
             The Paris Convention for the Protection of Industrial Property   134
             The Madrid Arrangement   135
             The Madrid Protocol   136
             GATT and the Agreement on Trade-related Aspects of
                 Intellectual Property Rights (TRIPS)   138

Appendix 1   TRADE MARKS ACT 1994   139

Appendix 2   THE TRADE MARKS RULES 1994   203

Appendix 3   FIRST COUNCIL DIRECTIVE OF 21 DECEMBER 1988 TO
APPROXIMATE THE LAWS OF THE MEMBER STATES
RELATING TO TRADE MARKS   231

Index   241

TABLE OF CASES

References are to paragraph numbers.

Ad-Lib Club Ltd v Granville [1971] 2 All ER 300, [1972] RPC 673, [1971] FSR 1   3.12
Advocaat, *see* Erven Warnink Besloten Vennootschap v J Townend & Sons (Hull)
American Cyanamid Co v Ethicon [1975] AC 396, [1975] 2 WLR 316, [1975] 1 All
    ER 504, HL   7.41
American Greetings Corpn's Application, Re [1984] 1 WLR 189, [1984] 1 All ER
    426, [1984] RPC 329, HL; *affirming* [1983] 1 WLR 912, [1983] 2 All ER 609,
    [1984] RPC 329, CA; *affirming* [1983] 1 WLR 269, [1983] 2 All ER 609, [1984]
    RPC 329   10.5
American Tobacco v Guest (1892) 9 RPC 218, ChD   8.1
Anheuser-Busch Inc v Budejovicky Budvar Narodni Podnik [1984] FSR 413, (1984)
    128 SJ 398, (1984) 81 LS Gaz 1369, CA   3.11, 12.6
Annabel's (Berkeley Square) Ltd v Schock (G) (trading as Annabel's Escort Agency)
    [1972] RPC 838, [1972] FSR 261, CA   3.9, 7.10
Anti-Monopoly [1978] BIE 39 (Holland)   7.21
Application by Union Inter-Syndicale des Marques Collectives, Re an [1922] 2 Ch
    653, (1922) 39 RPC 97   12.2, 12.12
Aquascutum v Cohen & Wilks (1909) 26 RPC 651, ChD   4.5
Argyllshire Weavers v A Macauley (Tweeds) Ltd [1964] RPC 477, 1965 SLT 21   12.4
Aristoc v Rysta [1945] AC 68, [1945] 1 All ER 34, (1945) 62 RPC 65, HL; *reversing sub*
    nom Rysta Ltd's Application, Re, Re Aristoc Ltd's Opposition [1943] 1 All ER 400,
    (1943) 60 RPC 87, CA   7.7
Associated Newspapers (Holdings) v Insert Media Ltd [1991] 1 WLR 571, [1991] 3
    All ER 535, [1991] FSR 380, CA; *affirming* [1990] 1 WLR 900, [1990] 2 All ER
    803, (1990) 134 SJ 636   3.13, 3.16
Athletes Foot Marketing Associates Inc v Cobra Sports Ltd [1980] RPC 343   3.11
Autodrome TM [1969] RPC 564, [1969] FSR 320   1.23
Avon TM [1985] RPC 43, Trade Marks Registry   5.17, 9.8

BAT Cigaretten-Fabriken GmbH v EC Commission [1985] ECR 363, [1985] 2
    CMLR 470, [1985] FSR 533, European Ct of Justice   13.22
Balden v Shorter [1933] Ch 427, [1933] All ER Rep 249, 102 LJ Ch 191   3.21
Bale and Church Ltd v Sutton, Parsons and Sutton and Astrah Products (1934) 51
    RPC 129, CA   5.29
Bali Trade Mark (No 2) [1978] FSR 192   5.26
Baume & Co v Moore (AH) [1958] Ch 907, [1958] 2 WLR 797, [1958] RPC 226, CA   8.11
Bayer Dental [1992] 4 CMLR 61   13.21
Bay-o-nox [1990] 4 CMLR 429   10.21, 13.21
Beecham v Sainsbury [1987] EIPR D-234   8.10
Bernadin (Alain) et Cie v Pavilion Properties Ltd [1967] RPC 581, [1967] FSR 341   3.11
Bestobell Paints Ltd v Bigg [1975] FSR 421, (1975) 119 SJ 678   3.21, 7.10
Betts v Wilmott (1871) LR 6 Ch App 239   4.12
Birmingham Vinegar Brewery Co v Powell [1897] AC 710, 66 LJ Ch 763, *sub nom*
    Powell v Birmingham Vinegar Brewery Co Ltd (1897) 14 RPC 720, HL   1.26, 3.10
Blue Paraffin TM [1977] RPC 473, CA   2.27

Bollinger (J) v Costa Brava Wine Co Ltd (No 3) [1960] Ch 262, [1959] 3 WLR 966,
    [1960] RPC 16   12.18
Bon Matin TM [1988] RPC 553   9.12
Bostik v Sellotape [1994] RPC 556, [1994] TLR 14, ChD   3.9, 3.14
Bostitch Trade Mark [1963] RPC 183, ChD   1.5, 1.26, 1.28
Boswell-Wilkie Circus (Pty) Ltd v Brian Boswell Circus (Pty) Ltd [1986] FSR 479,
    [1985] FSR 434, SC of S Africa Appellate Division   3.18, 4.7
Bristol Conservatories Ltd v Conservatories Custom Built Ltd [1989] RPC 455,
    CA   3.7, 3.13, 7.26
Bristol-Myers Co v RH Macy & Co 151 F Supp 513, 113 USPQ 274, (1957)   9.15
British Diabetic Association [1992] 11 EIPR D-242   4.2
British Legion v British Legion Club (Street) Ltd (1931) 48 RPC 555, (1931) 47 TLR
    571   3.12, 4.2
British Medical Association v Marsh (1931) 48 RPC 565, (1931) 47 TLR 572   3.12, 4.2
Bud TM [1988] RPC 535   5.38
Buler TM [1975] RPC 275   5.26
Bulmer (HP) Ltd and Showerings Ltd v J Bollinger SA and Champagne Lanson Pere
    et Fils [1978] RPC 79, [1977] 2 CMLR 625, CA; *affirming* [1976] RPC 97, [1975] 2
    CMLR 479   12.18
Burroughs (James) Distillers v Speymalt Whisky Distributors [1991] RPC 130,
    [1989] SLT 561, 1989 SCLR 255   4.8, 4.10

Cadbury Ltd v Ulmer GmbH [1988] FSR 385   3.17
Cadbury-Schweppes Proprietary Ltd v The Pub Squash Co Proprietary Ltd [1981] 1
    WLR 193, [1981] 1 All ER 213, [1981] RPC 429, PC; [1980] 2 NSWLR 864n   1.30, 3.9
Campari [1978] 2 CMLR 397   13.20
Canadian Shredded Wheat Co v Kellog Co of Canada Ltd [1938] 1 All ER 618,
    (1938) 55 RPC 125, PC   9.6
Caplets, *see* Johnson & Johnson Autralia Pty Ltd v Sterling Pharmaceuticals Pty Ltd
Carless, Capel & Leonard v Pilmore Bedford (1928) 45 RPC 205   7.33
Cassis de Dijon [1979] ECR 64, [1979] 3 CMLR 494   13.23
Celia Clarke, Re 17 USPQ 2d 1238 (Trademark Trial and Appeal Board, 1990)   2.4, 2.20
Centrafarm BV v American Home Products Corpn (No 3/78) [1978] ECR 1823,
    [1979] 1 CMLR 326, [1979] FSR 189   13.23
Centrafarm BV and Adriaan De Peijper v Winthrop BV (No 16/74) [1974] ECR
    1183, [1974] 2 CMLR 480, [1975] FSR 161   13.23
Champagne, *see* Bollinger (J) v Costa Brava Wine Co Ltd (No 3); Taittinger SA v
    Allbev Ltd
Cheetah TM [1993] FSR 263, ChD   1.23
Chelsea Man Menswear Ltd v Chelsea Girl Ltd [1987] RPC 189, CA; *affirming* [1985]
    FSR 567   3.11
Cheryl Playthings, Re [1962] 1 WLR 543; *sub nom* Cheryl Playthings' Application, Re
    [1962] 2 All ER 86, *sub nom* Rawhide TM [1962] RPC 133   12.26
Chunky TM [1978] FSR 322   2.26
Cnl Sucal v Hag, *see* SA-Cnl Sucal NV v Hag Gf AG
Coast to Coast, *see* Unidoor v Marks & Spencer
Coats (J & P) Ltd's Application [1936] 2 All ER 975, (1936) 53 RPC 355, 155 LT 127   2.26
Coca-Cola Co v AG Barr & Co [1961] RPC 387   3.9

Coca-Cola Trade Mark, Re [1986] 1 WLR 695, [1986] 2 All ER 274, [1986] RPC
    421, HL   2.7, 2.8, 2.15
Colgate-Palmolive Ltd v Markwell Finance Ltd [1989] RPC 497, CA; *affirming* [1988]
    RPC 283   1.13, 1.29, 4.8
Compaq Computers Corpn v Dell Computer Corpn [1992] FSR 93, [1992] BCC
    484   3.21
Consten and Grundig, *see* Etablissements Consten SARL and Grundig-
    Verkaufs-GmbH v EC Commission
Cos Trade Mark [1993] RPC 67   5.20
Creusois v Seguy [1982] 10 EIPR D-213 (France)   12.2
Crosfield's Application [1910] 1 Ch 130, (1909) 26 RPC 561   2.26

Dalgety Spillers Foods Ltd v Food Brokers Ltd [1994] FSR 504, (1993) *The Times*,
    2 December   3.9, 5.14
Dallas Cowboys Cheerleaders 604 F 2d 200, 203 USPQ 161   7.12, 7.30
Day v Brownrigg (1878) 10 ChD 294, 48 LJ Ch 173, 39 LT 553, CA   4.7
Dee Corp's Applications [1989] 3 All ER 948, [1990] RPC 159, CA; *affirming* [1989]
    FSR 266   1.18
Def Lepp Music v Stuart-Brown [1986] RPC 273   4.8
Deutsche Grammophon GmbH v Metro-SB-Grossmarkte GmbH & Co KG [1971]
    ECR 487, [1971] CMLR 631, ECJ   13.20, 13.23
Diamond T Motor Car Co's Application [1921] 2 Ch 583, (1921) 38 RPC 373   2.14, 5.23
Dome Blacklead, *see* James's TM
Dormeuil Freres SA v Feraglow [1990] RPC 449   7.40
Dunhill v Bartlett (1922) 39 RPC 426   3.9
Duracell International v Ever Ready [1989] FSR 71   7.37

Eastman Photographic Materials Co Ltd v Comptroller-General of Patents, Designs,
    and Trade-Marks, Solio Trade-Mark, Re [1898] AC 571, (1898) 15 RPC 476   2.28
Edwards' Application (1946) 63 RPC 19   2.33
Electrolux Ltd v Electrix Ltd (1954) 71 RPC 23, CA; *affirming* (1953) 70 RPC 127   6.9
Elida Gibbs v Colgate-Palmolive [1983] FSR 95   3.9
Erven Warnink Besloten Vennootschap v J Townend & Sons (Hull) [1979] AC 731,
    [1979] 3 WLR 68, [1980] RPC 31, 85, HL; *reversing* [1980] RPC 31, 55, [1978]
    FSR 473, CA; [1980] RPC 31, [1978] FSR 1   3.5, 3.7, 3.10, 3.13,
        3.17, 3.22, 4.2, 12.4, 12.18
Esso TM [1972] RPC 283, [1971] FSR 624   5.18
Etablissements Consten SARL and Grundig-Verkaufs-GmbH v EC Commission
    [1966] ECR 299, [1966] CMLR 419   13.20
Eurim-Pharm v Bundesgesundheitsamt (C-207/91) (1993) *Financial Times*, 13 July,
    ECJ   13.25
Eurofix and Bauco (UK) v Hilti AG [1989] 4 CMLR 677, [1988] FSR 473, EC
    Commission; appeal dismissed 2.3.1994, ECJ   13.22
Evans v Eradicure [1972] RPC 808, [1972] FSR 137   4.8
Everglide, *see* Unic SA v Lyndeau Products
Exxate TM [1986] RPC 567, ChD   5.18

Felix/Loesje [1993] IER 56 (Holland)   1.36

Ferodo Ltd's Application (1945) 62 RPC 111   12.30
Floradix TM [1974] RPC 583   5.31
Ford Motor Co [1994] RPC 545, QBD; [1993] RPC 399, Registered Designs
   Appeals Tribunal; (1994) *The Times*, 16 December, HL   1.3
Ford-Werke AG's Application (1955) 72 RPC 191   2.24, 5.12
Fyffes v Chiquita Brands International Inc [1993] FSR 83, ChD   11.10

GE Trade Mark, Re, *see* General Electric Co (of USA) v General Electric Co
Gallaher v Health Education Bureau [1982] FSR 464   7.5, 7.6
Games Workshop Ltd v Transworld Publishers Ltd [1993] FSR 705, CA   4.6, 7.16
General Electric Co (of USA) v General Electric Co [1972] 1 WLR 729, [1972] 2 All
   ER 507, 116 SJ 412, HL; *reversing sub nom* GE Trade Mark, Re [1970] RPC 339,
   [1970] FSR 113, CA   5.33, 6.12, 11.2
Glenlivet, The, TMs [1993] RPC 461, Board of Trade   1.25
Godiva/Dogiva 231 USPQ 562   7.12, 7.30
Golden Pages TM [1985] FSR 27, Sup Ct of Ireland   4.3
Goodwin v Ivory Soap (1901) 18 RPC 389   7.21
Guccio Gucci SpA v Paolo Gucci [1991] FSR 89   3.18, 4.7

Habib Bank Ltd v Habib Bank AG Zurich [1981] 1 WLR 1265, [1981] 2 All ER 650,
   [1982] RPC 19, CA; *affirming* [1982] RPC 1   3.19, 12.27
Hag, *see* SA-Cnl Sucal NV v Hag Gf AG
Hallelujah TM [1976] RPC 605, Trade Marks Registry   2.35
Handelskwerij G J Bier v Mines des Potasse d'Alsace [1976] ECR 1735   4.10
Harrods Ltd v R Harrod Ltd (1924) 41 RPC 74, (1924) 40 TLR 195, CA   1.17, 1.35, 3.9
Have a Break TM [1993] RPC 217, ChD   2.18
Hermes TM [1982] RPC 425, [1982] Com LR 98   6.8
Hodgkinson & Corby v Wards Mobility Services [1994] 1 WLR 1564, [1995] FSR
   169, [1994] TLR 446, ChD   2.11, 3.9, 3.14, 4.6
Hoffmann-La Roche & Co AG v Centrafarm Vertriebsgesellschaft Pharmazeu-
   tischer Erzeugnisse mBH (No 102/77) [1978] ECR 1139, [1978] 3 CMLR 217,
   [1978] FSR 598, European Ct   13.23, 13.24
Hoge Raad [1985] BIE 23 (Dutch Sup Ct)   2.12
Holly Hobbie Trade Mark, Re, *see* American Greetings Corpn's Application, Re
Hoover v Air-Way [1936] 1 All ER 466, (1936) 53 RPC 399   8.11
Hospital World TM [1967] RPC 595   4.3

IHT Internationale Heiztechnik v Ideal Standard [1995] FSR 59   9.17, 13.24
I.Q. TM [1993] RPC 379, Trade Marks Registry   2.25
I can't believe it's yogurt [1992] RPC 533, Board of Trade   2.18
Imperial Group v Philip Morris [1982] FSR 72, [1982] Com LR 95, CA; *affirming*
   [1980] FSR 146   3.9, 6.9
Imperial Group v Philip Morris [1984] RPC 293   5.12, 5.13
Ind Coope Ltd v Paine & Co Ltd [1983] RPC 326   7.4, 7.8
IRC v Muller & Co's Margarine Ltd [1901] AC 217, [1900–3] All ER Rep 413, 70
   LJKB 677, HL   3.6

Jaffa Cakes, *see* United Biscuits (UK) v Burtons Biscuits

James's TM (1886) 33 ChD 392   2.7, 2.8, 2.15
Jardex, *see* Edwards' Application
Jarman & Platt v I Barget Ltd [1977] FSR 260, CA   2.11
Jaybeam Ltd v Abru Aluminium Ltd [1976] RPC 308, [1975] FSR 334   8.8
Jellinek's Application (1946) 63 RPC 59   5.30, 5.31
Jif Lemon, *see* Reckitt & Colman Products v Borden Inc
Job TM [1993] FSR 118, Trade Marks Registry   10.16, 11.8
Johnson & Johnson Autralia Pty Ltd v Sterling Pharmaceuticals Pty Ltd (1991) 21
    IPR 1, Fed Ct of Australia   6.12, 7.17, 9.15

Karo Step TM [1977] RPC 255   5.37
Kat v Diment [1951] 1 KB 34, [1950] 2 All ER 657, 67 RPC 158   12.18
Kean v McGivan [1982] FSR 119, CA   3.12, 4.2
Keene v Paraglex 653 F 2d 822 (3rd Cir, 1981)   2.10
Kiku TM [1978] FSR 246   2.29
Kleenoff, *see* Bale and Church Ltd v Sutton, Parsons and Sutton and Astrah Products
Kodiak TM [1990] FSR 49, ChD   1.36, 6.4, 6.10

Lancer Trade Mark [1987] RPC 303, CA   5.29
Laura Ashley Ltd v Coloroll Ltd [1987] RPC 1   2.5
Lawton v Dundas (1985) *The Times*, 13 June   2.4
Lease Management Services Ltd v Purnell Secretarial Services Ltd; Canon (South
    West) Ltd, Third Party [1994] TLR 189, (1994) *The Times*, 1 April, CA   1.22
Legal and General Assurance Society v Daniel [1968] RPC 253, [1967] FSR 512,
    (1967) 111 SJ 808, CA; *reversing* [1968] RPC 253, [1967] FSR 481   1.17, 1.35
Lego System A/S v Lego M Lemelstrich [1983] FSR 155, Pat Ct   3.16, 4.4
Levi Strauss v Shah [1985] RPC 371   6.3, 7.21
Levi Strauss v Kimbyr [1994] FSR 335, High Ct of NZ   4.13
Levi Strauss v Wingate [1993] EIPR D-258, (1993) 26 IPR 215, Fed Ct of Aus   8.11
Levy v Walker (1890) 10 ChD 436   7.7
Lexis/Lexus 875 F 2d 1026   7.12, 7.27
London General Omnibus Co Ltd v Felton (1896) 12 TLR 213   3.9
Loudoun Manufacturing Ltd and Another v Courtaulds plc (trading as John Lean
    and Sons) [1994] TLR 74, (1994) *The Times*, 14 February, ChD   5.1, 11.2

McCain International v Country Fair Foods Ltd [1981] RPC 69, CA   2.27, 3.9, 4.5
McDonald's Hamburgers Ltd v Burgerking (UK) Ltd [1987] FSR 112, CA; *reversing*
    [1986] FSR 45, (1985) 4 Tr L 226   7.13
Manganin TM [1967] RPC 271   2.26
Manus v Fullwood (RJ) and Bland Ltd [1949] Ch 208, [1949] 1 All ER 205, (1949) 66
    RPC 71, CA; *affirming* (1948) 65 RPC 329   9.13
Mars GB v Cadbury [1987] RPC 387   7.16
Maxim's v Dye [1977] 1 WLR 1155, [1978] 2 All ER 55, [1977] FSR 364   1.36, 3.11
Millington v Fox (1838) 3 My & Cr 338, 40 ER 210   3.5
Mirage Studios v Counter-Feat Clothing [1991] FSR 145   1.36, 3.13, 3.16, 10.5
Mirage TM IPD 17013   9.14
Molyslip TM [1978] RPC 211, Trade Marks Registry   1.26, 10.16

Mothercare UK Ltd v Penguin Books Ltd [1988] RPC 113, CA   1.36, 4.6, 7.16, 8.11
Motor Lodge [1965] RPC 35   2.28
Murray v King [1986] FSR 116, Fed Ct of Australia   11.16
My Kinda Town v Soll and Grunts Investments [1983] RPC 407, CA; *reversing* [1983]
    RPC 15, [1982] FSR 147, [1981] Com LR 194   3.9

Naamlooze Vennootschap Fabriek van Chocolade en Suikerwerken JC Klene &
    Co's Application (1923) 40 RPC 103   11.17
National Phonograph Co of Australia Ltd v Menck (1911) 28 RPC 229, PC   4.12
Nationwide Building Society v Nationwide Estate Agents [1987] FSR 579, DC   2.35, 3.19
Naylor v Hutson [1994] FSR 63, ChD   1.1
Nerit, *see* Imperial Group v Philip Morris [1982]
Netherlands, Kingdom of v The EC Commission (No 11/76) [1979] ECR 245,
    European Ct   1.3
Nitedals Taendstikfabrik v R Lehmann & Co Ltd (1908) 25 RPC 793   7.8
Northern & Shell v Conde Nast (1994), 9 December, unreported   6.6, 7.54

Office Cleaning Services Ltd v Westminster Window and General Cleaners Ltd
    (trading as Office Cleaning Association) [1946] 1 All ER 320n, 174 LT 229, (1946)
    62 RPC 39, HL; *affirming* [1944] 2 All ER 269, 61 RPC 133, CA   4.5
Old Dutch Houses [1984] BIE 193   2.10
Orient Express Trading Co Ltd's TM [1992] 12 EIPR D-268, IPD 15124   6.10
Origins Natural Resources Inc v Origin Clothing Ltd (1994) 17 November,
    unreported   7.20, 8.11
Orlwoola [1910] 1 Ch 130, (1909) 26 RPC 683, 850   2.27
Oscar TM [1979] RPC 173   9.1, 12.8
Oven Chips, *see* McCain International v Country Fair Foods Ltd
Owens Corning, Re 774 F 2d 1116 (Fed Cir 1985)   2.9

Pagliero v Wallace China 198 F 2d 339 (9th Cir, 1952)   2.10
Pall Corpn v PJ Dahlhausen & Co (C-238/89) [1991] TLR 52, (1991) *The Times*,
    4 February, European Ct   7.52
Parfums Givenchy v Designer Alternatives [1994] RPC 243   3.16, 7.10
Parker-Knoll Ltd v Knoll International [1962] RPC 265, HL; *affirming* sub nom
    Parker-Knoll and Parker-Knoll (Textiles) v Knoll International Britain (Furniture
    and Textiles) [1961] RPC 346, CA; *reversing* [1961] RPC 31   4.7
Parker Knoll v Knoll International [1962] RPC 243, CA   3.18
Parker-Knoll v Knoll Overseas [1985] FSR 349   1.24
Paterson Zochonis & Co v Merfarken Packaging [1986] 3 All ER 522, [1983] FSR
    273, [1982] Com LR 260, CA   7.34
Payton & Co Ltd v Snelling, Lampard & Co Ltd [1901] AC 308, 70 LJ Ch 644, 17
    RPC 628, HL; (1900) 17 RPC 48, CA   3.17
Pepper (Inspector of Taxes) v Hart [1993] AC 593, [1992] 3 WLR 1032, [1993] 1 All
    ER 42, HL; *reversing* [1991] Ch 203, [1991] 2 WLR 483, CA; *affirming* [1990] 1
    WLR 204   1.3
Persil TM [1978] FSR 348, [1978] 1 CMLR 395, EC Commission   13.21
Pfizer v Eurim-Pharm GmbH (No 1/81) [1981] ECR 2913, [1982] 1 CMLR 406,
    [1982] FSR 269, European Ct   13.23

Pharmon BV v Hoechst AG (No 19/84) [1985] 6 ECR 2281, [1985] 3 CMLR 775,
    [1986] FSR 108, European Ct   8.11
Pianotist Co Ltd's Application (1906) 23 RPC 774, ChD   5.28, 7.23
Pickwick International Inc (GB) v Multiple Sound Distributors [1972] 1 WLR 1213,
    [1972] RPC 786, [1972] FSR 427   7.9
Pinto v Badman (1891) 8 RPC 181, (1891) 7 TLR 317, CA   11.1, 11.2
Pirie (Alex) and Son Ltd's Application (1933) 50 RPC 147, 149 LT 199, HL; [1932]
    WN 45, 146 LT 493, (1932) 49 RPC 195, CA   5.26
Polydor and RSO Records Inc v Harlequin Record Shops and Simons Records
    [1982] 2 ECR 329, [1982] 1 CMLR 677, [1982] FSR 358, European Ct   13.25
Pompadour Laboratories Ltd v Stanley Frazer [1966] RPC 7, ChD   1.24
Pound Puppies TM [1988] RPC 530, Board of Trade   2.26
Powell v Birmingham Vinegar Brewery Co Ltd, *see* Birmingham Vinegar Brewery Co
    v Powell
Practice Direction [1994] RPC 617   7.41
Pronuptia de Paris GmbH Frankfurt am Main v Schillgalis (No 161/84) [1986] 1
    ECR 353, [1986] 1 CMLR 414, European Ct   10.17
Provident Financial plc v Halifax Building Society [1994] FSR 81, ChD   1.36, 7.26

Qualitex Co v Jacobson Products Co 13 F 3d 1297, 29 USPQ 2d 1277 (CA 9 1994)   2.9

R v Kent County Council ex parte Price [1993] 9 EIPR D-224, (1994) 158 JPN 78   7.48
R v Veys [1993] FSR 366, CCA   5.37, 7.48
Radio Telefis Eireann v EC Commission (Magill TV Guide Intervening) [1991] II
    ECR 485, [1991] 4 CMLR 586, 669, 745, (1991) *The Times*, 21 October   13.22
Raffles, *see* Imperial Group v Philip Morris [1982]
Ravenhead Brick v Ruabon (1937) 54 RPC 341   7.21
Ravok (M) (Weatherwear) v National Trade Press [1955] 1 QB 554, [1955] 2 WLR
    583, (1955) 72 RPC 110   7.7
Rawhide TM, *see* Cheryl Playthings, Re
Reckitt & Colman Products v Borden Inc [1990] 1 All ER 873, [1990] RPC 341,
    (1990) 134 SJ 784, HL; *affirming* [1988] FSR 601, (1988) 8 Tr LR 97, CA   3.7, 3.8
Reddaway (Frank) & Co Ltd v George Banham & Co Ltd [1896] AC 199, [1895–9]
    All ER Rep 313, 13 RPC 218, HL   3.6, 3.9, 3.13, 9.6
Registrar of Restrictive Trading Agreements v Schweppes [1971] 1 WLR 1148, 115
    SJ 263; sub nom Schweppes Agreement (No 2), Re, Registrar of Restrictive
    Trading Agreements v Schweppes [1971] 2 All ER 1473   4.15
Renault v Thevenoux [1988] 3 CMLR 686   13.26
Reuter (R J) Co Ltd v Muhlens [1954] Ch 50, [1953] 3 WLR 789, 70 RPC 235, CA;
    affirming (1953) 70 RP Ct 102   3.9
Revlon Inc v Cripps & Lee [1980] FSR 85, (1979) 124 SJ 184, CA   4.12
Richards v Butler (1890) 7 RPC 288   7.7
Rickless v United Artists Corp [1988] QB 40, [1987] 2 WLR 945, [1987] FSR 362,
    CA   12.18
Roger's TM (1895) 12 RPC 149, ChD   11.5
RoHo, *see* Hodgkinson & Corby v Wards Mobility Service
Royal Baking Powder Co v Wright, Crossley & Co (1901) 18 RPC 95, HL   3.20

Rysta Ltd's Application, Re, Re Aristoc Ltd's Opposition, *see* Aristoc v Rysta

SA des Manufacturers de Glaces v Tilghman's Patent Sand Blast Co (1883) 25 ChD 1   4.12
SA-Cnl Sucal NV v Hag Gf AG [1990] 1 ECR 3711, [1990] 3 CMLR 571, [1991]
   FSR 99, ECJ   1.13, 13.24
Sabatier (K) TM [1993] RPC 97, Trade Marks Registry   4.10, 7.39
Sanders v Chichester [1994] TLR 620, (1994) *The Times*, 2 December, QBD   3.12
Sangamo-Weston's Application, Re, *see* Weston TM
Schweppes Agreement (No 2), Re, *see* Registrar of Restrictive Trading Agreements v
   Schweppes
Sea Island Cotton Certification Trade Marks [1989] RPC 87, Board of Trade   12.16
Sears plc v Sears Roebuck & Co and Others [1993] RPC 385, ChD   5.43
Sevcon v Lucas CAV [1986] 1 WLR 462, [1986] 2 All ER 104, [1986] RPC 609, HL   8.11
Sheen, *see* Coats (J & P) Ltd's Application
Sheraton Corpn of America v Sheraton Motels Ltd [1964] RPC 202   3.11
Shredded Wheat Co Ltd v Kellogg Co of Great Britain Ltd (1940) 57 RPC 137, HL   9.6
Shredded Wheat's TM No 500,671 'Shredded Wheat', Re; Kellogg Co of Great
   Britain Ltd's Application, Re (1938) 55 RPC 271, CA   9.6
Sinclair Ltd's TM (1932) 49 RPC 123   11.6
Sirdar and Phildar Trade Marks, Re [1975] 1 CMLR D93   13.21
Smith Kline & French Laboratories Ltd's Cimetidine TM [1991] RPC 17, ChD   5.1
Sodastream Ltd v Thorn Cascade Co Ltd [1982] RPC 459, Com LR 64, CA   3.9
Soflens TM [1976] RPC 694, Trade Marks Registry   2.27
Solio Trade-Mark, Re, *see* Eastman Photographic Materials Co Ltd v Comptroller-
   General of Patents, Designs, and Trade-Marks, Solio Trade-Mark, Re
Sony Corp v Anand (No 2) [1982] FSR 200   7.20
Sony KK v Saray Electronics (London) [1983] FSR 302, CA   3.13
Spalding (A G) & Bros v A W Gamage Ltd (1915) 84 LJ Ch 449, (1915) 32 RPC 273,
   31 TLR 328, HL   1.17, 1.27, 1.35, 8.11
Spalding Bros v A W Gamage [1914] 2 Ch 405, [1914–15] All ER Rep 847, 31 RPC
   421   3.6, 3.9, 3.13
Spar (UK) Ltd v Audits of Great Britain Ltd [1986] 5 EIPR D-74   12.1
Spillers' Application, Re, Hovis v Spillers (1954) 71 RPC 234, HL; *affirming* (1953) 70
   RPC 51, CA; *affirming* (1952) 69 RPC 327   7.8
Sport International Bussum BV v Hi-Tec Sports [1988] RPC 329, CA   10.6
Star Industrial Co v Yap Kwee Kor (trading as New Star Industrial Co) [1976] FSR
   256, PC   11.1
Stilton TM [1967] RPC 173, [1967] FSR 15   12.7
Stringfellow v McCain Foods (GB) Ltd [1984] RPC 501, 128 SJ 701, 81 LS Gaz
   2464, CA; *reversing* [1984] FSR 199   3.15, 4.4
Sunbeam Motor Car Company's Application (1916) 33 RPC 389, ChD   11.1

Taittinger SA v Allbev Ltd [1993] FSR 659, [1993] TLR 358, CA; [1993] FSR 641,
   [1993] TLR 62, ChD   2.35, 3.13, 3.16, 7.10, 12.3, 12.4
Taw Manufacturing Co v Notek Engineering Co (1951) 68 RPC 271   5.29
Terrapin (Overseas) v Terranova Industrie CA Kapferer & Co [1976] ECR 1039,
   [1976] 2 CMLR 482   13.24
Tyburn Productions v Conan Doyle [1991] Ch 75, [1990] 3 WLR 167, [1990] 1 All
   ER 909   4.8

Unic SA v Lyndeau Products [1964] RPC 37, ChD   2.5
Unidoor v Marks & Spencer [1988] RPC 275, ChD   1.36
Unilever plc's TM [1984] RPC 155, ChD   2.27
Unilever v Johnson Wax [1989] FSR 145   7.9
Unilever Ltd's (Striped Toothpaste No 2) TM [1987] RPC 13   2.27
UNIS, *see* Application by Union Inter-Syndicale des Marques Collectives, Re an
United Biscuits (UK) v Burtons Biscuits [1992] FSR 14, ChD   3.9, 5.14
Univer TM [1993] RPC 239, ChD   5.27

Val Marks, *see* Naamlooze Vennootschap Fabriek van Chocolade en Suikerwerken
    JC Klene & Co's Application
Visa TM [1985] RPC 323, ChD   1.17
Vitamin Ltd's Application, Re [1956] RPC 1, [1956] 1 WLR 1, [1955] 3 All ER 827   11.2
Volvo AB v Erik Veng (UK) Ltd [1988] ECR 6211, [1989] 4 CMLR 122   13.22

W & G du Cros Ltd's Application (1913) 30 RPC 661   2.25
Walker (John) & Sons Ltd v Henry Ost & Co Ltd [1970] 1 WLR 917, [1970] 2 All ER
    106, [1970] RPC 489   3.17, 4.9, 7.35
Walpamur v Sanderson (1926) 43 RPC 385   9.14
Weston TM [1968] RPC 167, [1968] FSR 77; sub nom Sangamo-Weston's
    Application, Re (1968) 112 SJ 270   11.1
White Horse Distillers Ltd v Gregson Associates Ltd [1984] RPC 61   3.17, 4.9, 7.35
Wilts United Dairies v Thomas Robinson, Sons & Co Ltd [1958] RPC 94, CA;
    affirming [1957] RPC 220   3.13, 3.20, 7.10

X v Caledonian Newspapers and Another [1994] TLR 81, (1994) *The Times*,
    16 February, Ct Sess (OH)   4.10

York Trailer Holdings v Registrar of Trade Marks [1982] 1 All ER 257, [1982] FSR
    111, (1982) 126 SJ 97, HL   2.26
Yorkshire Relish, *see* Birmingham Vinegar Brewery Co v Powell

TABLE OF STATUTES

References are to paragraph numbers.

Civil Jurisdiction and Judgments Act
  1982   4.10
Consumer Protection Act 1987
  s 2(1)   3.25
    (2)(b)   3.25, 10.1
  s 3(2)   10.1
Copyright, Designs and Patents Act
  1988   1.3, 7.43, 7.49
  s 16(4)   7.42
  s 97(2)   7.29
  s 99(4)   7.42
  Sch 4   8.5
Criminal Justice and Public Order Act
  1994
  s 165   7.49
Cutlers Company Act 1623   3.1, 3.3
Cutlers Company Act 1791   3.1, 3.3
Cutlers Company Act 1801   3.1, 3.3
Cutlers Company Act 1814   3.1, 3.3
Cutlers Company Act 1860   3.1, 3.3

Defamation Act 1952
  s 3(1)   3.20
Deregulation and Contracting Out Act
  1994   4.14, 4.15

Hallmarks Act 1973   3.2

Law of Property Act 1925
  s 76   11.10
  s 136   11.4
Law of Property (Miscellaneous
  Provisions) Act 1994   11.10

Merchandise Marks Act 1862   3.1, 3.3
Merchandise Marks Act 1887   3.1, 3.3

Patents Act 1977
  s 30(1)   11.4
  s 36   11.18

  s 70   8.5
Patents, Designs and Trade Marks Act
  1883   3.3
Patents, Designs and Trade Marks Act
  1986   1.17, 2.19, 3.3
Patents, Designs and Trade Marks
  Amendment Act 1888   3.3

Registered Designs Act 1949
  s 26   8.5
Restrictive Trade Practices Act 1976   4.14,
                             10.19, 12.23
  ss 6, 7   4.14
  s 9(3)   4.14
    (5)   4.14
  ss 11, 12   4.14
  s 18(2)   4.14
    (5)   4.14
  s 21(1), (2)   4.15
  s 27A   4.15
  Sch 3   4.15, 10.19
    para 4   4.14
    para 4(1)   4.14
    para 4(2)   4.14

Single European Act 1986   13.1

Trade Descriptions Act 1968   3.1, 3.22,
              5.37, 7.49, 7.51, 10.1, 12.18
Trade Descriptions Act 1972   3.1, 3.22,
                                      10.1
Trade Marks Act 1905   1.26, 3.3, 9.14,
                                      12.2
  s 2   1.4
  s 22   11.2
Trade Marks Act 1914   3.3
Trade Marks Act 1919   3.3
Trade Marks Act 1938   1.5, 1.18, 1.31,
         2.18, 2.26, 2.37, 3.3, 4.6, 5.2,
         5.15, 5.20, 5.31, 5.40, 5.42,
         5.44, 5.48, 6.12, 7.1, 7.3, 7.10,
         7.18, 7.20, 7.26, 8.11, 9.12, 9.16,
         11.3, 11.7, 11.17, 12.6, 14.2

Trade Marks Act 1938–(*contd.*)

s 1	2.19
s 4	7.4, 7.6
(1)	7.4, 7.5, 7.9
(b)	7.13
s 5(2)	7.10, 7.55
s 12	7.18
(1)	5.30
(2)	5.25
s 13	5.45
s 17(1)	11.2
s 18(1)	12.26
s 22(1)	11.2
(3)	11.7, 11.9
(4)	11.8
(7)	11.7, 11.8
s 26	7.18, 9.1
(1)	6.4, 9.14
s 27	12.30
(4)	9.1
s 28	1.5
(3)	10.9
(6)	10.5
s 29(1)(a)	11.3
s 32	9.1
s 33	5.23, 9.1
s 62	1.28
s 68(1), (2)	2.2
(2A)	7.9
Sch 1, para 1(3)	12.7
para 4	9.1

Trade Marks (Amendment) Act

1984	1.17, 3.3
Trade Marks Act 1994	1.2, 1.3, 1.16, 1.18, 1.19, 1.32, 1.34, 1.35, 2.29, 3.3, 4.1, 4.6, 5.2, 5.8, 5.9, 5.15, 5.20, 5.23, 5.31, 5.38, 5.40, 5.47, 5.48, 6.8, 6.11, 7.3, 7.7, 7.8, 7.9, 7.32, 10.7, 10.14, 12.1, 12.2, 12.6, 12.26, 12.31, 13.6, 14.2
s 1	2.1, 2.8, 2.18, 4.3, 9.6
(1)	2.19, 5.1, 9.6
(2)	12.9
s 2(1)	11.2
ss 3–6	9.6
s 3	2.22, 5.11, 9.7, 12.20
(1)	5.11
(a)	2.19
(b)	2.24, 4.5, 9.6
(c)	1.25, 2.26, 2.28, 4.5, 9.6, 12.9

(d)	2.31, 9.6
(2)	2.8, 2.13, 9.7
(c)	2.15
(3)	9.7
(a)	2.35
(b)	2.30, 9.7
(4)	2.35, 9.7
(5)	2.34, 9.9
(6)	5.1, 5.9
s 4	2.22, 2.34, 5.4, 9.9
(2)	2.34
s 5	2.22, 2.32, 7.18
(1)	5.28, 9.11
(2)	9.11
(3)	5.34, 9.11, 12.29
(4)	5.37, 9.11
(a)	5.37
(5)	5.27
s 6	2.32, 5.35, 5.39, 12.29
(2), (3)	5.36
s 7	5.25
ss 9–12	7.54
s 9	1.37, 4.6, 7.16
(1)	6.6, 7.6
s 10	1.23, 1.37, 4.3, 4.6, 6.7, 7.6, 7.24
(1)	7.19, 7.20, 7.21
(2)	7.19, 7.20, 7.22, 7.26
(a)	7.19
(b)	7.19, 7.54
(3)	4.4, 7.1, 7.19, 7.26, 7.27, 7.28, 7.29, 7.36, 7.46, 10.15
(4)	6.7, 7.33, 7.48
(a)	1.23
(d)	7.15
(5)	7.34, 7.35, 12.15
(6)	1.37, 4.6, 6.12, 7.15, 7.36, 7.37, 8.11, 10.4
s 11(1)	8.11
(2)(a)	4.7, 8.11
(b), (c)	8.11
(3)	8.11
s 12(1), (2)	8.11
s 13(1)(a)	2.13, 5.23
(b)	5.24
s 14	7.1, 7.54
(2)	7.1, 7.40
s 15	7.42
s 16	3.26, 7.43
s 18	7.44, 8.11

Trade Marks Act 1994—(*contd.*)

s 19	3.26, 7.43	(c)	5.17
(2)	12.15	s 43	5.44, 9.3
s 20	3.26, 7.43	(3)	9.3
s 21	8.3, 8.4	(5)	9.3
(1)	3.25	s 45	5.25, 5.27
(4)	8.7	(1)	9.1, 9.2
s 22	1.30, 3.24, 11.2, 11.4	(2)(b)	9.2
s 23	11.18	s 46	4.3, 6.6, 6.10, 8.11, 9.8,
s 24(1)	11.8		10.1, 12.16
(2)(a), (b)	11.8	(1)	9.13
(3)	11.4, 11.14	(a)	6.2, 6.6, 9.12, 9.13
(4), (5)	11.22	(b)	6.2, 9.13
(6)	11.5	(c)	6.2, 9.15
s 25(1)	11.13	(d)	6.2, 9.7, 9.8
(3)	11.13, 11.18	(2)	6.7
(a)	11.11	(3)	9.12
(b)	10.10	(4)(a), (b)	9.4
(4)	10.10, 11.13, 11.18	(5)	9.1, 9.12, 9.14
s 26(1)	11.11	(6)	9.5, 9.20
s 28(1)	10.12	s 47	9.8, 12.17
(a)	10.11	(1)	9.6
(b)	10.12, 10.13	(3)(a), (b)	9.4
(3), (4)	6.6	(5)	9.1
s 29(1)	10.8	(6)	9.4, 9.20
s 30(2)	10.9	s 48	8.11, 12.27
(4)	10.9	s 49	5.50, 12.19
(6)	10.9	s 50	5.50, 12.8
s 31	10.8	ss 53, 54	14.18
(1)	2.19, 10.8	s 55(1)(b)	7.32, 12.27
(3)	2.19, 10.8	s 56	4.8, 7.31, 7.32, 12.27, 12.28
(4)–(6)	10.8	(1)	7.31
s 32(2)	5.5	(2)	7.31, 12.27
(a)	5.1	(3)	7.31
(b)	5.1	s 57	2.34, 5.4, 7.39
(c)	5.1	s 58	2.34, 7.39
(d)	5.1	s 59	5.4
(3)	4.3, 5.1	s 60	4.10, 7.39
s 33(1)	5.6	s 64	9.19
(6)	11.21	(5)	9.19
s 34(2)	5.2	s 65	5.2
s 35	5.3	(3)–(5)	5.2
(4)	5.3	s 75	3.26, 7.1
s 36	5.3	s 76	5.42
s 38(1), (2)	5.40	(4)	5.42
(3)	5.40, 5.41	s 77	5.42
s 39(1)	5.21	s 84	3.29
(2)	5.20, 12.7	(4)	3.28
s 40(3)	5.6, 11.3	s 86	3.28
s 41(1)(a), (b)	5.22	s 88	3.29
		s 89	7.45, 12.15

Trade Marks Act 1994—(*contd.*)

ss 90, 91	7.49
s 92	3.27, 7.47, 7.48, 7.49
(4)	7.46
(5)	7.48
s 93	1.16, 7.49
(3)	7.49
ss 94, 95	7.52
s 96	7.49
ss 97, 98	7.51
s 100	6.5, 9.12
s 101	7.53
s 103(1)	4.3
(2)	2.4, 6.7, 7.33
s 105	3.2
Sch 1, para 3	12.20
para 3(1)	12.3
paras 5–8	5.50
para 5(1)	12.20
(2)	11.19, 12.21
para 7	12.22
para 9	12.22
para 10	11.19
para 11	12.22, 12.24
para 12	12.24
para 12(4)–(6)	12.24
Sch 2, para 2	12.9
para 3	12.9
para 3(1)	12.3
para 4	11.20, 12.10
para 5	12.7
paras 6–9	5.50
para 6	12.12
para 6(1)	12.10
para 6(2)	12.10, 12.11
para 7(1)(a)(ii)	12.11

para 7(1)(b)	12.10
para 7(2)	12.10
paras 9, 10	12.12
para 11	5.50, 12.13
para 12	11.20
paras 13, 14	12.15
para 15	12.16
Sch 3, para 2(1)	5.45
para 2(2)	5.46
para 2(3)	5.45
para 3	5.23
para 3(1)	5.45
para 3(2)	5.46
para 4	5.46
para 4(1)	7.3, 7.54
para 4(2)	7.54, 7.55, 8.11
para 8	11.23
para 8(1)	11.9
para 10	5.50
para 10(1), (2)	5.47
para 10(3)	5.45
para 11	5.47
para 15	5.46
para 17(2)	5.45, 12.30
para 19(1)	12.12
para 19(2)	12.13
para 20	3.2
Sch 4, para 7	4.14, 10.19
para 7(2)	12.23
Trade Marks Registration Act 1875	3.2, 3.3, 3.6, 11.2
s 10	3.2
Trade Marks Registration Amendment Act 1875	3.3
Trade Marks Registration Extension Act 1875	3.3

TABLE OF STATUTORY INSTRUMENTS

References are to paragraph numbers.

Rules of the Supreme Court 1965,
SI 1965/1776
  Ord 14   7.20

Trade Marks Act 1994 (Commencement)
  Order 1994, SI 1994/2550   1–2
Trade Marks Rules 1994, SI 1994/2583
  r 2   5.40
  rr 4, 5   5.1
  r 6   5.3
  r 7   5.2, 5.47
  r 8   5.1, 5.2
    (3)   5.2
  r 9   2.34, 5.4
  r 10   5.1
    (5)   5.1
    (7)   5.1
  r 11   5.5
  r 12   5.40
  r 13(1)–(3)   5.40
    (5), (6)   5.40
  r 14(1)   5.40
  r 15   5.40, 5.41
  r 17   5.20
    (4)   5.40
  r 18   5.20
  rr 19, 20   5.22
  r 21   5.17
  r 22   5.50, 12.10, 12.21
  r 23   5.50

  r 24   2.13, 5.23, 5.24
  r 26   9.2
    (1)   9.18
    (2)   9.2
  rr 27–30   5.44
  rr 29, 30   9.3
  r 31   9.19
    (1)–(5)   9.19
  r 32   2.19
  r 34   11.10
  r 35(1)   10.18
    (a)   11.13
    (e)   11.14, 11.15
    (2)   10.18, 11.13
    (3)   11.12
  r 40   5.2, 5.42
  r 41   5.42
  r 43   5.15
  r 49(2)   5.40
  r 50   5.40
  r 51   5.9, 5.40
  r 52   5.40
  r 53   5.9
  rr 54, 55   5.40
  rr 57–59   9.19
  r 62(3)   5.40
  r 63   5.1
  r 66   2.27, 5.7
  r 68   5.47
  Schs 3, 4   5.2

TABLE OF EUROPEAN LEGISLATION AND INTERNATIONAL TREATIES

References are to paragraph numbers.

Agreement on Trade-Related Aspects of
    Intellectual Property Rights (GATT
    Uruguay round) concluded on 15
    December 1993   1.2, 1.3, 12.29,
        14.21, 14.22
  Art 16.2   12.28
  Art 16.3   12.28

Brussels Convention on Civil Jurisdiction
    and Judgments of 27 September
    1968
  Art 5(3)   4.10
  Art 16(4)   4.10

EC Misleading Advertising Directive
  84/450/EEC   7.13, 7.15
EC Regulation 3842/86, OJ [1986]
  L 357/1 on measures to prohibit the
  free circulation of counterfeit
  goods
  Art 3(1)   7.45
EC Regulation 823/87, OJ [1987]
  L 84/59   2.35, 12.3
EC Regulation 2043/89, OJ [1989]
  L 202/1   12.3
EC Regulation 3295/94, OJ [1994]
  L 341/80   13.26
EC Trade Mark Regulation 40/94, OJ
  [1994] L 11/1   1.2, 1.3, 1.18, 7.24,
    8.11, 12.30, 13.1, 13.2, 13.18
  Art 1(2)   13.6
  Art 2   13.5
  Art 3   13.6
  Art 4   2.2
  Art 5   13.6
    (1)   13.6
  Art 7(2)   13.6
  Art 8(2)   13.6
  Art 8(4)   13.6
  Art 9   7.15
  Art 10   2.31, 6.12, 7.17, 13.6
  Art 11   13.6

Art 15   13.6
Art 16   13.15
Art 17   13.14
Art 21   13.15
Art 22   13.13
Art 23   13.13, 13.16
Arts 25–27   13.7
Art 29   13.8
Art 32   13.8
Art 34   5.35, 13.8
Art 35   5.35, 13.8
Arts 36–38   13.9
Art 39   6.9, 13.9
Art 40   13.9
Arts 41, 42   13.6, 13.9
Art 43   13.9
Art 51   13.6
Art 52   13.6
  (2)(b)   13.6
Arts 57–62   13.11
Art 63   13.5, 13.11
Arts 64–72   12.2, 13.6
Art 66(2)   13.6
Art 74   13.10
Art 75(1)   13.10
Art 76   13.10
Art 85   13.5
Arts 88, 89   13.7
Art 91   13.12
  (1)   13.12
Arts 93, 94   13.12
Art 94(2)   13.12
Art 99   13.12
Arts 108–110   13.6
Art 111   13.5
Art 115(2)   13.5
Art 115(3)   13.7
Art 116   13.5
Art 118   13.5
Arts 125–132   13.5

First Council Directive of 21 December
  1988 to approximate the laws of the
  Member States relating to trade

First Council Directive–(*contd.*)
marks (89/104/EEC), OJ [1988]
   L 40/1   1.2, 1.3, 2.22, 4.6,
         8.11, 10.14, 12.14, 13.1, 13.2,
                        13.3, 13.6
First Recital   13.1
Preamble   7.26
Preamble, para 10   1.13
Art 5   1.37, 4.6
  (1)   1.37, 7.19
  (2)   7.19, 7.26
  (3)(d)   7.15
  (5)   1.37, 4.6
Art 8   10.6
  (1)   10.12
Art 10(3)   6.6, 10.1
Art 12   9.17
Art 14   12.2

Madrid Agreement for the Repression of
  False or Deceptive Indications of
  Source of Goods 1891   14.10
Madrid Arrangement concerning the
  International Registration of Marks
  1891   14.10, 14.16–14.19
Art 1(2), (3)   14.10
Art 3   14.11
Arts 4, 5   14.12
Art 6(1)   14.14
  (3)   14.13
Art 7   14.14
Art 9   14.14
Madrid Protocol Relating to the
  International Registration of Marks
  of 27 June 1989   1.2, 3.3, 5.35,
             5.39, 13.17, 14.16–14.20
Art 2(1)   14.17
Art 5(2)(b)–(d)   14.17
Art 6(1)   14.17

Art 7(1)   14.17
Art 8(7)   14.17

Nice Agreement of June 1957   5.2

Paris Convention for the Protection of
  Industrial Property of 20 March
  1883   1.2, 5.3, 11.21, 12.6,
                12.26, 13.6, 14.8
Art 2   12.25
  (1)   12.26
Art 3   12.25
Art 6 bis   1.34, 5.35, 7.31, 12.6,
         12.25, 12.28, 12.29, 13.6
Art 6 ter   7.39
Art 6 septis   7.39
Art 7 bis   12.5, 12.19
Art 8   1.22
Art 10 bis   3.22
Art 10 ter   3.22

Treaty of Rome   4.11
Art 30   10.20
Arts 30–36   4.11, 13.1, 13.20, 13.23,
                     13.24
Art 59   13.1, 13.23
Art 85   4.11, 4.14, 8.13, 10.19,
       10.20, 13.1, 13.20, 13.21
  (3)   4.15
Art 86   4.11, 13.1, 13.22
Art 177   13.3
Art 222   13.12
Art 235   13.1

World International Property
  Organisation Trademark Law
  Treaty, adopted at Geneva on
  27 October 1994   13.4

Chapter 1

THE COMMERCIAL FUNCTIONS OF A TRADE MARK

INTRODUCTION

1.1 Human society uses signs, symbols or marks in many ways. Name tags, cattle brands and shipping symbols indicate ownership of chattels. Car registration numbers may be used to trace a person having charge of the vehicle, and 'special' or 'personalised' registration numbers are valued highly[1]. When a commercial undertaking provides goods or services, trade marks or brand names provide important information as to the nature and origin of those products. Such information is essential to the functioning of a competitive market[2]. This book seeks to explain how the indicative value of trade marks is protected by law in the UK and to outline the international systems and influences under which UK law operates.

---

1   As recognised in *Naylor v Hutson* [1994] FSR 63 ('1700 MG').
2   On the economic functions of trade marks, see Landes and Posner, 'The Economics of Trademark Law' (1988) 78 TMR 267; Economides, 'The Economics of Trademark Law' (1988) 78 TMR 523; Cornish and Phillips, 'The Economic Function of Trade Marks: An Analysis with Special Reference to Developing Countries' (1982) 13 IIC 41.

1.2 The Trade Marks Act 1994[1] makes major changes to the law of registered marks, bringing the UK into line with the European Community's First Council Directive[2] to approximate the trade marks laws of Member States. That, in turn, was designed to pave the way for a unitary system of Community trade mark protection[3]. The 1994 Act also enables the UK to take advantage of developments in the international filing of trade marks provided by the Madrid Protocol[4]. The 1994 Act demonstrates the UK's compliance with its obligations under the venerable Paris Convention for the Protection of Industrial Property[5] and under the more recent GATT/TRIPS agreement of 1993[6].

---

1   Commencement 31 October 1994: Trade Marks Act 1994 (Commencement) Order 1994.
2   89/104/EEC, OJ [1988] L 40/1 (also reproduced in the UK White Paper, 'Reform of Trade Mark Law' (1990) Cm 1203).
3   Council Regulation 40/94, OJ [1994] L 11/1 establishes that system. It is anticipated that applications for Community trade marks will be accepted from about January 1996. See, further, Ch 13.
4   Madrid Protocol Relating to the International Registration of Marks of 27 June 1989. The text is reproduced in *United Kingdom Trade Mark Handbook* (1991) vol 2. It is hoped that the UK will ratify the Protocol in early 1995. See, further, Ch 14.
5   Paris Convention for the Protection of Industrial Property of 20 March 1883 and revisions. On 26 February 1969, the UK ratified the 1967 Stockholm text, published in TS 61 (1970) Cmnd 4431. The text is also reproduced as Appendix 12 to T A Blanco White and R Jacob, *Kerly's Law of Trade Marks and Trade Names* (1986), 12th edn. See, further, Ch 14.
6   Agreement on Trade-Related aspects of Intellectual Property Rights (GATT Uruguay round) concluded on 15 December 1993 and signed at Marrakesh on 15 April 1994. The text is reproduced in

(1994) IIC vol 25 no 2, pp 209–237 and appears as a supplement to [1994] 11 EIPR. See J Worthy, 'Intellectual Property Protection after GATT' [1994] 5 EIPR, 185.

1.3   Interpretation of the Trade Marks Act 1994 by the courts will involve traditional techniques, together with the possibility of referring to Hansard in cases of ambiguity, obscurity or absurdity as outlined in *Pepper v Hart*[1]. In discerning the intention of Parliament, it will also be relevant to scrutinise the texts[2] of the Community Trade Mark Regulation and Directive and the preparatory works generated by the European institutions. For example, the Commission and Council prepared statements for inclusion in the minutes of adoption of the Regulation[3]; as a matter of Community law[4], these are available to guide the courts.

1   [1993] 1 All ER 42; applied to the construction of designs legislation in *Ford Motor Co* [1993] RPC 399, where the learned Deputy Judge remarked that some of the parliamentary debates were as obscure as the statute. On application for judicial review by Ford, the Divisional Court disapproved of references to Ministerial statements in Hansard. It seems that the Copyright, Designs and Patents Act 1988 was not sufficiently obscure or ambiguous: [1994] RPC 545. On appeal, Lord Mustill abandoned a literal construction but found no useful guidance in Hansard [1994] *The Times*, 16 December 1994.
2   Including the detailed preambles.
3   Conveniently collected together with texts of the Regulation, Directive and TRIPS agreement in *ECTA Law Book* (1994) European Communities Trade Mark Association.
4   See *Netherlands v The Commission* [1979] ECR 245, cited in S Smyth, 'Service Mark Registrations in Ireland: a Myth or a Reality?' [1994] 4 EIPR 167 at n 2.

1.4   In order to analyse the effects of the 1994 legislation and to identify areas of uncertainty or difficulty, it is useful first to examine the functions of trade marks. In previous statutes, trade marks were said to indicate a connection in the course of trade. Section 2 of the Trade Marks Act 1905[1] helpfully spelt out varieties of connection which a trade mark might indicate:

'manufacture, selection, certification, dealing with or offering for sale'.

1   Edw 7, c 15.

1.5   No such examples were listed in the Trade Marks Act 1938; by then it was recognised that patterns of trade develop and change. In particular, it was accepted that there could be an appropriate connection between a licensor and licensed goods, provided that adequate control was exercised over their quality[1].

1   Trade Marks Act 1938, s 28. On the effect of s 28 and decided cases, see H Norman, 'Trade Mark Licences in the United Kingdom: Time for Bostitch to be Re-evaluated?' [1994] 4 EIPR 155.

1.6   To indicate a trade connection, the mark must enable someone to distinguish goods or services which enjoy such a connection from those which do not. A good mark will be distinctive, attractive and memorable, generating a frisson of favourable associations.

1.7 The information carried by a trade mark is concentrated in concise, symbolic form. Like a poem, the information content and uses of a mark depend not just upon its inherent and perceptible features, but also on the characteristics of the perceiver, especially the extent to which she or he has been educated in the significance of the mark. Advertising influences the interpretation of a mark, but changing social conditions play their part. The effect of a mark may be altered by current affairs[1] and the activities of third parties[2], as well as by the activities of its proprietor. The owner must be particularly careful to avoid using the mark 'generically', as a product description[3]. At this stage, we will turn to the personalities interested in trade marks and the functions of a trade mark as between the various parties.

---

1 Eg, the oil spillage from the tanker Exxon Valdez must have reflected badly on Standard Oil's 'EXXON' mark.
2 The action for infringement enables a mark's proprietor to control third party use. See Ch 7.
3 Thus, marks such as 'Linoleum' and 'Aspirin' have fallen into general and commercial usage to denote a type of product, rather than the product of a particular company.

COMPETITORS AND CONSUMERS

1.8 At each link in a chain of commercial transactions the trade mark plays its part. Manufacturers, wholesalers, retailers, agents and consumers use marks to identify, order, catalogue, advertise, sell or buy products. The mark may also be used when returning faulty goods or complaining about unsatisfactory services. Figure 1 shows a single link in the chain of commerce and the relationship of relevant parties. For simplicity, it is assumed that the trader is the trade mark proprietor. The trader could, of course, be a formal licensee, or one who legitimately uses a mark to identify the proprietor's goods. A middleman acts both as customer and supplier; the trade mark enables him to select which products to stock or which services to recommend. He uses

Figure 1: Personalities interested in trade marks.

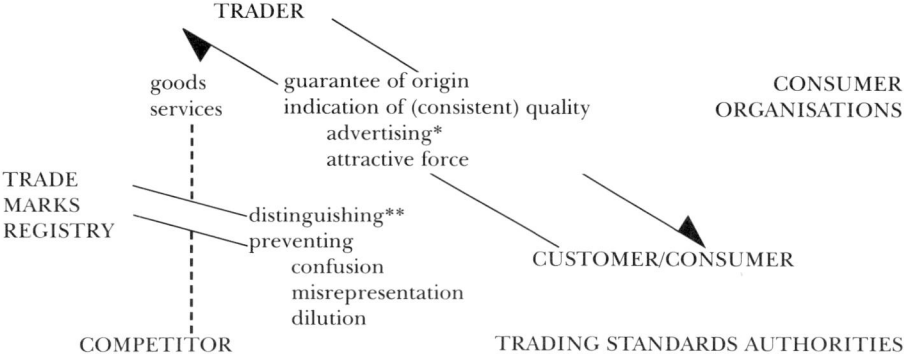

* Educates customers to recognise mark and stimulates them to buy.
** Distinguishes trader's products from competitor's and distinguishes between trader's own different ranges.

the drawing power of the mark to attract custom. In addition, a retailer's 'own-brand' goods may benefit from price comparisons with premium brands[1].

---

1   Legitimate unless the 'own brand' product is designed to look too similar to the premium brand. See, for example, D Franklin, 'Brands versus "Look-Alikes" in the UK' *Trademark World*, July/August 1994, p 10; A Spencer, 'Look-alikes and Private Label Competition' *Trademark World*, September 1994, p 14.

1.9   A trader uses a mark to educate customers as to the characteristics of the product; recognition of the mark will stimulate purchase. For a product which is bought repeatedly[1], customer satisfaction associated with the trade mark will encourage repeat purchases. For a major 'one-off' transaction, marks can act as a banner under which the consumer amasses information[2]. Where a product is new, advertising it under its new mark arouses the customer's curiosity[3]. The new mark may be combined with an established mark of the same proprietor, thus inspiring customer confidence[4]. Alternatively, an existing product may be given a new image by re-branding or by association with a fictional character[5].

---

1   Eg, 'Arctic Roll' ice cream dessert.
2   Thus a consumer may consider taking out a mortgage with the Halifax.
3   As in the case of many 'designer' soft drinks.
4   Motor manufacturers use a combination of house marks and model marks, thus 'Renault Clio', 'Renault Espace Quadra'. L Cohen calls these 'primary' and 'secondary' brands in, 'Brands and valuations' *Managing Intellectual Property*, June 1994, p 23.
5   Eg, use of the 'Sonic the Hedgehog' to re-vitalise the image of 'Fanta' soft drinks among young consumers.

1.10   The effect of the mark on customers and consumers varies not only with the type of product but also with time. A mark coined to intrigue at a product's launch may build up immense goodwill by virtue of customer satisfaction and eventually be used to launch new products and marks. Initially, that mark denotes a narrow product range, later it becomes a vehicle for diversification. At this stage in development, the fact that later products come 'from the same stable' as earlier products will carry much weight.

1.11   Thus, trade marks can function in a number of different ways. The functions and uses appear to fall into three main categories[1]:

(a)   advertising[2];
(b)   quality[3];
(c)   origin[4].

---

1   This scheme may be traced back to the influential work of F I Schechter, see especially, 'The Rational Basis for Trade Mark Protection' (1927) 40 Harv LR 813.
2   See, further, paras **1.30–1.31**.
3   See paras **1.27–1.29**.
4   Kamperman Sanders and Maniatis dub the trade mark which fulfils all three functions as the 'consumer trade mark': see 'A consumer trade mark: protection based on origin and quality' [1993] 11 EIPR 406. This article cites a number of classic and recent analyses of trade mark function; see in particular the American authors Schechter and Diamond.' See also paras **1.25–1.26** below.

1.12   Only the last, the origin function, is universally recognised as the proper object of protection by registration. Thus, in its explanatory memorandum on the creation of a Community trade mark[1], the EC Commission refers to a trade mark's function:

'of providing consumers with a guide to the particular origin of the product and its particular quality and characteristics, although these are not legally guaranteed'.

It then adds firmly:

'Both economically and legally the function of the trade mark as an indication of origin is paramount.... From this basic function of the trade mark are derived all the other functions which the trade mark fulfils in economic life'

before going on to admit:

'... the quality function predominates in the mind of the consumer and the publicity function predominates in the mind of the producer ...'

---

1   *Bulletin of the European Communities*, Supplement 8/76, paras 14 and 68.

1.13   However, a mark's operation as between traders, competitors and consumers was recognised by the European Court of Justice in *SA-Cnl Sucal v Hag*[1]:

'Consequently, as the court has stated on many occasions, the specific subject matter of a trade mark right is to grant the owner the right to use the trade mark for the first marketing of a product and, in this way, to protect him against competitors who would like to abuse the position and reputation of the mark by selling products to which the mark has been improperly affixed. To determine the exact effect of this exclusive right which is granted to the owner of the mark, it is essential to take account of the essential function of the mark, which is to give the consumer or final user the guarantee of the identity of the origin of the marked product by enabling him to distinguish, without any possible confusion, that product from others of a different provenance.'

One may go so far as to hope that in *Sucal v Hag*[2] and other cases[3] the European Court of Justice has so recognised the quality or 'guarantee' function of a trade mark as to accord it legal standing in EC law. In para 10 of the preamble to the Directive are the telling words:

'the registered trade mark, the function of which is *in particular* to guarantee the trade mark as an indication of origin' (emphasis added)

which, it is submitted, leave the UK free to retain the jurisprudence of *Colgate*[4] where the quality function of a registered mark was acknowledged.

---

1   [1990] 3 CMLR 571; [1991] FSR 99.
2   See H Norman, 'Trade Mark Licences in the United Kingdom: Time for Bostitch to be Re-evaluated?' [1994] 4 EIPR 155, n 23.
3   In particular, those on parallel imports: see paras **7.31** and **7.32**.
4   Para **1.29**, n 1.

1.14 As the quotations make clear, the chief effect of a mark as between a trader and a competitor is that of differentiation in the eyes of customers and consumers. Their respective marks distinguish them as distinct sources of goods or services. Trade journals and market advisers, as well as customers, can use the marks to categorise market shares and track fluctuations in sales. The Consumers' Association makes extensive use of marks to identify products which it evaluates[1]. In many spheres of commercial activity, one trader may offer different grades of a product at varying prices; the use of marks enables such products to be distinguished just as effectively as the products of different traders. It is important for the trader and the customers that the lines of demarcation remain clear.

1   See any issue of *Which?* magazine.

1.15 When a trader applies to register a mark[1], it may find that the application is refused by the Registry, or that a competing trader opposes registration. Even after the mark is accepted on to the register, someone may see fit to apply for revocation[2], on the grounds of invalidity or of non-use.

1   See Ch 5.
2   See Ch 9.

1.16 To protect its proper functions a trade mark may be litigated as between traders in the civil courts[1]. Weights and measures authorities exercising their powers to enforce local trading standards have a duty to enforce the criminal provisions of the 1994 Act[2]. Other agencies such as the National Consumer Council also oversee the consumer's interest in trade marks[3].

1   See Ch 7.
2   Trade Marks Act 1994, s 93.
3   The National Consumer Council's Working Paper No 6, 'Intellectual property – the consumer view of patents, copyright, trade marks and allied rights' (1991) is hostile to most intellectual property but sympathetic to trade marks.

GOODS AND SERVICES

1.17 Marks can serve to distinguish goods, services and whole businesses. All these possibilities have been recognised by the common law in passing off actions[1]. Until 1984, UK legislation provided only for the registration of marks for goods. Service marks could sometimes be protected indirectly by registering for goods used in the supply of the service[2], but the Trade Marks (Amendment) Act 1984 introduced service mark registration[3]. The Nice classification, which is used to categorise marks by product, has 34 classes for goods, but a mere eight for services: advertising and business, insurance and financial, construction and repair, communication, transportation and storage, material treatment, education and entertainment and 'other services'.

---

1   *Spalding v Gamage* (1915) 32 RPC 273; *Harrods* (1924) 41 RPC 74; *Legal and General* [1968] RPC 253.
2   As in *VISA TM* [1985] RPC 323.
3   The 1984 Act was itself amended before commencement by the Patents, Designs and Trade Marks Act 1986.

1.18   Where retailers sell a very wide range of products, they have to apply for and administer a huge number of registrations for the same mark in different classes to enjoy the benefits of registration across the product range. It is not surprising that they have tried to register their marks for 'retail services', arguing that by giving advice on prospective purchases and providing facilities such as credit, banking, mother and baby rooms, and so on, they offer a retailing service[1]. Such attempts were unsuccessful under the 1938 Act and Parliament debated whether to introduce specific wording in the 1994 Act to make sure that retail services were registrable[2]. The proponents of retail service mark registration argued that shop names and styles would thus gain protection and that registration for this category of service was available in France, Australia, New Zealand, the USA and other countries. Others took the view that retailers did and should register their distinctive signs for the various goods and services which they offered. There was some scepticism as to whether 'retail service' existed as a distinct service, a view shared by the European Commission and Council who prepared a statement for entry in the minutes of adoption of the Community Trade Mark Regulation[3]:

'The Council and the Commission consider that the activity of retail trading in goods is not as such a service for which a Community trade mark may be registered under this regulation.'

---

1   See J Olsen, 'Cinderella spurned: a retailer's lament' [1987] 9 EIPR 251. For examples of the various suggested components of retail services, see *Dee Corp's Applications* [1989] FSR 266.
2   See, especially, Hansard (Official Report, House of Lords) Parliamentary Debates, 6 December 1993, vol 550, no 10, cols 766–767; Public Bill Committee, 13 January 1994, cols 3–10.
3   Council Regulation 40/94, OJ [1994] L 11/1.

1.19   In the event, reference to retail services was omitted from the Trade Marks Act 1994. The problems of obtaining and administering marks will be alleviated under the 1994 Act by the possibility of multi-class applications and by the expanded definition of infringement: a registration may be used to prevent unauthorised use of a mark on the products for which it is registered, on similar products and, in certain circumstances, on dissimilar products[1]. The World Intellectual Property Organisation (WIPO) is reviewing the Nice classification of goods and services and may at some stage be persuaded to include retail services as a separate category.

---

1   See paras **7.13–7.15**.

1.20   Whereas goods may be marked physically with the trade mark, services are insufficiently tangible to be stamped or branded. Although one may watch a builder working on a neighbour's land, or admire a friend's haircut, services are usually more difficult to inspect than goods. Thus, the information carried by a service mark will be particularly important. Visual use of a mark in relation to services may be made on business signs and papers and in advertising.

PRODUCTS AND BUSINESSES

1.21   In some countries, business names are registrable, as distinct both from company names and trade marks. Often, of course, all three share a common main element. Thus, Jordan Publishing Limited is one of the companies which carries on business under the trading style 'Jordans', which is used as a trade mark on books, advertising literature and other items. In other cases, names and marks are different. For example, Marks & Spencer plc labels its goods with the mark 'St Michael'.

1.22   Companies House does not permit two or more companies to be registered with identical names, but similarity of company names is no bar to their respective registrations. The practice of registering company names emulating those of well-known but unconnected companies was deplored in *Lease Management Services Ltd v Purnell Secretarial Services Ltd; Canon (South West) Ltd, Third Party*[1]. Registration of business names is not at present required in the UK. Thus, registration of marks and the action for passing off[2] are needed to protect business names and trading styles from undue imitation.

---

1   (1994) *The Times*, 1 April, CA.
2   See para **3.5**. Art 8 of the Paris Convention obliges signatories to protect trade names, whether or not they form part of a trade mark.

1.23   Doubts have been expressed as to whether a company, such as Marks & Spencer, uses its name as a trade mark in relation to its products if the latter are labelled with another mark ('St Michael'). These doubts were implicit in the parliamentary debates on retail service marks[1]. A case which is often quoted in this regard is *Autodrome*[2], where the sale of used motor cars from premises called 'the Autodrome' was held not to be use of a registered mark. However, it is clear from the judgment that, had proper evidence been forthcoming as to the use of 'Autodrome' on invoices, the case would have been decided differently. More recently, in *Cheetah TM*[3] the court held that use of a mark on invoices and delivery notes was trade mark use. This is confirmed by s 10 of the 1994 Act. It is submitted that the wording of s 10(4)(a) of the Trade Marks Act 1994, which refers to offering or exposing goods for sale (etc) under the sign, is apt to include use on a shop sign or as a business name[4].

---

1   See para **1.11**, n 4.
2   [1969] RPC 564; [1969] FSR 320.

3   [1993] FSR 263.
4   See 'Reform of Trade Marks Law' 1990 Cm 1203, paras 3.26 and 3.27.

1.24   A related question arises when a company's trade mark is included as part of its company name: does use of the full name constitute use of the mark? Cases decided under the 1938 Act suggested not[1]. However, the European Commission's view was clearly to the contrary:

'It should be made clear in the text [of the Community Trade Mark Regulation] that the protection of the EEC trade mark also extends to its use as a part of a business name.'[2]

The outcome of any case is likely to depend upon the overall impression made by the way in which the name is used.

1   *Pompadour v Frazer* [1966] RPC 7, criticised in *Kerly's Law of Trade Marks* (1986) 12th edn, para 14.27; *Parker-Knoll v Knoll Overseas* [1985] FSR 349 at p 371.
2   Memorandum on the creation of an EEC trade mark, *Bulletin of the European Communities*, Supplement 8/76, para 109.

GUARANTEES OF ORIGIN

1.25   Origin is here used in the sense of commercial origin, rather than geographical origin. Usually, the two are mutually exclusive: s 3(1)(c) of the 1994 Act bars from registration a mark which consists exclusively of an indication of geographical origin. The latter may be protected as a certification mark[1]. Occasionally, the two connotations coincide: in *The Glenlivet*[2], a case about registration of the mark for mineral water, the court took the view that only someone seeking to trade on the applicant's reputation for whisky was likely to want to extract water from Glenlivet and to use that geographical name. The geographical name had become indicative of a specific commercial source. Conversely, a non-geographical name may carry geographical connotations: it may be assumed that a motor car bearing a French mark is manufactured in France, although this may not be justified[3].

1   See **1.32** and **12.7–12.18**.
2   [1993] RPC 461.
3   Comment made during the Trade Mark Bill's second reading in the House of Lords: Hansard, 6 December 1993, vol 550, no 10, col 758, Lord Peston.

1.26   Several points can be made about the concept of commercial origin. First, early passing-off cases[1] established that it does not matter whether the mark conveys the identity of its proprietor. Rather, it must indicate that a common source exists for the marked goods or services[2]. Secondly, as set out at para **1.8**, even though 'origin' implies a causal link between an act of the proprietor and the arrival of the products on the market, the link can take many forms. The trade mark's proprietor may manufacture or select goods[3], licence the provision of services under the mark, subject to the provision of know-how and quality control[4], or choose a licensee to manufacture goods who is competent to exercise quality control itself[5]. Although formal requirements as to quality control in licences have been dropped from the 1994 Act[6], the more tenuous the commercial connection, the more emphasis has traditionally been given to control of quality.

1   Eg *Powell v Birmingham Vinegar Brewery* [1897] AC 710 ('Yorkshire Relish').]
2   The EC Commission's explanatory memorandum, **1.12**, n 1 above, at para 68 echoes this: 'If the trade mark guarantees that the commercial origin *is the same*, the consumer can count on a similarity of composition and quality of goods bearing the trade mark'.
3   See the quotation in para **1.4** from the Trade Marks Act 1905.
4   See *Bostitch* [1963] RPC 183: provision of designs and know-how for the manufacture of goods.
5   *Molyslip* [1978] RPC 211.
6   The parties themselves are responsible for maintaining the integrity of a mark: see 'Reform of Trade Mark Law' (1990) Cm 1203, para 4.36. In practice, *de facto* quality control is likely to be as important as ever: see Norman, para **1.5**, n 1.

INDICATIONS OF QUALITY

1.27   Customers' use of a mark as indicating product quality contributes to the health of the market[1] and has long been recognised at common law. In *Spalding v Gamage*[2], supply of the plaintiff's obsolete goods, under the mark associated with its improved goods, was held to be passing off. Courts and commentators[3] have been slower to acknowledge such a function in the case of registered marks, although customer perception is hardly dependent on whether a mark is registered or not.

1   See the discussion and citations in Kamperman Sanders and Maniatis, 'A consumer trade mark: protection based on origin and quality' [1993] 11 EIPR 406 at pp 407–8.
2   (1915) 32 RPC 273.
3   Especially German: see Beier 'Territoriality of trade mark law and international trade' at (1970) 1 IIC 48. For the view of the European Commission and Court of Justice, see paras **1.12–1.13**.

1.28   What militates against legal recognition of the quality function of a registered mark? One argument is that the concept might be used against a mark's proprietor when, for whatever reason, he introduces quality changes. The Trade Marks Act 1938[1] made explicitly clear that a mere change in the form of connection between the proprietor and his goods or service would not invalidate a mark. In *Bostitch*[2], changes in methods and country of manufacture were held not to render the mark deceptive.

1   Section 62.
2   [1963] RPC 183.

1.29   However, it is submitted that this argument should not prevail where anyone uses a mark significantly to mislead customers as to quality. This need not open the floodgates to a deluge of capricious consumer litigation. At least in the context of infringement, the Court of Appeal has already confirmed that a mark's quality function may be protected by registration. In *Colgate-Palmolive v Markwell Finance*[1], Slade LJ said:

'I accept Mr Hobbs' submission that there is nothing incongruous in holding that a registered trade mark is infringed in relation to goods which do not conform to an identifiable quality which purchasing members of the public in this country ordinarily receive by reference to the mark.'

---

1   [1989] RPC 497 at p 527.

VEHICLES FOR ADVERTISING

1.30   A well-chosen mark can play a significant role in the success of a promotional campaign. Some marks are chosen to complement a proposed advertising theme, others are adopted to echo someone else's effective advertising[1]. Three particular situations may be singled out:

(a)   The proprietor of the mark uses it in advertising. There has been considerable debate as to whether the value of identified brands should be entered in their proprietors' trading accounts[2]. Whatever the outcome on that particular issue, it is beyond question that a good mark is of great value to its proprietor as an advertising tool. As indicated above, the meaning attributed to the mark by customers or the content of the advertising message it conveys can vary with time and place. The mark itself may undergo subtle alteration. With investment in advertising and in the quality and distribution of the product it denotes[3], a mark becomes an important asset. This is reflected in the proprietary nature of a registered mark, which is stated to be personal property[4], which may be assigned, disposed of by will or transmitted by operation of law[5].

(b)   A third party uses the mark to advertise its own products. In this case the proprietor's investment enures to the advertiser's benefit and the mark is likely to lose its power to denote the proprietor's goods or services. The proprietor may arrest this process by suing for trade mark infringement or passing off[6].

(c)   The mark is used in advertising by a third party to refer to the proprietor's products. In this way, retailers or distributors can inform the public of the availability of the proprietor's products. However, if there is a misrepresentation as to their quality or as to the business of the advertiser, the proprietor of the mark may sue as before.

---

1   As in *Cadbury-Schweppes v Pub Squash* [1981] 1 WLR 193; [1981] RPC 429.
2   For examples of this phenomenon and a summary of valuation methods, see M Birkin, 'Brand Valuation' in D Cowley, ed, *Understanding Brands* (1991). The papers in Cowley's book provides an excellent overview of trade marks from the advertiser's perspective. For a lawyer's view, see L Cohen, 'Brands and valuations' *Managing Intellectual Property*, June 1994, p 23. It appears that the Accounting Standards Board disapproves of the valuation of individual brands, regarding them as inseparable from goodwill: *Managing Intellectual Property*, March 1994, p 10.

3   A campaign will fail if contradicted by customer experience of the product. In 'Brands and the role of advertising' in D Cowley, ed, *Understanding Brands* (1991), G Duckworth cites as examples 'The wonder of Woolworths' and 'The age of the train'.
4   Trade Marks Act 1994, s 22.
5   See, further, Ch 11.
6   See Ch 7.

1.31   Alternatively, the advertiser may refer to the proprietor's trade mark, goods or services for the purposes of comparison, commonly to show that its own products are as good, but cheaper. Under the Trade Marks Act 1938 a mark registered in the former Part A of the register could be used to enjoin comparative advertising, even where the advertisement clearly distinguished between the products of the advertiser and the trade mark owner. The situation is now less clear and will depend upon the necessity, purpose and fairness of the comparison[1].

1   See paras **7.40–7.45**.

SPECIAL CATEGORY MARKS

1.32   Three special categories of mark are examined in Chapter 12: certification marks, collective marks and well-known marks. Certification marks are sometimes called 'guarantee marks' because they indicate that products comply with objective criteria as to quality, quantity, materials, geographic origin and so forth. Thus, the kite mark indicates compliance with the relevant British Standard, the wool-mark evidences all-woollen fabric or clothes, and 'Stilton' cheese is made by defined processes in a limited geographic region. Certification marks are owned and administered by independent bodies, which do not themselves trade in the products concerned. This is believed to ensure their impartiality in applying the rules by which products qualify to use the mark. Certification marks have long been registrable for goods and the 1994 Act provides for their registration in respect of services.

1.33   Small and medium-sized enterprises often collaborate to increase their competitiveness. Thus, grocery retailers join purchasing groups and travel agents spread the risks of their trade by joining associations which provide insurance against calamity or failure. To be effective, these organisations must be active in the commercial area concerned. Registration of their marks as collective marks is now possible; the right to use the mark is conferred by membership of the association.

1.34   Some trade marks gain international recognition. Art 6 *bis* of the Paris Convention[1] obliges signatories to protect such marks by preventing third parties from using or registering them in their territories. Art 6 *bis* is rather obscurely worded, but it is doubtful whether the UK previously complied with its obligations. A foreign plaintiff would fail in a passing-off suit if it did not trade within the jurisdiction, or at least have a good customer base[2]. Refusal of registration was left to the good sense and discretion of the Registrar. The 1994 Act gives statutory force to Art 6 *bis*.

1   For the protection of industrial property, 1883 and revisions.
2   See para **3.5**.

OTHER USES OF MARKS

1.35   Trade marks are powerful symbols, charged with meaning. All the uses discussed so far relate to the distinguishing function of marks in the course of trade: providing information about the goods, services and business of a proprietor or advertiser. These functions are protected by the Trade Marks Act 1994 and by the common law[1]. Non-commercial uses do not fall within the scope of that protection. If people choose to adorn their houses or themselves with images of famous marks, that is a matter for them. If someone makes up a story for a child in which a cat eats 'Paws' catfood, or a teenager makes disparaging remarks about a friend for wearing a cheap brand of jeans, such decorative, descriptive or social use is not in the course of trade and falls outside the proprietor's exclusive rights.

1   *Spalding v Gamage* (1915) 32 RPC 273 (goods); *Harrods v Harrod (R) Ltd* (1924) 41 RPC 74 (services); *Legal & General Assurance Society v Daniel* [1968] RPC 253 (businesses).

1.36   What if the trade mark is used decoratively on goods for which it is registered ('Kodak' on tee-shirts[1]) or to give colour to narrative in a 'blockbuster' novel ('. . . the morning after, Joanna realised that her job at the local branch of the "Halifax"[2] building society would never feel the same. The dinner at "Maxim's"[3], the journey home through the channel tunnel . . .')? In the former case the public may or may not imagine the tee-shirt to be connected with the trade mark proprietor[4] and any case will probably turn on this fact. In the latter scenario, there is unlikely to be any misapprehension as to the significance of the mark. In *Mothercare v Penguin Books*[5], the use of the title 'Mother Care/Other Care' on a book about the relative merits of maternal and other care of children was held to be accurately descriptive and not trade mark use. Thus, it was outside the scope of the rights conferred by the plaintiff's registration of 'Mothercare' for books. In The Netherlands, non trade mark use may be enjoined by a registered proprietor. Cases cited by a number of commentators[6] include *Philips*, where the electrical company's logo was altered to include a swastika and used to illustrate a magazine article about Philips's activities during the second world war, and *Alicia*, where a Coca-Cola bottle was used as a prop in an indecent film. However, in *Felix*, the proprietors of 'Felix' for cat food were unable to restrain a political poster referring to the activities of a politician called Felix[7]. Such broad scope of protection was initially rejected by the European Commission in its proposals for harmonisation but a discretionary provision allowing Member States to adopt or retain prohibition on non trade mark use was included in the trade marks harmonisation directive[8].

1   *Kodiak TM*; [1990] FSR 49; *'Coast to Coast' Unidoor v Marks & Spencer* [1988] RPC 275.
2   For curious trade mark infringement proceedings, see *Provident Financial plc v Halifax Building Society* [1994] FSR 81.

3   Subject of the passing off action in *Maxim's v Dye* [1977] 1 WLR 1155; [1975] FSR 364.
4   Contrast the doubts expressed in the *Kodiak* and *Coast to Coast* cases with judicial recognition of merchandising in *Mirage Studios v Counter-Feat Clothing* [1991] FSR 145.
5   *Mothercare v Penguin Books* [1988] RPC 113.
6   See, in particular, M Kniff, 'Selected Benelux cases' *Trademark World*, July/August 1994, p 14; A Kamperman Sanders, 'Trade mark dilution – the parting of the ways?' *Managing Intellectual Property*, March 1992, p 42.
7   *Felix/Loesje* [1993] IER 56 (in Dutch). The registered mark 'Felix' and a slogan meaning 'Ooh, that's tasty', were used on a poster by a non-profit-making organisation devoted to political witticism. The use made a clear reference to events at a Young Socialist's congress. The plaintiff's claims of infringement and unfair competition were rejected because the use was held not to be for economic purposes and no confusion was found. (Thanks to A Kamperman Sanders for information on this case.)
8   See C Gielen 'Harmonisation of Trade Mark Law in Europe' [1992] 8 EIPR 262.

1.37 This provision is Article 5(5) of the EC Trade Mark Directive, which states:

'Paragraphs 1 to 4 shall not affect provisions in any Member State relating to the protection against the use of a sign other than for the purposes of distinguishing goods or services, where use of that sign without due cause takes unfair advantage of, or is detrimental to, the distinctive character or repute of the trade mark.'

Textual comparison of Article 5 with the detailed infringement provisions in s 10 of the Trade Marks Act 1994 suggest that Article 5(5) has not been adopted directly. However, the House of Lords rejected amendments which would have expressly limited the trade mark proprietor's rights to trade mark use[1]. Another clue on the face of the 1994 Act is the statement in s 9 that the proprietor has exclusive rights in the use of the 'trade mark', rather than 'sign' as in Article 5(1) of the Directive. This author's view is that non-trade mark use of a mark, on its own, falls outside the scope of the 1994 Act. On this analysis, Mothercare and Felix could not prevent the use of their marks on books and political posters because such use is not a trade mark use[1]. However, if commercial use is made of the proprietor's product as well as the mark, a different result may apply, because the sign is acting as a mark in relation to the product shown[2].

The use of marks in the Warhol painting or the 'Alicia' film would fall within the proprietor's exclusive rights. At this point, s 10(6) of the 1994 Act would come into play. This subsection was introduced, ostensibly under Article 5(5), to enable a proprietor to restrain use of its mark in comparative advertising[3]. It is an amalgam of the last two lines of Article 5(5) (above) together with an added requirement that, to infringe, use must be otherwise than in accordance with honest practices in industrial or commercial matters. Applying these criteria, Coca-Cola might be able to restrain distribution of the 'Alicia' film but Campbell's could not complain of use of its soup tin imagery in Andy Warhol's work because there would be no detriment.

It was said to be implicit that trade mark use be present for statutory rights to be enforced[4].

---

1   House of Lords Public Bill Committee, 18 January 1994, cols 23–25.
2   See Ch 7.
3   House of Lords, 24 February 1994, cols 735–739. See, further, paras **7.36** and **7.37** below.
4   House of Lords, 24 February 1994, col 733, Lord Strathclyde citing the 15th recital to the Directive (Appendix 3).

Chapter 2

THE MARK ITSELF

IMPACT UPON THE SENSES

2.1 Section 1 of the 1994 Act defines a trade mark as:

'any sign capable of being represented graphically which is capable of distinguishing goods or services of one undertaking from those of other undertakings'.

2.2 For the sign to get its message through, it must be perceptible to the human senses. Although information is received through all five senses, the 1938 definitions of 'mark'[1] and 'use'[2] ensured that only visual marks were registered and only visual use infringed. Where 'Saab' advertised motor cars on television with a voice spelling out the mark in air traffic notation as 'Sierra, Alpha, Alpha, Bravo', the Ford Motor Co could not have relied on any registration of 'Sierra' to stop it. Have things changed? The 1994 Act names particular types of sign of which a trade mark may consist: words, designs, letters, numerals or the shape of goods and their packaging. All these are visual, although shapes may also be detected by touch. Will the *ejusdem generis* rule of statutory construction oust other varieties of mark? Apparently not; in the statements prepared for entry in the minutes of adoption of the Community Trade Mark Regulation the following appears:

'Re Article 4

(a)   The Council and the Commission consider that Article 4 does not rule out the possibility:
  – of registering as a Community trade mark a combination of colours or a single colour[3];
  – of registering in the future sounds as Community trade marks,
  provided that they are capable of distinguishing the goods or services of one undertaking from those of other undertakings.'

---

1   Trade Marks Act 1938, s 68(1).
2   Trade Marks Act 1938, s 68(2).
3   For references to US cases on the registration of colours, see para **2.9**, n 1.

2.3 The White Paper 'Reform of Trade Mark Law'[1] cites and endorses a statement from the European Commission's Explanatory Memorandum on the Community trade mark[2]:

'No type of sign is automatically excluded from registration.... Depending on the circumstances, therefore, the trade-marks office, the national courts, or in the last resort the Court of Justice will be responsible for determining whether, for example, solid colours or shades of colours, and signs denoting sound, smell or taste may constitute Community trade marks.'

---

1   (1990) Cm 1203, para 2.06.
2   *Bulletin of the European Communities*, Supplement 5/80, p 56.

2.4   Thus, it seems clear that distinctive[1] tactile, aural, olfactory and taste marks are
not excluded from registration, provided they can be represented graphically[2]. This
view is reinforced by s 103(2) of the 1994 Act, which establishes that use of a mark
includes use otherwise than by means of a graphic representation. Marks are often
chosen for their sound as well as their appearance; these sensible provisions mean that
the protection conferred by registration of a word mark extends to use on sound radio.
If a 'pure' sound mark can be registered, the distinctive 'jingle' by which a broadcaster
identifies its programme is less likely to be imitated[3]. Where touch, taste or smell are
concerned it may be more difficult to say that the information conveyed by those
senses has a trade mark significance. The sounds coming from a discotheque or the
smells wafting from a restaurant may draw in custom but are unlikely to be distinctive
of a particular establishment. Probably they amount to an eloquent description of the
services available inside. This, together with the problem of representing such marks
adequately for recording on the register[4], is likely to limit their number in practice.
One may imagine[5] applications to register the sound of a lion for films (but not a zoo);
a roughened disc tag for men's luggage (but not for power tools); a scent reminiscent of
roses for sewing thread but not for toilet water[6]; marracuya flavour for lipstick (but not
for yoghurt).

---

1   See para **2.15**.
2   'Reform of Trade Mark Law' (1990) Cm 1203, para 2.06. See also M Elmslie, 'The New UK Trade
    Marks Bill' [1991] 3 EIPR 119; D Lyons 'Sounds, Smells and Signs' [1994] 12 EIPR 540.
3   Although a jingle may be protected as a copyright musical work: see *Lawton v Dundas* (1985) *The Times*, 13
    June. Jingles have been registered in the USA; in 'Extending the Boundaries of Trademark Protection
    in the US' Part 2, *Copyright World*, September 1993, p 30, M S Sommers cites registration since the 1950s
    for the notes G, E and C 'played on chimes'.
4   See para **2.14**.
5   The registration of 'sensory marks' in the USA is discussed by M S Sommers, 'Extending the Boundaries
    of Trade Mark Protection in the US' *Copyright World*, July/August 1993, p 18 and September 1993,
    p 29.
6   *Re Celia Clarke* 17 USPQ 2d 1238, cited in Sommers, n 5 above.

2.5   Must the perceiver be conscious of the mark[1]? Would subliminal use of a visual
cue amount to trade mark use? Since subliminal advertising is not encouraged in the
UK, a judge might be moved to enforce a registered mark against a subliminal
infringer. However, in *Laura Ashley v Coloroll*[2], Whitford J gave short shrift to subliminal
experiments designed to establish confusion between the plaintiff's and defendant's
marks. His remarks suggest that the law would regard marks as operating only at the
level of conscious choice.

---

1   In *Everglide* [1964] RPC 37 the mark was just visible. The editors of *Kerly's Law of Trade Marks and Trade
    Names* (1986) 12th edn, doubt whether a registration would be infringed where the mark is so small as to
    be visible to the naked eye: para 17.19.
2   [1987] RPC 1.

SUITABILITY FOR MARKING AND THE 'INTEGRAL MARK' PROBLEM

2.6   Where a mark is to be applied to goods, it goes without saying that it must be possible to do so. An embossed crest is suitable for paper goods but not for diamonds. The mark should not interfere with the use of the product: an overly fancy shape would confer a very short working life on a bar of soap. Where services are requested by reference to the mark, it must be easy to pronounce, or bashful customers will make a different choice.

2.7   All these examples suggest that the mark is distinct from the basic product. A more subtle problem arises when the sign alleged to be a trade mark is the product itself, or its most striking feature. In *James's TM*[1] and *Coca-Cola TM*[2], the distinction was drawn between a mark applied to goods and the goods themselves. The dome shape of black lead blocks was refused registration in *James* and the ornate cola bottle and its shape in *Coca-Cola*.

---

1   (1886) 33 Ch D 392 ('dome blacklead').
2   [1986] 1 WLR 695.

SHAPES OF GOODS OR THEIR PACKAGING – FUNCTIONALITY AND SUBSTANTIAL VALUE

2.8   Insofar as *James* and *Coca-Cola* held that the shapes of objects or distinctive containers was unregistrable under their respective statutes, both decisions have been overtaken by s 1 of the 1994 Act. This is a welcome development; proving the distinctiveness of packaging has been an uphill task for plaintiffs in passing-off actions[1]. There is now an elaborate regime to allow registration of product and packing shapes whilst preventing monopolisation of some important types of feature. Section 3(2) of the 1994 Act prohibits the registration of signs which consist exclusively of certain shapes. First, there is the shape which results from the nature of the goods themselves. Thus, a spherical shape results from the nature of a ball.

---

1   Although many cases have special features which explain the plaintiff's failure: see B Mills, 'Just Pot Luck! The UK Cup Noodles Case' [1994] 7 EIPR 307. See also, J R Jeremiah, 'Passing off the "Buzzy Bee": when get-up can be functional' [1994] 8 EIPR 355.

2.9   Secondly, shapes which are necessary to obtain a technical result are excluded. Wheels must be round to achieve smooth and efficient locomotion; a sailboard needs a ball joint between hull and mast. What is not clear is the degree of 'necessity' which disqualifies the shape. If it is uniquely able to produce the technical result, it is clearly unregistrable. If it is not unique, the degree of design freedom will be relevant. What if applications are filed to register the only two available design solutions? The first applicant may persuade the Registry that another solution is available. But what about the second application? If registered, both possible solutions would be unavailable to competitors for a potentially infinite period. A similar line of reasoning has been used against the registration of colours in the USA, and the argument has been honoured with the title 'colour depletion theory'. US jurisprudence has shown[1] that the colour depletion objection may be overcome by evidence of distinctiveness.

---

1   *Re Owens Corning* 774 F 2d 1116 (Fed Cir 1985). Some courts have been reluctant to follow this ruling. For example, in *Qualitex Co v Jacobson Products Co*, an appeal has been lodged against the 9th circuit's decision that a single colour should not be registered since primary colours should not be monopolised and registration of other colours would lead to unnecessary arguments as to 'shade confusion': 13 F3d 1297; 29 USPQ 2d 1277 (CA 9 1994). For commentary on US cases, see Coleman, 'Color as trademarks: breaking down the barrier of the mere colour rule' [1992] JPTOS 345; Sommers, 'Extending the Boundaries of Trademark Protection in the US' Part 2, *Trademark World*, September 1993, p 29.

2.10   The third and last limb excludes shapes which give substantial value to the goods. This brings to mind examples such as the cut of a diamond or a very elaborate container holding a token quantity of alcoholic beverage[1]. Sommers describes and criticises the 'aesthetic functionality' doctrine as applied by some courts in the USA: he cites *Pagliero v Wallace China*[2] where a floral pattern on china was denied protection as a trade mark and *Keene v Paraglex*[3] where the doctrine was rejected.

---

1   As in the *Old Dutch Houses* case BIE 1984, 193 cited by A Kamperman Sanders in 'Some frequently asked questions about the Trade Marks Act 1994' [1995] 2 EIPR 67 at n 16.
2   198 F 2d 339 (9th Cir, 1952).
3   653 F 2d 822 (3rd Cir, 1981).

2.11   On this issue the troubled UK case-law on passing off by get-up[1] is relevant. The courts have to consider whether the appearance of a product acts as a trade mark in drawing custom, or whether it encourages purchase for other reasons. Thus, in *Jarman & Platt v Barget*[2], customers bought the plaintiff's 'Louis' chairs because they valued their appearance. In *Hodgkinson & Corby v Wards Mobility Services*[3], those ordering 'black egg-box' prosthetic cushions were held not to be 'moved by source'. In dismissing *Hodgkinson's* action, however, Jacob J rejected the distinction between capricious additions and integral features of products. It is clear that both may operate as marks.

---

1   For a fuller selection of cases, see T Blanco White and R Jacob, *Kerly's Law of Trade Marks and Trade Names* (1986) 12th edn, paras 16.67–16.70; C Wadlow, *The Law of Passing Off* (1995) 2nd edn, pp 426–450.
2   [1977] FSR 260.
3   [1995] FSR 169; A Firth, 'Cushions and confusion: the RoHo passing off care' [1994] 11 EIPR 494.

2.12   The Dutch Supreme Court has grappled with the distinction between the premium conferred on a product by the cachet of its mark and the 'substantial value' which renders a shape mark unregistrable. In a case involving 'twirled snacks'[1], it was held that the value of the crisp resided in its eating qualities and not in the fancy shape.

1   Hoge Raad, 11 November (1983), NJ (1984) 203; BIE (1985) 23. See, further, Kamperman Sanders, 'Some Frequently Asked Questions about the Trade Marks Act 1994' [1995] 2 EIPR 67.

2.13   The prohibitions of subs 3(2) are absolute; no amount of acquired distinctiveness can render these features of shape registrable on their own. But note the word 'exclusively': evidence of distinctiveness may be admissible to show that the features concerned do have a trade mark significance. Furthermore, a shape which consists of excluded features combined with other distinctive elements, can be registered as a whole. One hopes that in this area the Registry will encourage trade mark proprietors to make use of voluntary disclaimers[1].

1   Trade Marks Act 1994, s 13(1)(a) enables the applicant or proprietor to disclaim any right to the exclusive use of any specified element of the mark. There is no power in the Registry to require disclaimer. The applicant faced with refusal, or the litigant in danger of losing their mark by revocation for invalidity may, however, be moved to disclaim. Disclaimer is effected by notice in writing to the Registrar, who publishes it: r 24.

COMPOUND MARKS

2.14   Even where all individual features are excluded, is it open to an applicant for registration to argue that the particular combination of features is capable of being distinctive? Cases on disclaimers show that a mark composed of commonplace elements may be registrable as a whole. Thus, in *Diamond T*[1], the letter 'T' and the surrounding device of a diamond were disclaimed, but the mark as a whole was registered. It is submitted that where the combination is technically or functionally necessary, it will not be registrable. It would be artificial to allow an applicant to break down the product shape into its components. But where there is freedom to use different combinations, the whole may be capable of being distinctive.

1   [1921] 2 Ch 583; (1921) 38 RPC 373.

'SUBSTANTIAL VALUE' GENERALLY

2.15   The registration of shape marks consisting exclusively of signs which confer substantial value in use is expressly prohibited by subs 3(2)(c). The same problem may arise, however, in relation to smell, taste or sound marks. The distinctive scent of upmarket toiletries may confer substantial value, as may the smell of instant coffee or the taste of a soft drink. These features are important elements of the products. Likewise, the opening bars of a musical work may be compelling and distinctive but they are usually the most significant part of the work itself. It is submitted that the 'not-a-mark' argument of *James* and *Coca-Cola* will still be relevant in such cases.

2.16   In practice, the question as to whether the distinctive feature is a trade mark will be much affected by the way the goods or service has been advertised. If the feature is promoted as enhancing the functional or aesthetic qualities of the product, then it is unlikely to be accepted as a mark. This can be regarded as a form of estoppel. Promotion of the feature as a distinguishing sign constitutes a self-serving statement, to which little weight would normally attach. However, it may be relevant in educating the public to recognise the feature as distinctive. Such use may therefore be taken into account by the Registry or court in deciding whether the sign is a trade mark.

SUITABILITY FOR ADVERTISING

2.17   A trader adopting a mark should consider all likely advertising media and in particular those likely to reach the target market. A good mark can be long-lived; in the classic situation the product acts as its own advertisement. This has been overtaken by hoardings, print media, sound broadcasting, television, cablecasting and teletext. For some of these, a mark may be physically or morally[1] ill-suited.

---

1   See para **2.35**.

2.18   Conversely, an advertising technique may mature into a trade mark. It used to be doubted that advertising slogans were trade marks. Registration was refused to the Kit-Kat slogan *Have a Break*[1]. *I Can't believe it's yogurt*[2] was registered under the 1938 Act. Parliament rejected as unnecessary an amendment[3] to the Trade Marks Bill which would have added 'slogans' to the list of signs in s 1.

---

1   Reported at [1993] RPC 217, but decided in 1983.
2   [1992] RPC 533. Note that the requirement of distinctiveness will be absent where the slogan refers to the qualities of the service or goods: 'Where People Matter' *ITMA Information*, April/May 1994, p 1.
3   House of Lords Public Bill Committee Report, 13 January 1994, cols 10–11.

ENTERING ON THE REGISTER

2.19   To be registrable as a mark, a sign must be capable of graphic representation[1]. This requirement ensures that it can be entered upon the register. Although 'register' suggests a huge leather-bound book, the Patents, Designs and Trade Marks Act 1986 made clear[2] that the register need not be kept in documentary form. Since then, the Trade Marks Registry (a division of the Patent Office) has developed a computerised register[3]. Section 63(1) of the 1994 Act defines 'register' and s 63(3) merely provides that it be kept in such manner as may be prescribed. This is done in r 32 of the Trade Marks Rules 1994[4], which again states that it need not be kept in documentary form.

---

1   Trade Marks Act 1994, s 1(1). A mark which does not satisfy s 1(1) cannot be registered: s 3(1)(a).
2   By inserting a new s 1 into the Trade Marks Act 1938.

3   Known as OPTICS, for Office of Patents and Trade marks Integrated Computer Systems. There is also
    a database facility for devices dubbed TRIMS (Trade Marks IMaging System).
4   SI 1994/2583, appendix 2.

2.20   Words, devices, letters and numerals already have their graphical representation. Where packaging or product shapes are concerned, the representation may be
achieved by drawings or photographs, or by attaching the unfolded 'net' of a box to
the application. The Registry has indicated that representations up to A4 size can be
accepted[1]. The representation of sound, taste, smell and tactile marks may tax the
applicant's powers of description. A synthetic scent can be described by its chemical
formula, but that would unduly limit the scope of protection. *Re Celia Clarke*[2] used an
elaborate sensory definition: 'a high-impact, fresh, floral fragrance reminiscent of
plumeria blossom'.

1   Form TM3, note (h).
2   17 USPQ 2d 1238 (Trademark Trial and Appeal Board, 1990), cited by M Sommers, para **2.4**, n 5.
    According to *The Times* of 1 November 1994, p 7, an application to register the smell of Chanel No 5 was
    filed on 31 October 1994, the mark being described as: 'the scent of aldehyde-floral fragrance product,
    with an aldehydic top note from aldehydes, bergamot, lemon and neroli; an elegant floral middle note,
    from jasmine, rose, lily of the valley, orris and ylang-ylang; and a sensual feminine base note from
    sandal, cedar, vanilla, amber civet and musk. The scent also being known as Chanel No 5'. This may be
    contrasted with 'the smell of roses when applied to tyres'; ibid.

2.21   Sound marks may also be represented in a technical or in a descriptive way.
The notes 'GEC' played on chimes could be described as such. Alternatively, the
sound motif could be represented by a trace of its waveform. This is more precise but
more limiting when it comes to comparison[1] with other marks, for the purpose of
opposing later registration or in infringement proceedings. The sound of a horse
trotting may be described as 'clip, clop, clip, clop' but such a registration may not be
infringed by a long sequence of a trotting sound.

1   For comparison of marks, see paras **5.28** and **5.29**.

ABILITY TO DISTINGUISH

2.22   Capability of distinguishing is the fundamental characteristic of a trade mark.
Marks which are incapable of distinguishing therefore, cannot be registered; ss 3, 4
and 5[1] ensure this. The spirit of the Directive and the 1994 Act is to allow registration
of marks unless prohibited[2]. Thus, where evidence shows that a sign operates as a
distinctive mark, it will generally be possible to register the mark. The next section
analyses reasons why a sign may lack distinctiveness on a temporary or a permanent
basis.

1   'Absolute grounds for refusal of registration': s 3; 'specially protected emblems': s 4; and 'relative
    grounds for refusal of registration': s 5.

2   White Paper 'Reform of Trade Mark Law' (1990) Cm 1203, paras 2.06 and 3.07–09.

NON-DISTINCTIVE SIGNS

2.23   Non-distinctive signs fall logically into five categories.

The sign is incapable of conveying information

2.24   A short, isolated straight line or the single letter (and indefinite article) 'a' simply cannot carry a distinctive message. 'White' noise would be too complex to operate as a sound mark. Subsection 3(1)(b) prohibits registration of signs which are devoid of any distinctive character. However, this is subject to the proviso that the mark can be registered on proof of distinctiveness acquired through use. In the past, evidence of use has been accepted as evidence of distinctiveness. Does the proviso require proof of recognition of the mark as well? Common sense suggests that for a borderline mark, evidence of actual distinctiveness is desirable. For a 'stronger' mark, evidence of use may suffice to put its registrability beyond doubt. Secondly, is it necessary to show that the mark has become distinctive in the UK, or will proof of distinctiveness through use abroad be adequate? It is submitted that evidence of use abroad, especially in another Member State of the European Union, may be relevant to capability to distinguish, but could never be conclusive. Different linguistic and other conditions will pertain[1].

---

1   See *Ford-Werke* (1955) 72 RPC 191.

2.25   Past refusals to register which may exemplify this category include two- and three-letter combinations other than words[1]. The Registry now take the view that a three-letter non-words will not be refused and that pronounceable two-letter combinations may be registered[2]. Similar practices relate to numbers and combinations of letters and numbers.

---

1   *W&G* (1913) 30 RPC 661; *I.Q.* [1993] RPC 379. Monograms and other 'fancy' combinations were often registered, however.
2   Work Manual, Ch 6, Appendix I.

The sign is descriptive, ab initio, of the product

2.26   Subsection 3(1)(c) obliges the Registry to refuse to register marks which consist exclusively of signs which serve, in trade, to designate the kind ('frocks'), quality ('all wool'), quantity ('tonne'), intended purpose ('cat food'), value ('pound'[1]), geographical origin[2] ('Brighton' for rock), the time of production of goods or rendering of services ('24 hours'), or other characteristics of goods and services ('speedy', 'perfect'). This category is again subject to the proviso for acquired distinctiveness[3]. Dealing with the last examples first, UK law has traditionally been strict as to laudatory marks. In a classic case, registration was refused to 'Perfection'[4]. However, where words have been subtly rather than directly laudatory[5], registration has been allowed.

1 Although *Pound Puppies* was registered under the 1938 Act [1988] RPC 530 (Board of Trade).
2 The strength of a geographical objection will depend upon the size and importance of the geographical location and whether it does or could have a reputation for the product. The Registry has formulated guidelines for its staff: Work Manual, Ch 6, Appendix G.
3 Surprisingly descriptive words have been held to have acquired distinctiveness. *Manganin*, the name of an alloy, became distinctive of an applicant's products, [1967] RPC 271; whilst *York* was assumed to be 100% distinctive in fact (though not in law) for trailers, [1984] RPC 231.
4 *Crosfield's Application* [1910] 1 Ch 130; 26 RPC 561. In this case the judge recognised that a word could be simultaneously descriptive and distinctive.
5 As in *Sheen* for sewing thread (1936) 53 RPC 355 or *Chunky* for dog food [1978] FSR 322. For an interesting and detailed analysis of the registration of laudatory marks in Canada, see R M Colbert and E Manolakis, 'Laudatory Words in Trade Marks—are proper considerations being applied?' (1994) 10 CIPR 635.

2.27 Marketing departments seem extraordinarily fond of descriptive marks[1]. This is understandable in the case of new products, where advertising has to create recognition of the product as well as the mark. Unfortunately, a descriptive mark may be taken as a mere product description, and fail to achieve distinctiveness even through use[2]. Another common ploy is to misspell or combine descriptive words, or to use foreign words[3]. To date, the Registry has been quick to spot and refuse applications to register marks such as *Soflens*[4]. Device marks have also been refused as descriptive, as in *Unilever*[5]. However, if it can be shown that the descriptive symbol or word refers to a distinctive feature of the goods or services, then it can be registered[6].

1 For cautionary examples from US case-law, see any edition of Diamond, *Trade Mark Problems and How to Avoid Them*.
2 As in 'Oven Chips': *McCain v Country Fair* [1981] RPC 69.
3 The former requirement that foreign words or symbols be translated or transliterated has not been retained; presumably it is covered by the Registry's powers to call for translation of all or part of any document: Trade Marks Rules 1994, r 66.
4 For contact lenses [1976] RPC 694. See also *Orlwoola* [1910] 1 Ch 130; (1909) 26 RPC 683 and 850.
5 Representation of striped toothpaste [1984] RPC 155, and see [1987] RPC 13.
6 *Blue Paraffin* [1977] RPC 473; *Unilever Ltd's (Striped Toothpaste No 2) TM* [1987] RPC 13.

2.28 Marks in this category range from direct and overt descriptions (eg, *Motor Lodge*[1]), which are likely to fall foul of subs 3(1)(c) to 'covert and skilful allusions'[2] which will not be caught. The latter type of mark, suggestive rather than descriptive of a product's qualities, can be very effective.

1 [1965] RPC 35.
2 *Solio* [1898] AC 571; 15 RPC 476.

2.29 If a mark in a foreign language or script[1] is descriptive in its own language, its registrability in the UK will depend upon the degree of recognition of the language or script in the UK (residents of the UK are likely to be familiar with French, but not Lithuanian) and whether the language is customarily used for the products (eg, French for beauty products). It will also depend upon the degree of descriptiveness of the mark's meaning[2].

It is likely that more quasi-descriptive marks will be registered under the 1994 Act than formerly.

---

1   In which case, transliteration will be required: Work Manual, Ch 6, Appendix F.
2   See, eg, *Kiku* [1978] FSR 246, Japanese for 'Chrysanthemum'.

The sign is misdescriptive of the product

2.30   Subsection 3(3)(b) prohibits registration of marks which are of such a nature as to deceive the public, for instance as to the nature, quality or geographical origin of the product. Thus, 'babycare' would be misdescriptive of rat poison and 'all wool' deceptive if used in relation to synthetic fabrics. Sometimes, however, a misdescription is so fanciful as to avoid deceptiveness. Thus, 'North Pole' for bananas or 'Sahara' for ice cubes would deceive nobody as to geographical origin.

The sign was distinctive but has become descriptive

2.31   Just as a descriptive sign can become distinctive through use as a trade mark, so a trade mark can lose distinctiveness through misuse as a product description. Such marks are said to have become 'generic'. Where a mark has been registered whilst distinctive, only 'generic' use in the trade is sufficient to invalidate it[1]. What if the mark is not already on the Register, or registration is sought for further goods or services? Subsection 3(1)(d) denies registration to signs which have become customary in the current language or in the bona fide and established practices of the trade. It is submitted that these two limbs are distinct[2]; currency in the language may be established by dictionary entries[3].

---

1   See para **9.14**.
2   So that everyday language as well as trade usage counts.
3   Dictionary editors should always be encouraged to refer to trade marks as such. Specific provision is made for this in Art 10 of the Community Trade Mark Regulation 40/94, OJ [1994] L 11/1. A similar provision appeared in earlier drafts of the Directive (see, eg, Art 4 of the amended proposal published at OJ [1985] C 351/4) but was omitted from the final text.

The sign calls to mind the goods or services of others

2.32   Where the sign carries deceptive information as to the origin of the product, s 5 sets out the 'relative' grounds on which registration of a mark is to be refused. Fatal conflict can occur whether the prior mark is registered or not: s 6.

2.33   Confusion with other marks may also lead to deception as to the nature of the product. In some cases, this could pose a danger to consumers. Thus, an application to register 'Jardex' for disinfectant was refused by reason of a prior registration 'Jardox' for meat extract[1]. However, it was indicated in Parliament that the Registry no longer had a consumer protection role[2]. Furthermore, refusal to register would not prevent use and concomitant deception of the public[3]. It has recently been announced that the Registry will no longer search for and raise 'danger' citations[4].

1   (1945) 63 RPC 19.
2   House of Lords, vol 550, no 10, 6 December 1993, col 752.
3   House of Lords Public Bill Committee, 13 January 1994, cols 16–17.
4   *ITMA Information,* January/February 1995, p 3.

2.34   Also included in this category are cases where use of a sign suggests a connection with the Royal family, or resembles the Red Cross, a national flag or other State or international symbol. In these cases, registration is prohibited by ss 3(5), 4[1], 57[2] and 58[3] and r 9. The prohibitions may be overcome by authorisation from the appropriate State, organisation or member of the Royal family; in the case of UK and national flags, the Registrar is arbiter: subs 4(2).

1   Royal arms, crown, flags, likenesses etc; the union or national flags of the UK.
2   The national emblems of Paris Convention countries.
3   The names, abbreviations and emblems of international intergovernmental organisations of which one or more Paris Convention countries are members.

INAPPROPRIATE SIGNS

2.35   Where a mark is universally repellant, market forces will prevent its adoption. Sometimes, however, a 'bad' mark[1] will appeal to a target sector of the public. Subsection 3(3)(a) prohibits the registration of a trade mark which is contrary to public policy or to accepted principles of morality. This 'public order' exception is likely to be used sparingly. In the past, registration has been refused to 'Hallelujah' for jeans[2]; the mark had a powerful religious significance and was likely to offend. A more general exclusion is contained in subs 3(4): a mark shall not be registered if or to the extent that its use is prohibited in the UK by any enactment, rule of law or provision of Community law[3]. 'To the extent that' suggests that a mark whose use was wholly prohibited by, say, obscenity laws could not be registered at all. Conversely, an otherwise unobjectionable mark might be refused registration for products where its use was restricted. To take a historical example, assume that deregulation of the financial services sector had not occurred in 1986. Building societies would not be permitted to provide estate agency services. Use by the 'Nationwide'[4] building society of its mark in relation to estate agency would be prohibited within the meaning of subs 3(4), and the mark could not be registered for estate agency services. But this would not prevent its registration for, say, mortgage lending services.

1   Eg, 'Opium', 'Poison' for toiletries, 'Death' for cigarettes.
2   [1976] RPC 605.
3   For example, a registration of 'Champagne' for a different beverage; its use would contravene EC Reg 823/87. See *Taittinger v Allber* [1993] FSR 641 at p 672.
4   See *Nationwide* [1987] FSR 579, where the building society sued in passing off shortly before liberalisation to restrain use of 'Nationwide' by estate agents. An interlocutory injunction was refused but undertakings from the defendants not to expand further were accepted.

CHOOSING A MARK

2.36   A mark needs to be chosen for its intrinsic and extrinsic qualities. It must convey information but not be descriptive of the product. Keating[1] categorises marks as:

(a)   coined (the most enduring);
(b)   fanciful;
(c)   suggestive; and
(d)   descriptive.

The last should be avoided. Which of the other categories is used depends very much upon the characteristics of product and market. An allusive mark may be popular among young people, but its connotations may be liable to rapid change. A classical mark[2] may prove longer-lasting; its allusions may be more obscure but less prone to change.

1   Author of *Franchising Adviser* (1987).
2   Eg, those cited in Gredley, 'Is your trade mark classic?' *Managing Intellectual Property*, June 1993, p 31.

2.37   Before adoption of a new mark, a search of existing registrations for conflict with existing marks in use or on the UK or Community registers is essential. With a wider range of relevant prior registrations than under the 1938 Act and a wider range of signs which can be protected, the search will take on a new significance[1]. A search will indicate whether use of a mark is likely to infringe and whether registration is likely to be blocked by earlier marks.

1   For comments on the effect of new provisions on conflicting marks, see Spencer, 'European Harmonisation: Harmony – or confusion and conflict? *Trademark World*, December/January 1993/94, p 23.

Chapter 3

LEGAL MODES OF PROTECTION

HISTORICAL BACKGROUND

3.1   From the Middle Ages the Guild system controlled access to and the conduct of the various trades and professions. The weakening of those controls, together with the opportunities for profit and for cheating in the metal trades, seems to have led to the early enactment of protective statutes, the Cutlers Company Acts. These bolstered the powers of the Company to allot unique marks by prohibiting their unauthorised use. Other trades must have envied this system. In 1862, Parliament considered Bills for the registration of marks and for the protection of the public and traders from deceptive use of marks. The latter prevailed, and the Merchandise Marks Act 1862 passed on to the statute book. This was superseded by the Merchandise Marks Act 1887, and can be regarded as the precursor to the Trade Descriptions Acts 1968 and 1972.

3.2   In 1875 the Trade Marks Registration Act created a general Registry, providing for registration of marks for all classes of goods. To be registrable, the mark had to comprise at least one 'essential particular'[1], but any special or distinctive word or combination of figures or letters used as a trade mark before commencement was also registrable. Provision was made for co-ordination with the Cutlers system of allotting metal or 'Sheffield' marks; eventually the Sheffield Register became a limb of the general Register[2] and has been abolished as a separate category by the 1994 Act[3]. The 1875 Act stipulated that no action for infringement of an unregistered mark was to be brought. This was not, however, fatal to the general action in passing off[4].

---

1   An individual or firm name printed, etc, in some particular or distinctive manner, a written signature, a distinctive device, mark, heading label or ticket, plus any letters, words, etc: s 10.
2   For a history of the system, see Blanco White and Jacob, *Kerly's Law of Trade Marks and Trade Names* (1986) 12th edn, Ch 6.
3   Section 105 and Sch 3, para 20. Note also the existence of the Hallmarks Act 1973.
4   See paras **3.5–3.19**.

3.3   The Registry appears to have been inundated with applications to register textile marks[1], because the Acts of 1876 and 1877 extended transitional provisions for applicants of those marks waiting for registration. Amending and consolidating Acts followed fast upon the 1875–77 Acts, as shown in Table 1. The texts of subsequent Acts acknowledges a widening range of registrable marks and permissible transactions. The 1994 Act accelerates this process.

---

1   A distinct office was created in Manchester.

Table 1:   Trade mark legislation in the UK[1]

Date	Statute	Main effect
1623, 1791, 1801, 1814, 1860	Cutlers Company Acts	Empowered the Cutlers Company in Sheffield to allot marks to users for metal goods
1862	Merchandise Marks Act	Created criminal penalties for the deceptive use of marks on merchandise
1875	Trade Marks Registration Act	Introduced general registration system
1876	Trade Marks Registration Amendment Act	Suspended section one (no infringement of unregistered mark) to allow more time for registration of textile marks
1877	Trade Marks Registration Extension Act	As above
1883	Patents Designs and Trade Marks Act	Amended and consolidated law of registered marks
1887	Merchandise Marks Act	As above
1888	Patents, Designs and Trade Marks Amendment Act	Amended definition of registrable symbols and introduced disclaimers
1905	Trade Marks Act	Consolidated and amended; defined 'trade mark'; broadened criteria for registration
1914	Trade Marks Act	Amendments
1919	Trade Marks Act	Created Part B of register; provided for removal of generic marks
1938	Trade Marks Act	Liberalised licensing and assignment of registered marks; elaborated system for certification marks
1984	Trade Marks (Amendment) Act	Provided for registration of service marks
1986	Patents, Designs and Trade Marks Act 1986	Enabled register to be kept in non-documentary (ie computerised) form; consolidated Paris priority provisions into trade marks statute
1994	Trade Marks Act	Implements EC harmonisation Directive; enabling sections for Madrid Protocol, Community Trade Mark

1   For a fuller account of trade mark history, see S Ricketson, *The Law of Intellectual Property* (1984) paras 30.1–30.5; F I Schechter, *Historical Foundations of the Law Relating to Trade Marks* (1925). Statutes from 1875 are conveniently set out in appendices to *Kerly's Law of Trade Marks and Trade Names* (1986) 12th edn.

3.4   In parallel with the statutory measures and Guild controls, common law and equity provided redress for consumers and traders injured by the deceptive use of marks. The most important cause of action is passing off, considered together with other actions.

PASSING OFF AND OTHER TORTS

Passing off

3.5   Passing off appears to have developed[1] out of the tort of deceit, in which a customer could sue in respect of deceptive use of a badge of trade, to a situation where the presence of a confused customer[2] establishes an important element of the tort alleged by one trader against another. Initially, a plaintiff had to show actual intention to deceive on the part of the defendant, but by the mid-nineteenth century, Equity would intervene without such proof[3]. Objective likelihood of deception or confusion is now the benchmark[4].

---

1   See S Ricketson, *The Law of Intellectual Property*, paras **24.1–24.2**; C Wadlow *The Law of Passing Off* (1995) 2nd edn, pp 9–31.
2   Actual or potential.
3   Eg *Millington v Fox* (1838) 3 My & Cr 338, 40 ER 210.
4   Eg 'Advocaat' *Erven Warnink Besloten Vennotschap v J Townend & Sons* [1979] AC 731; [1980] RPC 31.

3.6   Passing off is said to protect a property right in the goodwill of the business carried on by reference to the mark, and not any property right in the mark as such[1]. Historically, this is not surprising, since the Trade Marks Registration Act 1875 and its successors made clear that there was no right to sue for infringement of an unregistered trade mark. Thus, the continued protection of marks by passing off had to be by way of protection of a different entity. In *Commissioners of Inland Revenue v Muller & Co's Margarine Ltd*[2], Lord Macnaughton said of goodwill:

'It is a thing very easy to describe, very difficult to define. It is the benefit and advantage of the good name, reputation and connection of a business. It is the attractive force which brings in custom. . . . It must be attached to a business.'

Actual or likely damage to goodwill is an essential element of passing off[3]. The existence of a misrepresentation, confusion or deceit is necessary but not sufficient.

---

1   Eg *Reddaway v Banham* [1896] AC 199; 13 RPC 218; *Spalding (AG) & Bros v Gamage (AW) Ltd* [1914] 2 Ch 405; 32 RPC 273.
2   [1901] AC 217 at 223.
3   Although where evidence shows an intention to pass off, the burden of proving damage is lightened.

Formulations of passing off

3.7   Two comparatively recent formulations of the tort of passing off, those of Lord Diplock in *Advocaat*[1] and of Lord Oliver in the *Jif Lemon* case[2], are regularly applied by the courts. Lord Diplock identified five factors present in all cases of passing off (although he warned that occasionally the factors could be present without amounting to passing off – the mysterious 'undistributed middle'[3]). His five factors are:

(a)   a misrepresentation;
(b)   by a trader in the course of trade;
(c)   to prospective customers or ultimate consumers;
(d)   which is calculated (objectively likely) to injure the plaintiff's goodwill or business; and
(e)   which causes actual damage, or a serious likelihood of damage in a *quia timet* action.

An alternative formulation by Lord Fraser in *Advocaat* has been held to apply in a more limited class of case[4] and is not discussed here.

---

1   [1979] AC 731; [1980] RPC 31.
2   *Reckitt & Colman v Borden* [1990] 1 All ER 873.
3   Their presence might indicate dishonest trading which is none the less permitted in the interests of competition – an economic policy exception. It is difficult to identify examples.
4   See *Bristol Conservatories v Conservatories Custom Built* [1989] RPC 455.

3.8   In *Jif*, Lord Oliver analysed passing off in terms of the 'classical trinity' often used in pleading:

(a)   goodwill or reputation attached to the goods or services supplied by reference to the distinctive mark;
(b)   a misrepresentation to the public;
(c)   causing actual or likely damage.

Badges of trade, reputation and goodwill

3.9   Starting with the question of reputation in a mark, passing off has been founded on all manner of insignia, including names (such as 'Harrods'[1] or 'Annabel's'[2]), words (such as 'Camel Hair Belting'[3] or 'New Orb'[4]), numbers (such as '4711'[5]), devices (such as an inlaid white spot[6]), colours (such as grey for gas cylinders[7]), the livery and uniforms of a bus company[8], the design of a restaurant[9], the style of an advertising campaign[10] or the shape and colour of packaging or containers ('Jif' lemons[11], 'Coca-Cola' bottles[12]). Where passing off by get-up is alleged, however, plaintiffs often find it difficult to persuade the courts that their get-up is distinctive and, if so, that an operative misrepresentation is being made[13]. In these cases, the totality of the plaintiff's and the defendant's respective get-up is taken into account; the defendant may avoid a finding of confusion by the use of one or more distinguishing features. Plaintiffs also tend to have an uphill struggle where a mark is not inherently distinctive, such as 'Oven Chips' for oven-ready chipped potatoes[14]. It is not sufficient to coin a new phrase or arrive first upon the market. Nor is long user and massive advertising enough when others use the mark in question[15].

---

1   *Harrods Ltd v Harrod (R) Ltd* (1924) 41 RPC 74.
2   *Annabel's (Berkeley Square) v Schock* [1972] FSR 261; [1972] RPC 838.

3 *Reddaway v Banham* [1896] AC 199.
4 *Spalding (AG) & Bros v Gamage (AW) Ltd* [1914] 2 Ch 405; 31 RPC 431.
5 *Reuter v Mulhens* (1953) 70 RPC 735; [1954] Ch 50.
6 *Dunhill v Bartlett* (1922) 39 RPC 426, although the defendant's spot was sufficiently different to avoid passing off.
7 *Sodastream v Thorn Cascade* [1982] RPC 459.
8 *London General Omnibus v Felton* 12 TLR 213.
9 *My Kinda Town v Soll* [1983] RPC 15.
10 *Cadbury-Schweppes v Pub Squash* suggests this, although there was held to be no passing off in that case. See also, *Elida-Gibbs v Colgate Palmolive* [1983] FSR 95.
11 Para **3.7**, n 2, injunction granted.
12 *Coca-Cola Co v Barr* [1961] RPC 387.
13 See, eg, *Jaffa Cakes* [1992] FSR 14; [1994] FSR 504; *Bostik v Sellotape* [1994] RPC 556; *Hodgkinson & Corby* [1995] FSR 169 and cases cited therein, discussed in A Firth 'Cushions and confusion' [1994] 11 EIPR 494; *Dalgety Spillers Foods v Food Brokers* [1994] FSR 199, discussed in B Mills, 'Just Pot Luck! The UK Cup Noodles Case' [1994] EIPR 307.
14 *McCain v Country Fair* [1981] RPC 69. Contrast 'Camel Hair Belting', found to have acquired distinctiveness in *Reddaway v Banham* [1896] AC 199.
15 So, in 'Raffles', *Imperial Group v Philip Morris* [1982] FSR 72, the presence on the market of other black and gold cigarette packs defeated the plaintiff's claim that 'Raffles' cigarettes were being passed off as 'John Player Specials'.

3.10 The mark may uniquely denote the plaintiff, or may denote a clearly delineated class to which the plaintiff belongs, but not the defendant. A class reputation was at issue in the *Advocaat* case. Note that the plaintiff's actual identity need not be known to consumers[1].

---

1 Eg, *Powell v Birmingham Vinegar Brewery* [1897] AC 710.

3.11 Because passing off protects goodwill rather than any proprietary interest in the mark itself, a plaintiff with reputation in a mark may none the less fail unless it has business in the UK. Thus, in *Budweiser*[1], the plaintiff enjoyed only minimal sales in the UK proper (US airbase and embassy sales were discounted) and failed in its action to restrain a rival 'Budweiser' beer. However, a number of decisions suggest that a customer base in the UK will suffice[2]; certainly a fairly slight business activity will do[3]. Where a localised reputation is enjoyed, it may none the less be protected by nationwide injunction, as in *Chelsea Man*[4].

---

1 *Anheuser-Busch v Budjovicky Budvar* [1984] FSR 413.
2 Eg, *Maxim's v Dye* [1977] FSR 364; *Sheraton Corp v Sheraton Motels* [1964] RPC 202; cf *Bernadin v Pavilion Properties* [1967] RPC 581; *Athletes Foot v Cobra Sports* [1980] RPC 343.
3 *Bernadin*, n 2, at p 584.
4 [1985] FSR 567.

3.12 The plaintiff may be a professional or other organisation which does not trade in the commonplace sense of the word; the courts will grant relief if use of a similar name by others is likely to tarnish its reputation or to discourage membership[1]. Lastly, goodwill may endure after cessation of a business, at least where there is some intention to resume. This was the case in *Ad-Lib Club*[2], where a club had closed because of noise problems.

---

1   Eg, *British Legion v British Legion Club (Street) Ltd* (1931) 48 RPC 555: ex-serviceman's organisation; *British Medical Association v Marsh* (1931) 48 RPC 565. Contrast *Kean v McGivan* [1982] FSR 119 ('SDP'); for an election case lost by the defendant's successor, see *Sanders v Chichester* (1994) *The Times*, 2 December.
2   *Ad-Lib Club v Granville* [1971] FSR 1; [1972] RPC 673.

Misrepresentation

3.13   Many kinds of misrepresentation have been enjoined in passing-off actions. The most common is probably that the defendant's goods emanate from the plaintiff[1]. It may also be passing off to represent that the plaintiff's goods or services were supplied by the defendant[2]. Many other forms have been recognised; Table 2 lists some varieties, together with examples of cases founded upon them.

---

1   Thus, in *Reddaway v Banham* it was stated that 'nobody has any right to represent his goods as the goods of somebody else': [1896] AC 199 at p 204.
2   *Bristol Conservatories v Conservatories Custom Built* [1989] RPC 455.

Table 2:   Forms of misrepresentation

Type of misrepresentation (D = defendant; P = plaintiff)	Case example
D's products emanate from P	*Reddaway v Banham*[1]
D's goods are of the same class as P's	*Advocaat*[2]
D's goods are in some way connected with the products or business which has the goodwill	*Taittinger v Allbev*[3]
P's products emanate from D	*Bristol Conservatories*[4]
P's goods are P's goods of a different quality	*Spalding v Gamage*[5]
P's altered or deteriorated goods are original quality	*Wilts United Dairies v Robinson*[6]
D is P's licensee	*Mirage Studios v Counterfeat Clothing*[7]
D's business is connected with P's, eg as authorised distributor	*Sony v Saray*[8]
P is in some way responsible for the quality of D's products or D's customers' products	*Associated Newspapers v Insert Media*[9]

---

1   [1896] AC 199.
2   [1979] AC 731; [1980] RPC 31.
3   [1993] FSR 641 at pp 668, 673.

4   [1989] RPC 455.
5   [1914] 2 Ch 405; plaintiff's superseded 'ORB' footballs sold as the new and improved product.
6   [1958] RPC 94; affirming [1971] RPC 220: old stocks of canned milk.
7   [1991] FSR 145; 'Teenage Mutant Ninja Turtles' clothing.
8   [1983] FSR 302.
9   [1991] FSR 380: suggestion that plaintiffs had approved insertion of additional material into its
    periodicals, news publishers taking responsible attitude to advertising.

3.14   In order to be actionable, the representation must be false and likely to have an effect on customers or consumers. Thus, where the term 'Gledhill coils' had come to denote paper rolls to fit the plaintiff's tills, rather than rolls manufactured by the plaintiff, there was no passing off. In *Hodgkinson & Corby v Wards Mobility Services*[1], the resemblance between the defendant's and the plaintiff's prosthetic cushions was not likely to confuse the careful purchasers. In that case and in 'Blue-tak'[2], the possibility of post-sale confusion did not assist the plaintiff.

1   [1995] FSR 169; A Firth, 'Cushions and confusion: the RoHo passing off case' [1994] 11 EIPR 494.
2   *Bostik v Sellotape* [1994] RPC 556.

Damage

3.15   Damage is an essential element and comes in a variety of forms. The defendant's misrepresentation may cause diversion of business – sales or members. Thus, customers wishing to buy traditional 'Advocaat' were likely to be diverted to the defendant's non-conforming drink by use of the mark. Conversely, Stringfellow's passing off action failed[1] because the judge was not persuaded that the defendant's use of 'Stringfellows' on chips had affected attendance at the plaintiff's nightclub. Less direct damage occurs when the plaintiff's reputation is tarnished or prejudiced in some way, which diminishes the attractive force of the mark. This often occurs because the defendant's product is inferior to the plaintiff's. The effect of prejudice to reputation is difficult to quantify, which factor may encourage the grant of an interlocutory injunction.

1   *Stringfellow v McCain* [1984] RPC 501.

3.16   Damage may also be sustained by a plaintiff where it is exposed to litigation or complaint. It may be necessary to mollify dissatisfied customers or consumers[1]. Where a mark is popular with customers, the courts recognise that a plaintiff may wish to exploit goodwill by diversifying its business under the mark. It may wish to expand its product range, or enter into licensing arrangements. Alternatively, it may deliberately refrain from so doing in order to maintain the mark's exclusivity. In recent years, the action for passing off has been used to protect these aspects of goodwill in a mark, with cases like *Lego*[2], *Mirage Studios*[3] and *Elderflower Champagne*[4]. The last case is significant in referring explicitly to the concept of dilution.[5]

1   See, eg, *Associated Newspapers v Insert Media* [1991] FSR 380.

2   *Lego v Lego M Lemelstrich* [1983] FSR 155. 'Lego' was a household name for toy bricks; the defendants were enjoined from using it on garden equipment.
3   [1991] FSR 145.
4   *Taittinger v Allbev* [1993] FSR 641 at 678; see also *Parfums Givenchy v Designer Alternatives* [1994] RPC 243.
5   See paras **7.10–7.12**.

3.17   A deceptive mark can cause damage at all stages of the chain of commerce. It may amount to a misrepresentation at one stage, but not another. This is recognised in the *Advocaat* case, where Lord Diplock refers to ultimate consumers as well as prospective customers for the plaintiff's products. A person who participates in use of a misleading mark may be liable for damage further down the line. In the most extreme case, a passing-off action may lie where consumers are outside the jurisdiction. In *John Walker v Ost*[1] and in *White Horse v Gregson*[2], the defendant's activities caused or enabled adulterated Scotch whisky to be passed off abroad as the real thing; injunctions were granted in both cases. However, a defendant will not be held liable if an unobjectionable mark is subsequently misused[3].

1   [1970] RPC 489.
2   [1984] RPC 61.
3   *Payton v Snelling* (1900) 17 RPC 628 at 635; see also *Cadbury v Ulmer* [1988] FSR 385.

Defences to passing off

3.18   Even if a plaintiff makes out a case in passing off, the defendant may argue that it has an independent or concurrent right to use the mark. Thus, a defendant may not be enjoined from making proper use of its own name and address, provided it makes sufficient distinction from the plaintiff. Occasionally it is difficult to see quite what the defendant can do to distinguish itself[1]. Where a defendant has been in breach of an injunction elsewhere, he may exceptionally be restrained from using his own name at all in a particular commercial sphere[2].

1   Eg *Boswell-Wilkie Circus (Pty) Ltd v Brian Boswell Circus (Pty) Ltd* [1986] FSR 479; *Parker-Knoll v Knoll International* [1962] RPC 243 at pp 257ff.
2   *Gucci v Gucci* [1991] FSR 89.

3.19   Equitable defences may be available, at least to the grant of an injunction. Thus, in *Habib Bank*[1], the defendant bank, which had previously been a branch of the plaintiff's predecessor, was able to defend the passing off action. Acquiescence, laches and estoppel were also pleaded; the question was whether it would be unconscionable for the plaintiff to succeed. In *Nationwide*[2], grant of an interlocutory injunction would have conferred an unfair commercial advantage upon the plaintiff.

1   [1982] RPC 1.
2   [1987] FSR 579; injunction refused.

Other torts

3.20 Misuse of another's mark may amount to an injurious or malicious falsehood[1]. In *Wilts United Dairies Ltd v Thomas Robinson Sons & Co Ltd*[2], old stock which had deteriorated was sold as current stock under the plaintiff's mark. There was no disclaimer as to its condition. This was held to be both passing off and malicious falsehood. The latter tort is committed when:

(a) a false statement is made of the plaintiff's goods, services or business;
(b) maliciously, that is without just cause or excuse; and
(c) causes special damage[3].

Proving the last element has been eased by subs 3(1) of the Defamation Act 1952 which dispenses with proof of special damage if the words in question are calculated to cause pecuniary damage to the plaintiff and are either in writing or other permanent form or are in respect of the plaintiff's office, profession, trade, calling or business carried on at the time of publication.

---

1 The terms 'trade libel' or 'slander of goods' are also used.
2 [1958] RPC 94, affirming [1957] RPC 220.
3 *Royal Baking Powder v Wright, Crossley* (1901) 18 RPC 95.

3.21 The meaning of malice was elaborated in *Balden v Shorter*[1]; it involves some dishonest or otherwise improper motive. Malicious falsehood is usually less attractive to a plaintiff than passing off. This is partly because of the need to show malice, and partly because a defence of justification may lie. A defendant who claims he will justify at trial will be able to avert an interlocutory injunction, as in *Bestobell Paint v Bigg*[2]. Statements which are true in context may amount to falsehood if taken out of context[3].

---

1 [1933] Ch 427.
2 [1975] FSR 421.
3 *Compaq Computer v Dell Computer* [1992] FSR 93.

3.22 In *Advocaat*[1], Lord Diplock referred to passing off as a form of unfair competition. However, a wider tort of unfair competition is not recognised in English law, despite periodic calls from commentators[2]. In other Member States of the European Union[3], unfair competition law is variously founded upon general provisions of a civil code as to damages[4] or fault[5] or is provided by a specific statute[6]. Article 10*bis* of the Paris Convention obliges members of the Paris Union to give protection[7] against unfair competition in its various forms, in particular:

'1. all acts of such a nature as to create confusion by any means whatsoever with the establishment, the goods, or the industrial or commercial activities, of a competitor;
2. false allegations in the course of trade of such a nature as to discredit the establishment, the goods, or the industrial or commercial activities, of a competitor;
3. indications or allegations the use of which in the course of trade is liable to mislead the public as to the nature, the manufacturing process, the characteristics, the suitability for their purpose, or the quantity, of the goods.'

In the UK, passing off is seen as dealing with 1 and 3, which are also prohibited by the criminal Trade Descriptions Acts 1968 and 1972. Malicious falsehood provides an avenue for preventing the second category of unfair conduct.

1   *Advocaat* [1980] RPC 31.
2   See G Dworkin, 'Unfair Competition – is the Common Law Developing a New Tort?' [1979] EIPR 241. The answer to date has been 'no' – see J Adams, 'Unfair Competition – Why a Need is Unmet' [1992] EIPR 259 and citations therein.
3   And many other countries throughout the world. For an overview see 'Protection Against Unfair competition – an Analysis of the World Situation' WIPO 1994.
4   As in France: Art 1382 of the civil code.
5   As in The Netherlands: Civil Code of 1992, Arts 6.162 and 6.194–6.
6   As in Germany's Law of 1909 or Belgium's law of trade practices and consumer legislation.
7   Art 10*ter* obliges such states to provide appropriate legal remedies.

REGISTRATION

3.23   The causes of action outlined above have considerable disadvantages. A passing-off action can prove very expensive, unless satisfactorily compromised at an early stage. Malicious falsehood has the additional difficulty of establishing malice. Other torts such as interference with contract or unlawful interference with trade are usually difficult to sustain where trade marks are concerned. One of the greatest advantages of registration lies in the simplification of infringement proceedings. Where an identical mark is used in relation to the goods or services for which a mark is registered, the plaintiff in an infringement action need prove neither reputation nor confusion. Where the marks or products are merely similar, likelihood of confusion must be established but not reputation. The latter need only be proved where the goods or services are not similar or it is sought to enjoin use in relation to the proprietor's own goods or services. In these cases the damage to distinctiveness or reputation must also be proved.

3.24   Other advantages to the proprietor of registration include the enhanced possibility of preventing subsequent registration of a similar mark by others. The registration acts as a repellent, since a search will reveal its existence to third parties. A registered mark is an object of property in its own right. Section 22 of the 1994 Act states that it is incorporeal moveable property in Scotland; elsewhere personal property. A registered mark can thus be assigned with or without goodwill, as opposed to a 'common law (unregistered) mark', for which assignment without goodwill is meaningless[1]. A licensee under a registered trade mark may enjoy rights of action for infringement, as well as sharing in the other benefits enjoyed by a proprietor.

1   See S Lane; 'The Status of Licensing Common Law Marks' (1991), p 10.

3.25   Competitors and others also benefit from registration. It is possible to conduct a search of the register when choosing a new mark and to avoid the possibility of infringement. Where unjustified threats of infringement proceedings are made, an aggrieved party may sue to restrain the threats and recover damages[1]. Consumers have a means of identifying the proprietor of the mark and may have redress in case of injury caused by defective goods[2].

1 Unless they relate to marking or importing of goods or the supply of services under the marks: s 21(1).
2 Consumer Protection Act 1987, s 2(1) and 2(2)(b).

CIVIL PROCEEDINGS FOR INFRINGEMENT

3.26 Infringement of registered trade mark is a tort and may also constitute a criminal offence. Civil proceedings for infringement are brought in the High Court in England and Wales and Northern Ireland and in the Court of Session in Scotland[1]. At present there is no such jurisdiction in the other civil courts, although county courts and sheriff courts can make orders for the delivery up and destruction of infringing goods, materials or articles[2].

1 Section 75 defines 'court' in these terms.
2 Sections 16, 19 and 20.

CRIMINAL SANCTIONS

3.27 Section 92 of the 1994 Act creates a number of criminal offences[1]. These are triable either way. Conviction may result in imprisonment, with a maximum of 6 months on summary conviction or 10 years on indictment, or a fine, or both. In addition, infringing goods and materials may be forfeit; in fact, forfeiture orders can be made without a conviction, providing the court is satisfied that an offence has been committed. This power will be useful to trading standards officers in possession of goods whose owners understandably do not wish to reappear to claim them.

1 See, further, paras **7.46–7.48**.

PERSONNEL OF TRADE MARK LAW

3.28 As under previous legislation, there are no restrictions on providing trade mark agency services. Anyone can act as a trade mark agent. For several reasons, however, it is desirable to employ a professionally qualified agent. First, registration of trade mark agents depends upon professional qualification; examinations are currently administered by a joint board of the Institute of Trade Mark Agents and the Chartered Institute of Patent Agents. Secondly, communications with a registered trade mark agent on matters relating to trade marks, passing off and designs are privileged in the same way as communications with a solicitor. This extends to communications with third parties for the purpose of obtaining information for instructing the agent or in response to such a request. Privilege also applies where the trade mark agent is a partnership of registered agents or a company entitled to call itself a registered trade mark agent[1]. A registered trade mark agent may be described as a 'trade mark attorney' without breaching rules otherwise restricting the term 'attorney' to solicitors[2].

1   In particular because all its directors are registered agents: s 84(4).
2   Section 86.

3.29   To preserve these important advantages, s 84 renders criminal the unjustified use of the terms 'registered trade mark agent' by unqualified persons. Proceedings must be brought within a year. The Registry may refuse to deal with a person who has been convicted of such an offence, as well as anyone whose conduct would render them liable to removal from the register of trade mark agents: s 88. The 1994 Act contains powers to prescribe rules for mixed partnerships. A number of solicitors also do trade mark work; a recent trend has been the employment of trade mark agents by firms of solicitors in order to provide clients with a 'one-stop shop' for trade mark matters.

Chapter 4

LIMITS TO TRADE MARK PROTECTION

INTRODUCTION

4.1   Registration and passing-off rights do not give a proprietor a monopoly over a mark in all circumstances. First, limits may be inherent in the mark or the rights themselves, or expressly imposed by the Trade Marks Act. These are described here as 'intrinsic limits'. Secondly, the sovereignty of Parliament and the jurisdiction of the courts are territorially limited, and rights may not extend throughout the jurisdiction. Lastly, the enjoyment and exercise of trade mark rights are subject to general rules of law and in particular those rules designed to ensure freedom of trade. This last category of limit is described here as 'extrinsic'.

INTRINSIC LIMITS

'In the course of trade'

4.2   Trade mark rights, not surprisingly, are generally confined to the commercial arena. This is certainly true of passing off[1]. A plaintiff's use of a mark is unprotected if there is no business activity to which goodwill can attach. Thus, a local political party[2] failed to gain protection for their name by suing in passing off. However, well-established professional and charitable organisations like the British Legion[3], the British Medical Association[4] and the British Diabetic Association[5] have succeeded – 'trade' may be given a generous interpretation. Likewise, the defendant's activities need to be commercial for a passing off action to lie. Lord Diplock in *Advocaat*[6] makes particular reference to misrepresentations by a trader in the course of trade.

---

1   In *Advocaat*, Lord Diplock referred to 'the trader by whom the action is brought' and Lord Fraser referred to the business of the plaintiff: [1980] RPC 31.
2   *Kean v McGivan* [1982] FSR 119 ('SDP').
3   *British Legion v British Legion Club (Street) Ltd* (1931) 48 RPC 555.
4   *BMA v Marsh* (1931) 48 RPC 565.
5   See [1992] 11 EIPR D-242.
6   See n 1.

4.3   Similar considerations apply to registered trade marks[1]. The acts amounting to infringement of a registered trade mark are elaborated in s 10 of the Trade Marks Act 1994, where all infringing acts are expressed to be in the course of trade. Curiously, the Act is less explicit when it comes to the activities of the registered proprietor. Section 1 refers to the trade marks distinguishing between 'undertakings', a phrase which suggests economic activity[2]. Subsection 32(3) specifies that an applicant for registration must state its use or intention to use the mark for the goods or services concerned, although the course of trade is not specified. Failure to make 'genuine' use of a registered mark is a ground for revocation: s 46. It is to be hoped that the Parliamentary draftsman's reticence here will leave it open for all trade mark users to register. Certainly the Act leaves little scope for the Registry to repeat its refusal to register 'Hospital World'[3] because the publication was funded by advertisements and distributed free to readers[4].

1   The 1994 Act refers to 'trade', which 'includes any business or profession': s 103(1).
2   See, eg, D Raybould and A Firth *Law of Monopolies* (1991), pp 211–212.
3   [1967] RPC 595.
4   Cf *Golden Pages* [1985] FSR 27 (Ireland), registered for directories delivered free. Latterly the UK Registry has followed this in practice: *UK Trade Marks Handbook*, CIPA/ITMA, para 6.33.

Similarity of product

4.4   Even where plaintiff and defendant are both traders, an action in passing off or for infringement of a registered trade mark generally requires a degree of similarity between the parties' goods or services. Unless this element is present, the likelihood of damage is remote[1]. If the mark is a 'household name', however, damage may be established and an injunction will lie[2].

1   Eg, *Stringfellow v McCain* [1984] RPC 501.
2   As in *Lego v Lego M Lemelstrich* [1983] FSR 155 (passing off); Trade Marks Act 1994, s 10(3).

Signs in common currency

4.5   Where a sign is wholly descriptive or one which traders at large have a legitimate right to use, the courts are slow to find passing off[1]. Even if one trader enjoys goodwill in such a mark, small differences will suffice to prevent misrepresentation by a rival trader[2]. A wholly descriptive mark is debarred from registration by subs 3(1)(b) and (c) of the 1994 Act, unless distinctive character has been acquired by use. Again, it seems likely that the scope of such a registered mark will be narrow; thus 'Aquatite' would not be an infringement of 'Aquascutum' for watertight garments[3].

1   As in *'Oven chips'*, *McCain v Country Fair* [1981] RPC 69.
2   *Office Cleaning Services Ltd v Westminster Window and General Cleaners* (1946) 62 RPC 39.
3   As in *Aquascutum v Cohen & Wilks* (1909) 26 RPC 651.

Non-trade mark use[1]

4.6   If the defendant does not use a sign as a trade mark, it is unlikely that a plaintiff in a passing-off action will succeed in establishing a misrepresentation[2]. The same was true of infringement actions under the 1938 Act[3]. What about the 1994 Act? The trade marks harmonisation Directive expressly does not affect provisions in a Member State relating to non-trade mark use, provided that use of the sign without due cause takes unfair advantage of, or is detrimental to, the distinctive character or repute of the mark[4]. Comparison of the text of Article 5 of the Directive with s 10 of the 1994 Act suggests that no new prohibition on non-trade mark use of a registered mark has been introduced, save possibly where a mark is used to refer to the proprietor's own goods or services[5]. This is reinforced by s 9, which confers exclusive rights in the 'trade mark' rather than in the 'sign'. This may be contrasted with the situation in The Netherlands, where non-trade mark use may be enjoined[6].

1   See paras **1.36** and **1.37**.
2   Eg, *Hodgkinson & Corby v Wards Mobility Services* [1995] FSR 169, discussed in A Firth, 'Cushions and confusion' [1994] 11 EIPR 494.
3   Eg, *Mothercare v Penguin Books* [1988] RPC 113; cf *Games Workshop v Transworld* [1993] FSR 705.
4   Art 5(5).
5   Section 10(6).
6   See, eg, the *Philips* case cited by M Kniff in 'Selected Benelux cases' *Trademark World*, July/August 1994, p 14.

Use of own name, address, etc

4.7   A variant of the above occurs when the mark, in which a plaintiff claims rights, constitutes the defendant's own name or address. This may provide a complete defence[1] or lead to a qualified injunction[2].

1   As in *Day v Brownrigg* (1878) 10 Ch D 294: adoption of house name, Trade Marks Act 1994, s 11(2)(a).
2   *Parker-Knoll v Knoll International* [1962] RPC 265; *Boswell-Wilkie Circus v Brian Boswell Circus* [1986] FSR 479; cf *Gucci v Gucci* [1991] FSR 89.

TERRITORIAL LIMITS

4.8   Passing off may be territorially limited in two respects. The plaintiff's goodwill may be limited to part of the country only. In *Evans v Eradicure*[1], the defendant's and plaintiff's businesses under similar names expanded until they overlapped. It was held that, in the area of overlap, they could restrain third parties but not each other from carrying on business under a similar mark. If the plaintiff does not carry on business in the UK, he may find it difficult to establish an actionable goodwill. Section 56 of the 1994 Act enables a foreign[2] plaintiff whose mark is well known in the UK to restrain confusing use even without a registration or passing off rights. As far as registered trade marks are concerned, the legislative powers of Parliament are territorially limited. This factor underlies the decision in *Burroughs v Speyside*[3], where allegedly infringing activities took place in Italy. A similar issue arose in *Colgate-Palmolive v Markwell Finance*[4]. The court at first instance pointed out that the mark which had been applied to the goods was the Brazilian 'Colgate' mark, and not the identical UK mark.

In *Def Lepp*[5], a copyright claim was struck out from English proceedings because it related to allegedly infringing acts which took place in Holland and Luxemburg. In *Conan Doyle v Tyburn*[6], the court declined jurisdiction in an action for a declaration as to whether acts committed in the US infringed US copyright.

---

1   [1972] RPC 808; [1972] FSR 137.
2   Section 56 is unlikely to avail a UK plaintiff, since it is designed to satisfy the UK's international obligations: see A Kamperman Sanders, 'Some Frequently Asked Questions about the Trade Marks Act 1994' [1995] EIPR 67 at n 43 for a textual argument.
3   *Burroughs (James) v Speymalt Whisky Distributors* [1991] RPC 130; where the right to sue in Scotland and to sue for the equivalent wrong in Italy were enjoyed by different parties. At the time of writing, Parliament is debating the Private International Law (Miscellaneous Provisions) Bill with a proposed abrogation of the 'double actionability' rule.
4   [1989] RPC 497.
5   *Def Lepp Music v Stuart-Brown* [1986] RPC 273.
6   *Tyburn Productions v Conan Doyle* [1990] 1 All ER 909, discussed by R Arnold in 'Can one sue in England for infringement of foreign intellectual property rights?' [1990] EIPR 254.

4.9   It may be noted that in the Scotch Whisky cases[1], injunctions were granted to restrain the defendants' conduct within the UK on the basis that it would lead to passing off in another jurisdiction, where it was also actionable. These cases may be distinguished from those cited above in that the acts alleged against the defendants took place in England. Furthermore, the courts in passing-off cases have always been astute to restrain passing off at source, even where confusion occurs further down the line[2].

---

1   *John Walker v Ost* [1970] RPC 489; [1970] FSR 63; *White Horse v Gregson* [1984] RPC 61.
2   See para **4.2**, n 1.

4.10   The situation is complicated by the Brussels Convention on Civil Jurisdiction and Judgments[1]. Article 16(4) confers on the UK courts exclusive jurisdiction as to the registration or validity of UK registered marks. Although pure issues of title usually fall outside this provision, in trade mark cases, title and validity are often interlinked[2]. The Convention is silent as to infringement; presumably jurisdiction in infringement follows the general tort criteria of defendant's domicile, the place of commission of the tort and (at least where damage is an integral element of the tort[3]) the place where damage is sustained[4]. It should be noted that in applying the Brussels Convention a court applies its own private international law. Thus, it is perfectly feasible for a UK court to decline jurisdiction over an infringement in, say, Germany[5], whilst a Netherlands court assumes jurisdiction[6]. In the latter case, however, the court is enforcing rights existing under the law of the jurisdiction in which the acts of infringement take place. The Brussels Convention does not extend the law of The Netherlands and any trade mark registrations effective there to Germany. It is submitted that the validity of any extra-territorial injunction would depend on the existence of parallel rights in the outside jurisdictions[7].

1 Of 27 September 1968; implemented in the UK by means of the Civil Jurisdiction and Judgments Act 1982 (in force from 1 January 1987). For helpful accounts, see N Rose, ed, *Pre-emptive Remedies in Europe* (1992); O'Malley & Layton *European Civil Practice* (1989).

2 Eg because an assignment has rendered a mark deceptive or because the wrong person has applied to register: *K Sabatier TM* [1993] RPC 97; Trade Marks Act 1994, s 60.

3 To allow proceedings wherever damage is felt, eg, because a bank account is maintained in a particular jurisdiction, would defeat the purpose of the Convention.

4 Art 5(3) refers to the place where the harmful event occurred; this has been used to sustain an action in the jurisdiction where pollution damage occurred, as opposed to the place where the causative discharge of pollutants took place: *Handelskwerij G J Bier v Mines des Potasse d'Alsace* [1976] ECR 1735.

5 See R Arnold [1990] EIPR 254.

6 Some courts in The Netherlands appear happy to hear cases and grant relief in respect of foreign infringements of intellectual property rights: for commentary see J J Brinkhof, 'Could the President of the District Court of the Hague take measures concerning the infringement of foreign patents?' [1994] EIPR 360.

7 Although Lord Coulsfield doubted in *Burroughs* whether this would satisfy the double actionability rule of UK private international law. For interlocutory enforcement proceedings, see *X v Caledonian Newspapers* (1994) *The Times*, 16 February.

EXTRINSIC LIMITS

4.11   The territorial nature of trade mark rights makes them apt to hamper trade. Although an established mark will not usually prevent a competitor from introducing a competing product into the market, the latter will have to gain customer acceptance in the face of the earlier brand. It is not surprising, therefore, that the exploitation of trade mark rights may be subject to the doctrine of restraint of trade, to national competition law and to the provisions of the EEC Treaty[1]. Where there is an actual or potential effect on trade between Member States, Article 85 of the Treaty as to restrictive practices, Article 86 on abuse of monopoly and Articles 30–36 on the free movement of goods[2] in particular will be relevant. In fact the competence of the European Commission, Council of Ministers, Parliament and Court of Justice to legislate and rule in trade mark and other intellectual property matters depends upon the effects on interstate trade.

1 For further detail on the effect of these provisions on intellectual property, see Ch 13 of D Raybould and A Firth *Law of Monopolies* (1991) Ch 7.

2 For recent developments, see G Tritton, 'Articles 30 to 36 and Intellectual Property: is the Jurisprudence of the ECJ now of an Ideal Standard? [1994] 10 EIPR 422.

4.12   As a matter of UK law, the territorial nature of trade marks and other intellectual property rights in principle makes it possible for the proprietor to control the movement of products between territories[1]. Where a proprietor fails in transactions to avail itself of the possibility of control, consent to movement will be implied. Thus, in *Betts v Willmott*[2], a patentee was held impliedly to consent to a movement of goods which was within its powers to prevent. The alternative doctrine of international exhaustion, in which enjoyment of rights in one State renders equivalent rights unenforceable in other States, was emphatically rejected by the Privy Council in *National Phonograph v Menck*[3]. The concept of implied consent does not seem to have developed in the same way in the rest of Europe, possibly because privity of contract and the corporate veil[4] do not have the same potency[5] as in the UK. However, the issue of consent is crucial to 'exhaustion' in the jurisprudence of the European Court.

1   Whether this remains true as between States making up the European single market is considered
    below.
2   (1871) LR 6 Ch App 239; cf *SA des Manufacturers de Glaces v Tilghman's Patent Sand Blast Co* (1883) 25 ChD 1.
3   (1911) 28 RPC 229.
4   The legal dividing line between a company, as a distinct legal entity, and its shareholders or members.
    'Piercing the corporate veil' – crossing the dividing line – is rarely achieved, unless the company is a
    sham.
5   However, the UK Registry and courts have not been overly strict in this regard. See, eg, *Revlon v Cripps &
    Lee* [1980] FSR 85.

4.13   The common law doctrine of restraint of trade will apply to trade mark transactions as to any other. Readers will recall that an agreement or term in restraint of trade will be void unless it is reasonably necessary to protect a legitimate interest – reasonable as between the parties and in the public interest. Given that trade mark restrictions would not normally fetter trade in the goods or services as such and given the public's particular interest in the indicative power of trade marks, it is not surprising that decisions in this area are uncommon. Indeed, in *Levi Strauss v Kimbyr*[1], the High Court of New Zealand rejected the argument that a trade mark was a form of monopoly:

'... the protection of genuine well-established trade marks such as Levi's pocket tab device from free riding competition is in the public interest and pro-competitive rather than the reverse ...'[2].

1   [1994] FSR 335, Williams J.
2   Ibid at p 368.

4.14   The Restrictive Trade Practices Act 1976[1] clearly contemplates that trade mark agreements may be registrable. Registration is required when two or more persons carrying on business in the UK accept certain kinds of restrictions[2]. However, Sch 3, para 4[3] provides exemption in certain cases. Para 4(2) exempts agreements authorising the use of certification and collective marks, provided that any relevant restrictions are permitted by the regulations approved for the use of those marks. Agreements authorising the use of ordinary registered marks are exempt under para 4(1), provided the relevant restrictions relate to the descriptions of goods or kinds of services for which the mark is to be used, the form or manner of provision of services and the processes of manufacture to be applied to goods marked or supplied. Presumably the wording is adequate to extend to all necessary types of quality control; quality control to British Standards or certain Trade Association standards is already accommodated by ss 9(5) and 18(5). Paragraph 4(1) does not refer to restrictions as to the manner of marking but these would probably fall to be disregarded by virtue of s 9(3) for goods and s 18(2) for services. Thus, to avoid registration for pure trade mark licences, it would not be necessary to locate a licensor off-shore or to ensure that only one party accepts restrictions[4].

1   For some time, it has been proposed to repeal this statute in favour of effects-based legislation along the lines of Art 85 of the Treaty of Rome: see White Paper, 'Opening Markets: new policy on restrictive trade practices' (1989) Cm 727. At the time of writing, however, the reforms were not in immediate prospect. See J Pratt, 'Changes in UK Competition Law: a wasted opportunity?' [1994] 2 ECLR 89. The Deregulation and Contracting Out Act 1994 amends the 1976 Act in several matters of detail.
2   See ss 6, 7, 11 and 12.
3   As substituted by Sch 4, para 7 of the Trade Marks Act 1994.
4   These tactics are effective and legitimate because the 1976 Act is form-based rather than effect-based.

4.15   The various classes of agreement exempted by Sch 3 are not cumulative[1]. However, a mixed know-how and trade mark licence, or a franchise agreement, is likely to be viewed sympathetically by the Office of Fair Trading[2]; the Registrar has discretion not to refer cases to the Restrictive Practices Court where they are exempt under Article 85(3)[3]. He may also be discharged from his duty to refer when an agreement is unlikely to be detrimental to competition[4]. A new s 27A has been inserted by the Deregulation and Contracting Out Act 1994. This empowers the Secretary of State by Order to render certain descriptions of agreement non-notifiable. Specific reference is made to size criteria and to Community law.

EC jurisprudence on trade marks is more extensive, and is discussed further in Ch 13.

1   *Re Schweppes Agreement (No 2)* [1971] 1 WLR 1148.
2   See M Howe, 'Franchising and restrictive practices law: the Office of Fair Trading view' [1988] ECLR 439.
3   Restrictive Trade Practices Act 1976, s 21(1).
4   Restrictive Trade Practices Act 1976, s 21(2).

Chapter 5

REGISTRATION

THE CRITERIA

5.1   To obtain registration, the following must be present:

(a)   a registrable mark; this in turn presupposes a sign[1], which
    (i)   functions as a trade mark[2],
    (ii)   is capable of being distinctive[3],
    (iii)   can be represented graphically[4], and
    (iv)   is not prohibited from registration on absolute grounds[5], nor on relative grounds[6];
(b)   an applicant with an address for service in the UK[7];
(c)   who uses the mark or has a bona fide intention to do so[8], in relation to;
(d)   stated goods and services[9], in a specified class or classes[10], for which;
(e)   a request for registration is made to the Registrar[11],
(f)   together with payment of fees[12].

A representation[13] of the mark must be attached to the relevant box on Form TM3, which is sent or delivered to the Patent Office[14].

---

1   See Trade Marks Act 1994, s 1(1); paras **2.1–2.4**.
2   See Ch 1; cf *Smith Kline & French Laboratories Ltd's Cimetidine TM* [1991] RPC 17.
3   See paras **2.32–2.34**.
4   See paras **2.19–2.21**.
5   See para **2.35**.
6   See paras **2.32–2.34**.
7   Trade Marks Act 1994, s 32(2)(b) and Trade Mark Rules 1994, r 10. Failure to provide an address for service may result in the application being treated as abandoned: r 10(6), although the Registrar will first of all give notice for the defect to be put right: r 10(6). An applicant does not have to show a proprietary interest: *Loudoun Manufacturing v Courtaulds* (1994) *The Times*, 14 February.
8   Section 32(3). If the stated intention is not bona fide, the application may be treated as made in bad faith, and may be refused, opposed or cancelled. See s 3(6) and para **5.40** and Ch 9.
9   Section 32(2)(c).
10   Rule 8.
11   Section 32(1) and (2)(a). The request is made on Form TM3: r 5.
12   Rule 4. Fees may accompany the application or be deducted from an account with the Registry.
13   Section 32(2)(d); although the box is small (8cm x 8cm), it appears that the Registry will accept representations of up to A4 size: Form TM3, note (h).
14   Rule 2(3). Rule 63 enables the Registry to offer service by electronic means.

5.2   Classification of goods and services is made according to the Nice system[1]; classes 1–34 comprise every imaginable variety of goods, whilst classes 35–42 are for services[2]. The classes are particularly useful for search purposes. Allocation of goods or services to a particular class is a matter solely for the Registrar[3]. It has no significance as far as infringement or other rights are concerned. At the date of commencement of the 1994 Act, some venerable registrations were classified according to an earlier scheme[4]; the Registrar is empowered by s 65 of the 1994 Act to re-classify these, with provision for advertisement and opposition[5]. Under the 1938 Act, a separate application had to be made for each class. Under the 1994 Act, a single application is possible for registration of a mark in a number of classes[6]. Where an application has listed goods or services in the wrong class, they may be moved, the application being amended to include the appropriate class where necessary[7]. However, it seems that it will not be possible for an applicant to broaden the scope his application by asking for additional rather than alternative classes. For example, building materials fall in different classes according to whether they are made of wood, metal, etc. An application for building materials in one class could not be amended to cover building materials in additional classes.

1   Agreed at Nice in June 1957 and revised in 1967 and 1977. As at 1 July 1994, 41 States had signed the Nice Agreement, but the classification is used by trade mark registries in many other States. The classification is given in Sch 4 to the Trade Marks Rules 1994 (SI 1994/2583) (Appendix 2 below).
2   WIPO publish detailed listings.
3   Section 34(2).
4   See r 7 and Sch 3.
5   Section 65(3)–(5) and r 40.
6   Rule 8; subject to payment of additional fees.
7   Rule 8(3), Form TM3A.

5.3   Section 35 allows an applicant to claim priority from the earliest application made in a Paris Convention country[1], provided that does not predate the UK application by more than six months[2]. The significance of a priority claim is that the mark is vulnerable only to applications or registrations made before the 'priority date'. Nor is the application affected by any use of the mark in the UK between the two dates. This is advantageous to an applicant where the use is by a third party but it means that use by the proprietor during the interim period cannot affect registrability. This may be disadvantageous where the applicant needs evidence of use to support the application[3]. If it is sought to rely on a Convention priority, additional documents must be filed[4]. Provided the UK application is for the same or a narrower specification of goods or services as the earlier Convention application, the whole will enjoy the earlier priority date. It is also possible to have one or more partial priority claims within a single application[5].

1   Priority for the Channel Islands, colonies and other territories are dealt with in s 36.
2   In accordance with Art 4. If the first application has failed without being used for priority, a second application date from the same country may be used: s 35(4).
3   See para **5.10**.
4   Rule 6.
5   Registry Work Manual, Ch 6, p 45.

5.4   Where the mark consists of or contains an emblem specially protected by s 4, for example Royal Arms, the appropriate consent to registration must also be filed[1].

---

1   Rule 9. Sections 57 and 59 also prohibit the registration of the emblems of Convention countries and international organisations unless authorisation is given or unnecessary.

5.5   If the application is defective, the Registrar will notify the applicant and give two months for the matter to be put right. The effect of failure to do so depends upon the defect in question[1]. Failure to supply the basic information specified in s 32(2) (request for registration, name and address, statement of goods and services and representation of the mark) means that the application is deemed never to have been made. Where the default is in the statement of use or of intention to use, or payment of application or class fees, the application is treated as abandoned. The difference is significant in that the abandoned mark will appear on a computer search and deter other applicants, whereas a void application will not.

---

1   Rule 11.

5.6   If and when all the requirements are satisfied, the application will be given a filing date[1] – the date upon which the application became complete. If the mark proceeds to registration, it will be deemed to have been registered as of the filing date[2], so that infringement rights will be retrospective.

---

1   Section 33(1).
2   Section 40(3).

THE PROCESS

5.7   The Registrar may require translation of any document or part document which is not in English[1]. This presumably applies where the mark itself appears to be in a foreign language or script. The Registry will then have regard to the meaning of the mark when assessing its registrability[2]. The strength of an objection based on a mark's meaning depends upon whether the language is familiar or unfamilar in the UK and on whether the language is commonly associated with the type of product, for example, French for fashion articles and toiletries.

---

1   Rule 66.
2   Registry Work Manual, Ch 6, Appendix F sets out detailed practice on this.

5.8   Assuming that all the paperwork is formally in order, it remains for the Registry to examine whether the application satisfies the substantive requirements of the 1994 Act, including carrying out a search for conflicting marks. The ways in which the application may proceed are mapped out in Figure 2.

Figure 2: Processes of registration

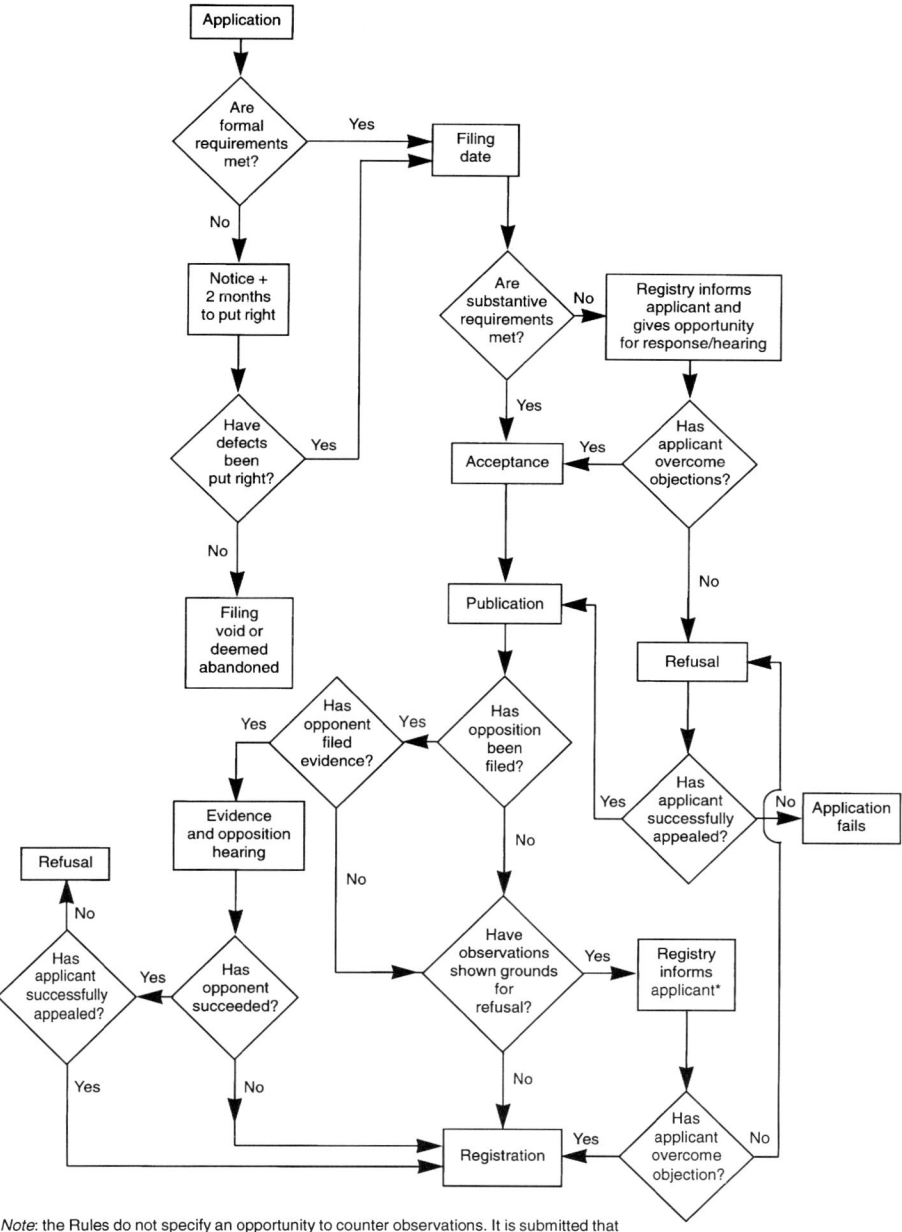

* *Note*: the Rules do not specify an opportunity to counter observations. It is submitted that natural justice demands it.

THE OBSTACLES

5.9   The Registry may raise objections to registrability, which may be inherent in the mark itself, as applied to the product in question, or based on extrinsic factors, in particular conflict with earlier marks. The latter is considered at para **5.28**. In the former case, the Registrar may argue that the alleged sign does not appear to function as a trade mark[1], or is descriptive, geographical, misleading or otherwise fails to satisfy the 1994 Act. When the Registry raises an objection, it will notify the applicant in writing and give an opportunity for the applicant to respond. This can be done informally, by correspondence. The applicant may also request an oral hearing. An appointment with a hearing officer is not held in public[2] and can be quite informal. Hearings may be conducted at the Patent Office in Newport, Wales, or by video conference link. Hearing accommodation has also been retained at the former Patent Office building in London. The applicant or their agent should consider whether any of the following ways of overcoming obstacles will be needed and prepare accordingly. The Registrar has the power to call for evidence or documents and may do so at the hearing[3]. If the Registrar suspects bad faith[4], he may call for evidence at an early stage.

---

1   See, eg, Registry Work Manual, Ch 6 at p 9.
2   As opposed to an inter partes hearing: r 53.
3   Rule 51.
4   An absolute ground of refusal: s 3(6).

OVERCOMING THE OBSTACLES

Argument

5.10   It may be possible to argue that the Registry is mistaken as to fact or law. The law will always be a matter for argument, but unless the Registrar is able to take 'judicial notice' of some factor overlooked, in practice evidence will be needed as to fact.

Evidence of use

5.11   A number of the objections under s 3 can be dispelled by evidence of distinctiveness in fact, acquired by use before the application date: proviso to subs 3(1). Such evidence may also be used to overcome an objection on the grounds of deceptiveness, if the mark has been used extensively without actually causing deception. Evidence of use after the date of application may be relevant on this point. It may also be possible to argue that distinctiveness acquired after the date of application is evidence of capability to distinguish.

5.12 It is submitted that evidence of distinctiveness in use outside the UK may be relevant. The section is not territorially limited, although traditionally the Registry and courts have been unenthusiastic as to evidence of foreign use[1]. If it can be shown that a mark has in fact become distinctive outside the UK, this may be persuasive as to capability of distinguishing in this country, but much will depend on linguistic and commercial factors. For this reason, it is unlikely that evidence of foreign use would be persuasive on the issue of deceptiveness.

Does the evidence have to prove distinctiveness, or will the Registry be prepared to infer distinctiveness from evidence of use? The Act does refer to the mark 'having acquired a distinctive character as a result of the use made of it'. As pointed out in the Registry Work Manual[2], long use of a sign common to the trade will not establish distinctiveness[3]. In a suitable case, it is likely that evidence of use will be accepted, especially if accompanied by evidence that no similar mark is in use on the market.

1 See *Kerly's Law of Trade Marks and Trade Names* (1986) 12th edn, para 8–6, citing *Ford-Werke* (1955) 72 RPC 191.
2 See Ch 6, p 18.
3 And see *Imperial Group v Philip Morris* [1984] RPC 293.

5.13 If evidence of distinctiveness is required, how may it be obtained? The courts have been hostile to market survey evidence in infringement actions, even where the survey has been properly conducted[1]. In the *Raffles* case[2], Whitford J gave guidance on what constituted the elements of a good survey:

(a)   representative sample;
(b)   statistically significant size;
(c)   fair conduct;
(d)   disclosure of all surveys and responses;
(e)   no leading questions[3];
(f)   recording of exact answers;
(g)   disclosure of instructions to interviewers;
(h)   disclosure of coding instructions where computer analysis is used.

1 For an excellent account of survey evidence in infringement cases, see the *UK Trade Mark Handbook* (CIPA/ITMA 1991 and releases) para 21.3.42.
2 *Imperial Group v Philip Morris* [1984] RPC 294.
3 On the design of survey questions to measure whether distinctiveness has been attained, see V Palladino 'Surveying Secondary Meaning' (1994) 84 TMR 155.

5.14 The court has pointed out[1] that evidence as to manner of sale or supply, and the circumstances in which confusion may arise, are helpful. Surveys may elicit this kind of information quite effectively. The Registry has traditionally been more receptive of survey evidence, provided of course that the survey is properly carried out. Survey evidence is much used by trade mark registries in continental Europe[2]. It seems unlikely that the UK Registry will engage in 'number-crunching' exercises.

---

1 *Dalgety Spillers Foods v Food Brokers* [1994] FSR 504, cf *United Biscuits v Burtons Biscuits (Jaffa Cakes)* [1992] FSR 14.
2 See, eg, A Kur, 'Well-known marks, highly renowned marks and marks having a (high) reputation – what's it all about?' (1992) 23 IIC 218.

5.15 In providing evidence of use, an applicant needs to consider whether any information is confidential. Under the new regime, all documents filed (whether in 1994 Act applications or in applications pending under the 1938 Act) will in principle be open to public inspection once the relevant stage of the procedure has been completed[1]. Although the rules permit an applicant to request and the Registrar to rule that a document or part of a document is confidential, it is thought that this power will be used sparingly. It is preferable to prepare evidence in such a way that confidential detail need not be disclosed.

---

1 Rule 43.

Other evidence

5.16 Other evidence relates to the way in which services or goods are marketed, used, ordered[1] or approved, the character of a geographical location and the likelihood of honest traders there being embarrassed by registration of a geographical mark, and so forth.

---

1 Eg, doctors are notorious for their bad handwriting on prescriptions.

Invoking an earlier registration

5.17 Where the same or a similar mark is already registered in the name of the applicant, he may wish to rely upon it in support of a later application. This tactic may backfire; the Registry has been known to comment darkly that the earlier registration might be invalid[1]. However, if a new mark is an equally distinctive variant of an earlier registration, it can help. Thus, a registration of 'Opx' might suggest the distinctiveness of 'Opk' but not 'Opt'. In fact, it is possible to register variants on a basic theme as a series of marks, all in the same application or registration[2]. For example, a mark may be accompanied by model numbers; all being registrable as a series. Thus, 'Cyclops 10', 'Cyclops 20', 'Cyclops 30'.

---

1 Eg, *Avon* [1985] RPC 43 at p 48 where an earlier registration had been obtained after creation of the County of Avon.
2 Section 41(1)(c) and r 21.

5.18   The Registry recognises that a trader may wish to extend the range of services or goods supplied under the mark. In *Esso*[1] the application for registration of the Esso[2] roundel for tyres was allowed in the light of existing registrations for lubricants and fuels. Tyres were fairly closely allied to the pre-existing fields of activity. However, registration was refused for parts and fittings for land and water vehicles.

---

1   [1972] RPC 283.
2   The problem with the mark was, of course, the phonetic equivalent of 'Esso' to the two letters 'SO'. For success with a similar mark from the same stable, see *Exxate* [1986] RPC 567 (equivalent to X8).

5.19   Where the objection is based on deceptiveness or public morality rather than distinctiveness, an earlier registration of the same mark will undoubtedly assist, especially if reinforced by evidence if lack of confusion or offence.

5.20   As well as invoking a prior registration of a similar mark, a different established mark could be used to support an application under the 1938 Act. This was because amendment of a mark was possible during prosecution of the application. If a mark was likely to be rejected due to lack of distinctiveness, it could sometimes be helped on to the register by adding an established sister or house mark. Thus, if Volkswagen were having difficulty in registering a model name, such as 'Golf' or 'Polo', it could amend the mark to 'Volkswagen Golf' or 'Volkswagen Polo'. This practice was sometimes known as 'adding an equity'. The tactic is not possible for 1994 Act applications, however, since the scope for amending marks is very restricted[1]. In any event, registration of a composite mark would not always help its elements to get on the Register at a later stage[2].

---

1   Section 39(2) permits amendment only when it does not substantially affect the mark's identity, and then only in respect of corrections to name, address or obvious errors of wording or other obvious mistakes. For practice on amendment, see rr 17 and 18.
2   Eg, in *Cos TM* [1993] RPC 67, the prior registration of 'Cos D'Estournel' did not overcome geographical objection to registration of 'Cos'.

Amend specification of goods or services

5.21   Amendment of the specification of goods or services is available under s 39(1). The objection may relate only to some of the goods or services concerned, which can be deleted. Since registration now confers infringement rights beyond the products for which the mark is actually registered, the usefulness of this practice[1] is likely to diminish.

---

1   Charmingly described as 'Penguin' practice: Registry Work Manual, Ch 6, Appendix K. Penguin was registered for books excluding those about penguins. However, 'Penguin' in the title of a book about penguins would probably not be regarded as use of a trade mark.

Division or merger of the application

5.22   Division of the application is less drastic than removing or excluding goods or services altogether. Instead, an application may be split[1] so that it may proceed swiftly to registration for the trouble-free goods or services, and the troublesome part of the application may be dealt with separately. The opposite, merger[2] of applications (or indeed registrations), is also possible. Where objections or disputes are anticipated, it may be wise to file separate applications on the same date. If and when the problems are overcome, merger can be sought. Once marks are registered, they can be merged even if their filing dates are different. The merged registration bears the date of registration of the latest component, and is subject to any disclaimer, limitation or licence affecting the component registrations.

1   Section 41(1)(a); r 19.
2   Section 41(1)(b); r 20.

Disclaimers and conditions

5.23   Former Registry practice was to impose conditions or a disclaimer on the registration of a doubtful mark. An example was the blank space condition, whereby registration was conditional upon the use only of non-trade mark matter in any blank space. Breach of condition was a ground for cancellation or variation of the registration[1]. The 1994 Act makes no provision for conditions; upon commencement, all conditions ceased to have effect[2]. Disclaimers were often used where a composite mark was made up of non-distinctive elements. The classic example was *Diamond T*[3], where the device of a 'T' in a diamond was registered but the applicant had to disclaim exclusive rights under the registration in the diamond or 'T' individually. Voluntary disclaimers are still possible[4], although it seems unlikely that an applicant would voluntarily disclaim exclusive rights in part of a mark without pressure from the Registry.

1   Trade Marks Act 1938, s 33.
2   Sch 3, para 3.
3   [1921] 2 Ch 583; 38 RPC 373.
4   Section 13(1)(a); r 24.

Limitations

5.24   A registration may be limited, territorially or otherwise[1], if agreed by the applicant. The registration could be limited to goods for export only. Service marks are more amenable than trade marks for goods to limitation to a particular locality.

1   Section 13(1)(b); r 24.

Honest concurrent user

5.25 Where the Registrar is satisfied that an applicant has made honest concurrent use of a mark, he may allow the application to proceed to advertisement[1]. It will then be up to the owner of the prior mark to oppose registration. This provision was introduced to compensate in part for the rigour of relative examination by the UK Registry. In Member States of the Community where no relative examination is carried out, a mark may be registered notwithstanding prior conflicting registrations. If the earlier proprietor acquiesces for five years in the use of the later registered mark, the earlier proprietor loses the right to challenge the later registration or to oppose further use of the later mark, unless he can show it was applied for in bad faith[2].

1 Section 7; practice follows that under s 12(2) of the 1938 Act.
2 Hansard (House of Lords) vol 553, no 55, 14 March 1994, col 72.
3 Section 45.

5.26 The criteria for registration of an honest concurrent user were considered in *Pirie's application*[1]. Relevant factors are:

(a) the length of use (2–3 years at least[2]);
(b) the volume of use and area of trade;
(c) the honesty of the concurrent user (knowledge of the earlier registration being pertinent but not conclusive[3]);
(d) the presence or absence of actual confusion[4];
(e) the degree of likely confusion; and
(f) whether that is tolerable to the public.

1 (1933) 50 RPC 147.
2 Just under three years in *Buler* [1975] RPC 225.
3 *Bali* [1978] FSR 192.
4 Not necessarily fatal to the later applicant: *Buler* [1975] RPC 225.

CONFLICT WITH EARLIER MARKS

5.27 Where an earlier mark raises a relative objection, a number of options are open. The most convenient, and powerful option is to obtain the consent of the earlier mark's proprietor[1]. An attempt to retain the discretion formerly enjoyed by the Registrar over this aspect of practice was soundly rejected by Parliament[2]. However, it was valuable in protecting the public from dangerous confusion[3]. Alternatively, the later applicant could seek assignment[4], surrender[5], revocation or invalidation[6] of the earlier trade mark.

1 Trade Marks Act 1994, s 5(5).
2 House of Lords Public Bill Committee, 13 January 1994, col 16.
3 See, eg, *Univer TM* [1993] RPC 239.
4 See Ch 11.

5   Section 45.
6   See Ch 9.

5.28   Section 5(1) prohibits the registration over an identical earlier mark for identical goods or services. This prohibition 'is absolute' in the words of the Directive, in that no confusion need be shown. If the marks and/or the goods or services are merely similar, then likelihood of confusion[1] is the determining factor. A test for comparison of word marks was set forth in *Pianotist*[2]. In this decision, oft cited in Registry proceedings, the following approach was recommended:

'You must take the two words. You must judge them, both by their look and by their sound. You must consider the goods to which they are to be applied. You must consider the nature and kind of customer who would be likely to buy those goods. In fact, you must consider all the surrounding circumstances; and you must further consider what is likely to happen if each of those trade marks is used in a normal way as a trade mark for the goods of the respective owners of the marks'.

1   'Including the likelihood of association': para **5.33**.
2   (1906) 23 RPC 774.

5.29   Both look and sound are important in gauging the probability of confusion. Where goods or services are expensive, bought with particular care – as the motor cars in *Lancer/Lancia*[1], where it was suggested that the marks would be pronounced alike – smaller differences will suffice to prevent confusion than when the goods are bought on impulse or by children. Although marks are invariably compared side by side by the Registry or court, in reality customers' recollection may be imperfect. Thus, the idea of a mark is an important additional factor[2]. Marks should be considered as a whole, although elements common to the trade would be given less weight than others[3]. The first syllables of words tend to be more prominent than later syllables.

1   [1987] RPC 303.
2   Eg, the idea of a cat in *Taw v Notek* (1951) 68 RPC 271.
3   *Kleenoff – Bale & Church v Sutton* (1934) 51 RPC 129.

5.30   Section 12(1) of the 1938 Act prohibited the registration of similar marks for goods or services of the same description, goods associated with the services in question, or vice versa. In deciding whether goods were 'of the same description', *Jellinek*'s case[1] described three important considerations:

(a)   the nature and composition of the goods;
(b)   their respective uses;
(c)   the trade channels through which they are bought and sold.

1   '*Panda*' (1946) 63 RPC 59 – shoes and shoe-polish not of the same description.

5.31 It seemed that identity of two out of the three might render the products 'of the same description'[1]. It is submitted that these factors remain relevant under the 1994 Act, although the comparisons might lead to a conclusion of 'similarity' for goods which were not 'of the same description'. In fact, the outcomes of decided cases under the 1938 Act were often difficult to reconcile.[2] The Registry has used an adaptation of the *Jellinek* tests in comparing services:

(a) the nature of the services;
(b) their respective purposes;
(c) the characteristics of their users;
(d) the normal kinds of business relationship involved[3].

1 *Floradix* [1974] RPC 583.
2 For examples, see *Kerly*, paras 10–15.
3 Registry Work Manual, Ch 6, p 30; see also Ch 11, p 26.

5.32 Apart from the possibility that goods might be similar to services and services to goods, it is clear that similarity of marks and similarity of products interact. Where marks are merely similar, small differences in the goods or services would render confusion unlikely, whereas with identical marks, there might be confusion if the marks were used on less closely allied products. The fame of the marks also affects the probability of confusion. These two forms of interaction are clearly contemplated in a somewhat rambling series of preambles to the Directive:

'Whereas the protection applies also in the case of similarity between the mark and the sign and the goods or services; whereas it is indispensable to give an interpretation of the concept of similarity in relation to the likelihood of confusion; whereas the likelihood of confusion, the appreciation of which depends on numerous elements and, in particular, on the recognition of the trade mark in the market, of the association which can be made with the used or registered sign, of the degree of similarity between the trade mark and the sign and between the goods or services identified, constitutes the specific condition for such protection.'

5.33 It is submitted that gauging the likelihood of confusion is a matter of common sense; judges have always treated it as a 'jury' question[1]. More metaphysical is the question of likelihood of association: is it merely a factor in establishing confusion, or does it take the arena of conflict beyond mere confusion? Arguments on this issue are considered at paras **7.24–7.26**; identical rules of comparison are used for registration over earlier marks and for infringement. The Registry has adopted a sensible policy of keeping to previous practice where the way ahead is unclear; the issues are likely to be fought out between competing interests in opposition and infringement proceedings.

1 Eg, *GE Trade Mark* [1973] RPC 297.

5.34 The same pragmatic attitude is apparent in the Registry's approach to the third category of conflict, set out in s 5(3). Where the earlier mark has a reputation, registration of the later mark should not be allowed if or to the extent that use of the later marks on dissimilar goods or services would take unfair advantage of, or be detrimental to, the distinctive character or repute of the earlier mark. Since no guidance is given to the strength of reputation involved, and since the Registry staff have no means of knowing which marks in fact have a reputation, it is impossible for them to apply s 5(3) in ex parte proceedings[1]. So it will be up to the owners of such marks to keep a watch on the register and to oppose later applications where appropriate. The Registry will confine itself to searching for identical or similar marks for goods and services in the same and related classes.[2]

The date at which conflict is assessed is the filing date, or the priority date, if different[3].

1   The Directive does not purport to affect national procedural rules 'whereas the ways in which likelihood of confusion may be established, and in particular the onus of proof, are a matter for national procedural rules which are not prejudiced by the Directive'.
2   Registry Work Manual, Ch 6, p 31.
3   See Ch 5.

5.35   The 'earlier trade marks' which can block a later application are defined in s 6. First, there are UK registrations and applications with an earlier filing or priority date, similar Community trade mark registrations or applications[1] and UK registrations or applications resulting from a Madrid Protocol filing[2]. Secondly, there are Community trade marks which have a valid claim to 'seniority', from an earlier UK mark or international filing designating the UK. This anticipates the coming into operation of Arts 34 and 35 of the community Trade Mark Regulation: if the proprietor of a national registration applies for and registers a Community trade mark, he can let the national registration lapse but retain equivalent rights in the State of registration. Lastly, 'earlier trade mark' includes a mark which is entitled to protection as a well-known trade mark under Art 6*bis* of the Paris Convention[3]. Protection must be afforded to such marks even where they are not registered. In practice, it is likely that many of the marks which would qualify for this category are already registered in the UK.

1   When in existence, paras **13.5–13.17**.
2   When available, paras **14.7–14.20**.
3   See, further, paras **12.25–12.31**.

5.36   The effect of an earlier registration endures for a year after its expiry, unless it can be shown to have been out of use for at least the preceding two years[1]. The effect of an application is subject to its maturing into a registration: s 6(2).

1   Section 6(3).

5.37   Where an earlier mark is not registered, a proprietor of goodwill with 'passing off rights' may prevent the later registration under s 5(4)(a). Other 'rules of law' which might be invoked to protect an unregistered mark include malicious falsehood and the Trade Descriptions Act 1968, which makes it an offence to apply a false trade description to goods or services. It is interesting to speculate whether a registration which is proceeding because of consent by the earlier proprietor[1] might none the less be blocked on this ground. Not all uses of a trade mark involve a 'trade description'[2]. Earlier rights of copyright, design right or registered designs are catered for in s 5(4)[3].

1 See para **5.27**.
2 *R v Veys* [1993] FSR 366.
3 Copyright in a pictorial mark was invoked in *Karo Step* [1977] RPC 255. For an Australian perspective, see D Lyons, 'Copyright in Trade Marks' [1994] 1 EIPR 21.

5.38 Where applications are co-pending, the application with the earlier filing date or priority date will be unaffected by the later application, but may be cited against the latter. There are no provisions for the Registry to give notice to applicant of later co-pending applications. The Registry's former practice was described as sensible in *Bud TM*[1]; in that case a passing off action had established that both applicants had goodwill in the mark; both were allowed to proceed to registration. It is difficult to see how a similar decision could be reached under the 1994 Act, unless the earlier applicant were to consent to registration by the second proprietor.

1 *BUD TM* [1988] RPC 535.

Examples of potential conflict

5.39 Assume that by 31 January 1996, the Community trade mark and Madrid Protocol systems are fully in operation. On that date, Albert applies to register 'Grit' for men's toiletries. A search reveals the following, all applications or registrations in the name of third parties:

(a) a UK registration filed on 31 October 1994[1] of 'Grid' for aftershave;
(b) Cecilia filed in France to register 'Grince' for soap. On 28 September 1995 she applied to the International Bureau under the Madrid Protocol, designating the UK;
(c) a UK application dated 1 March 1995 to register 'Prit' for toiletries; fees were not paid and the application is deemed abandoned;
(d) a Community trade mark application filed on 1 February 1996 claiming priority from a Convention filing in Australia on 30 October 1995, 'Grif' for talcum powder.

All except 'Prit' are earlier marks within the meaning of s 6.

1 The first day for filing under the 1994 Act.

OPPOSITIONS AND OBSERVATIONS

5.40   Once the Registry has decided to accept an application, it is published in the *Trade Marks Journal*[1]. Interested parties then have three months[2] in which to file opposition to registration or to make informal observations to the Registrar[3]. It is at this stage that objections based on earlier marks registered for dissimilar goods or services, well-known marks and honest concurrent user are likely to arise. The proportion of marks which are opposed will probably be higher under the 1994 Act than the 1–2 per cent reported under the 1938 Act, but lower than the 80 per cent anticipated for Community trade marks[4]. Anyone may oppose registration. The opposition is filed on Form TM7, together with a statement of the grounds on which the opposition is based. These are then sent by the Registry to the applicant, who has three months[5] in which to file a counter-statement[6]. There is then a round of evidence, with evidence in support of opposition, counter-statement and, if necessary, reply. Up to three months are allowed for each stage[7] of evidence. Failure to file evidence in support of the opposition will result in its being deemed abandoned: r 17(4). Either party may request a hearing which, being inter partes, is open to the public[8]. The Registrar, in the shape of a hearing officer, may hear oral evidence and call for such documents, information or evidence as he thinks fit, being invested with all the powers of an official referee of the Supreme Court[9]. The hearing officer will normally reserve his decision; parties will be sent notice of the outcome, with reasons[10]. The Registry have power to award reasonable costs and to require security for costs[11].

1   Section 38(1); Rules 12 and 2.
2   Rule 13(1), with no extension: r 62(3). A would-be opponent who misses the deadline will have to seek a declaration of invalidity of the mark once registered: see Ch 9.
3   Section 38(2) and (3); r 15.
4   White Paper, paras 4.11 and 4.14.
5   Rule 13(2), again, no extensions are allowed: r 62(3).
6   Form TM8.
7   Rule 13(3), (5), (6).
8   Rule 53.
9   Rules 49(2), 51 and 52. The power to call for evidence is quite general.
10 Rule 14(1).
11 Rules 54 and 55.

5.41   It is also possible during the opposition period for an objector to make informal written observations to the Registrar[1], who sends a copy to the applicant. The observer does not become a party to proceedings on the application. Although there are no formal requirements, it is unlikely that the Registrar will give much weight to unsubstantiated allegations in deciding what effect, if any, the observations have.

1   Section 38(3), r 15.

APPEALS AND STAYS

5.42   Appeals from a refusal to register, an adverse decision in opposition proceedings or other decision[1] of the Registrar may be made to the court[2] or to a person appointed by the Lord Chancellor under s 77. The latter has a discretion to refer the appeal to the court where requested or if an important point of law is involved, but otherwise will hear and determine the appeal. The appointed person's judgment is final[3]. This arrangement was introduced into the 1994 Act to replace a similar appeal mechanism under the 1938 Act, to the 'Secretary of State', latterly in the shape of Robin Jacob QC (now Jacob J) and Hugh Laddie QC, which proved popular with users in recent years[4].

1   Not as to classification: rr 40, 41.
2   High Court in England and Wales and Northern Ireland, the Court of Session in Scotland: s 76.
3   Section 76(4).
4   House of Commons Standing Committee B, 17 May 1994, col 13.

5.43   At this point, it should be noted that a stay of Registry proceedings may be sought where there is litigation in court relating to the issue in question[1].

1   In *Sears v Sears Roebuck* [1993] RPC 385, it was held that the court has powers to restrain Registry proceedings by interlocutory injunction, even where the Registrar had refused a stay.

DURATION AND RENEWALS

5.44   Under the 1938 Act, the first period of registration of a mark was 14 years, with subsequent renewal periods of 7 years. A registration can be renewed indefinitely, although the registration may become vulnerable to attack. Under the 1994 Act, the first period of registration is shorter, at 10 years, and the period between renewals is longer, also 10 years. This is a welcome simplification. Renewal can be effected up to six months before the due date, and for six months after on payment of an additional fee[1]. Where the renewal fee is not paid within these time-limits, the Registrar removes the mark from the Register. Where the circumstances of failure to renew warrant sympathy, the proprietor has a further six months from removal to seek restoration to the register[2].

1   Section 43 and rr 27–29.
2   Section 43 and r 30.

TRANSITIONAL PROVISIONS

5.45   Some provisions of the 1994 Act had immediate effect on existing registrations and applications. Thus, the division of the Register into Parts A and B was abolished[1].

Conditions of use and associations between marks ceased to have effect on commencement[2], although pending applications relating to breach of conditions continue
under the old law. The old presumption of valid registration after seven years[3]
disappeared, along with the possibility of registering well-known words 'defensively'[4].

---

1   Sch 3, para 2(1).
2   Sch 3, paras 3(1), 2(3) and 10(3).
3   Trade Marks Act 1938, s 13.
4   For a eulogy on defensive registration, see R Wheeldon, 'The Community Trade Mark and the concept
    of dilution: was the case for defensive trademarks adequately considered?' *Trademark World*, November
    1994, p 12. The existence of defensive registration is preserved for five years from attack on the ground
    of non-use: Sch 3, para 17(2).

5.46   Series of marks and disclaimers were transferred to the new register[1]. The new
infringement provisions apply to all acts after commencement, subject to a transitional
defence in the case of existing registrations[2]. Where an existing mark is still in its first
period of registration, the former period of 14 years will continue to apply. Otherwise
the new periods of first registration and renewal apply, thus extending the registration
of marks already into a seven-year renewal period[3].

---

1   Sch 3, paras 2(2) and 3(2).
2   Sch 3, para 4: use which did not infringe before commencement may be continued.
3   Sch 3, para 15.

5.47   Pending applications already advertised at 31 October 1994 are subject to the
old law[1]. Where the pending application has not been advertised before commencement, the applicant has a choice: either to leave the application to proceed under the
old law, save that the new period for opposition would apply[2], or to give notice for the
pending application to be determined according to the 1994 Act. Such notice must be
given in the six months following commencement, and once given is irrevocable[3]. A
converted application is deemed to have been filed on 31 October 1994.

---

1   Sch 3, para 10(1).
2   Sch 3, para 10(2) and r 7.
3   Sch 3, para 11 and r 68.

5.48   The decision whether to convert depends on the nature of the mark and nature
of any difficulty anticipated. For marks which could be registered under the 1938 Act,
the possibility of amendment of the mark during prosecution, and the likelihood that
conflict with earlier marks would be more problematic under the 1994 Act might
militate against conversion.

5.49   Happily, the Registry was able to preserve familiar form numbers. Transitional
provisions as they relate to infringement, licences and assignment are dealt with in
later chapters.

SPECIAL CATEGORY MARKS

5.50 The procedures for registering collective and certification marks largely follow those for ordinary trade marks, except that regulations to govern the use of the mark must be filed within nine months of the application to register and approved by the Registrar[1]. The regulations can be amended only upon application to the Registrar, who will advertise the amendments for opposition[2]. Certification and collective marks are considered further in Chapter 12.

---

1   Sections 49 and 50; Sch 1, paras 5–8; Sch 2, paras 6–9; r 22.
2   Sch 3, para 10, Sch 2, para 11 and r 23.

Chapter 6

USING THE MARK

INTRODUCTION

6.1 A registered mark may be turned to account by its proprietor in a number of ways. First, it can be used by the proprietors to distinguish their own services or goods. Secondly, it can be used to pursue infringers[1]. A third possibility is that of licensing the mark for use by others[2]. Lastly, the marks may be assigned outright[3]. This chapter deals briefly with exploitation by use.

---

1 See Ch 7.
2 See Ch 10.
3 See Ch 11.

THE SIGNIFICANCE OF USE

6.2 Proper use of a mark is significant in a number of ways. Different aspects of use are scattered throughout the 1994 Act, and can briefly be summarised as follows:

(a) actual use or a bona fide intention to use on the goods or services in question is a prerequisite for registration[1];
(b) failure to make genuine use of the mark is a ground for removal of the mark from the register: s 46(1)(a) and (b)[2];
(c) misuse by the proprietor or failure to restrain misuse by others may render the mark liable to revocation[3], either because it has lost its distinctiveness or because it has become deceptive: s 46(1)(c) and (d).

---

1 See Ch 5.
2 See Ch 9.
3 See Ch 9.

MANNER OF USE

6.3 Use should normally be of the mark as registered, although use of a mark differing in elements which do not affect its distinctiveness may suffice to prevent revocation on the ground of non-use. If development of the mark is desired, applications should be made to register the new form. However, the mark may be used with additional indicia. In *Levi Strauss v Shah*[1], use of a tab mark with additional legend was held to be use of the registered mark.

---

1 [1985] RPC 371.

6.4 The mark should be used on all the goods or services for which it is registered; failure to do so may lead to partial cancellation for those products. Although this was possible under the 1938 Act[1], it is likely to become more common. This is because the proviso to s 26(1) of the 1938 Act, whereby use on goods or services of the same description could save a mark, has been repealed and not replaced.

---

1 Eg, *Kodiak* [1990] FSR 49.

6.5 Use should be documented. Section 100 of the 1994 Act provides that where a question arises in civil proceedings as to the use of a mark, it is for the proprietor to show what use has been made.

6.6 By whom is use made? Article 10(3) of the Directive provides that use of the trade mark with the consent or authority of the proprietor shall be deemed to constitute use by the proprietor. The 1994 Act approaches the question partially and obliquely. Section 9(1) refers twice to lack of the proprietor's consent in defining infringement[1]. Subsection 28(3) ensures that where the context so requires, the phrase 'consent of the proprietor' will include a predecessor in title[2]. Section 28(4) allows a licensor to permit sub-licensing. Section 46 refers to use by the proprietor or with his consent. Nowhere is there a statement in terms as general as those of Article 10(3)[3].

---

1 As noted by Jacob J in *Northern & Shell v Conde Nast* (9 December 1994, as yet unreported).
2 Unless the licence provides otherwise.
3 An amendment to introduce a definition of 'use' elsewhere was rejected by the House of Lords: Hansard vol 553, no 55, 14 March 1994, col 76. Lord Strathclyde did, however, say 'the all-embracing statement in [what is now s 46(1)(a)] applies throughout the Bill, but appears where it really matters when dealing with revocation': col 77.

6.7 Nor does the Act contain a comprehensive definition as to what activities constitute use. Pointers are to be found in a number of sections:

(a) s 103(2) states that use of a sign includes use otherwise than by way of a graphic representation[1];

(b) s 10(4) shows that, for the purposes of s 10 (infringement) a person uses a sign if, in particular, he:
   (i) affixes it to goods or packaging,
   (ii) offers or exposes goods for sale, puts them on the market, stocks them for such purposes as supplies services under the sign,
   (iii) imports or exports goods under the sign,
   (iv) uses the sign on business papers or in advertising;

(c) s 46(2) states that use in the UK includes affixing the trade mark to goods or to the packaging of goods in the UK solely for export purposes.

---

1 For example, where a trade mark is encoded electronically in a video cassette: House of Lords, Hansard vol 552, no 46, 24 February 1994, col 740.

6.8   As regards goods, it is clear that the mark need not be attached physically, although that is of course desirable. Nor do goods have to be on the market at the time the mark is used on papers or in advertising[1]. The 1994 Act appears to have preserved the decision in *Hermes*[2], where use of a mark on orders during preparations to re-launch a product was sufficient to avert expunction from the register.

---

1   A Spencer, in 'European Harmonisation: use it or lose it' *Trademark World*, May 1994, p 24 points out
    that mere advertising is insufficient under the WIPO Model Law.
2   [1982] RPC 425.

6.9   To avoid challenge on the ground of non-use, the use must be genuine. This echoes the criterion of 'genuine commercial use' which was the benchmark in cases under the previous legislation. In *Nerit*[1], token use of a 'ghost mark', registered to protect the unregistrable sign 'Merit', was insufficient to save the mark. In *Electrolux v Electrix*[2], use of the mark 'Electrux' on household electrical goods was held to be genuine commercial use, even though the primary purpose was to preserve the mark and enable the proprietors to sue for infringement. Also of interest on this point is the explanatory memorandum to Article 39 of the Community Trade Mark Regulation[3], which makes clear that a single instance of use may suffice.

---

1   *Imperial Group v Philip Morris* [1982] FSR 72.
2   [1954] RPC 23.
3   *Bulletin of the European Communities*, Supplement 5/1980, p 69.

6.10   Does use have to be use as a trade mark? The dangers of generic use as a product description are described below. The question as to whether use on tee-shirts was trade mark use in relation to the tee-shirts was in issue in *Kodak/Kodiak*[1]. It is submitted that s 46 refers clearly to genuine use of 'it' (the trade mark) and therefore trade mark use is required. If the mark forms part of a company's name, use of that name may not constitute use of the mark[2].

---

1   [1990] FSR 49.
2   *Orient Express Trading Co Ltd's TM* [1992] 12 EIPR D-268; IPD 15124.

6.11   In the author's view the 1994 Act is unsatisfactory on the question of use. Problems may arise as to its proper construction. However, several practical problems can clearly be identified and are discussed below.

PROBLEMS OF USE

6.12   Particular pitfalls to avoid or restrain are:

(a)   Generic use by the proprietor, where the mark is used as a product description. This may bar registration or lead to revocation. If the recommendations set out in para **6.14** are followed, proprietor's use should avoid this trap. Unfortunately, marketing departments often diverge from good trade mark practice in their enthusiasm to secure acceptance for products.

(b) Generic use by others is even more of a problem. Where use relates to the proprietor's own goods or services, there might be some comfort in s 10(6)[1], since generic use will certainly be detrimental to a mark's distinctive character. However, it will be difficult to show that the use was for the purpose of identifying the goods as those of the proprietor. In relation to other goods or services, it is submitted that the 1994 Act provides exclusive rights over trade mark use only, so infringement will be difficult to prove[2]. A rival may set out deliberately to scupper another's trade mark by using it generically[3].

(c) Generic use in dictionaries should be discouraged. The Community Trade Mark Regulation, Article 10, applies where the reproduction of a mark in a dictionary or similar publication gives the impression that it constitutes the generic name of the goods or services. The proprietor can call upon the publisher, at latest in the next edition, to include an indication that the mark is a registered trade mark. The Directive and Act have no similar provision, but proprietors should adopt similar arguments against errant publishers of hard-copy, CD or on-line reference works. Most publishers in practice are likely to be conscientious in this regard.

Use as in (b) or (c) prior to application is likely to prevent a mark's registration[4]. Once on the register, however, it will only be removed if the mark is used generically in the trade and in consequence of the acts or inactivity of the proprietor[5].

(d) Deceptive use should be guarded against. The main danger here is that of uncontrolled licensing, which may lead to deceptiveness as to origin and/or quality[6]. Deceptive use by a third party is usually easier to restrain than generic use because it will usually involve infringement.

---

1   See paras **7.36** and **7.37**.
2   See Ch 1.
3   See 'caplets': *Johnson & Johnson Australia Pty Ltd v Sterling Pharmaceuticals Pty Ltd* (1991) 21 IPR 1 (Fed Ct of Aus). The author's colleague Ellen Gredley coined the phrase 'reckless endangerment' to describe this kind of misuse.
4   Para **2.31**.
5   For discussion on this point, see House of Lords Public Bill Committee, 19 January 1994, col 82–83.
6   Conversely, maintenance of quality control can maintain validity, even where confusion as to origin may occur: *'GE' TM* [1973] RPC 297; see C Morcom 'The Trade Marks Act 1938 – twenty years of decisions of the House of Lords' [1994] 2 EIPR 67.

EDUCATING CUSTOMERS AND CONSUMERS

6.13   In the author's view, educating customers and consumers may best be achieved by vigilance and example. Customers and competitors who recognise that a sign is a trade mark, jealously guarded, are likely to respect the mark and use it properly. Proprietors should school their employees, agents, distributors, stockists and advertisers in the basic rules for trade mark use.

6.14   First, the mark should be used as an adjective, together with a noun or phrase to describe the product, for example:

Take 'Aspirin' painkillers
Buy our 'Linoleum' floor coverings
Wash your hair with 'Tessarae' shampoo

and not as a noun or verb, as in

Take an aspirin
Treat yourself to new linoleum
Tessarae your hair

Secondly, it is as well to emphasise the trade mark significance, by use of capital letters or different typeface and/or symbols: 'R' (if registered) or 'TM' in a circle. Alternatively, an asterisk may be used to refer to explanatory wording.

Finally, misuse should be corrected, by advertisement if necessary.

Chapter 7

PURSUING INFRINGEMENTS

INTRODUCTION, ROUTES AND REMEDIES

7.1   As under the Trade Marks Act 1938, actions for infringement under the 1994 Act are brought in the High Court in England and Wales and Northern Ireland and in the Court of Session in Scotland[1]. Section 14(2) provides that relief is available as for infringement of any other property right. As with other statutory intellectual property rights, infringement is actionable without proof of damage[2].

---

1   The governing section, s 14, does not actually say so, but 'the court' is defined thus in s 75.
2   Save, perhaps under s 10(3), see below.

7.2   Some specific remedies are also provided by the statute: erasure, destruction and delivery up. Remedies are discussed further below. Infringement is actionable by 'the proprietor of the trade mark', but this expression includes a licensee in appropriate circumstances[1]. It is also possible for parties in a trade mark dispute to agree that the matter be resolved by arbitration[2]. The Chartered Institute of Arbitrators now has an intellectual property section and the World Intellectual Property Organisation has set up an arbitration centre for private intellectual property disputes.

---

1   See Ch 10.
2   For the relative merits of arbitration, mediation and litigation, see M Alexander, 'Settlement in Intellectual Property Disputes', *Trademark World*, December/January 1992/93, p 26.

THE EXCLUSIVE RIGHTS OF THE PROPRIETOR UNDER THE 1938 AND 1994 ACTS

7.3   Regarding infringement as a cause of action, the 1938 Act had a number of disadvantages when it came to pursuing infringers. The old provisions continue to apply in actions where the alleged acts of infringement took place before commencement of the 1994 Act on 31 October 1994[1]. The new provisions apply to acts taking place on or after 31 October.

---

1   Sch 3, para 4(1). See, further, paras **7.54** and **7.55**.

7.4   One problem with the 1938 Act was the famous obscurity of its elaborate infringement provisions in s 4. The general first part of s 4(1), rarely relied upon, conferred exclusive rights on the proprietor to use the mark in relation to the goods or services for which it was registered. This general right was held infringed in *Ind Coope v Paine*[1], where the proprietor of 'John Bull' for beer was able to restrain the defendant (who was proprietor of the mark for beer kits) from instructing kit purchasers how to make 'John Bull' beer. The mark was indeed used in relation to beer, although the defendant's trade was in beer kits.

---

1   [1983] RPC 326.

7.5   In fact the general words of s 4(1) did not specifically require the use to be in the course of trade. On a similarly worded statute, the Irish court made a finding of infringement where a mark registered for cigarettes was used on packets which resembled cigarette packs but in fact contained anti-smoking campaign material[1].

---

1   *Gallagher v Health Education Bureau* [1982] FSR 464.

7.6   Although the general infringement provisions (the first sentence of s 9(1) of the 1994 Act) are in much the same terms[1] as the introductory words to s 4 of the 1938 Act, the later sentence states:

'The acts amounting to infringement, if done without the consent of the proprietor, are specified in section 10.'

All the operative sections of s 10 are qualified by 'in the course of trade'. It is submitted that *Gallagher* could not be decided in the same way under the 1994 Act.

---

1   Though more simply expressed.

7.7   The 1994 Act does not specify that the trade has to be trade in the goods or services for which the mark is registered. The editors of *Kerly* refer to pre-1938 cases[1] and cite the later case of *Ravok v National Trade Press*[2] in support of the proposition that the trade in which the mark was used must be trade in the goods (or services) for which the mark is registered; otherwise there was no infringement[3] (under pre-1994 Acts, a mark was infringed only in relation to the products for which it was registered). However, a number of other decisions were inconsistent with this proposition, although consistent with a somewhat broader one:

'If the mark is registered for goods or services X, to be infringed it must be used on *or* in relation to X. The dependant's trade must be at least in one of the products on which the mark is used, or the products in relation to which the mark is used.'

---

1   *Kerly's Law of Trade Marks and Trade Names*, para 14–06, n 14: *Levy v Walker* (1890) 10 ChD 436; *Richards v Butcher* (1890) 7 RPC 288.
2   (1955) 72 RPC 110. Trade marks were registered in the name of the plaintiffs for various goods. They were listed in the defendants' directory, which attributed them to another firm. Held: no infringement. The publication was not regarded as 'use' of the mark.
3   *Ravok* in turn cited *Aristoc v Rysta* (1945) 62 RPC 65 for this proposition. However, the decision in *Aristoc* was based on the temporary nature of a repair service for stockings.

7.8   Examples include:

(a)   *Nitedals v Lehmann*[1]: a cow mark was registered for matches. A cow mark was used in advertisements for Cow brand milk, carried on match boxes. Held: infringement.

(b)   *Ind Coope v Paine*[2]: 'John Bull' was registered for beer. It was used on beer kits in relation to beer. The trade was in beer kits. Held: infringement.

(c)   *Spillers*[3]: 'Hovis' was registered for flour. It was used on baking tins to impress the words on loaves. The trade was in loaves. Held: no use in relation to flour, but observed that wording such as 'made from Hovis flour' would be use in relation to flour (though doubted whether this would infringe).

The following decision from The Netherlands is also consistent with this test:

(d)   *Alicia*[4]: 'Coke' was registered for cola. It was used on a cola bottle in an indecent film sequence. The defendant's trade was in films. Held: infringement.

It is submitted that these cases would be decided in the same way under the infringement provisions of the 1994 Act; (b) and (c) probably involve use on 'similar' goods.

---

1   (1908) 25 RPC 793.
2   [1983] RPC 326.
3   (1954) 71 RPC 234.
4   Dutch decision of 1974, cited by M Knijff, 'Selected Benelux cases' *Trademark World*, July/August 1994, p 14 and by D W Feer Verkade in 'Unfair use of and damage to the reputation of well-known trademarks, trade names and indications of source – a combination from the Benelux' (1986) 17 IIC 768. In this author's view a number of the cases Feer Verkade classes as 'non-designatory use' would constitute infringement on the above test.

7.9   The specific rights conferred on the proprietor by s 4(1) were to exclude others from using the trade mark or a closely resembling mark in the course of trade in relation to the goods or services for which is was registered:

(a)   as a trade mark; or
(b)   to import a reference to the proprietor.

'Closely resembling' was defined in terms of the likelihood of deception or confusion: s 68(2A). No rights were given in relation to goods or services for which the mark was not registered. This strict rule of 'specialism' has been relaxed in the 1994 Act[1].

---

1   For an example of the contortions it caused, see *Pickwick International v Multiple Sound Producers* [1972] RPC 786; [1972] FSR 427: music cassettes within the specification 'apparatus for wireless telegraphy; parts and fittings therefor'; *Unilever v Johnson Wax* [1989] FSR 145: whether Toilet Duck a common soap or detergent.

7.10   Apart from identical marks, and for all Part B marks[1], infringement under the 1938 Act was effectively based on confusion. There was no scope under the 1938 Act to restrain dilution, whereby a mark suffers attrition of its distinctive character by

others' use on related or non-related (and hence non-competing) products, in circumstances where no confusion occurs or is likely[2]. Nor was there a remedy under the 1938
Act for such use which prejudiced reputation by inferior or unsavoury connotations.
The latter is probably recognised in passing off: *Annabel's*[3]. The former was regarded
as an arguable category of damage in the *Elderflower Champagne*[4] passing off case
although in that case there was also a finding of confusion.

1   For which s 5(2) provided a defence to relief if a defendant showed that there was no likelihood of
    confusion.
2   Although where there was an arguable case of infringement, likely erosion of distinctiveness was held
    relevant to the grant of an interlocutory injunction: *Parfums Givenchy v Designer Alternative* [1994] RPC 243.
3   *Annabel's v Schock* [1972] FSR 261; [1972] RPC 838.
4   *Taittinger v Allbev* [1993] FSR 641.

7.11   Dilution is established in US law, not federal but State law with many States
having specific anti-dilution laws[1]. Gilson points out that the courts have applied the
statutes 'neither eagerly nor broadly'[2]. The scope for suing for defamation in the US is
less than in the UK, partly due to constitutional protection of free speech. This also
gives rise to a defence of parody in US trade mark cases[3]. Some cases which are
litigated under US anti-dilution laws might well be actionable in the UK as injurious
falsehood. However, the 'defamation' defence of justification may inhibit the courts in
granting interlocutory injunctions[4]. This reduces the attractiveness of malicious
falsehood as a cause of action. Plaintiffs tend to plead passing off or occasionally
both[5].

1   For an excellent account, see Gilson, *Trade Mark Protection and Practice*, para 5.05.
2   For criticism of dilution remedies as opposed to the registration of defensive marks, see R Wheeldon,
    'The Community Trademark and the concept of dilution: was the case for defensive registration
    adequately considered?' *Trademark World*, November 1994, p 12.
3   On which see A Langvardt, 'Protected marks and protected speech' (1992) 82 TMR 671.
4   *Bestobel v Biggs* [1975] FSR 421.
5   *Wilts United Dairies v Robinson* [1958] RPC 94.

7.12   Three examples of US dilution cases may be used to illustrate dilution. The first
is *Godiva/Dogiva*[1], in which use of 'Dogiva' on dog treats was enjoined as eroding the
distinctiveness of the mark 'Godiva' for chocolates. In *Dallas Cowboys Cheerleaders*[2], the
plaintiff's uniforms were used as costumes for the participants in a rude film. This was
enjoined as detrimental to the plaintiff's reputation in the appearance of their
costumes. Lastly, in *Lexis/Lexus*[3], it was alleged that use of 'Lexus' on Toyota motor
cars would dilute the distinctiveness of 'Lexis' for legal information services. This was
held improbable, given the specialist nature of the market for 'Lexis'.

1   231 USPQ 562.
2   604 F 2d 200, 203 USPQ 161.
3   875 F 2d 1026.

COMPARATIVE ADVERTISING

7.13   The provisions of s 4(1)(b) were used to restrain comparative advertising, which uses the proprietor's mark to identify the proprietor's products for the purposes of comparison. If this actually led to confusion, it was actionable in passing off[1] and would infringe both Part A and Part B marks. Comparative advertising could also infringe a Part A mark even if there were no confusion. The actionability of comparative advertising depended on registration of the mark in Part A. Proposed amendments to EC Directive 84/450/EEC on misleading advertising would permit the necessary use of marks in comparative advertising subject to safeguards.

1   *McDonalds v Burger King* [1987] FSR 112.

7.14   The amendments adopted by the European Parliament in 1992 prohibited the use of trade marks in comparative advertising except where necessary to identify the compared goods or services, where the comparison did not extend to the competitor's person or circumstances, and where justification was ready to be produced within 24 hours. More recently, it was proposed that:

'comparisons must not present goods or services as imitations or replicas of goods or services which are already protected by registered trade marks, trade names and/or designations of origin.'[1]

1   Hansard, House of Commons, vol 241, no 85, 18 April 1994, col 684.

7.15   The statement for entry in the minutes of the EC Council meeting at which the Community Trade Mark Regulation was adopted says of Article 9 of the Regulation, which is in identical terms to Article 5(3)(d) of the Directive and s 10(4)(d) of the 1994 Act:

'The Council and the Commission consider that the reference to advertising in paragraph 2(d) does not cover the use of a Community trade mark in comparative advertising.'

It is submitted, however, that in enacting s 10(4)(d) and s 10(6) of the 1994 Act, Parliament was also endeavouring to comply with the spirit of the proposed amendments to the EC Misleading Advertising Directive and was thus implementing the Directive in a proper and appropriate way. Subsection 10(6) is further discussed in paras **7.36** and **7.37**.

NON TRADE MARK USE

7.16   In *Mothercare v Penguin Books*[1], it was held that use of the registered mark as part of the book title 'Mothercare/Other Care', which aptly described the book's contents, did not infringe because the use was not trade mark use[2]. Section 9 refers to the proprietor's exclusive rights in the *trade mark*; it is submitted that some such significance will always be required for infringement under s 9[3].

1   [1988] RPC 113; see also *Mars v Cadbury* [1987] RPC 387 – 'Treets' not infringed by 'Treat-size'.

2   For a case where a book series title was held capable of acting as a trade mark, see *Games Workshop* [1993] FSR 705.
3   See paras **1.36** and **1.37**.

7.17   However, if non trade mark use is not prohibited, it may cause difficulties, for example to proprietors whose marks are being used 'generically', by competitors[1] or in dictionaries[2].

1   As in 'caplets': *Johnson & Johnson Australia v Sterling Pharmaceuticals* (1991) 21 IPR 1.
2   Cf Art 10 of the Community Trade Mark Regulation; para **13.5**.

COMPARISON OF MARKS AND PRODUCTS UNDER THE 1994 ACT

7.18   The tests which the Registry will use to compare marks, goods and services for conflict under s 5 of the 1994 Act are described at paras **5.28–5.33**. It is likely that the court will take similar factors into account; the rules of comparison are identical for refusal and for infringement. As noted above, registration under the 1938 Act gave infringement rights only in relation to the goods or services for which the mark was registered. This was in contrast to its use to block subsequent registrations (s 12) and the use which was needed to keep the mark on the register (s 26).

7.19   The tests for comparison in infringement are spelt out in subss 10(1), (2) and (3), which enact Articles 5(1) and 5(2) of the Directive. Their effect is summarised in Table 2.

Table 2:   Comparisons for infringement

Marks	ID	Similar – Confusion	Similar – Association	Dissimilar
Goods / Services				
ID	10(1)	10(2)	10(2)	–
Similar – Confusion	10(2)(a)	10(2)(b)	10(2)(b)	–
Similar – Association	10(2)(a)	10(2)(b)	10(2)(b)	–
Dissimilar	10(3)*	10(3)*	10(3)*	–

* Additional elements: reputation, detriment, lack of due cause.

7.20   Section 10(1) ensures that use in the course of trade of an identical mark on identical goods or services will infringe the registration. There is no need to prove confusion, damage or intention. This case will continue to be suitable for summary judgment under Order 14 of the Rules of the Supreme Court[1]. Only one uncertainty is present – does 'identical' mean 'similar in every respect'[2]? Or would partial identity, such as phonetic identity of word marks, suffice[3]? Since the latter case is adequately covered in s 10(2), it is submitted that 'identical' means 'in every respect'.

If this view is correct, 'Scarlet Rain' would not be infringed by 'Scarlett Reign', nor 'Swallow Hole' by 'Swallow Whole'. Although phonetically identical, the spelling and ideas of the respective marks are different.

1 See *Sony v Anand* [1982] FSR 200 (1938 Act): In *Origins Natural Resources Inc v Origin Clothing Ltd* (Jacob J, 17 November 1994, as yet unreported), summary judgment was given under s 10(2) of the 1994 Act ('*Origins* versus *Origin*').
2 Parliament wished to avoid lawyers 'stumbling' over this point: Hansard (House of Lords), vol 552, no 46, 24 February 1994, col 731.
3 See para 8 of the Preamble to 1991 draft of Community Trade Mark Regulation, cited by Adrian Spencer in *Trademark World*, December/January 1993/94, p 26, especially:

   'trade mark must be viewed as a whole. In order to determine whether a Community trade mark and a sign consisting of words are *the same or are at any rate phonetically similar*, it is not possible to disregard the fact that the Community exists and that the public is increasingly aware of the correct pronunciation of words in the languages which are spoken therein.'

7.21 What account should be taken of any additional matter used by the defendant in conjunction with the mark as registered? In the past, UK trade mark law has disregarded additions, at least where they did not swamp the identity of the mark in suit. Thus, 'Sanrus' was held to infringe 'Rus'[1], but 'Ivory' was not too close to 'Ivy'[2]. In *Levi Strauss v Shah*[3], a blank 'tab' mark was registered for jeans. The plaintiffs and the defendants both used tabs in the position for which it was registered, on the rear pocket of jeans, but with words on the tab. It was held that both were using the registered mark. If this continues to be good law, additional material will not affect infringement under s 10(1) unless it changes the identity of the mark. On this analysis, 'Anti-Monopoly' for board games would probably infringe 'Monopoly' and 'Union Soleure' would infringe 'Union'. It seems clear from the analysis of those cases by Dutch authors[4] that a different view on identity may be taken elsewhere.

1 *Ravenhead Brick v Ruabon* (1937) 54 RPC 341.
2 *Goodwin v Ivory Soap* (1901) 18 RPC 389.
3 [1985] RPC 371.
4 C Gielen [1992] 8 EIPR 262; M Knijff *Trademark World*, July/August 1994, p 14. Cf G Wurtenberger, 'Determination of risk of confusion in trade mark infringement proceedings in the European Union: the Quattro decision' [1994] 7 EIPR 302 who criticises the European Commission for requesting comparison of 'Espace Quadra' and 'Audi Quattro' in their entirety. The Dutch court, however, indicated that 'Anti' before 'Monopoly' would not suggest a different source: [1978] BIE 39 (in Dutch – thanks to A Kamperman Sanders for assistance).

7.22 Section 10(2) provides that where the mark and sign and/or the respective goods or services of the plaintiff and defendant are not identical but merely similar, infringement is based on the likelihood of confusion on the part of the public, which includes the likelihood of association. Confusion is a familiar test. Of course, comparison of marks will interact with comparison of products to produce likelihood of confusion. The distinctiveness or strength of the mark will also be relevant. Figure 3 shows the way in which similarity of marks and products may be expected to interact for the purposes of s 10(2).

Figure 3:   Comparison of marks interacts with comparison of products

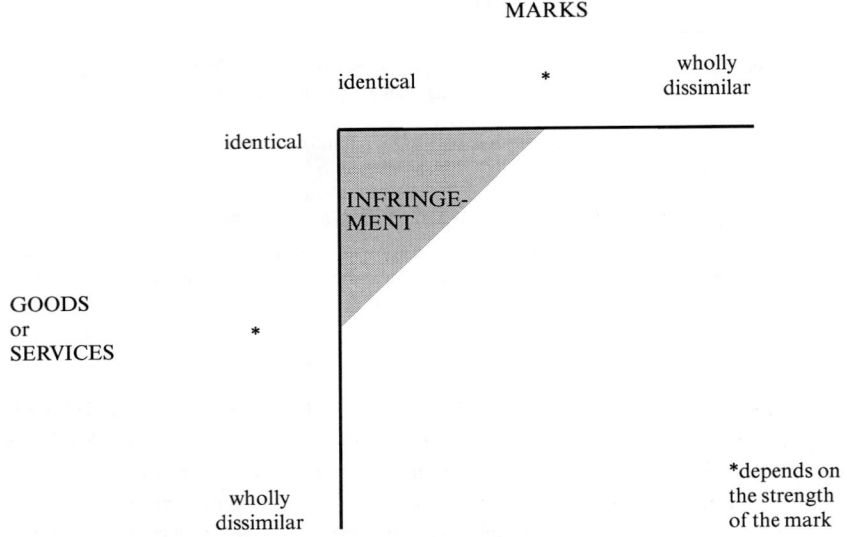

MARKS

7.23   Does confusion of the public at large have to be shown? It is submitted that 'the relevant public', those members of the public who are likely to buy or use the goods or services, are the proper group for which to estimate whether confusion is likely[1]. Surveys[2] can be helpful in identifying witnesses, although the courts do not always find survey evidence helpful.

---

1   *Pianotist* (1906) 23 RPC 774, paras **5.28** and **5.29**.
2   See paras **5.13** and **5.14**.

7.24   A difficult question is whether the inclusion of 'association' within 'confusion' extends the latter beyond confusion as traditionally understood. A statement for entry in the minutes of the EC Council meeting at which the Community Trade Mark Regulation was adopted reads:

'The Council and the Commission note that 'likelihood of association' is a concept which has been developed by Benelux case-law.'

However, it appears from Benelux cases that association is an extension of traditional confusion, rather than a subspecies or element[1]. This interpretation is also consistent with the scheme of s 10. If association were given a limited meaning, there would be a remedy for dilution by use on dissimilar products but not on similar products.

---

1   C Gielen, 'Harmonisation of Trade Mark Law in Europe' [1992] 8 EIPR 262; A Kamperman Sanders, 'Some frequently asked questions about the 1994 UK Trade Marks Act' [1995] 2 EIPR 69.

7.25 However, a wide interpretation of confusion/association not only increases the sphere in which a mark is protected against infringement, but also extends the zone of conflict at the registration stage. Many more marks would meet with opposition if the test were widely drawn. Probably a reference to the European Court of Justice will be needed to clarify this issue.

7.26 To summarise, the arguments for association being a mere subset of confusion are:

(a) the literal wording of s 10(2);
(b) the wording of the preamble to the Directive[1];
(c) the fact that too wide an interpretation of 'association' will lead to difficulty in registering and using marks[2];

The arguments for association meaning something different from traditional confusion, more akin to dilution (see below) are:

(a) there is a separate non-mandatory provision in the Directive, Article 5(2), which is enshrined in s 10(3). This provides for infringement of non-similar products and does not require confusion, although there are additional elements;
(b) the Commission has stated that 'association' comes from Benelux law;
(c) in the Benelux, 'association' seems to be recognised as distinct from confusion[3];
(d) The Netherlands appears to be a favoured forum for litigation, thus Benelux law may have a disproportionate influence on the interpretation of the infringement provisions.

Finally, can confusion or association work both ways? That was the case for infringement under the 1938 Act and in passing off[4].

---

1 App 3, p 96.
2 The problems of over-wide protection are mentioned in the Commission's memorandum on the creation of an EEC trade mark, *Bulletin of the European Communities*, Supplement 8/76, para 38.
3 See, eg, A Kamperman Sanders, 'Trade mark dilution – the parting of the ways?' *Managing Intellectual Property*, March 1992, p 42.
4 *Provident Financial plc v Halifax Building Society* [1994] FSR 81; *Bristol Conservatories* [1989] RPC 455. For a US perspective, see T Long and A Marks, 'Reverse confusion: fundamentals and limits' (1994) 84 TMR 1.

MARKS WITH A REPUTATION

7.27 Section 10(3) provides for infringement by use of the identical or a similar mark on non-similar goods. There is no specific requirement of confusion or association, although it is submitted that a mark can only be 'similar' to the registered trade mark if it calls it to mind in some way. To enjoy protection under s 10(3), the mark must enjoy a reputation in the UK. There is no indication as to the degree of reputation required[1]. It is submitted that decisions on passing off[2] will give excellent guidance here; clearly the reputation must be sufficient to support a finding of advantage to the defendant or detriment to the mark[3].

1   The White Paper 'Reform of Trade Marks Law' used the phrase 'wide repute': paras 3.17–3.19. For a
    helpful article, see A Kamperman Sanders, 'Some frequently asked questions about the Trade Marks
    Act 1994' [1995] 2 EIPR 67. See also A Kur, 'Well-known marks, highly renowned marks and marks
    having a (high) reputation – what's it all about?' (1992) 23 IIC 218.
2   See para **3.5ff**.
3   Not the case in *Lexis/Lexus* 875 F 2d 1026.

7.28   To infringe under s 10(3), the use of the mark must be 'without due cause'. This
suggests that there should be no justification for the defendant's use, which would
make restraint unreasonable[1]. It is difficult to imagine due causes which are not
provided as express defences to infringement, as outlined below. In *Claeryn*, the
Benelux Court of Justice had to consider the related concept of lack of 'valid reason' to
use, and held that such a reason would only be present:

'if the user is under such a compulsion to use this very mark that he cannot honestly be asked to
refrain from doing so regardless of the damages the owner of the mark would suffer from such
use.'[2]

1   See A Kamperman Sanders, para **7.27**, n 1 above.
2   See DW Feer Verkade, 'Unfair use of and damage to the reputation of well-known trademarks, trade
    names and indications of source – a contribution from the Benelux' (1986) 17 IIC 768.

7.29   There is a further requirement of unfair advantage to the defendant or
detriment to the distinctive character or repute of the trade mark. The first alternative
might be made out where a defendant unfairly took advantage of a plaintiff's
advertising campaign by using the mark[1]. A parallel may be drawn with the concept of
additional damages in copyright.[2] The editors of *Copinger and Skone James on Copyright*[3]
opine that such damages would be available where a defendant adopts a policy of
systematic infringement, but an injunction is not appropriate because the defendant
reproduces different material each time. By analogy, it is submitted that systematic use
of marks on different products might bring a defendant within s 10(3).

1   For further examples of 'free-riding' from German case-law and economic and legal arguments against
    the practice, see M Lehmann, 'Unfair use of and damage to the reputation of well-known marks, names
    and indications of source in Germany. Some aspects of law and economics' (1986) 17 IIC 746.
2   Copyright Designs and Patents Act 1988, s 97(2):

    'The court may in an action for infringement of copyright having regard to all the circumstances, and in
    particular to—

    (a) the flagrancy of the infringement, and
    (b) any benefit accruing to the defendant by reason of the infringement

    award such additional damages as the justice of the case requires.'
3   (1991) 13th edn, para 11–66.

7.30   The next two alternatives, detriment to the distinctive character or to the
repute of the mark, closely resemble two of the forms of dilution recognised in the US

and elsewhere (see above). Langvardt points out[1] that lessening of distinctiveness is most likely where the defendant uses the mark in a trade mark sense[2]. Prejudice to reputation usually operates by the trade mark becoming associated in customer's minds with the defendant's deleterious use.[3]

---

1   82 TMR 671 at 697.
2   Eg, *Godiva/Dogiva* 231 USPQ 562.
3   As in *Dallas Cowboys* 604 F 2d 200, 203 USPQ 161.

WELL-KNOWN MARKS

7.31   Section 56 provides a cause of action for the proprietor of a well-known mark within the meaning of Art 6*bis* of the Paris Convention. The mark has to be well known in the UK as the mark of a person who is a national of, domiciled in, or who has a real and effective commercial presence in, a Paris Convention country. That person can sue to restrain use in the UK, on identical or similar goods or services, of the same or an essentially identical or similar mark. The likelihood of confusion must be established. This special cause of action does not require business or goodwill in the UK[1]. It is subject to the defences of acquiescence and of *bona fide* continuing use[2].

---

1   Section 56(1).
2   Section 56(2) and (3).

7.32   Section 56 raises the questions of whether the mark has to be registered in its country of origin, and how well-known status may be established. In some countries, there is an administrative mechanism for declaring marks to be well known. No such proposals are contained in the 1994 Act. Furthermore, it appears that a UK national or resident cannot rely upon s 56. According to s 55(1)(b), 'Convention country' means a country other than the UK. However, someone established in the UK would probably enjoy rights to sue in passing off.

MANNER OF INFRINGING USE

7.33   Subsection 10(4) lists activities which may infringe. Affixing the sign to goods or packaging, offering, displaying, marketing or stocking goods under the sign all constitute use of the sign. So does importing or exporting under the sign, or using it on business papers or in advertising. It should be noted that the activities do not all require visual use of the offending sign; s 103(2) confirms that non-graphic use counts. Oral or other sensory use may suffice. Where a device mark represents a shape or form, an old case suggests that use of the form may infringe. In *Carless, Capel & Leonard v Pilmore Bedford*[1], the plaintiff's mark, registered for petroleum oil, included a lighthouse device. The defendants sold petrol from lighthouse-shaped pumps. It was held that the defendants did not infringe because the pumps did not, in fact, indicate the origin of the petrol to purchasers. It was recognised, however, that there could in principle be infringement by use of a form represented in a mark.

---

1   (1928) 45 RPC 205.

7.34   Subsection 10(5) is a curious subsection which makes someone party to infringing use by others. It applies where the person applies the registered mark to material intended to be used:

(a)   for labelling or packaging goods[1];
(b)   as a business paper; or
(c)   for advertising goods or services.

---

1   In *Paterson Zochonis v Merfarken Packaging* [1983] FSR 273, a packaging manufacturer was held not liable for copyright infringements.

7.35   The printing of the labels, stationery or advertising material are not rendered directly infringing, but the printer is made a party to infringing use of the material by others and will therefore incur potential liability. This subsection must be causing great concern to the printing and packaging industry, who may be liable for acts over which they have no control. It is reminiscent of the tort of causing and enabling passing off, as exemplified by the *Scotch Whisky* cases[1]. However, the person concerned will only be treated as party to infringing use if he knows or has reason to believe that the application of the mark was not duly authorised by the proprietor or a licensee. The best defence under this subsection is therefore vigilance in enquiry; if a customer warrants that use of any mark is duly authorised, at best the printer will be able to rely on it as a defence, at worst claim an indemnity. Professor John Adams has posited the case of a printer who makes labels at the request of the proprietor and then supplies some of these to an infringer. This case seems unlikely to be caught by s 10(5).

---

1   See para **4.9**, n 1.

USE IN RELATION TO THE PROPRIETOR'S GOODS OR SERVICES

7.36   Subsection 10(6) exempts from infringement the use of a mark to identify goods or services as those of the proprietor or a licensee, if that be the case. The last proviso is not expressed, but must be implicit. Section 10(6) is subject to an express proviso which disapplies it where the use is:

(a)   not in accordance with honest practices in industrial or commercial matters;
(b)   without due cause; and
(c)   takes unfair advantage of, or is detrimental to, the distinctive character or repute of the trade mark.

The last two factors have been considered above in the context of s 10(3). 'Not in accordance with honest practices' appears to be a subjective test, difficult of elucidation[1]. The complexity of the subsection, and in particular the combination of negatives, make it difficult to be sure on whom the burden of proof lies. It is submitted that a wise plaintiff who wishes to allege infringement by use on her own goods or services will proffer evidence on all three factors in the proviso. As honest practices, it would be helpful to rely upon industry guidelines, such as the Advertising Standards Authority's codes of practice.

1   House of Lords Public Bill Committee, 18 January 1994, cols 38–44. On 24 February 1994 (Hansard), vol 552, no 46, col 738, Lord Strathclyde said 'as a matter of principle we should leave industry and commerce to determine those matters themselves'.

7.37   Section 10(6) is most likely to be invoked in comparative advertising cases; at least the following questions may arise:

(a)   'Without due cause' – why is it necessary to use the mark to identify comparator product? Does the mark denote the only product previously available[1]?
(b)   'Takes unfair advantage of' – why compare, save to free-ride on the trade mark's reputation?
(c)   'Is detrimental to' – are the comparisons derogatory?
(d)   'The distinctive character' – the more distinctive the mark, the less justified the comparison.
(e)   'Or repute of the trade mark' – the less deserved the mark's repute, the easier it will be to make this out.

It appears that s 10(6) will be of most assistance to someone who wishes to engage in comparative advertising using an obscure comparator with a deservedly high reputation where the advertiser's own product comes out second best. Will anyone wish to enjoy this privilege?

Other savings from infringement are considered in Chapter 8.

1   Eg, *Duracell v Ever Ready* [1989] FSR 71.

OTHER CAUSES OF ACTION

7.38   Actions for infringement of a registered trade mark may be combined with other causes of action such as passing off[1] or malicious falsehood[2]. It is likely that this practice will continue, especially while uncertainties remain as to the scope and extent of infringement rights.

1   Paras **3.5ff**.
2   Paras **3.20** and **3.21**.

7.39 Three other special actions for injunctions may be mentioned briefly here. Sections 57, 58 and 60 implement articles 6*ter* and 6*septies* of the Paris Convention. Sections 57 and 58 enable the competent authority to restrain unauthorised use of flags and other emblems of States and international organisations. Section 60 enables the 'true' proprietor of a mark which has been wrongly registered in the name of an agent to restrain the agent's use and to call for transfer or invalidation[1] of the mark.

---

1   See *K Sabatier TM* [1993] RPC 97.

REMEDIES AND SEIZURE PROVISIONS

7.40 Section 14(2) makes all the usual remedies available to the court in infringement actions. These include damages; infringement cases are normally fought on specimen instances of infringement. The enumeration of all like acts of infringement and the estimation of damages[1] are usually postponed to a subsequent inquiry as to damages. An account of the defendant's profits from infringement may be claimed as an alternative to damages.

---

1   On the basis of profits lost by the plaintiff, or a notional royalty: *Dormeuil v Feraglow* [1990] RPC 449.

7.41 Injunctions are specifically mentioned: orders that the defendant refrain from infringing being particularly important to a proprietor who wishes to protect a mark. These include final injunctions, granted after judgment, and the interlocutory injunctions, designed to protect the applicant pending trial. The principles on which an interlocutory injunction[1] are granted were set forth by the House of Lords in *American Cyanamid v Ethicon*[2]. Other interlocutory orders such as *Mareva* injunctions[3] and *Anton Piller* orders[4] are also available. For further details of remedies and procedures, the reader is referred to specialist works[5].

---

1   Interim interdict in Scotland.
2   [1975] AC 396: the applicant must show that he has an arguable case, that damages would be an inadequate remedy pending trial, he must offer a cross-undertaking in damages which is adequate to protect the defendant. The court will also take into account the status quo, the effect of an injunction on third parties and, as a last resort, the relative strength of the parties' cases.
3   To preserve assets to meet judgment; see Practice Direction at [1994] RPC 617.
4   To preserve evidence; see Practice Direction at [1994] RPC 617.
5   Such as *Kerly*, paras 15–58 to 15–87; N Bean, *Injunctions* (1994) 6th edn; Burrows, *Remedies in breach of contract and tort* (1994) 2nd edn.

7.42 Section 15 provides a new statutory remedy of erasure, removal or obliteration of marks or, if those are impracticable, for the destruction of goods or materials. The defendant may be ordered to carry out these procedures, or to deliver them up to someone else for the purpose. Section 15 makes no explicit reference to general powers of the court to order thus, particularly in support of an injunction[1]; presumably inherent powers are not affected.

---

1   Contrast s 16(4) and s 99(4) of the Copyright, Designs and Patents Act 1988.

7.43   There are also specific new orders for delivery up and disposal, conferred by ss 16, 19 and 20 on county courts in Northern Ireland[1] and Sheriff courts in Scotland, as well as the High Court and Court of Session. As with the equivalent provisions of the Copyright, Design and Patents Act 1988, it is not clear whether these are meant as free-standing remedies; this must be the case, since county or sheriff courts do not otherwise have jurisdiction over civil infringements.

---

1   But not, it appears, in England and Wales.

7.44   There is a limitation period of six years on statutory delivery up, by virtue of s 18. It is submitted that this is inappropriate for trade marks, where *use* of a mark rather than the marking of goods constitutes the real mischief. The general powers of the courts are not limited if a mark used six years after products are marked.

7.45   A trade mark proprietor may give notice to Customs under s 89 of the impending arrival of infringing goods from outside the European Economic Area (EEA) or from inside the EEA if the goods have not yet been entered for free circulation. These may then be treated as prohibited goods. This procedure is supplanted when Article 3(1) of EC Regulation 3842/86 (see, now, Regulation 3295/94) entitles the proprietor to apply to restrain release for free circulation.

CRIMINAL PROVISIONS

7.46   Criminal sanctions[1] are applied to certain forms of infringement in relation to goods but not services. The offences relate only to use of a mark on or in relation to the goods for which the mark is registered, unless the trade mark has a reputation in the UK[2]. In that case, the offences can be made out if the use takes unfair advantage of, or is detrimental to, the distinctive character or repute of the goods[3]. Note that in the latter case, the prosecution does not have to establish that use was without due cause[4]. In this case, the reputation of and effect on the mark have to be shown whether the goods are similar or dissimilar to those for which the mark is registered. It appears unlikely that the prosecution could make out an offence beyond reasonable doubt where dissimilar goods were concerned.

---

1   For discussion, see P Rawlinson 'The UK Trade Marks Act 1994: It's criminal' [1995] 1 EIPR 54.
2   Section 92(4).

3   For discussion of these criteria, see Ch 7.
4   Contrast s 10(3). However, there is a defence that the accused believed on reasonable grounds that the
     use was not infringing; this would presumably cover any possible justification for the use.

7.47   Section 92 does not specify that use has to be trade mark use, but since
non-trade mark use probably does not infringe, the defence of reasonable belief of
non-infringement may be made out.

The s 92 offences have the following elements:

(a)   positive or negative commercial purpose ('with a view to gain for himself or with
       intent to cause loss to another');
(b)   lack of consent from the trade mark proprietor;
(c)   infringing acts, including:
       (i)   application of sign to goods, packaging or materials,
       (ii)   application to and use of business papers,
       (iii) commercial dealing or possession of marked goods or materials,
       (iv)   making tools (articles) for the above;
(d)   all in relation to an identical mark or one likely to be mistaken for the registered
       mark.

7.48   There is no element of intent to infringe but a defence that the accused believed
on reasonable grounds that use of the mark did not infringe: s 92(5). Curiously, the
'contributory' forms of offence seem wider than their civil equivalents under s 10(4).
Section 92 was intended to overcome difficulties with enforcement of the Trade
Descriptions Acts and in particular the decision in *Price's*[1] case, where it was held that a
disclaimer 'brand copies' could negate the falsity of a marking.

---

1   *R v Kent CC ex parte Price* [1993] 9 EIPR D-224; (1994) 158 JPN 78. See also *R v Veys* [1993] FSR 366.

7.49   Section 93 imposes a duty[1] on local weights and measures authorities (trading
standards officers) in England and Wales[2] to enforce s 92 and gives them like powers to
those they enjoy under the Trade Descriptions Act 1968 to make test purchases, enter
premises, and so forth. Section 90 enables regulations to be made and s 91 enables
Customs to disclose information for prosecutions under s 92 or the Trade Descriptions
Act 1968.

---

1   An amendment to similar effect of the Copyright Designs and Patents Act 1988 is contained in the
     Criminal Justice and Public Order Act 1994, s 165.
2   The Department of Economic Development has the duty in Northern Ireland (s 93(3)) and powers to
     extend time for summary proceedings are conferred in Scotland (s 96).

7.50   All offences are triable either way, with a maximum level of fine and/or six
months' imprisonment on summary conviction or a maximum of ten years' imprisonment and/or a fine on indictment.

7.51 Forfeiture may be ordered under ss 97 and 98 (Scotland). Under s 97, once proceedings have started, or otherwise by complaint, showing that an offence has been committed, the court has powers to order forfeiture or destruction or obliteration before return. This was introduced to obviate problems which arise when undoubtedly counterfeit goods had been seized but were not subject of a conviction, or where the owner of the infringing goods for obvious reasons makes himself scarce. The criminal courts also have general powers to order forfeiture and compensation in respect of convictions. Relevant offences are those under s 97, the Trade Descriptions Act 1968 or any offence involving dishonesty or deception.

7.52 There are other offences, of falsification of the register[1] and of falsely representing a trade mark as registered[2]. The latter cannot be made out where the mark is indeed registered somewhere in the European Union: see *Pall v Dahlhausen*[3].

1   Section 94.
2   Section 95.
3   (1991), *The Times*, 4 February.

7.53 Section 101 expressly imposes liability upon partners and upon company officers for their firms' and companies' crimes.

INFRINGEMENT – TRANSITIONAL PROVISIONS

7.54 Sections 9–12 and 14 apply to infringements of existing marks committed after commencement[1]. However, where a mark was registered before commencement, or is re-registered after commencement in substantially the same form and for the same goods or services, Sch 3, para 4(2) applies. Thereby, it is not an infringement to continue after commencement any use which did not amount to infringement under the old law. Exactly what amounts to continued use may present problems but, in *Northern & Shell v Conde Nast*[2], Jacob J held that para 4(2) applied to the continued import and sale of monthly magazines.

Example: A's mark is registered for sherry. B has used a similar mark for port since 1950. Even though port and sherry are probably sufficiently similar for infringement to be established under s 10(2)(b), B may continue using the mark on port (but not begin to use it on sherry or Madeira).

1   Sch 3, para 4(1).
2   9 December 1994, as yet unreported.

7.55 Section 5(2) of the Trade Marks Act 1938 spared an unauthorised user of a Part B mark if he could show that his use was not likely to deceive or cause confusion or be taken as indicating a connection with the proprietor or a registered user. Section 5(2) did not act as a defence to infringement, but only to remedy. Thus, Sch 3, para 4(2) may not permit continuation of such use.

Chapter 8

DEFENDING INFRINGEMENT PROCEEDINGS

PRIOR CONSIDERATIONS; THREATS

8.1 Prospective defendants in infringement proceedings should consider whether the action is worth defending at all. If the mark is of no great importance to them, it might be worth offering the trade mark proprietor all that he might achieve at trial: a prospective defendant can undertake to stop using the mark, to sticker catalogues, to return goods to suppliers or at least not part with them until the mark has been removed, and offer information as to the source of infringing articles. This may be the best course for a retailer or service provider in a small way of business. If this is done, the defendant is unlikely to incur costs in any proceedings, especially if the infringement was unwitting[1].

---

1   And even more so if proceedings were started without notice, eg *American Tobacco v Guest* (1892) 9 RPC 218.

8.2 The fact that this is so means that there is a temptation for proprietors to make extravagant threats against retailers. Indeed, this may be the only way to trace infringing goods to their source. Traders are unlikely to 'shop' their suppliers unless threatened with something worse. But over-zealous pursuit may cause damage to suppliers.

8.3 The use of unjustified threats was seen as a problem, in particular for small businesses.[1] Parliament accordingly enacted s 21, which provides a remedy for groundless threats of proceedings for infringement of a registered trade mark. Anyone aggrieved by the threat, be it the recipient or their supplier or some other person affected by the threat, can apply to the court for a declaration that the threat is unjustifiable, an injunction to restrain repetition and damages for any loss sustained. The burden of justifying the threat lies on the person making it; if that burden is not discharged, the plaintiff in threats proceedings is entitled to succeed. Even if justification can be made, it falls away if the registration is invalid or liable to be revoked in a material respect.

---

1   House of Lords Public Bill Committee, 19 January 1994, col 68. For an excellent account, see Lim HG 'The "threats" section in the UK Trade Marks Act 1994: can a person still wound without striking?' [1995] 3 EIPR 138.

8.4 Section 21 is a very powerful mechanism. Where used by the recipient of the threats, he can take the initiative in litigation but the proprietor still has to establish infringement, to escape liability for the threat.

8.5 The action is not available where the threats relate to the application of the mark to goods, the import or export of marked goods or the provision of services under the mark. In this respect, it resembles the remedies for unjustified threats of patent[1] and design[2] infringement. But here the mischief with which infringement proceedings are concerned is the use of the mark rather than characteristics of products themselves. Provided retailers can obliterate marks, sticker catalogues, and so forth, the goods are not 'sterilised' in their hands.

1　Patents Act 1977, s 70.
2　Registered Designs Act 1949, s 26 (note the act as amended appears as Sch 4 to the Copyright Designs and Patents Act 1988).

8.6　The effect of invalidity on the threats proceedings is probably designed to discourage covetously broad registrations being sought and abused.

8.7　Mere notification that the mark is registered is not a threat[1]. A suggested amendment to the Trade Marks Bill expressly to allow the proprietor to ask for the name of the supplier was not taken up[2].

1　s 21(4).
2　House of Lords Public Bill Committee, 19 January 1994, cols 66–67.

8.8　Could the proprietor allege passing off, threaten proceedings for passing off and also give notice of the trade mark registration? The latter is likely to be regarded as a threat, as in the copyright and design case of *Jaybeam v Abru*[1].

1　[1976] RPC 308.

CHALLENGING THE CLAIMS

8.9　Attack may be the best form of defence. Before or during proceedings, the defendant should consider whether there are grounds to attack the registration, ab initio for invalidity or by way of revocation for non-use, deceptiveness or because it has become generic in the trade. If the claim is by a licensee, it may be possible to challenge their standing to sue. In a case which will turn on confusion, the defendant can log calls and correspondence for any complaints, and seek the views of representatives and customers.

INTERLOCUTORY TACTICS

8.10　A defendant faced with an application for an interlocutory injunction or other relief has a number of options. He may seek to undermine the plaintiff's substantive case or raise effective defences. He may also avert an interlocutory injunction by persuading the court that damages would be perfectly adequate to compensate the plaintiff pending trial. Tactics include establishing that the defendant's products are not inferior, offering to log any shift to the defendant's goods or services (and conceding that damages would be available if so[1]), showing that the defendant is good for damages, or offering to make payments into an account in the name of the defendant's solicitors (or both). If these are ineffective, it may be preferable to give undertakings pending trial.

---

1   This ploy was used to good effect in *Beecham v Sainsbury* [1987] EIPR D-234.

JUSTIFYING USE – SUBSTANTIVE DEFENCES

8.11   A number of specific defences come under this general heading. They will be useful at trial and in showing an arguable defence to avert summary judgment. They are, briefly:

(a)   The defendant may be able to show that the goods or services which he identifies by the mark are those of the proprietor or a licensee – that they are genuine. This will call s 10(6) into play. As discussed at para 7–36, there is an elaborate proviso by which a proprietor may make out a claim of infringement. Examples include the use of the mark on second-hand goods. Cases in passing off[1] show that descriptions like 'factory reconditioned Hoovers' may be actionable, because members of the public would imagine reconditioning to have been done by or on behalf of the mark's proprietor, with original spares. Contrast 'We recondition vacuum cleaners – all makes – Hoover, Electrolux, Goblin, etc', which would probably pass muster under s 10(6).

(b)   If the proprietor's rights are restricted[2] by disclaimer or limitation, the defendant may be able to argue that his activities fall within that disclaimer, and thus cannot be enjoined. A defendant should get sight of the registration certificate or entry in the *Trade Mark Journal* as quickly as possible, to ascertain whether the plaintiff's rights may be limited in this way.

(c)   The defendant's products may be 'parallel imports' – goods marketed elsewhere by or with the consent of the plaintiff. If such goods emanate from the European Economic Area, s 12(1) provides a defence. The background to this section is discussed in Chapter 13. It appears that the consent has to be voluntary[3]. Section 12(2) disapplies 12(1) where there are legitimate reasons to oppose further dealings, especially where the condition of goods is changed/impaired.

(d)   If the defendant has a concurrent registration for the goods or services in question, s 11(1) provides that use within the scope of the registration will not infringe other marks. This is subject to validity of the registration relied upon, so it is not absolute. It may become so as set out in the next defence.

(e)   Where the defendant has registered and used the mark in suit and the plaintiff has been aware of its use but has acquiesced in that use for a continuous period of five years, s 48 applies. It provides a defence to the plaintiff's claims and disables the plaintiff from applying for a declaration of invalidity. Section 48 does not, however, preclude an application for revocation under s 46.

(f)   The defendant may be able to show an earlier local right in the mark, for example to sue in passing off. If so, s 11(3) provides a defence in that locality. Note that the text of s 11(3) diverges mysteriously from that of the trade marks harmonisation Directive by substitution of 'locality' for 'territory' at the end of the first sentence.

(g)   Non-trade mark use – see paras **1.36** and **7.16**.

   Note that the savings (h), (i) and (j) must be shown to be in accordance with honest practices in industrial or commercial matters which replaces 'bona fide'[4] in equivalent provisions of the 1938 Act.

(h)   Use of own name and address: s 11(2)(a). This appears to apply to all persons and not just individuals, notwithstanding the following statement for inclusion in the minutes of adoption of the Community Trade Mark Regulation.

   'The Council and Commission consider that the words 'his own name' in subparagraph (a) apply only to natural persons.'

   In practice, the court will recognise the ease with which company names can be changed; use of a company's own name may be permitted only in the short term. The name must be used in full[5].

(i)   If the allegations relate to a descriptive mark or part of a mark, a defendant may be permitted to continue use as a descriptive indication by virtue of s 11(2)(b). In *Mothercare*[6], the use of the trade mark in a book title was held to be descriptive rather than trade mark use.

(j)   Use of a mark will also be permitted to indicate the purpose of other goods or services. Section 11(2)(c) makes particular reference to accessories or spare parts; repairs and servicing also come to mind: 'spares for all Rover models' 'we repair Canon cameras' would be permitted under s 11(2)(c), but probably not 'Rover spares' for other manufacturers' parts for 'Rover' cars or 'Canon repairs'.

(k)   The Limitation Acts apply to infringement just as to any other torts. The limitation period of six years will apply to debar any instances of infringement occurring more than six years prior to the writ[7]. A six-year limitation period is also built into the special provisions on delivery up in s 18.

(l)   Innocence is not, strictly speaking, a defence in civil proceedings, since no requirement of intention or knowledge is built into the definitions of infringement. It may incline the court to refuse a discretionary remedy such as an account of profits, but will not deflect a claim to damages[8].

(m)   Non-infringing use started prior to commencement of the 1994 Act can be continued, by virtue of Sch 3, para 4(2). This applies where the mark was registered prior to commencement, or a new registration was obtained for essentially the same mark, for the same goods and services. It compensates for the broadening of the infringement provisions. See, further, paras **7.54** and **7.55**.

---

1   Eg, *Hoover v Air-Way* (1936) 53 RPC 399 ('reconditioned Hoover'); *Levi Strauss v Wingate* [1993] EIPR D-258, (1993) 26 IPR 215 (Fed Ct of Aus).
2   Section 13.
3   Cf *Pharmon v Hoechst* [1985] 3 CMLR 775 where a compulsory licence was in effect.
4   'The honest use by the person of his own name without any intention to deceive anybody or without any intention to make use of the goodwill which has been acquired by another trader': *Baume v Moore* [1958] RPC 226 at 235.
5   *Origins Natural Resources Inc v Origin Clothing Ltd*, Jacob J, 17 November 1994 (as yet unreported).
6   [1988] RPC 113.
7   For a patent case in which the defendant's acts were statute-barred before grant of the patent, see *Sevcon v Lucas* [1986] RPC 609.
8   *Spalding v Gamage* (1915) 32 RPC 273.

ATTACKING THE MARK

8.12   Invalidity may be raised by way of defence, but the defendant who challenges validity will probably counterclaim for a declaration of invalidity and/or for revocation. These are considered further in Chapter 9.

SETTLEMENT

8.13   Compromise of litigation is always desirable[1] but those seeking to settle a trade mark infringement action must be particularly careful. Inappropriate partitioning arrangements may offend against Article 85 of the Treaty of Rome[2]. Furthermore, a settlement agreement which involves licensing the defendant to continue to use the mark in some way may endanger the mark's validity by rendering it deceptive[3].

---

1   For a detailed account, see D Foskett 'The law of compromise' (1991 and supplements) 3rd edn; M Alexander, 'Settlement in intellectual property disputes' *Trademark World*, December/January 1992/93, p 26.
2   See Ch 13; S Singleton 'Intellectual property disputes: settlement agreements and ancillary licences under EC and UK competion law' [1993] 2 EIPR 48.
3   See Ch 10 on licensing.

Chapter 9

CANCELLATION OF REGISTRATION

INTRODUCTION

9.1   Under the 1994 Act, anyone[1] may seek removal of a trade mark from the Register, in respect of some or all of the goods or services for which it is registered[2]. In contrast, under the 1938 Act, a person applying for removal of a mark had to be a 'person aggrieved'[3]. This status was normally shown by the citation of the mark against an application, or threat of infringement proceedings[4]. It remains to be seen whether the liberality of the new provisions will lead to vexatious applications, or to the use of nominees in attacking marks.

1   An attempt to limit the possibility to those with a bona fide interest in removal of the mark from the register was rejected in Parliament: Hansard, House of Lords, vol 553, no 55, 14 March 1994, col 78.
2   Sections 45(1), 46(5), 47(5).
3   Trade Marks Act 1938, ss 26, 27(4), 32, 33 and Sch 1, para 4.
4   For a case in which the applicant for removal of a mark failed to satisfy this requirement, see *Oscar TM* [1979] RPC 173.

9.2   The proprietor himself may apply to the Registry to surrender the registration[1]. In this case, the 1994 Act recognises that licensees or those with a security or other interest in the registration might be affected[2]. The proprietor is required to give the name and address of any person having a registered interest in the mark and to certify that they have received three months' notice of the application. The proprietor must further certify either that such persons are not affected[3] by surrender or that they have given consent. Licensees or chargees should register[4] their interests in order to enjoy this (and other) protection. It appears that the Registry need not look behind the certificate, nor notify the registered interests directly[5].

1   Trade Marks Act 1994, s 45(1); Trade Marks Rules 1994, r 26.
2   Section 45(2) (B) and r 26(2).
3   Eg, the surrender may be for goods or services subject to the licence.
4   See paras **10.10**, **11.13** and **11.22**.
5   Unless they have filed a request for information, or 'caveat' on Form TM31C.

9.3   In lieu of surrender, the proprietor may simply fail to renew the registration. This requires no forms or consents; it is free and reversible. Section 43 provides for submission of the request for renewal up to six months after expiry[1] and for restoration of marks after that date[2].

1   Section 43(3) and r 29; there is an additional fee to renew the mark after expiry.
2   Section 43(5) and r 30 – if the Registrar is satisfied that it is just to restore the mark to the register.

9.4   Applications by third parties to remove a mark may be divided into two categories; both can be made to the Registry or to the court[1]. The first category of application, for a declaration of invalidity, is based on grounds existing at the time of registration. If the application is successful, in relation to some or all of the goods or services, the registration will be deemed never to have been made, subject to 'transactions past and closed'[2]. The Registrar himself may apply to the court for cancellation on the ground of bad faith.

1   To the court if proceedings are pending there: s 47(3)(a) and s 46(4)(a). The Registrar may transfer applications to the court: s 47(3)(b) and s 46(4)(b).
2   Section 47(6).

9.5   The second category is the application for revocation. This is based on grounds arising after registration: non-use, deceptiveness or a shift to generic meaning. The revocation may take effect from the date of the application, or from an earlier date at which the grounds for revocation subsisted[1].

1   Section 46(6).

GROUNDS – INVALIDITY

9.6   The grounds of invalidity include all those which could form a basis for refusal under ss 3 to 6. The applicant for a declaration of invalidity may allege that the registered sign does not satisfy s 1, because it is not a sign capable of graphic representation. At first glance, this seems a hopeless objection, because a graphic representation of something must have been entered on the register. However, it may still be open to argue that the representation is embarrassingly inadequate, and fails to show in what sign the proprietor has exclusive rights. Another ground based on s 1 is that of non-distinctiveness. If the mark is shown incapable of being distinctive[1] or devoid of distinctive character[2], then the registration may be declared invalid. Where invalidity is based on s 3(1)(b) or s 3(1)(c) and (d) (descriptive and generic marks) the proprietor may be able to show that the mark has acquired distinctiveness after registration by virtue of use, on the goods or services for which it is registered[3]. The case-law of passing off[4] shows that a descriptive mark may indeed acquire 'secondary meaning'. Difficulty arises, however, where the proprietor faces no competition. In *Shredded Wheat*[5], the mark was held to be non-distinctive[6] despite long and extensive use for breakfast cereal. This was partly because the product had been patented, so no other manufacturer could compete directly while the patent was in force, and partly because the proprietors' advertising had highlighted the descriptiveness of the name. By analogy, it may be more difficult to show acquired distinctiveness in a mark which has been protected by registration than in an unregistered mark.

1   Contrary to s 1(1).
2   Contrary to s 3(1)(b).

3 Section 47(1).
4 The classic example being 'Camel Hair Belting': *Reddaway v Banham* [1896] AC 199; 13 RPC 218.
5 (1938) 55 RPC 125 (Canada) and (1938) 55 RPC 271 (UK) and (1940) 57 RPC 137.
6 And therefore invalidly registered.

9.7 Other provisions in s 3 will provide grounds for invalidity: that the mark is merely a prohibited shape[1], is contrary to public order or accepted morals[2] or has always been deceptive at the date of application[3]. In practice, evidence of the way the mark has been used and perceived may be relevant to these issues as well as that of distinctiveness. The applicant for invalidity may further argue that the use of the mark is prohibited by UK or Community law[4]. For example, there may be some infraction of labelling laws.

---

1 See s 3(2).
2 Section 3(3).
3 Section 3(3)(b). Deceptiveness subsequent to registration is a ground for revocation under s 46(1)(d), referred to below.
4 Section 3(4).

9.8 Neither s 47 nor s 46 appears to cater for removal of a mark on the ground that its use has subsequently become contrary to public order or morality. Presumably the assumption is that standards in these matters usually relax rather than tighten. This is not true of legal rules, especially those designed to protect the health and safety of the consumer. Nor is there the possibility of invalidity proceedings if the mark acquires an overpowering geographical significance because of news coverage of disasters or the reorganisation of local government[1].

---

1 'Avon', for example became the name of a county as well as of a river [1985] RPC 43. However, a mark which becomes geographically deceptive by virtue of the proprietor's use may be liable to revocation: s 46(1)(d).

9.9 Where the mark is or incorporates one of the specially protected emblems referred to in ss 3(5) and 4, a declaration of invalidity may be sought.

9.10 The applicant in invalidity proceedings may argue that the mark has been applied for in bad fatih. This is likely to overlap with other grounds for removal, such as failure to use the mark. It may also coincide with relative grounds of refusal – that the mark was unregistrable over an earlier mark, especially a well-known earlier mark.

9.11 Validity may be impugned on the basis of identity or similarity to an earlier mark, where registration was prohibited by subss 5(1), (2), (3), or where the proprietor of an earlier right in passing off, copyright or design could prevent use and registration[1]. The applicant need not be the proprietor of such a right, although a third party might have greater difficulty in proving that it should have barred registration. For further details of 'relative' grounds for refusal and techniques for comparison of marks, goods and services, see Chapter 5 (registration) and Chapter 7 (infringement).

---

1   See s 5(4).

GROUNDS – REVOCATION

9.12   Revocation may be sought instead of or in addition to a declaration of invalidity. The first ground for revocation, and the one likely to be employed most frequently, is non-use. There are two possibilities. First, the applicant[1] may allege that the mark has not been put to genuine[2] use, by the proprietor or with his consent, for at least five years since it was placed on the register[3]. Alternatively, the revocation may be sought on the ground that the mark has been out of use for an uninterrupted period of five years. Once an allegation of non-use has been made in revocation proceedings, it is for the proprietor to show what use has in fact been made. This is the effect of s 100, which appears to require the trigger of (civil) proceedings. Unless use is shown on all the goods or services for which the mark is registered, its registration is liable to be revoked in whole or in part[4]. Where use is resumed after five or more years' non-use, the mark may be saved. Use in the three months prior to the application for revocation is disregarded, unless preparations were made before the proprietor became aware that the application might be made[5]. This is designed to enable the applicant to approach the proprietor with a view to compromise, in the knowledge that commencement of use will not count after warning is given.

---

1   There is no provision for ex officio revocation by the Registry.
2   For a discussion of 'genuine', see para **6.9**.
3   Section 46(1)(a) refers to five years following the date of completion of the registration procedure; the latter was held to be the relevant starting point under the 1938 Act: *Bon Matin* [1988] RPC 553.
4   Section 46(5).
5   Section 46(3).

9.13   Subsections 46(1)(a) and (b) refer to proper reasons for non-use. Although it may be for the applicant to establish that there are no proper reasons for non-use, a wise proprietor will be prepared to justify failure to use. Parliament declined to particularise the proper reasons which might subsist[1]; construction of s 46(1) and the provisions of the Directive on which it was based is therefore left to the courts. In the past, reasons for non-use had to be fairly extreme to save a mark: 'special circumstances in the trade' such as wartime prohibitions[2]. If the goods or services are very valuable, sales may be sporadic. Lack of demand may be a legitimate reason for non-use[3]. In its explanatory memorandum to Art 13 of the 1980 draft of the community trade mark regulation, the European Commission suggested that a manufacturer of pharmaceuticals who was prevented from using a mark because of marketing constraint would not be liable to lose the mark for non-use[4].

---

1   House of Lords Public Bill Committee, 19 January 1994, col 84.
2   *Manus v Fullwood & Bland* (1948) 65 RPC 329; (1949) 66 RPC 71.

3 A Spencer, 'European harmonisation use and abuse' *Trademark World*, May 1994 at p 27, citing section 30 of the WIPO Model Law.
4 Bulletin of the European Communities, suppl 5/1980, p 61.

9.14 Where a mark is used on some but not all of the goods for which it is registered, partial revocation is possible[1]. Consider a mark registered in class 18 for umbrellas, parasols and riding whips which is used only on umbrellas. Revocation may be sought in respect of parasols and riding whips. Section 26(1) of the Trade Marks Act 1938 contained a discretionary proviso whereby a mark could remain on the register if used for goods and services of the same description[2]. In our example, this would probably have saved the mark for parasols but perhaps not for riding whips. There is no equivalent provision in the 1994 Act. In its memorandum on the creation of an EEC trade mark the European commission wrote:

'If a trade mark is used only for some of the goods for which it is registered, it should be maintainable . . . only for those goods. In the case of proceedings for invalidation or cancellation, the remaining goods should be removed from the list of goods. This strict provision does not prejudice the rule that the protection of a trade mark extends to goods which are similar to the used goods. However, if use for similar goods were sufficient to maintain the registration for unused goods, the result would be an extension of the trade mark right beyond what is fair and reasonable.'

If use for similar goods were sufficient to maintain a mark for unused goods, the protection would extend to goods similar to those on which the mark is not used. In our example, the proprietor might attempt to rely on the decision in *Walpamur v Sanderson*[3], where use on enamel was held sufficient to sustain a registration for 'paints, enamels and varnishes', all of which were customarily sold together in a range.

1 Section 46(5).
2 For tests, see paras **5.30–5.31**.
3 (1926) 43 RPC 385, decided under the Trade Marks Act 1905, which did not have a saving proviso. Cf *Mirage TM* IPD 17013.

9.15 A mark which has become 'generic' in the trade (used by traders as the common name for a product or service for which it is registered) is vulnerable to revocation under s 46(1)(c). The applicant must show that the mark has become generic by virtue of the proprietor's acts or inactivity. A proprietor who has used his own mark in a generic way, or has stood idly by[1] whilst others do so is likely to lose the registration, but a vigilant if ineffective proprietor may be able to keep the mark on the register. The 1994 Act does not provide effective means to prevent generic use by other traders. The Australian *Caplets*[2] case shows that this can be a problem; such use may be quite deliberate. By contrast, in the USA, anti-dilution laws may be used to prevent misuse which is likely to lead to a mark becoming generic[3].

1 As Lord Trowie of Troon remarked whilst the Trade Marks Bill was in committee stage, proprietors whose marks become generic may (misguidedly) be 'quite pleased': House of Lords Public Bill Committee, 19 January 1994, col 83.

2   *Johnson & Johnson v Sterling Pharmaceuticals* (1991) 21 IPR 1.
3   J Gilson 'Trade mark protection and practice' (1977 and releases) para 2.02[7] citing *Bristol-Myers Co v RH Macy & Co* 151 F Supp 513, 113 USDQ 274 (SDNY 1957) and other cases.

9.16   Where, after registration, a mark merely loses its distinctiveness, as opposed to becoming generic or becoming deceptive[1], it is not liable to be revoked. This is in accordance with the law under the Trade Marks Act 1938[2].

1   See para **9.16**.
2   See *Kerly's Law of Trade Marks and Trade Names*, paras 11–17 and cases cited therein.

9.17   Registration of a mark may be revoked on the ground that use has rendered it misleading to the public, particularly as to the nature, quality or geographical origin of the goods or services concerned. The wording of this subsection follows that of Article 12 of the Directive. It is submitted that other forms of deceptiveness, especially as to commercial origin, are not excluded[1].

1   See H Norman, 'Trade mark licences in the United Kingdom' [1994] 4 EIPR 154. It is interesting to speculate whether the splitting assignment in *IHT Internationale Heiztechnik v Ideal Standard* [1995] FJR 59 might render the marks vulnerable to attack on this ground.

PROCEDURES

9.18   Surrender of a mark is straightforward, subject to notification of those with a registered interest in the mark, and to provision of the necessary names, addresses and certificates[1]. Form TM22 is used for total surrender, while Form TM23 is prescribed for partial surrender, in respect of only some of the goods and services[2].

1   See para **9.2**.
2   Rule 26(1).

9.19   Applications for revocation and for declarations of invalidity are rather more elaborate. Rule 31(1) prescribes the use of Form TM26 for these, as well as for application to rectify the register in the case of error or omission[1]. Rule 31 provides for transmission of the application to the registered proprietor[2], who may file a counter-statement on Form TM8. If the application is for revocation on the ground of non-use, and the proprietor fails to file a counter-statement, or to provide evidence of uses, the application will be granted and the mark revoked[3]. Any other interested party may file for leave to intervene, using Form TM27[4]. Thereafter, the rules for grounds of evidence, and hearings follow those for opposition proceedings[5]. Appeals may be made to the court or to the appointed person[6], again as for oppositions.

1   Pursuant to s 64. The Registrar may also delete apparently obsolete matter of his own initiative: s 64(5).

2 Unless made by the proprietor: r 31(2).
3 Rule 31(3), proviso and r 31(4).
4 Rule 31(5).
5 Rule 31(4); for oppositions, see para **5.40**.
6 Rules 57–59.

9.20 Where an application is made to surrender[1] a registration, in whole or in part, the proprietor should date and submit Form TM22 (surrender) or Form TM23 (partial surrender) as at the date on which surrender is sought. Subject to the interests of others, surrender will take effect as from that date[2]. Successful application to invalidate[3] a registered mark takes effect ab initio, but subject to 'transactions past and closed'[4]. An application to revoke[5] can take effect, if successful, from the date of application or an earlier date on which the grounds for revocation existed[6]. There is no provision to restore any such marks, but the former proprietor may make a subsequent application to re-register the mark, if it is 'recaptured' from a generic usage or it otherwise becomes registrable once more.

1 Paras **9.2–9.3** and **9.17**.
2 The author is grateful to the Trade Marks Registry for help on this point.
3 Paras **9.6–9.11** and **9.18**.
4 Proviso to s 47(6).
5 Paras **9.12–9.18**.
6 Section 46(6).

Chapter 10

LICENSING OTHERS TO USE THE MARK

INTRODUCTION

10.1   Article 10(3) of the trade marks harmonisation Directive states that use of a trade mark with the consent of the proprietor[1] shall be deemed to constitute use by the proprietor. Article 10(3) appears to relate to the use necessary to maintain a mark and is integrated into s 46 of the 1994 Act. In this context the attribution of use to a proprietor is a privilege. However, use by licensees should be properly controlled for a number of reasons. Inappropriate use may render the mark liable for revocation on the ground that it has become deceptive or generic. A trade mark licensor may incur liability for defective products by virtue of the Consumer Protection Act 1987[2]. It is possible that use of a mark in such a way as to deceive the public amounts to a false trade description within the meaning of the Trade Descriptions Acts 1968–72[3]. Even if these extreme consequences do not occur, improper use may diminish or destroy the goodwill and value of the mark. The Trade Marks Act 1994 deregulated trade mark licensing, Parliament relying upon the self-interest of proprietors to maintain their marks[4].

---

1   Or use of a collective or certification mark with the appropriate authorisation.
2   Sections 2(2)(b) and 3(2). See, further, D Good and C Easter, 'Product safety and product liability: the implications for licensing' [1993] 1 EIPR 10.
3   See para **7.48**.
4   See White Paper 'Reform of Trade Marks Law' 1990 Cm 1203, para 4.36; Hansard, House of Lords, vol 550, no 10, 6 December 1993, col 752.

10.2   The effect of licensing marks at common law is uncertain. Lane sums up the prevailing uncertainty thus:

'Under British law as it presently stands, it is quite possible that a licence over an unregistered mark (or other passing off subject matter) is a thing writ in water.'[1]

---

1   S Lane, *The Status of Licensing Common Law Marks* (1991), p 1.

10.3   This state of affairs is unsatisfactory, particularly for franchisors licensing their business formats. These can involve many badges of trade, some registered and some not. Lane makes an extensive survey of cases and concludes that the law has fallen into the error of concluding that the licensing of a trademark was unlawful at common law. These arguments can be prayed in aid by a litigant who has to fall back on the common law. It is preferable, however, for trade mark proprietors and licensees to shelter in the relative certainty of statute law.

10.4   Trade mark licences fall into four broad categories. First, the proprietor may authorise a manufacturer to apply the mark on the proprietor's behalf. In this case, the proprietor is effectively subcontracting the use, which will enure to him in any event. Secondly, use in relation to the proprietor's own goods does not infringe in normal circumstances[1]. Whether this is use 'by or with the consent of the proprietor' is a nice point; presumably consent will be implied into the circumstances of trade. Thirdly, the trade mark owner may license use of the mark on goods or services in which he has a direct commercial interest. Many business format franchises fall into this category. The proprietor will have considerable incentive to exercise control over the quality of such goods or services. Lastly, the proprietor may regard the trade mark as an asset from which a return may be made by licensing. Into this category come most aspects of character merchandising[2].

---

1 Section 10(6).
2 See J Adams, *Character Merchandising* (1987); R Bagehot and G Nuttall *Sponsorship, Endorsement and Merchandising: A Practical Guide* (1990).

10.5 Dealing with a mark as a commodity in its own right was regarded as 'trafficking' under the Trade Marks Act 1938[1]; the Registrar was required to refuse applications to register such licences[2]. However, the public has come to recognise the activity of licensing; such appears from the decision in the 'Ninja Turtles Case', *Mirage Studios v Counter-feat Clothing*[3]. Where the mark is registered, along with details of licences, the public has a means of identifying those connected with the goods or services supplied under the mark.

---

1 Section 28(6).
2 See *Holly Hobbie TM* [1984] 1 WLR 189; [1984] FSR 199.
3 [1991] FSR 145; Lord Strathclyde put it thus, reiterating para 4.36 of the White Paper 'Reform of Trade Marks Law' 1990 Cm 1203:

   'the public have grown accustomed to goods and services being supplied under licence from the trade mark owner for example as part of a franchise operation.' (Hansard, House of Lords, vol 550, no 10, 6 December 1993, col 752.)

10.6 Where a licensee's conduct takes him outside the scope of the trade mark, use of the mark constitutes infringement as well as breach of contract. As a matter of English law, this was confirmed in *Inter Sport*[1]: the licensee argued unsuccessfully that use after termination was not infringement. It is also spelt out in Article 8 of the Directive.

---

1 *Sport International Bussum v Hi-Tec Sports* [1988] RPC 329.

THE LICENSEE

10.7 Given that the ethos of the 1994 Act is to cast responsibility for the mark upon the parties concerned, it behoves a trade mark owner to exercise considerable care in the choice of a licensee. A good licensee will be solvent, reliable, have good distribution arrangements, advertising policy and other business methods. The licence may indeed specify such matters[1].

---

1   In practice, a short form of licence may be prepared for filing at the Registry. This can then be scheduled to a more elaborate agreement with all ancillary detail. This course has the advantage that confidentiality of the latter can be protected, although the Registrar has power to give directions as to confidentiality: r 45.

10.8   The licence may be exclusive[1], sole[2], or non-exclusive. Subject to the terms of the licence agreement, an exclusive licensee has all the rights and remedies of an assignee[3], except title. He can bring infringement proceedings in his own name[4] against anyone except the proprietor[5]. Where the proprietor has acted in breach of the agreement by authorising a third party to use the mark, the licensee's remedy is in contract against the proprietor[6]. The exclusive licensee must be joined in infringement proceedings brought by the proprietor where they have concurrent rights of action.

---

1   Authorising the licensee to use the mark to the exclusion of all others, including the proprietor: s 29(1).
2   So that use of the mark is limited to the licensee and the proprietor.
3   Section 31.
4   The proprietor should be joined as co-plaintiff or nominal defendant: s 31(4) and (5), although interlocutory relief may be sought prior to joinder. The court apportions pecuniary relief: s 31(6).
5   Section 31(1).
6   Since the third party may defend infringement proceedings by referring to the proprietor's consent: s 31(3).

10.9   A sole or non-exclusive licensee may also bring proceedings for infringement, unless the agreement provides to the contrary[1]. The licensee must first call upon the proprietor to take proceedings. If the proprietor fails to do so within two months, or refuses to do so, the licensee is then free to start litigation. This represents an improvement upon the 1938 Act, whereunder the licensee had to wait for two months even if the proprietor expressly refused to institute proceedings[2]. The proprietor must be joined, although the licensee may seek interlocutory relief prior to joining the proprietor[3]. Where the proprietor brings proceedings, the court has powers to order that pecuniary relief be held on behalf of licensees[4].

---

1   Section 30(2).
2   Trade Marks Act 1938, s 28(3).
3   Section 30(4).
4   Section 30(6).

10.10   In order to enjoy rights of action, the licensee must be registered as such[1]. Delay beyond six months in registering the licence may limit the licensee's ability to recover damages or claim an account of profits[2].

1   Trade Marks Act 1994, s 25(3)(b).
2   Section 25(4).

GENERAL AND LIMITED LICENCES

10.11   The licence may be general or limited to some of the goods or services for which the mark is registered[1]. Preferably the licence should be explicit on this point.

1   Section 28(1)(a).

10.12   Territorial limitations may also apply, as specifically provided by s 28(1)(b). Product and territorial limitations as envisaged by s 28(1) are referred to in Article 8(1) of the harmonisation Directive.

10.13   The licence may be limited to use of the mark in a particular manner[1]. For example, where a mark is registered without reference to colour or typescript, the licence may relate to use in a particular colour and/or a particular script. It may also be wise for the proprietor to specify that the mark be used in a minimum size and to restrict the use of other marks in combination with that licensed. It may not be in a licensee's interest to use her own mark in conjunction with the licensed mark; the latter may become difficult to use independently.

1   Section 28(1)(b).

10.14   So far, 'manner of use' has been interpreted in terms of mode of display of the mark. It may or may not extend to field of use, for example, where the proprietor supplies one sector, say the veterinary sector, while the licensee supplies a different sector, say the retail sector. This really amounts to market sharing. Neither the Directive nor the 1994 Act refers to limitations by customer type. In principle, a licence could be thus limited, but care should be taken when negotiating any limitation or restriction to avoid infringements of competition law (see para **10.19**).

QUALITY CONTROL

10.15   Control by the proprietor of the quality of goods or services supplied under the mark maintains a nexus between the proprietor and those products. It thus supports the 'origin' function of the trade mark, as well as its 'quality' function[1]. Quality control is important in maintaining the goodwill and reputation of a trade mark. Failure to control quality may diminish the mark's value or render it deceptive[2]. Loss of reputation may also affect the proprietor's ability to sue under s 10(3) to restrain use on dissimilar services or goods[3].

1   See Ch 1.
2   For a discussion, see H Norman 'Trade mark Licences in the United Kingdom: Time for Bostitch to be Reevaluated?' [1994] 4 EIPR 155.
3   See para **7.27**.

10.16   Quality control[1] may be carried out by the proprietor[2], by a third party equipped to do so[3] or in an exceptional case by the licensee[4].

1   For a discussion as to the optimum level of quality control, see W Borchard and A Lewis 'The US experience with quality control in trade mark licensing' (1994) 11 CIPR 3.
2   Who will need provisions in the agreement for the taking of samples for analysis. This on its own will not suffice unless it leads to regular contact with the licensee: *Job TM* [1993] FSR 118.
3   Eg, a laboratory or testing station.
4   See, eg, *Molyslip* [1978] RPC 211.

10.17   Standards of quality may be set by reference to a British or European standard for goods or services, or by setting out objective standards. Where this is impossible, it may be necessary to place restrictions on the licensee's suppliers[1].

1   A standard may be impossible to set, as in the fashion industry: *Pronuptia v Schillgalis* [1986] ECR 353; [1986] 1 CMLR 414 at para [21], or may be impossible to enforce in practice. In these circumstances, restriction may be valid notwithstanding competition laws – see below.

OTHER TERMS

10.18   A licence agreement should adequately identify the marks, registrations, and names and addresses of the parties. A licensee can register its interest without the cooperation of the licensor, but it is preferable for the licensor to agree to take whatever steps as are reasonably required to effect registration[1]. The licence should give particulars of consideration, whether by way of royalty or lump sum, of duration of the licence and of provisions for termination in the event of breach or insolvency[2].

1   Or at least agree to sign Form TM50, by which the licensee applies to register the licence: see r 35(1) and (2).
2   Much detailed guidance on licensing can be found in N Byrne 'Licensing Technology' (1994).

IMPACT OF COMPETITION LAWS

10.19   Both EC and UK competition laws govern the licensing of trade marks. Where two or more UK-based parties accept restrictions, the Restrictive Trade Practices Act 1976 may apply[1]. Pure trade mark licences with restrictions which relate strictly to the goods or services supplied under the mark are exempted by Sch 3 to the 1976 Act[2]. Agreements with an actual or potential effect on interstate trade are subject to Article 85 of the Treaty of Rome. There is no block exemption specifically for trade mark licences, although trade mark licences which are ancillary to franchising arrangements, patent licences or know-how licences may enjoy the benefit of the block exemptions for those kinds of licence[3]. These laws apply equally to licensing arrangements reached in compromise of litigation[4].

1   See para **4.14**.
2   As substituted by Sch 4, para 7 to the Trade Marks Act 1994.
3   EC Regulations 4087/88, 2449/84 and 556/89 respectively. A 'technology transfer' Regulation is proposed to replace the patent and know-how block exemptions. For comment on the preliminary draft, see R Whaite, 'The draft technology transfer block exemption' [1994] 7 EIPR 259; V Korah, 'The preliminary draft of a new EC group exemption for technology licensing' [1994] 7 EIPR 263.
4   See para **8.13**.

10.20   If trade is significant in the European market, a territorial licence which restricts the right of the licensee to make passive or unsolicited sales outside the territory may fall foul of competition law, particularly under Article 85 of the EEC Treaty; enforcement may be contrary to Article 30.

10.21   Field of use restrictions are usually regarded by the European Commission as disguised market partitioning arrangements[1]. Field of use and customer sharing restrictions should be approached with particular caution[2].

1   See, eg, *Bay-o-nox* [1990] 4 CMLR 429.
2   For a very useful note, see *ITMA Information*, No 5/94, June 1994, p 1.

Chapter 11

ASSIGNMENT OF MARKS

MARKS AND GOODWILL

11.1   As noted in Chapter 3, after the enactment of trade marks legislation in 1875, the action for passing off was used to protect property in goodwill. No property right in a trade mark per se is now recognised at common law[1]. In order validly to transfer a mark at common law, goodwill must be transferred. In fact, assignment of goodwill is deemed to include assignment of any marks used in the course of the business[2] or part of the business in question[3]. An attempt to assign a mark 'in gross' results in deemed abandonment of the mark by the vendor[4]; the purchaser may gain immunity from suit by the vendor, but no right to sue third parties[5].

1   For contrary views on historical causes, see C Wadlow, *Passing Off* (1995), pp 17–18 and K Lupton, 'Trade Marks as Property' (1991) 2 IPJ, pp 29–34 (Aus).
2   *Kerly*, para 13–04, citing *Weston* [1968] RPC 167 at 183.
3   *Kerly*, para 13–05, citing *Sunbeam* (1916) 33 RPC 389. For a critical analysis of the *Sunbeam* case, see S Lane, *The Status of Licensing Common Law Marks* (1991) at pp 18–19 and 22–23.
4   See *Star Industrial v Yap Kwee Kor* [1976] FSR 256 on loss of passing off rights by abandonment.
5   *Pinto v Badman* (1891) 8 RPC 181.

11.2   Registration, however, confers a property right in the mark itself[1]. This was also the case under previous statutes[2], although in *GE TM*[3] Lord Diplock expressed the view that the 1875 Act did not create property rights in marks because they were previously recognised at common law. The 1938 Act had a curious provision requiring the applicant for registration to claim to be 'the proprietor' of the mark[4]. The meaning of this was particularly obscure in the case of an unused mark. Section 17(1) was considered by Aldous J in *Loudoun Manufacturing Co v Courtaulds*[5]: it required merely a bona fide intention to use, and did not require the applicant to show that it had originated the mark[6].

1   Trade Marks Act 1994, ss 2(1) and 22.
2   See Trade Marks Act 1938, s 22(1): registered trade marks assignable and transmissible with or without goodwill; Trade Marks Act 1905, s 22: trade mark assignable and transmissible, but only with goodwill; see also *Pinto v Badman* (1891) 8 RPC 181.
3   [1973] RPC 297.
4   Section 17(1).
5   (1994) *The Times*, 14 February.
6   Cf *Vitamin Ltd's Application* [1956] RPC 1; [1956] 1 WLR 1.

11.3   Not surprisingly, the 1938 Act contained no provision for the assignment of an application to register. This was alleviated somewhat by the effect of s 29(1)(a), which enabled an application to be made with the intention of assigning it to a company not yet incorporated. The 1994 Act goes further in stating that the sections as to assignment and so forth apply, with necessary modifications, to applications to register. Thus, it appears that applications are an evanescent form of property, vanishing if the application fails to mature into a registration, but hardening into personal property if and when it does. This has logic, because once a mark is registered, rights date back to the application date, deemed to be the date of registration[1]. Where evidence of use by the assignor is likely to be important in securing registration, the assignee of an application should seek to acquire goodwill, so that he may rely upon the use.

---

1   Section 40(3).

11.4   Section 22 of the Trade Marks Act 1994 states that a registered mark is personal property or, in Scotland, incorporeal moveable property. From an English viewpoint one may note that s 22 does not state whether or not a mark is to be considered as a chose in action. This is in contrast to a patent, which is stated not to be a chose in action[1]. The editors of the *UK Trade Marks Handbook* express the view that as property a trade mark is sui generis, neither a chose in possession (because it is intangible) nor a chose in action[2]. The trade mark does have one important characteristic of a chose in action: any assignment must be in writing[3], signed by the proprietor[4].

---

1   Patents Act 1977, s 30(1).
2   Para 16.1.3.
3   See Law of Property Act 1925, s 136.
4   Trade Marks Act 1994, s 24(3); an assent must likewise be in writing.

ASSIGNMENT WITH BUSINESS GOODWILL

11.5   Section 24(6) makes clear that the Act does not affect the assignment or transmission of unregistered marks along with the goodwill of a business. As noted above, assignment of goodwill will transfer marks in the absence of contrary intention[1]. Provided that the assignment is in writing, this may be effective to transfer registered marks, although it is always desirable to identify these clearly by reference to registration numbers. Where the assignment is expressed not to include marks, it is unlikely that an assignor retains any common law right to protect them. In the case of registered marks which are retained, the assignor of goodwill will enjoy continued proprietorship unless the marks become vulnerable by reason of deceptiveness or non-use.

---

1   *Kerly* at para 13–04 citing *Roger* (1895) 12 RPC 149. For a discussion of the decision in *Roger* see S Lane, *The Status of Licensing Common Law Marks* (1991), pp 32–33.

11.6   Where part only of the goodwill is transferred, it is a delicate question as to whether the business can be severed in an appropriate way. Thus, in *Sinclair Ltd's TM*[1], an attempt was made to transfer the mark together with that portion of goodwill as attached to the mark. The assignor's interest in the business was otherwise unchanged. The assignment was held to be void. However, assignment without goodwill has since been made possible by statute, as outlined below.

1   (1932) 49 RPC 123.

ASSIGNMENT WITHOUT BUSINESS GOODWILL

11.7   The 1938 Act broke with common law tradition by permitting the assignment of registered marks without goodwill. The interest of the public in avoiding confusion or deception was protected by conferring on the Registrar the power to direct advertisements; unless and until such directions were sought[1] and complied with, the assignment was ineffective. If advertisements were duly made, the assignment was effective to transfer not only the registered marks but any unregistered marks used in the same business as the registered marks and transferred with those registered. This was achieved by virtue of subs 22(3) of the 1938 Act; that subsection was of general application but it is difficult to envisage a transfer of goodwill which was effective to transfer registered but not unregistered marks.

1   Within the six months' time-limit afforded to the assignee: s 22(7).

11.8   The White Paper, 'Reform of Trade Marks Law'[1] observed that the advertisement requirements of s 22(7) were 'of little practical effect as a safeguard to the public' and proposed their removal[2]. This has been done; s 24(1) of the Trade Marks Act 1994 states that a trade mark is transmissible, by assignment, testamentary disposition or operation of law, in connection with the goodwill of a business or independently. The assignment may effect a transfer of the mark for all or only some of the goods or services for which it is registered[3] or for a particular manner or territory of use[4]. There are no requirements for advertising an assignment without goodwill, nor is there any prohibition upon an assignment which would lead to the likelihood of deception or confusion[5]. The lack of restriction on transfer does not ensure, however, that an assignee will always enjoy the fruits of the assignment. There may be defects to title which undermine the transaction, while the assignment may render the mark deceptive and liable to revocation[6].

1   (1990) Cm 1203, para 4.46.
2   For arguments that trade mark provisions designed to protect the consumer should generally be repealed, see MD Pendleton, 'Excising Consumer Protection – the Key to Reforming Trade Mark Law' (1992) 3 AIPJ 110 (Aus).
3   Section 24(2)(a).
4   Section 24(2)(b).
5   Contrast s 22(4) of the Trade Marks Act 1938, which prohibited assignments resulting in a deceptive split of ownership for the same products or descriptions of product.
6   The decision in *JOB* [1993] FSR 118 illustrates the dangers of careless transactions.

11.9 Furthermore, there is no longer any provision for the assignment of unregistered marks along with registered marks when the assignment is without goodwill[1].

---

1 Cf s 22(3) of the 1938 Act which applied to transactions prior to commencement but not thereafter? Sch 3, para 8(1).

FORMALITIES AND PITFALLS

11.10 The essential elements of an assignment of a registered mark may be summarised[1] as:

(a) an identified mark;
(b) registered and transferred for identified goods or services;
(c) as of a specified date;
(d) the number of the registration;
(e) identification of the assignor;
(f) a statement that the assignor conveys the property 'with full title guarantee'[2];
(g) name and address of the assignee;
(h) identification of the territory for which the mark is to be assigned[3];
(i) consideration (unless under seal);
(j) details of any goodwill transferred;
(k) stamp duty, where payable.

---

1 See, in particular, r 34.
2 Formerly 'as beneficial owner', which implied covenants including full power to convey, quiet possession, and freedom from encumbrance under s 76 of the Law of Property Act 1925. That was repealed by the Law of Property (Miscellaneous Provisions) Act 1994 with effect from 3 November 1994.
3 For a case where arguments on territory were canvassed, see *Fyffes v Chiquita* [1993] FSR 83.

11.11 What if the assignor's title is defective? Where the assignor is registered as proprietor, there may be equitable interests in the mark, which are not registrable[1]. The assignee will take subject to any registered assignment, licence, security interest, assent or court order. He will not take subject to any such interest for which an application to register has not been made, unless he has knowledge of it[2].

---

1 Section 26(1).
2 Section 25(3)(a) actually says that an unregistered transaction is ineffective against a person taking a conflicting interest in ignorance of it, which suggests absence of actual knowledge.

11.12 Where the assignor can show good title which has not been registered, it seems that it is sufficient for the Registrar to be satisfied that a valid chain of transactions leads to the assignee. The Registrar also needs to be satisfied that any instrument subject to stamp duty has been duly stamped[1].

11.13   Once a mark has been assigned, the assignee or any other person claiming to be affected by the transaction may apply to register it[1]. Registration is desirable for a number of reasons: it protects the assignee against inconsistent transactions after the application to register[2]; the assignee will be able to prove title in infringement proceedings by putting in evidence a certificate of registration. Where the assignee fails to register within six months, damages and accounts of profits are unavailable until registration is effected[3]. Preferably, the assignor should sign the application to register the transaction; otherwise it must be accompanied by adequate documentary evidence[4].

1   Section 25(1), on Form TM16: r 35(1)(a).
2   Section 25(3), which is curiously worded. It suggests that an unregistered transaction is ineffective as against a person acquiring a conflicting interest. Presumably this is not so until the latter is registered; otherwise unregistered transactions would enjoy reverse priority.
3   Section 25(4) – unless the court is satisfied that it was not practicable to apply to register before.
4   Rule 35(2).

SPECIFIC CASES AND TRANSACTIONS

Transmission by testamentary disposition

11.14   Property rights in the mark will devolve upon the testator's personal representatives. The latter's assent must be made in writing and signed by or on behalf of the personal representative[1]. For the reasons indicated above, the assent should be registered[2].

1   Section 24(3).
2   By filing Form TM24: r 35(1)(e).

Transmission by operation of law

11.15   This is likely to arise in one of three circumstances: intestacy, insolvency or partnership. In the first two cases, the former proprietor is unable to co-operate in the registration of the transaction. In the latter case, an order of the court may form part of the chain of transmission. Registration of the order of a court or other authority competent to effect transfer is applied for on Form TM24[1]. Form TM16 (assignments) is also used for transactions not allotted a separate form.

1   Rule 35(1)(e).

11.16   Intellectual property generally may pass by operation of partnership law[1]. However, the enjoyment of a trade mark by a partnership will normally involve use on goods or services emanating from the partnership. That case is suitable for joint proprietorship, paras **11.17–11.18**.

---

1   *Murray v King* [1986] FSR 116 (copyright Fed Ct of Australia).

Jointly owned trade marks

11.17   The 1938 Act permitted the registration of marks in joint names, but only when the relationship between the proprietors was such that they each used the mark on behalf of them all or the mark indicated a connection with all of them[1]. Annand and Norman[2] point out that this ensured joint tenancy in the marks. This was desirable when the joint owners were actually trading under the mark, but was not necessarily suitable for other forms of exploitation, such as the grant of an exclusive licence to a third party.

---

1   Not necessarily the same connection for each joint owner: *Val Marks* (1923) 40 RPC 103 (manufacturer and distributor).
2   R Annand and H Norman, *Blackstone's Guide to the Trade Marks Act 1994* (1994) Ch 11.

11.18   Section 23 of the 1994 Act refers to the grant of a mark to two or more persons 'jointly', but goes on to say that each is entitled to an equal undivided share. This smacks of a tenancy in common[1], which may be more suitable where marks are held as assets or by way of security, but less suitable where the proprietors use the marks. Subsections 25(3) and (4) limit the powers of the co-proprietors to deal with the mark as they please; each is entitled to use the mark for his own benefit without accounting to the others for its use, but a licence, assignment or charge[2] requires the consent of co-proprietors. This arrangement is similar to that for patents[3].

---

1   See, eg, Annand and Norman, *Blackstone's Guide to the Trade Marks Act 1994* (1994) Ch 11, where an unattractive scenario is outlined.
2   But not transmission by operation of law, at least in the case of insolvency: Hansard, House of Lords, vol 552, no 46, col 745.
3   Patents Act 1977, s 36.

Collective marks[1]

11.19   There is no special regime for the transfer of collective marks. However, the rules governing the use of the mark must specify the persons authorised to use the mark[2]; any change will necessitate amendment of the regulations and acceptance of the amended regulations by the Registrar[3].

---

1   See, further, Ch 12.
2   Sch 1, para 5(2).
3   Sch 1, para 10.

Certification marks[1]

11.20 The proprietor must not trade in the goods or services of the kind certified[2]. It is not surprising, therefore, that the Registrar's consent is required for any assignment or other transmission[3].

1 See, further, Ch 12.
2 Sch 2, para 4.
3 Sch 2, para 12.

Assignment of the right of priority

11.21 The right of priority is the right to claim the priority date of a first filing within the preceding six months in another Paris Convention country[1]. This may be assigned, with or without the application on which it is based[2]. Thus, applicant A in France may assign to B the right to use the French filing date as priority date for a UK application.

1 See, generally, paras **5.3** and **14.8**.
2 Section 33(6).

Security interests over trade marks

11.22 A trade mark may be subject to a fixed or floating charge[1] or may be assigned by way of security[2]. In the latter case, it will usually be appropriate for the assignee to grant a licence back. In any event, all registrable elements of the transaction should be registered, for the reasons outlined above[3].

1 Section 24(5).
2 Section 24(4).
3 See para **11.13**.

TRANSITIONAL PROVISIONS

11.23 Transitional provisions are spelt out in Sch 3, para 8 to the 1994 Act. The new law applies to transactions effected after commencement, and to applications made after commencement to register prior transactions. Applications made prior to commencement but not yet determined by the Registrar are also dealt with under the new law.

Chapter 12

SPECIAL CATEGORY MARKS

INTRODUCTION

12.1 Although the proprietor of a mark has exclusive control over the use of a mark, there are a number of ways in which more than one person can legitimately use a mark. The proprietor may grant licences[1], or several persons may be registered as co-proprietors of a registered mark[2]. This chapter outlines two more systems for multiple use, the certification mark and the collective mark. A collective mark signifies that the goods or services are connected with a member of the association which owns the mark. The latter may or may not trade in the goods or services in question. Thus, the collective mark indicates origin, although the association may include quality standards as a condition of membership[3]. Registration of collective marks was introduced by the 1994 Act. Collective purchasing organisations[4] and other groups of small enterprises may find them particularly useful.

---

1 As outlined in Ch 10.
2 See paras **11.17** and **11.18**.
3 Subject to the rules of competition law: see White Paper, para 5.02.
4 For brief details of such an organisation, see *Spar (UK) Ltd v Audits of Great Britain Ltd* [1986] 5 EIPR D-74.

12.2 A certification mark indicates that the services or goods are certified as to some quality by the association which owns the mark. In this case, the proprietor must not trade; it would be inappropriate for one trader to certify the products of a competitor. Certification marks for goods have been registrable in the UK since 1905; the 1994 Act has extended them to services.

Both collective and certification (or 'guarantee') marks are permitted by Article 14 of the Directive. The Community Trade Mark Regulation[1] provides for the registration of Community collective marks, but not certification marks. However, Dawson[2] has observed that the distinction between collective and certification marks is not clear. Use of a collective mark may involve formal certification of goods or services or may carry informal connotations of quality in just the same way as an ordinary trade mark[3]. Indeed, it appears that the Trade Marks Act 1905, as liberally construed, may have permitted registration of what we now call collective marks. In *Re an Application by Union Inter-Syndicale des Marques Collectives*[4], reference was made to the exercise of

'a sufficient supervision and control over the affixing of marks upon goods by … the careful selection and control of members of the association or other persons who are permitted to affix the mark.'

---

1 Articles 64–72; see, generally, paras **13.5–13.17**.
2 N Dawson, *Certification Trade Marks: Law and Practice*, p 84, citing *Creusois v Seguy* [1982] 10 EIPR D-213 (France).
3 See Ch 1.

4   '*UNIS*' [1922] 2 Ch 653; (1922) 39 RPC 97, discussed by Dawson, *Certification Trade Marks: Law and Practice* (1988) at pp 17–20.

12.3   Conversely, a certification mark may indicate geographical origin, as may a collective mark[1]. Appellations of origin or geographical indications of origin are protected by distinct regimes in other countries and for some product sectors there are EC Regulations[2]. In *Taittinger v Allbev*[3] the Court of Appeal held that EC Regulation 823/87[4] was contravened by the sale of 'Elderflower Champagne' and would be enforced by injunction.

1   Sch 1, para 3(1); Sch 2, para 3(1).
2   See M Kolia [1992] 9 EIPR 333; D Ryan 'The protection of geographical indications in Australia under the EC/Australia wine agreement' [1994] 12 EIPR 521.
3   [1993] FSR 641 at pp 673, 674, 679.
4   Amended by reg 2043/89.

12.4   This chapter outlines the registration and infringement of collective and certification marks. Where these are not registered, or protected by other regulations, the users may build up a collective goodwill in the mark such as to found an action in passing off to restrain improper use. This was the case in *Taittinger*[1], in *Advocaat*[2] discussed in Chapter 3. Passing off may also be actionable at the suit of authorised users of a certification mark[3].

1   Para **12.3**, n 3.
2   *Erven Warninck v Townend* [1980] RPC 31.
3   N Dawson, *Certification Trade Marks: Law and Practice* (1988) at pp 77–78, discussing *Argyllshire Weavers v A Macauley (Tweeds) Ltd* [1964] RPC 477.

12.5   Collective marks are referred to in Art 7*bis* of the Paris Convention for the Protection of Industrial Property[1], which states:

'The Countries of the Union undertake to accept for filing and to protect collective marks belonging to associations the existence of which is not contrary to the law of the country of origin, even if such associations do not possess an industrial or commercial establishment.'

1   Of 1883, with revisions in 1900, 1911, 1925, 1934, 1958 and 1967.

12.6   The third 'special' category of mark, the 'well-known' mark, is also a creature of the Paris Convention. By Art 6*bis*, Paris Union members undertake to protect well-known marks against use and registration by another person. Although the Registry could exercise its discretion against registration under the 1938 Act, there was specific provision only for the 'defensive registration' of invented word marks. Where a foreign trade mark owner with reputation but no (or minimal) trade in this country was concerned, the action in passing off did not assist[1]. The 1994 Act explicitly discharges the UK's obligation to protect the well-known marks of other countries[2].

1   See the 'Budweiser' case: *Anheuser-Busch v Budjovicky Budvar* [1984] FSR 413 and other 'foreign plaintiff' cases discussed in Ch 3.
2   See Hansard, House of Lords, vol 550, no 10, 6 December 1994, col 753.

CERTIFICATION MARKS

12.7   The certification trade mark system has been used to register marks such as the woolmark, 'Lurpak' and other 'Lur' marks for Danish butter and dairy products, 'Stilton' for blue cheese made in the Melton Mowbray region of England[1] and the British Standards Institute's kite marks for all manner of goods. The marks are administered by the proprietor associations. Sometimes the mark itself suggests the qualities of the product which are certified, but usually these are found in the regulations governing use of the mark[2], in the regulations or statutory order establishing the proprietor, or in the relevant British or European standard. In the past, the Registry has often required that the phrase 'certification mark' be used upon the goods to indicate the kind of mark involved[3]. Similar requirements are set out in the 1994 Act[4]; exceptionally, amendment of the mark during the application procedure may be made to meet these[5].

1   Although the cheese had not actually been manufactured in Stilton: [1967] RPC 173.
2   Hansard, House of Lords, vol 552, no 46, 24 February 1994, col 730.
3   See Trade Marks Act 1938, Sch 1, para 1(3).
4   Sch 2, para 5.
5   Cf s 39(2); para **5.20**.

12.8   The qualities which are certified are objectively verifiable, rather than subjective standards like 'good design'[1]. An organisation seeking to promote subjective qualities of products could resort to a prize or award system[2] or to business format franchising. Section 50 of the Trade Marks Act 1994 sets out the qualities which a certification mark may indicate; most certification marks signify more than one of these[3]; the examples given in Table 3 below are by way of illustration only.

1   N Dawson, *Certification Trade Marks: Law and Practice* (1988), p 103, citing the Molony Committee on Consumer Protection (1962) Cmnd 1781, para 373.
2   For the tribulations of 'Oscar', see [1979] RPC 173.
3   See N Dawson, *Certification Trade Marks: Law and Practice* (1988), pp 50–54.

12.9   Unless otherwise specified, the general criteria of the 1994 Act apply to certification marks[1]. Special conditions which appertain are set out in Sch 2. The mark must be capable of graphical representation and of distinguishing the certified

Table 3:   Qualities and Certification Marks

Quality certified (s 50)	*Example mark*
Origin	'Lurpak'
Material	Woolmark
Mode of manufacture of goods	'Harris Tweed' orb mark
Mode of performance of services	British Standard mark for firms
Quality (specific qualities)	'Commanderia' wines
Accuracy	National Physical Laboratory (NPL)
Other characteristics	British Standard safety mark

goods and services from those not certified[2]. Absolute and relative grounds for refusal appear to follow those for trade marks in general, save that geographical indications are expressly permitted, with a saving for bona fide use by others[3]. Concern was expressed in Parliament that the other exclusions of s 3(1)(c)[4] would prevent the registration of certification marks. An assurance was given that this would not be the case[5].

---

1   Section 1(2).
2   Sch 2, para 2.
3   Sch 2, para 3; see para **12.3**.
4   Kind, quality, quantity, intended purpose, value, or time of production of goods or of rendering of services or other characteristics.
5   Hansard, House of Lords, vol 552, no 46, 24 February 1994, col 730.

12.10   The applicant/proprietor must not carry on a business involving the supply of goods or services of the kind certified.[1] The applicant applies in the normal way, giving name and address, details of the goods and services[2] and a representation of the mark applied for. Within nine months of filing for registration of a certification mark, the applicant must file a copy of the regulations governing use of the mark[3]. These must show who is entitled to use it. Some certification marks are used only by members of the association owning the mark[4], some are merely licensed to third parties and some may be used by members or non-members. The regulations should spell out the characteristics to be certified, and how the certifying body is to test those characteristics and supervise the use of the mark[5]. The applicant will need to satisfy the Registry that it is competent[6] and prepared to do so, fairly, with the support of the industry in question. In the past, an applicant has usually been required to show that it is representative of 80 per cent of the trade in question. With such high representation it is not surprising that the Department of Trade and Industry have been alert to the anti-competitive potential of certification marks.

---

1   Sch 2, para 4.
2   There does not appear to be anything in theory to prevent a multi-class application. In practice,

however, the regulations governing the use of the mark are likely to differ significantly from product to product.

3   Sch 2, para 6(1); Trade Marks Rules 1994, r 22; the relevant form is Form TM35. Failure to file regulations results in deemed withdrawal of the application: Sch 2, para 7(2).
4   The 'Board of Trade', latterly the Consumer Affairs Division of the Department of Trade and Industry (White Paper 'Reform of Trade Mark Law' 1990 Cm 1203, para 5.01), has shown itself strict in ensuring that certification is open to all qualified persons: N Dawson *Certification Trade Marks: Law and Practice* (1988), p 32. Rules for membership need to be clear on this point.
5   Sch 2, para 6(2).
6   Sch 2, para 7(1)(b).

12.11   The regulations must stipulate the fees (if any) to be paid in connection with the operation of the mark. There is no statutory requirement for the operation to be non profit-making, although this has often been required in practice[1]. A mechanism for the resolution of disputes must be established[2]. Finally, the regulations must comply with public policy and accepted principles of morality[3].

1   N Dawson, para **12.10**, n 4, p 33; see Trade Marks Registry Work Manual, Ch 23.
2   Sch 2, para 6(2).
3   Sch 2, para 7(1)(a)(ii).

12.12   Once a certification mark has been accepted, it is published in the normal way, together with the regulations, and open for opposition[1]. If it survives the opposition process, it is registered in the normal register. The regulations are open to public inspection[2].

1   The *UNIS* case, para **12.2**, n 4, involved opposition. For procedure, see paras **5.40–5.41**. Opposition or observations may also be based on the content of the regulations: Sch 2, para 9.
2   Sch 2, para 10. Regulations filed prior to commencement will be treated as if filed under Sch 2, para 6: Sch 3, para 19(1).

12.13   The mark may be assigned or transmitted only with the consent of the Registrar[1]. Amendment of the regulations also requires approval[2].

1   Although transmission by operation of law would appear to be automatic: see Hansard, House of Lords, vol 552, no 46, 24 February 1994, col 745 on the related issue of jointly owned marks in the case of insolvency.
2   Sch 2, para 11. The application to amend is filed on Form TM36. Requests for amendment filed before commencement of the 1994 Act will be dealt with under the old law: Sch 3, para 19(2).

12.14   Infringement of a certification mark is governed by the general provisions. As noted above, the Act is silent as to whether only trade mark use infringes[1]. It was stated in Parliament that was 'implicit'[2]. It is submitted that use which suggests any kind of trade mark function – as indicating origin, quality or certification – should be capable of 'implicitly' infringing a certification mark.

1   See paras **7.16** and **7.17**.
2   Hansard, House of Lords, vol 552, no 46, 24 February 1994, col 733, referring to the recital of the Directive.

12.15   Authorised users are equated for most purposes to licensees under 'ordinary' trade marks[1]. However, an authorised user has no right of action for infringement. Such right was proposed in an early version of the Trade Marks Bill, but removed by amendment[2]. The registered proprietor only can sue[3]. In proceedings brought by the proprietor the court may take into account any loss or likely loss to authorised users, and can order the plaintiffs to hold the proceeds of pecuniary remedies on behalf of authorised users[4].

1   Sch 2, para 13 specifically applies ss 10(5), 19(2) and 89. The last appears to enable an authorised user to request Customs stoppage of infringing goods, which is odd, since the user has no right to sue for infringement.
2   Hansard, House of Lords, vol 553, no 55, 14 March 1994, col 88–89, reversing 24 February 1994, col 748.
3   If the proprietor will not sue, the user may have a remedy in passing off, see para **12.4**, n 3.
4   Sch 2, para 14.

12.16   Revocation of a certification mark may be sought on all the grounds specified in s 46[1] and additionally on the following grounds[2]:

(a)   the proprietor is trading in the goods or services concerned;
(b)   the proprietor has used the certification mark in such a way that the public is liable to be misled as to its nature[3];
(c)   the regulations have not been observed or enforced[4];
(d)   an inappropriate amendment of the regulations has been made;
(e)   the proprietor is no longer competent to certify.

1   See para **9.12ff**.
2   Sch 2, para 15.
3   Ie not a certification mark.
4   For an application to revoke a certification mark on this basis, see 'Sea Island Cotton' Certification Trade Marks [1989] RPC 87; N Dawson, 'The West Indian Sea Island Cotton Association's certification trade mark: application to expunge' [1989] EIPR 375.

12.17   A declaration of invalidity may be sought on the grounds set forth in s 47[1] and also on the grounds that:

(a)   the proprietor traded in the products;
(b)   the public is liable to be misled as to the nature of the mark;
(c)   the regulations do not conform to the requirements.

1   See paras **9.6–9.11**.

12.18   An interesting question raised by Dawson[1] is whether a civil action lies for breach of statutory duty where the Trade Descriptions Act 1968 has been contravened by misuse of a certification mark. The prevailing view in England[2] appears to be that an injured trader cannot sue under the Act to restrain false trade descriptions[3]. The cases cited pre-date the decision in *Rickless v United Artists*[4], in which it was held that a performer's personal representatives could sue for breach of the Performers' Protection Acts (criminal statutes). However, if the ethos of the Trade Descriptions Act 1968 is protection of the consumer[5], *Rickless* will not avail the trader.

1   N Dawson, *Certification Trade Marks: Law and Practice* (1988), pp 63–64.
2   Contrast the situation in Ireland, Dawson, p 64.
3   Dawson, citing *Kat v Diment* [1951] 1 KB 34; *Bollinger v Costa Brava* [1959] 3 All ER 800; *Bulmer and Showerings v Bollinger* [1978] RPC 79; *Erven Warninck v Townend* [1979] 2 All ER 927; [1980] RPC 31.
4   [1988] QB 40; [1987] FSR 362.
5   See Dawson, p 63 at n 6.

COLLECTIVE MARKS

12.19   Collective marks are defined, in s 49, as marks distinguishing the goods or services of members of the association which is the proprietor from those of other undertakings. The first question this raises is whether collective marks may be registered in the name of an association of non-traders. It will be recalled that Art 7*bis* of the Paris Convention requires them to be protected even if the association does not possess an industrial or commercial establishment[1]. Gilson[2] says of the collective mark in the USA:

'It is also widely used by fraternal organisations, service clubs, automobile clubs and the like to indicate membership, where the members do not engage in any kind of commercial activity under the mark.'

It is submitted that a generous construction of s 49 is called for; this would be consistent with the wide interpretation of 'undertaking' in EC law[3].

1   See para **12.5**.
2   J Gilson, *Trade Mark Protection and Practice*, para 1.02[2] (US).
3   See, eg, D Raybould and A Firth, 'Law of Monopolies' (1991), pp 211–212.

12.20   An association seeking to register a collective mark is not prohibited from trading, however. As with certification marks, geographical indications are permitted, subject to bona fide use by others[1]. It is submitted that the other prohibitions in s 3 should be applied to collective marks in the same way as to ordinary trade marks [2]. As mentioned previously, the mark should not mislead as to its nature and can be amended during prosecution to ensure this[3].

1   Sch 1, para 3.
2   Contrast certification marks, para **12.9**.
3   Sch 1, para 5(1), see para **12.7**.

12.21   The mode of application for registration is similar to that for certification marks. Regulations governing use of the mark must be filed[1] specifying the persons authorised to use the mark and the conditions of membership of the association. This is rather oddly worded, since the collective mark is designed for use by members of the association. Perhaps different categories of membership are envisaged for different categories of user. If that is so, it may be difficult to ensure that the public is properly educated or informed as to the nature of the mark. Schedule 1, para 5(2) refers to 'any sanctions against misuse'. It is to be hoped that the Registry will insist, in practice, upon sanctions for misuse[2].

1   Sch 1, para 5(2); Trades Marks Rules 1994, r 22, Form TM35.
2   Although in the context of conflicting marks, Parliament observed that the Registrar was no longer to have a consumer protection role: Hansard, House of Lords, vol 550, no 10, 6 December 1993, col 752.

12.22   The regulations must be approved by the Registrar, who shall allow the applicant the opportunity to make representations or amendments[1]. Assuming that everything is in order, the collective mark and regulations are published and opponents may formally oppose and file observations as before[2]. Unless refused as a result of opposition or observations, the mark will proceed to registration and the regulations will be open to inspection[3]. Fees for use are not specifically mentioned. The regulations should, presumably, provide a fee structure for membership of the association. Any amendment to the regulations is subject to acceptance by the Registrar[4].

1   Sch 1, para 7.
2   See above at paras **12.12** and **5.40**.
3   Sch 1, para 9.
4   Sch 1, para 10, who has a discretion to publish the changes for opposition.

12.23   Where the extent of change is unclear, it is likely that the Registrar will follow previous relevant practice until otherwise directed by the courts. If the practice for collective marks follows the general pattern established for certification marks, their regulations are likely to ensure that competition laws are not breached. The amendment to the Restrictive Trade Practices Act 1976 made by Sch 4, para 7(2) of the 1994 Act appears to assume this, by equating collective with certification marks. If, however, a more *laissez faire* approach by the Registry develops, in keeping with the de-regulatory ethos of the 1994 Act, proprietors and users of collective marks need to pay especial attention to compliance with competition law[1].

1   On which, see Chs 4 and 13.

12.24 Infringement of a collective mark appears to follow that for trade marks in general[1]. Unlike certification marks, but like ordinary trade marks, collective marks confer on their authorised users the right to sue for infringement if the proprietor refuses, or fails to do so within two months of a request[3]. The proprietor must be joined[4]. In infringement proceedings brought by the proprietor, the court may direct that proceeds be held on behalf of authorised users[5].

1   See Sch 1, para 11, and Chs 7 and 8 above.
2   See para **12.15**.
3   Sch 1, para 12.
4   As a plaintiff or nominal defendant: Sch 1, paras 12(4) and (5). Interlocutory relief may be sought before the proprietor is joined.
5   Sch 1, para 12(6).

WELL-KNOWN MARKS

12.25   Art 6*bis* of the Paris Convention provides:

'(1) The countries of the Union undertake, ex officio if their legislation so permits, or at the request of an interested party, to refuse or to cancel the registration, and to prohibit the use, of a trade mark which constitutes a reproduction, an imitation, or a translation, liable to create confusion, of a mark considered by the competent authority of the country of registration or use to be well known in that country as being already the mark of a person entitled to the benefits of this Convention[1] and used for identical or similar goods. These provisions shall also apply when the essential part of the mark constitutes a reproduction of any such well-known mark or an imitation liable to create confusion therewith.
(2) A period of at least five years from the date of registration shall be allowed for requesting the cancellation of such a mark. The countries of the Union may provide for a period within which the prohibition of use must be requested.
(3) No time limit shall be fixed for requesting the cancellation of the prohibition of the use of marks registered or used in bad faith.'

1   Ie nationals of Union countries or those who are domiciled or have real and effective industrial or commercial establishments in the territories of one of the Paris Union Countries: Arts 2 and 3.

12.26   The UK, as a signatory to the Paris Convention, is obliged to provide such protection to nationals of, and those domiciled or established in, other Convention countries[1]. As noted above, prior to enactment of the Trade Marks Act 1994, such protection was afforded informally, by exercise of the Registrar's discretion[2] and by virtue of the action in passing off.

1   Art 2(1).
2   Eg, in calling for evidence of use or intention to use, advertising a mark before acceptance under the proviso to s 18(1) of the Trade Marks Act 1938, or refusing to register on judicial grounds: *Rawhide TM* [1962] RPC 133.

12.27 The 1994 Act defines a well-known mark in s 56 as the mark which is well-known in the UK as being the mark of a person national, domiciled or established in a Convention country other than the UK[1], whether or not that person carries on business, or has goodwill, in the UK. That person may sue for an injunction to restrain use of the mark[2] on identical or similar goods or services where the use is likely to cause confusion. The plaintiff does not have to show lack of consent, although it is submitted that a defence of estoppel would lie where consent has been given[3]. There is explicit application of the defence of five years' acquiescence in s 48; to make out that defence, however, the defendant has to have registered the mark in question.

1 Section 55(1)(b).
2 Or a similar mark: s 56(2).
3 For the equitable defences of estoppel, acquiescence and laches, see *Habib Bank Ltd v Habib Bank AG* [1981] 1 WLR 1265; [1982] RPC 1.

12.28 Section 56 thus goes beyond Art 6*bis* in protecting well-known marks for goods and for services. Thus, if 'Coca-cola' is a well-known mark for soft drinks, its use can be enjoined on restaurant services. In this the UK already complies with Article 16.2 of the GATT Agreement on Trade-Related Aspects of Intellectual Property Rights (TRIPS)[1]. Article 16.3 requires application of Art 6*bis* to goods or services which are not similar to those for which the mark is registered[2], provided use would indicate a connection and be deleterious to the owner of the registered mark; this is considered further below.

1 Reproduced as a supplement to [1994] 11 EIPR.
2 Presumably in the country where protection is sought.

12.29 The registration of a well-known mark by someone else is prevented by including the well-known mark within the definition of 'earlier trade mark' in s 6[1]. In effect, this will give the 'proprietor' of the well-known mark a ground for opposition[2]. The provisions of s 5(3) are more generous than those of Art 6*bis* or of TRIPS.

1 See para **5.35**.
2 The Registry will not attempt to examine marks for conflict against well-known marks which are not registered in the UK for the same or similar products: see Work Manual, Ch 6, pp 31 and 32.

12.30 A limited class of well-known marks was afforded some protection under s 27 of the Trade Marks Act 1938. Where an invented word mark had become so well known in respect of the words for which it was registered and used that its use on other goods was likely to be taken as indicating a connection in the course of trade with the proprietor, he could register for those other goods, notwithstanding that there was no use made or proposed. Such defensive registration served to block subsequent attempts to register and could be used to restrain infringements in the usual manner.

Defensive registration was sparingly granted, however[1], and the system was therefore little used in the UK and other countries with related legislation[2]. It is gradually being abandoned elsewhere. The system did, however, have the merit of comparative certainty for owners of defensive marks and for their competitors. Wheeldon[3] has pointed out that defensive trade mark legislation was interpreted more generously in South Africa, and regrets that it was not seriously considered to prevent dilution under the Community Trade Mark Regulation. No further defensive marks will be registered under the 1994 Act. Existing defensive registrations will be immune from revocation on the ground of non-use for a period of five years from commencement[4].

1 See, eg, *Ferodo Ltd's Application* (1945) 62 RPC 111.
2 M Tierney, *Irish Trade Marks Law and Practice* (1987) at p 106 reported no defensive marks on the Irish Register.
3 R Wheeldon, 'The Community Trademark and the concept of dilution: was the case for defensive trademarks adequately considered?' *Trademark World*, November 1994, p 12.
4 Sch 3, proviso to para 17(2).

12.31   The most difficult question lies with the definition of 'well known'. It is not defined in the Trade Marks Act 1994. Clearly, the world's 'top 20' marks are likely to be regarded as well known[1]. But beyond that, it is a matter for national decision-making[2]; markets, awareness, language and legal attitudes are so diverse that international harmonisation would seem impossible. In countries like Japan, the trade mark administration declares marks to be well known. A glance at the listings in any issue of the journal *AIPPI Japan* will suggest that awareness of marks is high and/or the threshold for 'well-known' status is low. In countries like Germany, the Registrar and courts use consumer awareness surveys to determine degrees of reputation[3].

1 See R Abnett 'AIPPI: Famous trademarks require a new legal weapon' *Trademark World*, December 1990/January 1991, p 23.
2 See country reports to question 100 (1990) AIPPI Annual Report (Barcelona, 1990).
3 See, eg, A Kur 'Well-known marks, highly renowned marks and marks having a (high) reputation – what's it all about? (1992) 23 IIC 218 and citations therein; M Lehmann, 'Unfair use of and damage to the reputation of well-known marks, names and indications of source in Germany. Some aspects of law and economics' (1986) 17 IIC 746.

Chapter 13

TRADE MARKS IN EUROPE

INTRODUCTION

13.1   Trade marks, like other areas of intellectual property law[1], have been influenced profoundly by European Community law in recent years. The programme of intellectual property measures designed to hasten the single market in the wake of the Single European Act[2] was based on the premise that disparities in national laws impeded the free movement of goods and services[3]. Free movement is one of the cornerstones of the EEC Treaty[4] and has been held to affect the exercise of trade mark rights, along with the competition laws prohibiting restrictive practices (Art 85 of the Treaty) and abuse of dominant position (Art 86). However, the ideal of a single, unitary, Community trade mark system[5] has been under consideration for many years. Preliminary proposals were prepared in 1964[6] and published in 1973[7]. In 1980 proposals for a Community Trade Mark Regulation and harmonisation Directive were published[8] and subsequently considered by the Economic and Social Committee and the European Parliament[9]. After further deliberation the proposals came to fruition as the Community Trade Mark Regulation[10] and the First Council Directive[11].

---

1   For other areas, see, eg, A Booy and A Horton, *EC Intellectual Property Materials* (1994). Useful tables showing the progress of EC legislation are published monthly in EIPR.
2   On which see, eg, J Steiner, *Textbook on EC Law* (1992) 3rd edn.
3   See First Recital to the Trade Marks Harmonisation Directive, 89/104/EEC.
4   And is governed by Arts 30–36 for goods and Art 59 for services.
5   And harmonised national laws.
6   By a Trade Mark Working Group convened in 1961.
7   By HMSO in unofficial translation. See Memorandum on the creation of an EEC Trade Mark 1976, *Bulletin of the European Communities*, Supplement 8/76, paras 3–6.
8   In the Bulletin of the European Communities, Supplement 5/1980.
9   OJ [1980] C 310/22 and OJ [1983] C 307/46. See also revised proposal at OJ [1984] C 230/1 and opinion at OJ [1991] C 280/153.
10   Council Regulation No 40/94, OJ [1994] L11/1, based on Art 235 of the EEC Treaty.
11   Promulgated somewhat sooner on 21 December 1988.

IMPLEMENTATION OF THE DIRECTIVE AND ENFORCEMENT OF TRADE MARK RIGHTS IN OTHER EUROPEAN UNION MEMBER STATES

13.2   The Directive governs the definition and registrability of marks, the grounds for refusal of registration, for revocation and invalidity. It touches upon licensing and sets out exhaustive criteria for infringement. It does not purport to affect registry or court procedures, or national rules as to ownership. It leaves Member States free to recognise rights acquired by use, save where they interact with registered marks, and to protect marks by national rules as to unfair competition, civil liability and consumer protection.

13.3 The date for implementation[1] of the Directive is well past. Where national laws are touched by the Directive, one may expect a convergence, assisted in areas of difficulty by decisions of the European Court of Justice[2]. The court can become seised of trade mark issues by way of reference under Article 177[3] from national courts and in review of decisions of the Community Trade Mark Regulation. Most Member States have now implemented the Directive[4]. Several have also taken steps to amend their civil procedure as it relates to trade mark infringement. Thus, new investigative measures to obtain information prior to action and interlocutory injunctions have been introduced in Spain[5]. France has opened up infringement actions to exclusive licensees, and clarified the law relating to temporary injunctions in trade mark cases[6]. Oppositions are being introduced in France and postponed until after registration in Germany. Italy's reform of civil procedure is likely to be advantageous at the preliminary stages of trade mark infringement proceedings[8].

1   31 December 1992.
2   For this reason, Parliament was inclined to follow the wording of the Directive: House of Lords Public Bill Committee, 13 January 1994, col 11.
3   Of the Treaty of Rome. In principle the court rules on the interpretation of the Treaty and legislation thereunder, whilst national courts apply the ruling to the facts. For a comment on recent blurring of this distinction, see C Worth and K Warburton, 'ECJ v National Courts: the Division of powers after Clinique' [1994] 6 EIPR 247.
4   For problems occasioned by delay in Ireland, see S Smyth, 'Service Mark Registrations in Ireland: A Myth or a Reality' [1994] 4 EIPR 167.
5   N Jenkins, 'Pre-action Proof of Facts and Preliminary Measures under the New Spanish Industrial and Intellectual Property Acts' [1993] 9 EIPR 347. Spain amended its trade mark law in 1988.
6   C Le Stanc, 'The enforcement of trade mark rights in France' [1994] 8 EIPR 352. France's new trade mark law came into effect in 1992.
7   M Fammler, 'The new German Act on marks: EC harmonisation and reform' [1995] 1 EIPR 22.
8   M Franzosi and G de Sanctis, 'Intellectual and industrial property litigation in Italy: a change for the better?' [1994] 9 EIPR 392.

13.4 Although trade mark registration procedures are not affected by the Directive, a parallel development may ultimately lead to a worldwide harmonisation. A diplomatic conference of the World Intellectual Property Organisation has concluded a Trademark Law Treaty to this end[1].

1   WIPO Trademark Law Treaty, adopted at Geneva on 27 October, 1994 and Regulations thereunder. See [1995] 34(1) Industrial Property and Copyright, p 62 and Laws and Treaties section.

THE COMMUNITY TRADE MARK

13.5 EC Council Regulation No 40/94 of 20 December 1993 establishes a unitary system for registration of marks throughout the European Community. It creates a

Community trade marks office, the 'Office for Harmonisation in the Internal Market (Trade Marks and Designs)'[1] (hereafter 'the Office') which is located in Alicante, Spain. It is an EC body with legal personality[2], and subject to legal control by the EC Commission[3] where not under the general jurisdiction of the European Court of Justice[4]. The Office has a President, two Vice-Presidents and an administrative board. Its work is to be carried out[5] by examiners, opposition divisions[6], an administration of trade marks and a legal division, cancellation divisions and boards of appeal. Implementing regulations are being drafted at the time of writing, and applications may be accepted from early 1996 in readiness for an opening date later in 1996[7]. The Office has five official languages: English, French, German, Italian and Spanish[8]. There is considerable leeway as to the language of proceedings and publications and entries in the register are to be made in all official languages of the Community[9]. The Office will publish a *Bulletin* and an *Official Journal*[10].

---

1 Art 2. On the proposed Community Design, see A Horton, 'European Design Law and the Spare Parts Dilemma: the Proposed Regulation and Directive' [1994] 2 EIPR 51.
2 Art 111.
3 Art 118.
4 The power of the court to review decisions of the Boards of Appeal is spelt out in Art 63.
5 Arts 125–132.
6 Since about 80 per cent of applications are expected to be opposed and each opposition division consists of three members, one legally qualified, there will be a considerable deployment of personnel in opposition.
7 M Todd, of the Intellectual Property Policy Directorate, speaking at Queen Mary and Westfield College on 15 December 1994.
8 Art 115.2.
9 Art 116. Although the text in the language of filing is taken as authentic in cases of doubt.
10 Art 85.

13.6 The Community trade mark is designed to be an indivisible entity, having equal effect throughout the Community. It can be registered, transferred, surrendered or revoked only for the whole Community[1]. The definition of a trade mark, the criteria for registration, duration, renewals, restoration, restrictions on amendment of applications and marks, the rules of comparison for infringement, defences to infringement, arrangements for surrender and the grounds of revocation or invalidity closely parallel those of the Directive and hence of the 1994 Act. Some differences are:

(a) There are specific provisions as to who can apply: natural or legal persons[2] who are nationals of Member States or of a Paris Convention country or who have a real and effective establishment in a Convention country, together with nationals of other states which 'according to published findings' afford national treatment to nationals of all Member States and recognise the Community trade mark as equivalent to registration in a country of origin[3].
(b) Absolute grounds will block registration even if they pertain only in part of the Community[4].
(c) Bad faith is not mentioned in the absolute grounds for refusal but appears as an absolute ground of invalidity in Article 51.

(d) Earlier trade marks or applications which can block a later Community application comprise[5] Community trade marks, marks registered in Member States or the Benelux and international registrations having effect in a Member State, and well-known marks within the meaning of Art 6*bis* of the Paris Convention[6].

(e) The proprietor of rights acquired by use can only oppose a Community trade mark if his mark is 'of more than mere local significance'[7].

(f) An opponent must have standing and may oppose only on relative grounds[8], but any person may make observations objecting to registration on absolute grounds[9].

(g) There is a specific provision to restrain the use of Community marks in dictionaries without indicating their trade mark status[10].

(h) A proprietor may oppose use of a mark registered in the name of his agent or representative[11].

(i) Use in part of the Community will be sufficient to maintain the mark on the register[12].

(j) Invalidity can be based on a right of personal portrayal[13].

(k) As mentioned in Chapter 12, there is provision for Community collective marks[14], but not certification marks[15].

(l) A Community trade mark or application may be converted into one or more national trade mark applications[16]. This is convenient where an application is refused by virtue of earlier national or Benelux registrations.

---

1 Art 1(2). A problem may arise when new members join the Community. However, Sweden, Finland and Austria are likely to join before the system begins to operate. It is unlikely that Norway, Iceland, Switzerland or former Eastern bloc countries will join for some time; by then a solution may have been devised.

2 On which see Art 3.

3 Art 5(1). Art 5 also contains provisions as to stateless persons and as to reciprocity arrangements in non-EC, non-Paris Convention countries.

4 Art 7(2).

5 Art 8(2).

6 Paras **12.25–12.31**.

7 Art 8(4).

8 Art 42 spells out the classes of prior right owner able to oppose.

9 Art 41.

10 Art 10.

11 Art 11.

12 Art 15 refers merely to 'genuine use in the Community', but the statement for inclusion in the minutes of adoption of the Regulation reads:

    'The Council and the Commission consider that use which is genuine within the meaning of Art 15 in one country constitutes genuine use in the Community.'

13 Art 52.2(b). The possibility of preventing use by a right to a name, copyright or industrial property right are also listed in Art 52 as grounds of invalidity, but do not appear under relative grounds for refusal. They do not appear to be available for opposition, but only cancellation, which is to be regretted.

14 Arts 64–72.

15 'Community guarantee-marks' were included in earlier drafts, see, eg, Art 86 of the proposal published at *Bulletin of the European Communities*, Supplement 5/1980, p 18. It is clear from a statement prepared for inclusion in the minutes of adoption of the Regulation that collective marks are not intended to include certification marks:

'the Council and Commission consider that a collective mark which is available for use only by members of an association which owns the mark is liable to mislead within the meaning of Art 66(2) if it gives the impression that it is available for use by anyone who is able to meet certain objective standards'.

16   Arts 108–110.

Application procedure

13.7   Application for a Community trade mark may be made direct to the Office or through a national registry, which will forward it to the Office[1]. The applicant need not be represented unless it lacks domicile or establishment in the Community[2]. The application must request registration of the mark in the name of an identified applicant for listed goods or services and bear a representation of the trade mark[3]. The application may be made in any official Community language, but must also specify a second language from the five Office languages as a possible language for opposition, revocation and invalidity[4]. The Office may also use this language for written communications to the applicant. Fees should be paid within one month of filing[5] to establish the filing date.

1   Art 25; the application should reach the Office within two weeks and is deemed to have been withdrawn if it reaches the Office more than one month after filing. This seems harsh on applicants with tardy national offices and will doubtless encourage direct filing.
2   Art 88; natural or legal persons may be represented by an employee. Professional representation is governed by Art 89.
3   Art 26.
4   Art 115(3).
5   Art 27.

13.8   Priority may be claimed from a regular national filing[1]; conversely, the Community trade mark application is deemed to be equivalent to a national filing in the Member States[2] and thus may be used to claim priority outside the Community. The proprietors of national marks are encouraged to file for Community trade marks by a 'seniority' provision. If the national mark is surrendered or allowed to lapse subsequently to registration of an identical Community trade mark for the same or a broader range of goods or services, the Community trade mark provides the same cover as the earlier trade mark[3]. Seniority may also be claimed after registration of an identical mark for identical products[4].

1   Art 29.
2   Art 32.
3   Art 34, unless the national trade mark is declared to have been revoked or invalidated.
4   Art 35.

13.9   The Office will examine the application as to form[1], entitlement[2] and on absolute grounds[3]. A search of the Community register will be carried out and those national offices which have opted to search their registers will be apprised of the application[4]. Results of the Community and any national searches will be communicated to the applicant, but no examination on relative grounds will be carried out by the Office itself. Instead, the application will proceed to publication and opposition or observations[5]. Opponents have three months in which to file written notice of opposition. Where opposition is based on an earlier Community or national trade mark, the opponent may be put to proof of genuine use within the Community or in the Member State in question over the preceding five years.

1   Art 36.
2   Art 37.
3   Art 38.
4   Art 39.
5   Arts 40–43.

Evidence

13.10   As regards relative grounds for refusal, the Office is restricted to the parties' cases as adduced. Otherwise, the Office may examine facts of its own motion[1]. Oral hearings are provided for[2] and evidence may be adduced by way of requests for information, documents and exhibits, live witnesses, expert opinions and written affidavits.

1   Art 74.
2   Art 75(1) and 76.

Appeals

13.11   Appeals to a Board of Appeal are governed by Articles 57 to 62. Where a decision is not final, it may be appealed along with a final decision, or with leave. The department whose decision is contested on appeal may voluntarily rectify its decision. From the Board of Appeal a further review may be sought before the European Court of Justice. The party or parties adversely affected by the Board of Appeal's decision have standing. There is no provision in Article 63 for the party successful before the Board of Appeal to appear in the Court of Justice to argue for dismissal. It is hoped that a formula may be found which will enable the other party to appear, and not have to rely upon the Office to maintain its decision.

Court proceedings

13.12   Member States are required to designate courts of first and second instance as 'Community Trade Mark Courts'[1]. These courts are to have jurisdiction in matters of infringement and validity[2] over the whole Community[3]. Choice of court is based on the Member State of the defendant's domicile or, if none, establishment[4]. If neither applies, the State of domicile or establishment of the plaintiff has jurisdiction. In the last resort, the Spanish Community Trade Mark Court has jurisdiction. It is also possible to sue in the court of the State where infringement occurs, but in that case jurisdiction is limited to that State[5].

1   Art 91.
2   But not, it seems, over ownership, which is conspicuously absent from the statement for inclusion in the
    minutes of adoption of the Regulation regarding Art 91(1):

    'The Council and the Commission consider that the functions assigned by the Regulations to Com-
    munity trade mark courts cover only infringement and validity actions together with the provisional,
    including protective, measures referred to in Article 99.'

    This is consistent with Art 222 of the EEC Treaty, but disregards the fact that where trade marks are
    concerned, ownership and validity are interlinked. See para **4.10**.
3   Art 94.
4   Art 93.
5   Art 94(2).

Licences and assignments

13.13   Licences are governed by Articles 22 and 23. A licence may be granted, for all or some of the goods or services, for the whole or part of the Community, exclusively or non-exclusively. An exclusive licensee may sue for infringement if the proprietor fails to do so; a non-exclusive licensee may bring infringement proceedings with the proprietor's consent. This could be given in the licence agreement, or subsequently. A licensee who contravenes his licence agreement may be liable for infringement.

13.14   A Community trade mark may be assigned with or without the proprietor's business or undertaking[1]. A transfer of the whole undertaking is deemed to transfer the Community mark unless the contrary appears from the agreement or circumstances. Unless made by order of the court, an assignment must be in writing and signed by the parties. The Office has power to refuse to register a transfer or to limit registration where the public is likely to be misled as a result of the transfer.

1   Art 17.

13.15   For the purposes of property and transactions, a Community trade mark is dealt with as a national trade mark registered in the State where the proprietor has its seat or domicile on the relevant date, or if none, where the proprietor has an establishment or, failing that, Spain[1]. This has the curious effect that the proprietary status and location of the Community trade mark can shift with the proprietor. Other provisions are necessarily arbitrary; where a mark is jointly owned, the domicile, etc of the first-named is used first. Where bankruptcy proceedings are filed[2], the Community mark may only be involved in the proceedings commenced first[3].

1   Where the Office has its seat: Art 16.
2   In the absence of harmonisation of insolvency laws.
3   Art 21.

13.16   Unless a whole undertaking is transferred, assignments, security interests and licences are effective against third parties only after registration, although a party acquiring rights with knowledge of the transaction will be subject to it[1].

1   Art 23.

13.17   A prospective Community trade mark applicant has a choice, either to make national applications in all or some Member States or to apply under the Madrid arrangement or protocol for an international registration[1]. Choice of route will depend upon the likelihood of conflict in the Community system, the relative levels of fees, and preference as to working languages.

1   See Ch 14.

FREE MOVEMENT AND COMPETITION RULES

13.18   Trade marks do not prevent the marketing or movement of goods or services as such, but the existence of a strong brand may constitute a significant barrier to a new-comer wishing to compete. Trade mark registrations can be renewed indefinitely, so any effect on competition is long-lasting. It might be supposed that the European Community would be altogether hostile to marks. However, they are recognised as playing an important positive role in a competitive market, in facilitating identification and choice by consumers[1]. The Community trade mark was intended to achieve this without some of the disadvantages of national marks. However, the Community Trade Mark Regulation has been a long time coming. National trade mark systems will still be required for those marks which are unable to get on to the Community register because of conflict with marks in other States, for marks which are linguistically or otherwise unsuitable as Community marks, and for the benefit of localised trading interests.

1   Memorandum on the creation of an EEC trade mark, *Bulletin of the European Communities*, Supplement 8/76, paras 11–14.

13.19   National trade mark rights can, in principle, be used to prevent the movement of goods and services across borders. The advantages of trade marks can be used to tie others to restrictive agreements or to practise discrimination. The European Court of Justice has had to reconcile the effect of trade mark laws with the principles of the single market. The remainder of this chapter reviews a number of decisions relevant to trade marks; for a more comprehensive view of EC law in this area the reader is referred to specialist works[1].

1   Such as Bellamy and Child *Common Market Law of Competition* (1993) 4th edn; V Korah *An Introductory Guide to EC Competition Law and Practice* (1994) 5th edn; D Raybould and A Firth *Law of Monopolies* (1991); R

Whish *Competition Law* (1993) 3rd edn. See, also, N Macfarlane, C Wardle and J Wilkinson 'The tension between national intellectual property rights and certain provisions of EC law' [1994] EIPR 525.

Article 85

13.20 Early decisions were based upon Article 85 of the EEC Treaty, which prohibits agreements which may affect interstate trade and which have an object or effect deleterious to competition. In *Consten v Grundig*[1], a trade mark agreement had the effect of partitioning the market between the parties. It was held contrary to Article 85[2]. The court made a distinction between the existence of national rights, which were preserved by the Treaty, and their exercise, which was subject to control by EC law[3]. Although this doctrine has recently been criticised as illogical[4] and obsolete[5], the distinction proved very potent in enabling the court to rule on the effect of national rights.

1   [1966] ECR 299.
2   See also the trade marks licensing case of *Campari* [1978] 2 CMLR 397.
3   A distinction made in *Deutsche Grammophon v Metro-Grossmarkte* [1971] ECR 487; [1971] CMLR 631.
4   C G Miller, 'Magill: time to abandon the "Specific Subject-matter" concept' [1994] 10 EIPR 415.
5   G Tritton, 'Articles 30 to 36 and intellectual property: Is the jurisprudence of the ECJ now of an Ideal Standard?' [1994] 10 EIPR 422.

13.21 Excessively restrictive repackaging bans[1] and field-of-use restrictions[2] have been found to fall foul of Article 85. Trade mark delimitation agreements which seek to reduce confusion between conflicting marks have also been subjected to scrutiny under Article 85. In *Re the agreement of Sirdar Ltd*[3], an opposition was settled on the basis that one company would use the marks 'Phildar' and 'Le Fil D'Art' in France, and the other would use 'Sirdar'. It was held that this would prevent cross supplies – supplies of products into the others' territories – and that the agreement should not be exempt from Article 85. Where cross supplies are feasible, and confusion prevented by distinguishing means, the agreement will not infringe[4].

1   *Bayer Dental* [1992] 4 CMLR 61.
2   *Bay-o-nox* [1990] 4 CMLR 429.
3   [1975] 1 CMLR D93.
4   *Persil* [1978] 1 CMLR 395.

Article 86

13.22 A rights holder who enjoys a dominant position in the market for a product in a substantial part of the Community must take care to avoid abuse of that position contrary to Article 86 of the EEC Treaty. Market definitions tend to be narrowly drawn[1]. Forms of abuse which may infringe include the limitation of production or markets, discriminatory practices, the imposition of unwanted obligations and refusals to supply. Although a mere refusal to grant a licence may not infringe[2], it may do so if accompanied by other forms of abuse[3] or possibly if it prevents the creation of a separate market[4]. Oppressive use of opposition procedure was held contrary to Article 86 in *BAT v Commission*[5]. The marks concerned were 'Toltecs' and 'Dorcet'.

1 Eg, *Eurofix and Bauco v Hilti* [1989] 4 CMLR 677; appeal dismissed 2 March 1994; see S Topping, 'Finally Nailed Down: The Hilti Appeal to the ECJ' [1994] EIPR 543.
2 Eg, *Volvo v Veng* [1989] 4 CMLR 122, a principle reiterated in the Advocate-General's opinion in *Magill*, n 4 below; see C Miller, para **13.20**, n 4.
3 Eg, *Hilti*, n 1 above.
4 *Magill – Commission v Radio Telefis Eireann and Others* [1991] 4 CMLR 586, 669, 745.
5 [1985] 2 CMLR 470.

Articles 30–36 and 59[1]

13.23 Articles 30–36 of the Treaty of Rome prohibit quantitative restrictions on import, export and measures having like effect, unless they can be justified on the grounds set out in Article 36, including the protection of industrial property[2]. In the context of trade marks, Article 30 may be used to suppress the exercise of trade mark rights in order to prevent imports from other Member States in the following classes of case:

(a) The imports are the proprietor's own products or those of a related company[3] or licensee: *Deutsche Grammophon v Metro-Grossmarkte*[4]. Having enjoyed the benefit of the trade mark in marketing the goods in one Member State, the proprietor has 'exhausted' his rights throughout the Community.
(b) The proprietor has adopted different marks in different Member States deliberately to partition the market and the importer substitutes the local mark: *Centrafarm v American Home Products*[5].
(c) The importer repacks the proprietor's products without affecting the quality of the goods and makes his activities clear to the proprietor and consumers: *Hoffmann-La Roche v Centrafarm*[6]; *Pfizer v Eurimpharm*[7].

1 It has been suggested that Art 59 on the free movement of services should be applied analogously to Arts 30–36. See, eg, L Defalque 'Copyright, free movement of goods and territoriality: recent developments' [1989] 12 EIPR 435.
2 Plus grounds of fiscal supervision, public health, fairness of commercial transactions or the defence of the consumer when 'measures' are not overtly discriminatory: *Cassis de Dijon* [1979] ECR 649; [1979] 3 CMLR 494; see also Commission notice at [1981] 1 CMLR 177.
3 *Centrafarm v Winthrop* [1974] ECR 1183; [1974] 2 CMLR 480; [1975] FSR 161.
4 Para **13.20**, n 3.
5 [1978] ECR 1823; [1979] 1 CMLR 326.
6 [1978] ECR 1139; [1978] 3 CMLR 217; [1978] FSR 598.
7 [1981] ECR 2913; [1982] 1 CMLR 406; [1982] FSR 269.

13.24 Articles 30 to 36 do not appear to apply to the following classes of case.

(a) The goods are repackaged in a way which affects their quality: *Hoffman-La-Roche v Centrafarm*[1].

(b) Different marks were chosen in different States for objectively justifiable reasons: *Centrafarm*[2].
(c) The goods were put on the market by someone entirely unconnected with the trade mark proprietor: *Terrapin v Terranova*[3].
(d) Ownership of the mark was previously split by expropriation: *CNL-Sucal v Hag*[4].
(e) Ownership of the mark was split due to financial difficulties: *Ideal Standard*[5].

The last decision may represent a relaxation in the attitude of the European Court of Justice to the exercise of intellectual property and if so, diminish the attractiveness of the Community trade mark.

1   Para **13.23**, n 6.
2   Para **13.23**, n 5.
3   [1976] ECR 1039; [1976] 2 CMLR 482.
4   [1990] 3 CMLR 571; [1991] FSR 99.
5   [1995] FSR 59; para **13.20**, n 5.

13.25   It should be noted that the free movement provisions now extend to the European Economic Area (EEA); the factors noted above are likely to apply equally to movement across EEA boundaries[1].

1   *Eurimpharm v Bundesundheitsamt* Case 207/91, 1 July 1993. Cf EFTA *Polydor v Harlequin* [1982] ECR 329. For a commentary, see C Worth, 'Free trade agreements and the exhaustion of rights principle' [1994] 1 EIPR 40.

ANTI-COUNTERFEITING MEASURES

13.26   The progressive reduction in customs tariffs and barriers and the principles of free movement mean that goods may circulate freely inside the single market. The corollary is that counterfeit products are unlikely to meet with obstacles to movement. Although a defendant who relies on free movement may be required to show lawful manufacture and sale in the common market[1], positive measures to restrain counterfeiting are seen as necessary[2]. Council Regulation (EC) No 3295/94[3] lays down measures, including custom's retention upon request or ex officio, to prohibit the release for free circulation of counterfeit and pirated goods.

1   *Renault v Thevenoux* [1988] 3 CMLR 686.
2   Concern over counterfeiting is widespread: see D P Harvey, 'Efforts under GATT, WIPO and other multinational organisations against trade mark counterfeiting' [1993] 12 EIPR 446.
3   Of 22 December 1994, OJ 1994 L 341/8.

Chapter 14

TRADE MARKS WORLDWIDE

VARIETIES OF SYSTEM

14.1   The World Intellectual Property Organisation has recently concluded a trade mark registration treaty which is now open for signature[1]. Ultimately, this may result in uniformity of the procedural aspects of trade mark registration. In the meantime, however, an immense variety of systems are to be found worldwide. For details, compendious works such as that by Horwitz[2] may be consulted.

---

1   Para **13.4**, n 1.
2   *World Trademark Law and Practice* (Matthew Bender).

14.2   Most systems can be classified as either first-to-file or first-to-use. In the former case, trade mark rights may only be acquired by registration. The first person to apply for a particular mark for certain goods or services becomes the proprietor; only prior registrations are able to block a subsequent application. Examples of this kind of system may be found in France or in the Benelux countries. The first-to-use country may require actual use before application (as was formerly the case in the USA) or registration. Alternatively, it may give precedence to the earlier user, even of an unregistered mark, in the event of conflict – as under the Trade Marks Act 1938. The UK has moved somewhat from that position under the Trade Marks Act 1994. In a letter to *The Times*[1] on the subject of the 1994 Act, Christopher Morcom QC commented:

'The most fundamental change is shifting the emphasis from common law action for passing off to the protection of marks by registration, which has become considerably easier and more effective. The risk of failing to register marks has undoubtedly increased.'

---

1   22 November 1994.

14.3   Another distinction is between countries that undertake a thorough examination of applications and those which leave any objections to be raised in cancellation proceedings, often in the courts rather than in the trade marks office. Systems which do not provide substantive examination of applications are sometimes called deposit systems, although the applications will in practice always receive a degree of inspection as to form, not least to ensure that the registry receives its fees.

14.4   All or most of the following elements are to be found in any trade mark registration system[1]:

(a)   filing;
(b)   search;
(c)   examination as to form;

(d)   substantive examination: absolute grounds;
(e)   substantive examination: relative grounds;
(f)   publication;
(g)   opposition;
(h)   use;
(i)   registration;
(j)   refusal.

The order in which these steps appear varies considerably from country to country.

---

1   The author is indebted to Richard Gallafent for this analysis.

14.5   Other features of individual systems include the registration of service as well as trade marks, provision for collective marks and/or certification marks, distinct schemes for trade names. The kinds of mark eligible for registration, the classification systems for products and the possibility of multi-class applications also vary, as do renewal frequency, use requirements and procedures for cancellation. Some countries permit licensing with or without registration of the licensee, others do not.

14.6   It will be evident to the reader that the skill and money needed to obtain and maintain an international portfolio of marks is considerable. Local agents usually have to be retained, and translations of documents filed. Enforcement also has its vagaries; rules of comparison of marks and products differ from jurisdiction as do court procedures and remedies.

14.7   Several mechanisms exist which reduce the problems of obtaining protection internationally. The first is the regional system. A single registry handles applications for the whole region, which enjoys a uniform law. A number of regional systems exist, including the Benelux, OAPI[1] and the Community trade mark. Secondly, international agreements facilitate direct registration into other systems. Thirdly, international registration of marks is possible through the Madrid mechanism.

---

1   French-speaking Africa. An ARIPO system in English-speaking Africa is being set up.

THE PARIS CONVENTION FOR THE PROTECTION OF INDUSTRIAL PROPERTY

14.8   The Paris Convention[1] had 129 members as at 1 January 1995. By establishing the principle of national treatment it obviates discrimination in its signatory States between domestic and foreign applicants. It also contains a number of specific provisions which are considered elsewhere[2]. It is administered by the World Intellectual Property Organisation, which became a specialised agency in the United Nations system of organisations in 1974. Its headquarters are in Geneva, Switzerland.

1 Of 1883, with revisions in 1900, 1911, 1925, 1934, 1958 and 1967.
2 Paras **2.34, 3.22, 5.4, 5.36, 7.31–7.32, 7.39, 11.21, 12.5–12.6, 12.25–12.31, 13.6.**

14.9 The next two categories of agreement are open to members of the Paris Union.

THE MADRID ARRANGEMENT

14.10 The Madrid Arrangement concerning the international registration of marks[1] was concluded in 1891[2]. It has more than 40 members, mainly civil law countries and their former dependencies. It can be used by natural and legal persons whose country of origin is in one of the contracting States[3]. 'Country of origin' is defined precisely. If a person has an industrial or commercial establishment in one of the States, that is the country of origin. If not, the State of domicile may be used, if applicable. If not, the country of which the person is a national can be considered the country of origin. These strict rules serve to prevent a user 'shopping' for the State where registration is most easily obtained. This is relevant because a national registration in the country of origin must be secured as a basis for the international filing. This makes the arrangement less suitable for countries where examination is strict, because the base registration takes longer to procure and is likely to be narrower in scope.

1 Note that there is another 'Madrid Agreement' of 1891, for the Repression of False or Deceptive Indications of Source on Goods: see WIPO (World Intellectual Property Organisation, otherwise OMPI) General Information, 1994, p 23.
2 And revised in 1900, 1911, 1925, 1934, 1957, 1967 and 1979.
3 Art 1(2) and (3).

14.11 Next, an international application[1] is filed in the country of origin[2]. The application must be in French, the official language of the system. It identifies the applicant, the mark, the base registration(s), any priority claimed, and the goods or services for which international registration is sought[3]. It also designates the countries where protection is sought. The national trade mark office then sends the application to the international bureau in Geneva. The bureau enters it in the international Register, publishes it in 'Les Marques Internationales' and forwards the application to the designated countries.

1 Art 3.
2 Which is examined for formal compliance. A fee may be charged.
3 The specification must be within the scope of the base registration(s).

14.12 The receiving countries then have one year in which to issue a refusal[1]. This is rather a short time for countries with full examination systems, although an initial objection counts as a 'refusal' for these purposes. If a refusal is not issued within the year, the registration is deemed to take effect in the designated country as if it were a national registration[2]. A refusal in one designated country does not affect protection in others. The receiving trade mark office may limit the specification of goods or services; again this does not affect the position in other countries.

---

1   Art 5.
2   Art 4.

14.13   If the base registration is invalidated, then the international registration fails and protection in all designated countries is lost[1]. This drastic process is known as 'central attack'. After five years, the international registration gains independence from the base registration and is no longer vulnerable to central attack.

---

1   Art 6(3).

14.14   Once the international registration achieves independence, it becomes freely assignable for some or all of the designated countries[1], but only to a person who is entitled to file an international application[2]. The initial registration endures for 20 years[3] and is renewable thereafter for further periods of 20 years[4].

---

1   Art 9. Assignment in the first five years requires consent of the assignee's country of origin.
2   See above.
3   Art 6(1).
4   Art 7, effected at the International Bureau.

14.15   Additional countries may subsequently be designated. The fees payable by the applicant depend on the number of countries designated and the number of classes in which registration is sought. A comparatively small proportion of the fees finds its way to the participating trade mark offices. For this reason the system is not attractive to countries operating a full examination system.

14.16   The Madrid Arrangement is very convenient for users, with a single application procedure, communications via the international bureau and central renewal. However, for the reasons outlined above, it has not commended itself to countries like the UK which have a full examination system. A parallel agreement, the Madrid Protocol, was devised to cater for such countries.

THE MADRID PROTOCOL

14.17   The Madrid Protocol was concluded in 1989. It shares many of the features outlined above under the Madrid Arrangement. Applications may be filed either in English or in French and may be based on a trade mark application[1] rather than a registration in the country of origin. The Protocol application can also be based upon a Community trade mark application. Participating States may opt for an extended period of 18 months in which to issue refusals and may refuse the mark beyond the time-limit on the basis of an opposition notified within the limit[2]. If the base application fails to mature into a registration, or is cancelled, the international registration may be converted into a series of national applications whose filing date is deemed to be that of the international registration. The fee structure will enable higher fees to be charged by receiving countries[3]. Thus countries with more rigorous examination procedures will be able to recoup proportionate fees. Duration and renewals will be for 10 years[4] rather than 20.

---

1   Art 2(1).
2   Art 5(2)(b), (c) and (d).
3   Art 8(7).
4   Arts 6(1) and 7(1).

14.18   The Trade Marks Act 1994, ss 53 and 54 contains provision for ratification of the Madrid Protocol. Rules will have to be promulgated. The Protocol will come into force when ratified by four States, at least one of which is a member and one a non-member of the Madrid Arrangement. At the time of writing, only Spain has ratified. The USA is unlikely to ratify in the near future, for political reasons[1]. It is hoped that Canada, Australia[2] and Japan will join at an early stage.

---

1   For the perceived merits for the USA, see IJ Kaufman, 'Madrid Agreement: will reform proposals attract more members?' [1990] 11 EIPR 407; IJ Kaufman, 'The Madrid Protocol: Should the United States be swept up in the rising tide?' *Trademark World*, October 1991, p 27.
2   T Stevens, 'The Madrid Protocol and its likely effect on trade mark owners and trade mark practitioners in Australia' (1993) 4 AIPJ 48.

14.19   The usefulness of the Madrid Protocol will also depend on ratification by existing members of the Madrid Arrangement. The common administrative system should provide a significant incentive. The complexities of the combined system have been discussed in a number of articles by G Kunze[1].

---

1   Eg, Kunze, 'Madrid Protocol's practical impact' Managing Intellectual Property, March 1994, p 50; G Kunze, 'The Madrid system for the international registration of marks as applied under the protocol' [1994] 6 EIPR 223.

14.20   When operative, the Madrid Protocol is likely to prove very attractive to UK trade mark owners. Its simplicity in terms of procedure and language compare favourably with the Community trade mark.

GATT AND THE AGREEMENT ON TRADE-RELATED ASPECTS OF INTELLECTUAL PROPERTY RIGHTS (TRIPS)

14.21   During the course of the Uruguay round of the General Agreement of Tariffs and Trade (GATT), impatience with the dearth of intellectual property rights in many countries and with the lack of national and international mechanisms for enforcement led to the conclusion of the TRIPS agreement. Trade mark provisions of the so-called 'Dunkel draft' which formed the basis of TRIPS were based upon European trade mark texts. Consequently, European and UK trade mark laws are already in conformity with TRIPS. The agreement will, however, be significant for UK trade mark interests internationally. At the time of writing, the European Union's role in GATT and TRIPS has been clarified by the European Court of Justice in a way which suggests that EU competence in intellectual property matters is shared with Member States[1]. This may have a significant effect within the Union as time goes by.

---

1   Opinion 1/94 of 15 November 1994.

14.22   At the conclusion of the Uruguay round, the World Trade Organisation was established as a permanent body in Geneva. Relations between the World Trade Organisation and World Intellectual Property Organisation will be a matter of considerable interest in coming years. The World Trade Organisation has jurisdiction over intellectual property disputes between States. The World Intellectual Property Organisation has set up an arbitration centre for private intellectual property disputes.[1]

---

1   (1995) 34(2) *Industrial Property and Copyright*, pp 117–123.

APPENDIX 1

Trade Marks Act 1994
(1994 c. 26)

ARRANGEMENT OF SECTIONS

Part I

REGISTERED TRADE MARKS

Introductory

		Page
1	Trade marks	143
2	Registered trade marks	143

Grounds for refusal of registration

3	Absolute grounds for refusal of registration	144
4	Specially protected emblems	144
5	Relative grounds for refusal of registration	145
6	Meaning of 'earlier trade mark'	146
7	Raising of relative grounds in case of honest concurrent use	146
8	Power to require that relative grounds be raised in opposition proceedings	146

Effects of registered trade mark

9	Rights conferred by registered trade mark	147
10	Infringement of registered trade mark	147
11	Limits on effect of registered trade mark	148
12	Exhaustion of rights conferred by registered trade mark	149
13	Registration subject to disclaimer or limitation	149

Infringement proceedings

14	Action for infringement	149
15	Order for erasure, etc. of offending sign	149
16	Order for delivery up of infringing goods, material or articles	150
17	Meaning of 'infringing goods, material or articles'	150
18	Period after which remedy of delivery up not available	151
19	Order as to disposal of infringing goods, material or articles	151

20 Jurisdiction of sheriff court or county court in Northern Ireland   152
21 Remedy for groundless threats of infringement proceedings   152

Registered trade mark as object of property

22 Nature of registered trade mark   152
23 Co-ownership of registered trade mark   152
24 Assignment, etc. of registered trade mark   153
25 Registration of transactions affecting registered trade mark   153
26 Trusts and equities   154
27 Application for registration of trade mark as an object of property   155

Licensing

28 Licensing of registered trade mark   155
29 Exclusive licences   155
30 General provisions as to rights of licensees in case of infringement   155
31 Exclusive licensee having rights and remedies of assignee   156

Application for registered trade mark

32 Application for registration   157
33 Date of filing   157
34 Classification of trade marks   157

Priority

35 Claim to priority of Convention application   158
36 Claim to priority from other relevant overseas application   158

Registration procedure

37 Examination of application   159
38 Publication, opposition proceedings and observations   159
39 Withdrawal, restriction or amendment of application   159
40 Registration   160
41 Registration: supplementary provisions   160

Duration, renewal and alteration of registered trademark

42 Duration of registration   160
43 Renewal of registration   160
44 Alteration of registered trade mark   161

Surrender, revocation and invalidity

45 Surrender of registered trade mark   161
46 Revocation of registration   161
47 Grounds for invalidity of registration   162
48 Effect of acquiescence   163

Collective marks

49 Collective marks   163

Certificate marks

50 Certification marks   163

PART II

COMMUNITY TRADE MARKS AND INTERNATIONAL MATTERS

Community trade marks

51 Meaning of 'Community trade mark'   163
52 Power to make provision in connection with Community Trade Mark Regulation 164

The Madrid Protocol: international registration

53 The Madrid Protocol   164
54 Power to make provision giving effect to Madrid Protocol   164

The Paris Convention: supplementary provisions

55 The Paris Convention   165
56 Protection of well-known trade marks: Article 6*bis*   165
57 National emblems, etc. of Convention countries: Article 6*ter*   166
58 Emblems, etc. of certain international organisations: Article 6*ter*   166
59 Notification under Article 6*ter* of the Convention   167
60 Acts of agent or representative: Article 6*septies*   167

Miscellaneous

61 Stamp duty   168

PART III

ADMINISTRATIVE AND OTHER SUPPLEMENTARY PROVISIONS

The registrar

62 The registrar   168

The register

63 The register   168
64 Rectification or correction of the register   168
65 Adaptation of entries to new classification   169

Powers and duties of the registrar

66 Power to require use of forms   169
67 Information about applications and registered trade marks   169
68 Costs and security for costs   170
69 Evidence before registrar   170
70 Exclusion of liability in respect of official acts   170

71 Registrar's annual report   170

Legal proceedings and appeals

72 Registration to be prima facie evidence of validity   171
73 Certificate of validity of contested registration   171
74 Registrar's appearance in proceedings involving the register   171
75 The Court   171
76 Appeals from the registrar   171
77 Persons appointed to hear and determine appeals   172

Rules, fees, hours of business, etc.

78 Power of Secretary of State to make rules   172
79 Fees   173
80 Hours of business and business days   173
81 The trade marks journal   173

Trade mark agents, etc.

82 Recognition of agents   173
83 The register of trade mark agents   173
84 Unregistered persons not to be described as registered trade mark agents   174
85 Power to prescribe conditions, etc. for mixed partnerships and bodies corporate 174
86 Use of the term 'trade mark attorney'   175
87 Privilege for communications with registered trade mark agents   175
88 Power of registrar to refuse to deal with certain agents   175

Importation of infringing goods, material or articles

89 Infringing goods, material or articles may be treated as prohibited goods   176
90 Power of Commissioners of Customs and Excise to make regulations   176
91 Power of Commissioners of Customs and Excise to disclose information   177

Offences

92 Unauthorised use of trade mark, etc. in relation to goods   177
93 Enforcement function of local weights and measures authority   178
94 Falsification of register, etc.   178
95 Falsely representing trade mark as registered   179
96 Supplementary provisions as to summary proceedings in Scotland   179

Forfeiture of counterfeit goods, etc.

97 Forfeiture: England and Wales or Northern Ireland   179
98 Forfeiture: Scotland   180

PART IV

MISCELLANEOUS AND GENERAL PROVISIONS

Miscellaneous

 99 Unauthorised use of Royal arms, etc.   182
100 Burden of proving use of trade mark   182

101 Offences committed by partnerships and bodies corporate   182

Interpretation

102 Adaptation of expressions for Scotland   183
103 Minor definitions   183
104 Index of defined expressions   184

Other general provisions

105 Transitional provisions   185
106 Consequential amendments and repeals   185
107 Territorial waters and the continental shelf   185
108 Extent   185
109 Commencement   185
110 Short title   185

SCHEDULES

Schedule 1—Collective marks   186
Schedule 2—Certification marks   189
Schedule 3—Transitional provisions   191
Schedule 4—Consequential amendments   197
Schedule 5—Repeals and revocations   201

An Act to make new provision for registered trade marks, implementing Council Directive No 89/104/EEC of 21 December 1988 to approximate the laws of the Member States relating to trade marks; to make provision in connection with Council Regulation (EC) No 40/94 of 20 December 1993 on the Community trade mark; to give effect to the Madrid Protocol Relating to the International Registration of Marks of 27 June 1989, and to certain provisions of the Paris Convention for the Protection of Industrial Property of 20 March 1883, as revised and amended; and for connected purposes.   [21 July 1994]

PART I

REGISTERED TRADE MARKS

Introductory

1 Trade marks

(1) In this Act a 'trade mark' means any sign capable of being represented graphically which is capable of distinguishing goods or services of one undertaking from those of other undertakings.

A trade mark may, in particular, consist of words (including personal names), designs, letters, numerals or the shape of goods or their packaging.

(2) References in this Act to a trade mark include, unless the context otherwise requires, references to a collective mark (see section 49) or certification mark (see section 50).

2 Registered trade marks

(1) A registered trade mark is a property right obtained by the registration of the trade mark under this Act and the proprietor of a registered trade mark has the rights and remedies provided by this Act.

(2) No proceedings lie to prevent or recover damages for the infringement of an unregistered trade mark as such; but nothing in this Act affects the law relating to passing off.

3 Absolute grounds for refusal of registration

(1) The following shall not be registered—

    (a) signs which do not satisfy the requirements of section 1(1),

    (b) trade marks which are devoid of any distinctive character,

    (c) trade marks which consist exclusively of signs or indications which may serve, in trade, to designate the kind, quality, quantity, intended purpose, value, geographical origin, the time of production of goods or of rendering of services, or other characteristics of goods or services,

    (d) trade marks which consist exclusively of signs or indications which have become customary in the current language or in the *bona fide* and established practice of the trade:

Provided that, a trade mark shall not be refused registration by virtue of paragraph (b), (c) or (d) above if, before the date of application for registration, it has in fact acquired a distinctive character as a result of the use made of it.

(2) A sign shall not be registered as a trade mark if it consists exclusively of—

    (a) the shape which results from the nature of the goods themselves,

    (b) the shape of goods which is necessary to obtain a technical result, or

    (c) the shape which gives substantial value to the goods.

(3) A trade mark shall not be registered if it is—

    (a) contrary to public policy or to accepted principles of morality, or

    (b) of such a nature as to deceive the public (for instance as to the nature, quality or geographical origin of the goods or service).

(4) A trade mark shall not be registered if or to the extent that its use is prohibited in the United Kingdom by any enactment or rule of law or by any provision of Community law.

(5) A trade mark shall not be registered in the cases specified, or referred to, in section 4 (specially protected emblems).

(6) A trade mark shall not be registered if or to the extent that the application is made in bad faith.

4 Specially protected emblems

(1) A trade mark which consists of or contains—

    (a) the Royal arms, or any of the principal armorial bearings of the Royal arms, or any insignia or device so nearly resembling the Royal arms or any such armorial bearing as to be likely to be mistaken for them or it,

    (b) a representation of the Royal crown or any of the Royal flags,

    (c) a representation of Her Majesty or any member of the Royal family, or any colourable imitation thereof, or

    (d) words, letters or devices likely to lead persons to think that the applicant either has or recently has had Royal patronage or authorisation,

shall not be registered unless it appears to the registrar that consent has been given by or on behalf of Her Majesty or, as the case may be, the relevant member of the Royal family.

(2) A trade mark which consists of or contains a representation of—

    (a) the national flag of the United Kingdom (commonly known as the Union Jack), or

(b) the flag of England, Wales, Scotland, Northern Ireland or the Isle of Man,

shall not be registered if it appears to the registrar that the use of the trade mark would be misleading or grossly offensive.

Provision may be made by rules identifying the flags to which paragraph (b) applies.

(3) A trade mark shall not be registered in the cases specified in—

section 57 (national emblems, etc. of Convention countries), or
section 58 (emblems, etc. of certain international organisations).

(4) Provision may be made by rules prohibiting in such cases as may be prescribed the registration of a trade mark which consists of or contains—

(a) arms to which a person is entitled by virtue of a grant of arms by the Crown, or
(b) insignia so nearly resembling such arms as to be likely to be mistaken for them,

unless it appears to the registrar that consent has been given by or on behalf of that person.

Where such a mark is registered, nothing in this Act shall be construed as authorising its use in any way contrary to the laws of arms.

5   Relative grounds for refusal of registration

(1) A trade mark shall not be registered if it is identical with an earlier trade mark and the goods or services for which the trade mark is applied for are identical with the goods or services for which the earlier trade mark is protected.

(2) A trade mark shall not be registered if because—

(a) it is identical with an earlier trade mark and is to be registered for goods or services similar to those for which the earlier trade mark is protected, or
(b) it is similar to an earlier trade mark and is to be registered for goods or services identical with or similar to those for which the earlier trade mark is protected,

there exists a likelihood of confusion on the part of the public, which includes the likelihood of association with the earlier trade mark.

(3) A trade mark which—

(a) is identical with or similar to an earlier trade mark, and
(b) is to be registered for goods or services which are not similar to those for which the earlier trade mark is protected,

shall not be registered if, or to the extent that, the earlier trade mark has a reputation in the United Kingdom (or, in the case of a Community trade mark, in the European Community) and the use of the later mark without due cause would take unfair advantage of, or be detrimental to, the distinctive character or the repute of the earlier trade mark.

(4) A trade mark shall not be registered if, or to the extent that, its use in the United Kingdom is liable to be prevented—

(a) by virtue of any rule of law (in particular, the law of passing off) protecting an unregistered trade mark or other sign used in the course of trade, or
(b) by virtue of an earlier right other than those referred to in subsections (1) to (3) or paragraph (a) above, in particular by virtue of the law of copyright, design right or registered designs.

A person thus entitled to prevent the use of a trade mark is referred to in this Act as the proprietor of an 'earlier right' in relation to the trade mark.

(5) Nothing in this section prevents the registration of a trade mark where the proprietor of the earlier trade mark or other earlier right consents to the registration.

6   Meaning of 'earlier trade mark'

(1) In this Act an 'earlier trade mark' means—

  (a) a registered trade mark, international trade mark (UK) or Community trade mark which has a date of application for registration earlier than that of the trade mark in question, taking account (where appropriate) of the priorities claimed in respect of the trade marks,

  (b) a Community trade mark which has a valid claim to seniority from an earlier registered trade mark or international trade mark (UK), or

  (c) a trade mark which, at the date of application for registration of the trade mark in question or (where appropriate) of the priority claimed in respect of the application, was entitled to protection under the Paris Convention as a well known trade mark.

(2) References in this Act to an earlier trade mark include a trade mark in respect of which an application for registration has been made and which, if registered, would be an earlier trade mark by virtue of subsection (1)(a) or (b), subject to its being so registered.

(3) A trade mark within subsection (1)(a) or (b) whose registration expires shall continue to be taken into account in determining the registrability of a later mark for a period of one year after the expiry unless the registrar is satisfied that there was no *bona fide* use of the mark during the two years immediately preceding the expiry.

7   Raising of relative grounds in case of honest concurrent use

(1) This section applies where on an application for the registration of a trade mark it appears to the registrar—

  (a) that there is an earlier trade mark in relation to which the conditions set out in section 5(1), (2) or (3) obtain, or

  (b) that there is an earlier right in relation to which the condition set out in section 5(4) is satisfied,

but the applicant shows to the satisfaction of the registrar that there has been honest concurrent use of the trade mark for which registration is sought.

(2) In that case the registrar shall not refuse the application by reason of the earlier trade mark or other earlier right unless objection on that ground is raised in opposition proceedings by the proprietor of that earlier trade mark or other earlier right.

(3) For the purposes of this section 'honest concurrent use' means such use in the United Kingdom, by the applicant or with his consent, as would formerly have amounted to honest concurrent use for the purposes of section 12(2) of the Trade Marks Act 1938.

(4) Nothing in this section affects—

  (a) the refusal of registration on the grounds mentioned in section 3 (absolute grounds for refusal), or

  (b) the making of an application for a declaration of invalidity under section 47(2) (application on relative grounds where no consent to registration).

(5) This section does not apply when there is an order in force under section 8 below.

8   Power to require that relative grounds be raised in opposition proceedings

(1) The Secretary of State may by order provide that in any case a trade mark shall not be refused registration on a ground mentioned in section 5 (relative grounds for refusal) unless

objection on that ground is raised in opposition proceedings by the proprietor of the earlier trade mark or other earlier right.

(2) The order may make such consequential provision as appears to the Secretary of State appropriate—

  (a) with respect to the carrying out by the registrar of searches of earlier trade marks, and
  (b) as to the persons by whom an application for a declaration of invalidity may be made on the grounds specified in section 47(2) (relative grounds).

(3) An order making such provision as is mentioned in subsection (2)(a) may direct that so much of section 37 (examination of application) as requires a search to be carried out shall cease to have effect.

(4) An order making such provision as is mentioned in subsection (2)(b) may provide that so much of section 47(3) as provides that any person may make an application for a declaration of invalidity shall have effect subject to the provisions of the order.

(5) An order under this section shall be made by statutory instrument, and no order shall be made unless a draft of it has been laid before and approved by a resolution of each House of Parliament.

  No such draft of an order making such provision as is mentioned in subsection (1) shall be laid before Parliament until after the end of the period of ten years beginning with the day on which applications for Community trade marks may first be filed in pursuance of the Community Trade Mark Regulation.

(6) An order under this section may contain such transitional provisions as appear to the Secretary of State to be appropriate.

Effects of registered trade mark

9   Rights conferred by registered trade mark
(1) The proprietor of a registered trade mark has exclusive rights in the trade mark which are infringed by use of the trade mark in the United Kingdom without his consent.

  The acts amounting to infringement, if done without the consent of the proprietor, are specified in section 10.

(2) References in this Act to the infringement of a registered trade mark are to any such infringement of the rights of the proprietor.

(3) The rights of the proprietor have effect from the date of registration (which in accordance with section 40(3) is the date of filing of the application for registration):
  Provided that—

  (a) no infringement proceedings may be begun before the date on which the trade mark is in fact registered; and
  (b) no offence under section 92 (unauthorised use of trade mark, etc. in relation to goods) is committed by anything done before the date of publication of the registration.

10   Infringement of registered trade mark
(1) A person infringes a registered trade mark if he uses in the course of trade a sign which is identical with the trade mark in relation to goods or services which are identical with those for which it is registered.

(2) A person infringes a registered trade mark if he uses in the course of trade a sign where because—

    (a) the sign is identical with the trade mark and is used in relation to goods or services similar to those for which the trade mark is registered, or

    (b) the sign is similar to the trade mark and is used in relation to goods or services identical with or similar to those for which the trade mark is registered,

there exists a likelihood of confusion on the part of the public, which includes the likelihood of association with the trade mark.

(3) A person infringes a registered trade mark if he uses in the course of trade a sign which—

    (a) is identical with or similar to the trade mark, and

    (b) is used in relation to goods or services which are not similar to those for which the trade mark is registered,

where the trade mark has a reputation in the United Kingdom and the use of the sign, being without due cause, takes unfair advantage of, or is detrimental to, the distinctive character or the repute of the trade mark.

(4) For the purposes of this section a person uses a sign if, in particular, he—

    (a) affixes it to goods or the packaging thereof;

    (b) offers or exposes goods for sale, puts them on the market or stocks them for those purposes under the sign, or offers or supplies services under the sign;

    (c) imports or exports goods under the sign; or

    (d) uses the sign on business papers or in advertising.

(5) A person who applies a registered trade mark to material intended to be used for labelling or packaging goods, as a business paper, or for advertising goods or services, shall be treated as a party to any use of the material which infringes the registered trade mark if when he applied the mark he knew or had reason to believe that the application of the mark was not duly authorised by the proprietor or a licensee.

(6) Nothing in the preceding provisions of this section shall be construed as preventing the use of a registered trade mark by any person for the purpose of identifying goods or services as those of the proprietor or a licensee.

    But any such use otherwise than in accordance with honest practices in industrial or commercial matters shall be treated as infringing the registered trade mark if the use without due cause takes unfair advantage of, or is detrimental to, the distinctive character or repute of the trade mark.

11   Limits on effect of registered trade mark

(1) A registered trade mark is not infringed by the use of another registered trade mark in relation to goods or services for which the latter is registered (but see section 47(6) (effect of declaration of invalidity of registration)).

(2) A registered trade mark is not infringed by—

    (a) the use by a person of his own name or address,

    (b) the use of indications concerning the kind, quality, quantity, intended purpose, value, geographical origin, the time of production of goods or of rendering of services, or other characteristics of goods or services, or

    (c) the use of the trade mark where it is necessary to indicate the intended purpose of a product or service (in particular, as accessories or spare parts), provided the use is in accordance with honest practices in industrial or commercial matters.

(3) A registered trade mark is not infringed by the use in the course of trade in a particular locality of an earlier right which applies only in that locality.

For this purpose an 'earlier right' means an unregistered trade mark or other sign continuously used in relation to goods or services by a person or a predecessor in title of his from a date prior to whichever is the earlier of—

(a) the use of the first-mentioned trade mark in relation to those goods or services by the proprietor or a predecessor in title of his, or

(b) the registration of the first-mentioned trade mark in respect of those goods or services in the name of the proprietor or a predecessor in title of his;

and an earlier right shall be regarded as applying in a locality if, or to the extent that, its use in that locality is protected by virtue of any rule of law (in particular, the law of passing off).

12 Exhaustion of rights conferred by registered trade mark

(1) A registered trade mark is not infringed by the use of the trade mark in relation to goods which have been put on the market in the European Economic Area under that trade mark by the proprietor or with his consent.

(2) Subsection (1) does not apply where there exist legitimate reasons for the proprietor to oppose further dealings in the goods (in particular, where the condition of the goods has been changed or impaired after they have been put on the market).

13 Registration subject to disclaimer or limitation

(1) An applicant for registration of a trade mark, or the proprietor of a registered trade mark, may—

(a) disclaim any right to the exclusive use of any specified element of the trade mark, or

(b) agree that the rights conferred by the registration shall be subject to a specified territorial or other limitation;

and where the registration of a trade mark is subject to a disclaimer or limitation, the rights conferred by section 9 (rights conferred by registered trade mark) are restricted accordingly.

(2) Provision shall be made by rules as to the publication and entry in the register of a disclaimer or limitation.

Infringement proceedings

14 Action for infringement

(1) An infringement of a registered trade mark is actionable by the proprietor of the trade mark.

(2) In an action for infringement all such relief by way of damages, injunctions, accounts or otherwise is available to him as is available in respect of the infringement of any other property right.

15 Order for erasure, etc. of offending sign

(1) Where a person is found to have infringed a registered trade mark, the court may make an order requiring him—

(a) to cause the offending sign to be erased, removed or obliterated from any infringing goods, material or articles in his possession, custody or control, or

(b) if it is not reasonably practicable for the offending sign to be erased, removed or obliterated, to secure the destruction of the infringing goods, material or articles in question.

(2) If an order under subsection (1) is not complied with, or it appears to the court likely that such an order would not be complied with, the court may order that the infringing goods, material or articles be delivered to such person as the court may direct for erasure, removal or obliteration of the sign, or for destruction, as the case may be.

16   Order for delivery up of infringing goods, material or articles

(1) The proprietor of a registered trade mark may apply to the court for an order for the delivery up to him, or such other person as the court may direct, of any infringing goods, material or articles which a person has in his possession, custody or control in the course of a business.

(2) An application shall not be made after the end of the period specified in section 18 (period after which remedy of delivery up not available); and no order shall be made unless the court also makes, or it appears to the court that there are grounds for making, an order under section 19 (order as to disposal of infringing goods, etc.).

(3) A person to whom any infringing goods, material or articles are delivered up in pursuance of an order under this section shall, if an order under section 19 is not made, retain them pending the making of an order, or the decision not to make an order, under that section.

(4) Nothing in this section affects any other power of the court.

17   Meaning of 'infringing goods, material or articles'

(1) In this Act the expressions 'infringing goods', 'infringing material' and 'infringing articles' shall be construed as follows.

(2) Goods are 'infringing goods', in relation to a registered trade mark, if they or their packaging bear a sign identical or similar to that mark and—

- (a) the application of the sign to the goods or their packaging was an infringement of the registered trade mark, or
- (b) the goods are proposed to be imported into the United Kingdom and the application of the sign in the United Kingdom to them or their packaging would be an infringement of the registered trade mark, or
- (c) the sign has otherwise been used in relation to the goods in such a way as to infringe the registered trade mark.

(3) Nothing in subsection (2) shall be construed as affecting the importation of goods which may lawfully be imported into the United Kingdom by virtue of an enforceable Community right.

(4) Material is 'infringing material', in relation to a registered trade mark if it bears a sign identical or similar to that mark and either—

- (a) it is used for labelling or packaging goods, as a business paper, or for advertising goods or services, in such a way as to infringe the registered trade mark, or
- (b) it is intended to be so used and such use would infringe the registered trade mark.

(5) 'Infringing articles', in relation to a registered trade mark, means articles—

- (a) which are specifically designed or adapted for making copies of a sign identical or similar to that mark, and

(b) which a person has in his possession, custody or control, knowing or having reason to believe that they have been or are to be used to produce infringing goods or material.

18 Period after which remedy of delivery up not available

(1) An application for an order under section 16 (order for delivery up of infringing goods, material or articles) may not be made after the end of the period of six years from—

    (a) in the case of infringing goods, the date on which the trade mark was applied to the goods or their packaging,

    (b) in the case of infringing material, the date on which the trade mark was applied to the material, or

    (c) in the case of infringing articles, the date on which they were made,

except as mentioned in the following provisions.

(2) If during the whole or part of that period the proprietor of the registered trade mark—

    (a) is under a disability, or

    (b) is prevented by fraud or concealment from discovering the facts entitling him to apply for an order,

an application may be made at any time before the end of the period of six years from the date on which he ceased to be under a disability or, as the case may be, could with reasonable diligence have discovered those facts.

(3) In subsection (2) 'disability'—

    (a) in England and Wales, has the same meaning as in the Limitation Act 1980;

    (b) in Scotland, means legal disability within the meaning of the Prescription and Limitation (Scotland) Act 1973;

    (c) in Northern Ireland, has the same meaning as in the Limitation (Northern Ireland) Order 1989.

19 Order as to disposal of infringing goods, material or articles

(1) Where infringing goods, material or articles have been delivered up in pursuance of an order under section 16, an application may be made to the court—

    (a) for an order that they be destroyed or forfeited to such person as the court may think fit, or

    (b) for a decision that no such order should be made.

(2) In considering what order (if any) should be made, the court shall consider whether other remedies available in an action for infringement of the registered trade mark would be adequate to compensate the proprietor and any licensee and protect their interests.

(3) Provision shall be made by rules of court as to the service of notice on persons having an interest in the goods, material or articles, and any such person is entitled—

    (a) to appear in proceedings for an order under this section, whether or not he was served with notice, and

    (b) to appeal against any order made, whether or not he appeared;

and an order shall not take effect until the end of the period within which notice of an appeal may be given or, if before the end of that period notice of appeal is duly given, until the final determination of abandonment of the proceedings on the appeal.

(4) Where there is more than one person interested in the goods, material or articles, the court shall make such order as it thinks just.

(5) If the court decides that no order should be made under this section, the person in whose possession, custody or control the goods, material or articles were before being delivered up is entitled to their return.

(6) References in this section to a person having an interest in goods, material or articles include any person in whose favour an order could be made under this section or under section 114, 204 or 231 of the Copyright, Designs and Patents Act 1988 (which make similar provision in relation to infringement of copyright, rights in performances and design right).

20   Jurisdiction of sheriff court or county court in Northern Ireland
Proceedings for an order under section 16 (order for delivery up of infringing goods, material or articles) or section 19 (order as to disposal of infringing goods, etc.) may be brought—

(a)   in the sheriff court in Scotland, or
(b)   in a county court in Northern Ireland.

This does not affect the jurisdiction of the Court of Session or the High Court in Northern Ireland.

21   Remedy for groundless threats of infringement proceedings
(1) Where a person threatens another with proceedings for infringement of a registered trade mark other than—

(a)   the application of the mark to goods or their packaging,
(b)   the importation of goods to which, or to the packaging of which, the mark has been applied, or
(c)   the supply of services under the mark,

any person aggrieved may bring proceedings for relief under this section.

(2) The relief which may be applied for is any of the following—

(a)   a declaration that the threats are unjustifiable,
(b)   an injunction against the continuance of the threats,
(c)   damages in respect of any loss he has sustained by the threats;

and the plaintiff is entitled to such relief unless the defendant shows that the acts in respect of which proceedings were threatened constitute (or if done would constitute) an infringement of the registered trade mark concerned.

(3) If that is shown by the defendant, the plaintiff is nevertheless entitled to relief if he shows that the registration of the trade mark is invalid or liable to be revoked in a relevant respect.

(4) The mere notification that a trade mark is registered, or that an application for registration has been made, does not constitute a threat of proceedings for the purposes of this section.

Registered trade mark as object of property

22   Nature of registered trade mark
A registered trade mark is personal property (in Scotland, incorporeal moveable property).

23   Co-ownership of registered trade mark
(1) Where a registered trade mark is granted to two or more persons jointly, each of them is entitled, subject to any agreement to the contrary, to an equal undivided share in the registered trade mark.

(2) The following provisions apply where two or more persons are co-proprietors of a registered trade mark, by virtue of subsection (1) or otherwise.

(3) Subject to any agreement to the contrary, each co-proprietor is entitled, by himself or his agents, to do for his own benefit and without the consent of or the need to account to the other or others, any act which would otherwise amount to an infringement of the registered trade mark.

(4) One co-proprietor may not without the consent of the other or others—

(a) grant a licence to use the registered trade mark, or

(b) assign or charge his share in the registered trade mark (or, in Scotland, cause or permit security to be granted over it).

(5) Infringement proceedings may be brought by any co-proprietor, but he may not, without the leave of the court, proceed with the action unless the other, or each of the others, is either joined as a plaintiff or added as a defendant.

A co-proprietor who is thus added as a defendant shall not be made liable for any costs in the action unless he takes part in the proceedings.

Nothing in this subsection affects the granting of interlocutory relief on the application of a single co-proprietor.

(6) Nothing in this section affects the mutual rights and obligations of trustees or personal representatives, or their rights and obligations as such.

24   Assignment, etc. of registered trade mark

(1) A registered trade mark is transmissible by assignment, testamentary disposition or operation of law in the same way as other personal or moveable property.

It is so transmissible either in connection with the goodwill of a business or independently.

(2) An assignment or other transmission of a registered trade mark may be partial, that is, limited so as to apply—

(a) in relation to some but not all of the goods or services for which the trade mark is registered, or

(b) in relation to use of the trade mark in a particular manner or a particular locality.

(3) An assignment of a registered trade mark, or an assent relating to a registered trade mark, is not effective unless it is in writing signed by or on behalf of the assignor or, as the case may be, a personal representative.

Except in Scotland, this requirement may be satisfied in a case where the assignor or personal representative is a body corporate by the affixing of its seal.

(4) The above provisions apply to assignment by way of security as in relation to any other assignment.

(5) A registered trade mark may be the subject of a charge (in Scotland, security) in the same way as other personal or moveable property.

(6) Nothing in this Act shall be construed as affecting the assignment or other transmission of an unregistered trade mark as part of the goodwill of a business.

25   Registration of transactions affecting registered trade mark

(1) On application being made to the registrar by—

(a) a person claiming to be entitled to an interest in or under a registered trade mark by virtue of a registrable transaction, or

(b) any other person claiming to be affected by such a transaction, the prescribed particulars of the transaction shall be entered in the register.

(2) The following are registrable transactions—

(a) an assignment of a registered trade mark or any right in it;

(b) the grant of a licence under a registered trade mark;

(c) the granting of any security interest (whether fixed or floating) over a registered trade mark or any right in or under it;

(d) the making by personal representatives of an assent in relation to a registered trade mark or any right in or under it;

(e) an order of a court or other competent authority transferring a registered trade mark or any right in or under it.

(3) Until an application has been made for registration of the prescribed particulars of a registrable transaction—

(a) the transaction is ineffective as against a person acquiring a conflicting interest in or under the registered trade mark in ignorance of it, and

(b) a person claiming to be a licensee by virtue of the transaction does not have the protection of section 30 or 31 (rights and remedies of licensee in relation to infringement).

(4) Where a person becomes the proprietor or a licensee of a registered trade mark by virtue of a registrable transaction, then unless—

(a) an application for registration of the prescribed particulars of the transaction is made before the end of the period of six months beginning with its date, or

(b) the court is satisfied that it was not practicable for such an application to be made before the end of that period and that an application was made as soon as practicable thereafter,

he is not entitled to damages or an account of profits in respect of any infringement of the registered trade mark occurring after the date of the transaction and before the prescribed particulars of the transaction are registered.

(5) Provision may be made by rules as to—

(a) the amendment of registered particulars relating to a licence so as to reflect any alteration of the terms of the licence, and

(b) the removal of such particulars from the register—

(i) where it appears from the registered particulars that the licence was granted for a fixed period and that period has expired, or

(ii) where no such period is indicated and, after such period as may be prescribed, the registrar has notified the parties of his intention to remove the particulars from the register.

(6) Provision may also be made by rules as to the amendment or removal from the register of particulars relating to a security interest on the application of, or with the consent of, the person entitled to the benefit of that interest.

26 Trusts and equities

(1) No notice of any trust (express, implied or constructive) shall be entered in the register; and the registrar shall not be affected by any such notice.

(2) Subject to the provisions of this Act, equities (in Scotland, rights) in respect of a registered trade mark may be enforced in like manner as in respect of other personal or moveable property.

27   Application for registration of trade mark as an object of property

(1) The provisions of sections 22 to 26 (which relate to a registered trade mark as an object of property) apply, with the necessary modifications, in relation to an application for the registration of a trade mark as in relation to a registered trade mark.

(2) In section 23 (co-ownership of registered trade mark) as it applies in relation to an application for registration the reference in subsection (1) to the granting of the registration shall be construed as a reference to the making of the application.

(3) In section 25 (registration of transactions affecting registered trade marks) as it applies in relation to a transaction affecting an application for the registration of a trade mark, the references to the entry of particulars in the register, and to the making of an application to register particulars, shall be construed as references to the giving of notice to the registrar of those particulars.

Licensing

28   Licensing of registered trade mark

(1) A licence to use a registered trade mark may be general or limited.

A limited licence may, in particular, apply—

   (a)   in relation to some but not all of the goods or services for which the trade mark is registered, or
   (b)   in relation to use of the trade mark in a particular manner or a particular locality.

(2) A licence is not effective unless it is in writing signed by or on behalf of the grantor.

Except in Scotland, this requirement may be satisfied in a case where the grantor is a body corporate by the affixing of its seal.

(3) Unless the licence provides otherwise, it is binding on a successor in title to the grantor's interest.

References in this Act to doing anything with, or without, the consent of the proprietor of a registered trade mark shall be construed accordingly.

(4) Where the licence so provides, a sub-licence may be granted by the licensee; and references in this Act to a licence or licensee include a sub-licence or sub-licensee.

29   Exclusive licences

(1) In this Act an 'exclusive licence' means a licence (whether general or limited) authorising the licensee to the exclusion of all other persons, including the person granting the licence, to use a registered trade mark in the manner authorised by the licence.

The expression 'exclusive licensee' shall be construed accordingly.

(2) An exclusive licensee has the same rights against a successor in title who is bound by the licence as he has against the person granting the licence.

30   General provisions as to rights of licensees in case of infringement

(1) This section has effect with respect to the rights of a licensee in relation to infringement of a registered trade mark.

The provisions of this section do not apply where or to the extent that, by virtue of section 31(1) below (exclusive licensee having rights and remedies of assignee), the licensee has a right to bring proceedings in his own name.

(2) A licensee is entitled, unless his licence, or any licence through which his interest is derived, provides otherwise, to call on the proprietor of the registered trade mark to take infringement proceedings in respect of any matter which affects his interests.

(3) If the proprietor—

(a) refuses to do so, or
(b) fails to do so within two months after being called upon,

the licensee may bring the proceedings in his own name as if he were the proprietor.

(4) Where infringement proceedings are brought by a licensee by virtue of this section, the licensee may not, without the leave of the court, proceed with the action unless the proprietor is either joined as a plaintiff or added as a defendant.

This does not affect the granting of interlocutory relief on an application by a licensee alone.

(5) A proprietor who is added as a defendant as mentioned in subsection (4) shall not be made liable for any costs in the action unless he takes part in the proceedings.

(6) In infringement proceedings brought by the proprietor of a registered trade mark any loss suffered or likely to be suffered by licensees shall be taken into account; and the court may give such directions as it thinks fit as to the extent to which the plaintiff is to hold the proceeds of any pecuniary remedy on behalf of licensees.

(7) The provisions of this section apply in relation to an exclusive licensee if or to the extent that he has, by virtue of section 31(1), the rights and remedies of an assignee as if he were the proprietor of the registered trade mark.

31   Exclusive licensee having rights and remedies of assignee

(1) An exclusive licence may provide that the licensee shall have, to such extent as may be provided by the licence, the same rights and remedies in respect of matters occurring after the grant of the licence as if the licence had been an assignment.

Where or to the extent that such provision is made, the licensee is entitled, subject to the provisions of the licence and to the following provisions of this section, to bring infringement proceedings, against any person other than the proprietor, in his own name.

(2) Any such rights and remedies of an exclusive licensee are concurrent with those of the proprietor of the registered trade mark; and references to the proprietor of a registered trade mark in the provisions of this Act relating to infringement shall be construed accordingly.

(3) In an action brought by an exclusive licensee by virtue of this section a defendant may avail himself of any defence which would have been available to him if the action had been brought by the proprietor of the registered trade mark.

(4) Where proceedings for infringement of a registered trade mark brought by the proprietor or an exclusive licensee relate wholly or partly to an infringement in respect of which they have concurrent rights of action, the proprietor or, as the case may be, the exclusive licensee may not, without the leave of the court, proceed with the action unless the other is either joined as a plaintiff or added as a defendant.

This does not affect the granting of interlocutory relief on an application by a proprietor or exclusive licensee alone.

(5) A person who is added as a defendant as mentioned in subsection (4) shall not be made liable for any costs in the action unless he takes part in the proceedings.

(6) Where an action for infringement of a registered trade mark is brought which relates wholly or partly to an infringement in respect of which the proprietor and an exclusive licensee have or had concurrent rights of action—

(a) the court shall in assessing damages take into account—

(i)   the terms of the licence, and

(ii)   any pecuniary remedy already awarded or available to either of them in respect of the infringement;

(b)   no account of profits shall be directed if an award of damages has been made, or an account of profits has been directed, in favour of the other of them in respect of the infringement; and

(c)   the court shall if an account of profits is directed apportion the profits between them as the court considers just, subject to any agreement between them.

The provisions of this subsection apply whether or not the proprietor and the exclusive licensee are both parties to the action; and if they are not both parties the court may give such directions as it thinks fit as to the extent to which the party to the proceedings is to hold the proceeds of any pecuniary remedy on behalf of the other.

(7) The proprietor of a registered trade mark shall notify any exclusive licensee who has a concurrent right of action before applying for an order under section 16 (order for delivery up); and the court may on the application of the licensee make such order under that section as it thinks fit having regard to the terms of the licence.

(8) The provisions of subsections (4) to (7) above have effect subject to any agreement to the contrary between the exclusive licensee and the proprietor.

Application for registered trade mark

32   Application for registration

(1) An application for registration of a trade mark shall be made to the registrar.

(2) The application shall contain—

(a)   a request for registration of a trade mark,

(b)   the name and address of the applicant,

(c)   a statement of the goods or services in relation to which it is sought to register the trade mark, and

(d)   a representation of the trade mark.

(3) The application shall state that the trade mark is being used, by the applicant or with his consent, in relation to those goods or services, or that he has a *bona fide* intention that it should be so used.

(4) The application shall be subject to the payment of the application fee and such class fees as may be appropriate.

33   Date of filing

(1) The date of filing of an application for registration of a trade mark is the date on which documents containing everything required by section 32(2) are furnished to the registrar by the applicant.

If the documents are furnished on different days, the date of filing is the last of those days.

(2) References in this Act to the date of application for registration are to the date of filing of the application.

34   Classification of trade marks

(1) Goods and services shall be classified for the purposes of the registration of trade marks according to a prescribed system of classification.

(2) Any question arising as to the class within which any goods or services fall shall be determined by the registrar, whose decision shall be final.

Priority

35   Claim to priority of Convention application

(1) A person who has duly filed an application for protection of a trade mark in a Convention country (a 'Convention application'), or his successor in title, has a right to priority, for the purposes of registering the same trade mark under this Act for some or all of the same goods or services, for a period of six months from the date of filing of the first such application.

(2) If the application for registration under this Act is made within that six-month period—

   (a) the relevant date for the purposes of establishing which rights take precedence shall be the date of filing of the first Convention application, and
   (b) the registrability of the trade mark shall not be affected by any use of the mark in the United Kingdom in the period between that date and the date of the application under this Act.

(3) Any filing which in a Convention country is equivalent to a regular national filing, under its domestic legislation or an international agreement, shall be treated as giving rise to the right of priority.

   A 'regular national filing' means a filing which is adequate to establish the date on which the application was filed in that country, whatever may be the subsequent fate of the application.

(4) A subsequent application concerning the same subject as the first Convention application, filed in the same Convention country, shall be considered the first Convention application (of which the filing date is the starting date of the period of priority), if at the time of the subsequent application—

   (a) the previous application has been withdrawn, abandoned or refused, without having been laid open to public inspection and without leaving any rights outstanding, and
   (b) it has not yet served as a basis for claiming a right of priority.

   The previous application may not thereafter serve as a basis for claiming a right of priority.

(5) Provision may be made by rules as to the manner of claiming a right to priority on the basis of a Convention application.

(6) A right to priority arising as a result of a Convention application may be assigned or otherwise transmitted, either with the application or independently.

   The reference in subsection (1) to the applicant's 'successor in title' shall be construed accordingly.

36   Claim to priority from other relevant overseas application

(1) Her Majesty may by Order in Council make provision for conferring on a person who has duly filed an application for protection of a trade mark in—

   (a) any of the Channel Islands or a colony, or
   (b) a country or territory in relation to which Her Majesty's Government in the United Kingdom have entered into a treaty, convention, arrangement or engagement for the reciprocal protection of trade marks,

a right to priority, for the purpose of registering the same trade mark under this Act for some or all of the same goods or services, for a specified period from the date of filing of that application.

(2) An Order in Council under this section may make provision corresponding to that made by

section 35 in relation to Convention countries or such other provision as appears to Her Majesty to be appropriate.

(3) A statutory instrument containing an Order in Council under this section shall be subject to annulment in pursuance of a resolution of either House of Parliament.

Registration procedure

37 Examination of application

(1) The registrar shall examine whether an application for registration of a trade mark satisfies the requirements of this Act (including any requirements imposed by rules).

(2) For that purpose he shall carry out a search, to such extent as he considers necessary, of earlier trade marks.

(3) If it appears to the registrar that the requirements for registration are not met, he shall inform the applicant and give him an opportunity, within such period as the registrar may specify, to make representations or to amend the application.

(4) If the applicant fails to satisfy the registrar that those requirements are met, or to amend the application so as to meet them, or fails to respond before the end of the specified period, the registrar shall refuse to accept the application.

(5) If it appears to the registrar that the requirements for registration are met, he shall accept the application.

38 Publication, opposition proceedings and observations

(1) When an application for registration has been accepted, the registrar shall cause the application to be published in the prescribed manner.

(2) Any person may, within the prescribed time from the date of the publication of the application, give notice to the registrar of opposition to the registration.

The notice shall be given in writing in the prescribed manner, and shall include a statement of the grounds of opposition.

(3) Where an application has been published, any person may, at any time before the registration of the trade mark, make observations in writing to the registrar as to whether the trade mark should be registered; and the registrar shall inform the applicant of any such observations.

A person who makes observations does not thereby become a party to the proceedings on the application.

39 Withdrawal, restriction or amendment of application

(1) The applicant may at any time withdraw his application or restrict the goods or services covered by the application.

If the application has been published, the withdrawal or restriction shall also be published.

(2) In other respects, an application may be amended, at the request of the applicant, only by correcting—

(a) the name or address of the applicant,
(b) errors of wording or of copying, or
(c) obvious mistakes,

and then only where the correction does not substantially affect the identity of the trade mark or extend the goods or services covered by the application.

(3) Provision shall be made by rules for the publication of any amendment which affects the representation of the trade mark, or the goods or services covered by the application, and for the making of objections by any person claiming to be affected by it.

40   Registration

(1) Where an application has been accepted and—

(a) no notice of opposition is given within the period referred to in section 38(2), or

(b) all opposition proceedings are withdrawn or decided in favour of the applicant,

the registrar shall register the trade mark, unless it appears to him having regard to matters coming to his notice since he accepted the application that it was accepted in error.

(2) A trade mark shall not be registered unless any fee prescribed for the registration is paid within the prescribed period.

If the fee is not paid within that period, the application shall be deemed to be withdrawn.

(3) A trade mark when registered shall be registered as of the date of filing of the application for registration; and that date shall be deemed for the purposes of this Act to be the date of registration.

(4) On the registration of a trade mark the registrar shall publish the registration in the prescribed manner and issue to the applicant a certificate of registration.

41   Registration: supplementary provisions

(1) Provision may be made by rules as to—

(a) the division of an application for the registration of a trade mark into several applications;

(b) the merging of separate applications or registrations;

(c) the registration of a series of trade marks.

(2) A series of trade marks means a number of trade marks which resemble each other as to their material particulars and differ only as to matters of a non-distinctive character not substantially affecting the identity of the trade mark.

(3) Rules under this section may include provision as to—

(a) the circumstances in which, and conditions subject to which, division, merger or registration of a series is permitted, and

(b) the purposes for which an application to which the rules apply is to be treated as a single application and those for which it is to be treated as a number of separate applications.

Duration, renewal and alteration of registered trade mark

42   Duration of registration

(1) A trade mark shall be registered for a period of ten years from the date of registration.

(2) Registration may be renewed in accordance with section 43 for further periods of ten years.

43   Renewal of registration

(1) The registration of a trade mark may be renewed at the request of the proprietor, subject to payment of a renewal fee.

(2) Provision shall be made by rules for the registrar to inform the proprietor of a registered trade mark, before the expiry of the registration, of the date of expiry and the manner in which the registration may be renewed.

(3) A request for renewal must be made, and the renewal fee paid, before the expiry of the registration.

Failing this, the request may be made and the fee paid within such further period (of not less than six months) as may be prescribed, in which case an additional renewal fee must also be paid within that period.

(4) Renewal shall take effect from the expiry of the previous registration.

(5) If the registration is not renewed in accordance with the above provisions, the register shall remove the trade mark from the register.

Provision may be made by rules for the restoration of the registration of a trade mark which has been removed from the register, subject to such conditions (if any) as may be prescribed.

(6) The renewal or restoration of the registration of a trade mark shall be published in the prescribed manner.

44 Alteration of registered trade mark
(1) A registered trade mark shall not be altered in the register, during the period of registration or on renewal.

(2) Nevertheless, the registrar may, at the request of the proprietor, allow the alteration of a registered trade mark where the mark includes the proprietor's name or address and the alteration is limited to alteration of that name or address and does not substantially affect the identity of the mark.

(3) Provision shall be made by rules for the publication of any such alteration and the making of objections by any person claiming to be affected by it.

Surrender, revocation and invalidity

45 Surrender of registered trade mark
(1) A registered trade mark may be surrendered by the proprietor in respect of some or all of the goods or services for which it is registered.

(2) Provision may be made by rules—

(a) as to the manner and effect of a surrender, and
(b) for protecting the interests of other persons having a right in the registered trade mark.

46 Revocation of registration
(1) The registration of a trade mark may be revoked on any of the following grounds—

(a) that within the period of five years following the date of completion of the registration procedure it has not been put to genuine use in the United Kingdom, by the proprietor or with his consent, in relation to the goods or services for which it is registered, and there are no proper reasons for non-use;
(b) that such use has been suspended for an uninterrupted period of five years, and there are no proper reasons for non-use;
(c) that, in consequence of acts or inactivity of the proprietor, it has become the common name in the trade for a product or service for which it is registered;
(d) that in consequence of the use made of it by the proprietor or with his consent in relation to the goods or services for which it is registered, it is liable to mislead the public, particularly as to the nature, quality or geographical origin of those goods or services.

(2) For the purposes of subsection (1) use of a trade mark includes use in a form differing in

elements which do not alter the distinctive character of the mark in the form in which it was registered, and use in the United Kingdom includes affixing the trade mark to goods or to the packaging of goods in the United Kingdom solely for export purposes.

(3) The registration of a trade mark shall not be revoked on the ground mentioned in subsection (1)(a) or (b) if such use as is referred to in that paragraph is commenced or resumed after the expiry of the five year period and before the application for revocation is made:

Provided that, any such commencement or resumption of use after the expiry of the five year period but within the period of three months before the making of the application shall be disregarded unless preparations for the commencement or resumption began before the proprietor became aware that the application might be made.

(4) An application for revocation may be made by any person, and may be made either to the registrar or to the court, except that—

(a) if proceedings concerning the trade mark in question are pending in the court, the application must be made to the court; and

(b) if in any other case the application is made to the registrar, he may at any stage of the proceedings refer the application to the court.

(5) Where grounds for revocation exist in respect of only some of the goods or services for which the trade mark is registered, revocation shall relate to those goods or services only.

(6) Where the registration of a trade mark is revoked to any extent, the rights of the proprietor shall be deemed to have ceased to that extent as from—

(a) the date of the application for revocation, or

(b) if the registrar or court is satisfied that the grounds for revocation existed at an earlier date, that date.

47 Grounds for invalidity of registration

(1) The registration of a trade mark may be declared invalid on the ground that the trade mark was registered in breach of section 3 or any of the provisions referred to in that section (absolute grounds for refusal of registration).

Where the trade mark was registered in breach of subsection (1)(b), (c) or (d) of that section, it shall not be declared invalid if, in consequence of the use which has been made of it, it has after registration acquired a distinctive character in relation to the goods or services for which it is registered.

(2) The registration of a trade mark may be declared invalid on the ground—

(a) that there is an earlier trade mark in relation to which the conditions set out in section 5(1), (2) or (3) obtain, or

(b) that there is an earlier right in relation to which the condition set out in section 5(4) is satisfied,

unless the proprietor of that earlier trade mark or other earlier right has consented to the registration.

(3) An application for a declaration of invalidity may be made by any person, and may be made either to the registrar or the court, except that—

(a) if proceedings concerning the trade mark in question are pending in the court, the application must be made to the court; and

(b) if in any other case the application is made to the registrar, he may at any stage of the proceedings refer the application to the court.

(4) In the case of bad faith in the registration of a trade mark, the registrar himself may apply to the court for a declaration of the invalidity of the registration.

(5) Where the grounds of invalidity exist in respect of only some of the goods or services for which the trade mark is registered, the trade mark shall be declared invalid as regards those goods or services only.

(6) Where the registration of a trade mark is declared invalid to any extent, the registration shall to that extent be deemed never to have been made:

Provided that this shall not affect transactions past and closed.

48   Effect of acquiescence

(1) Where the proprietor of an earlier trade mark or other earlier right has acquiesced for a continuous period of five years in the use of a registered trade mark in the United Kingdom, being aware of that use, there shall cease to be any entitlement on the basis of that earlier trade mark or other right—

(a)   to apply for a declaration that the registration of the later trade mark is invalid, or
(b)   to oppose the use of the later trade mark in relation to the goods or services in relation to which it has been so used,

unless the registration of the later trade mark was applied for in bad faith.

(2) Where subsection (1) applies, the proprietor of the later trade mark is not entitled to oppose the use of the earlier trade mark or, as the case may be, the exploitation of the earlier right, notwithstanding that the earlier trade mark or right may no longer be invoked against his later trade mark.

Collective marks

49   Collective marks

(1) A collective mark is a mark distinguishing the goods or services of members of the association which is the proprietor of the mark from those of other undertakings.

(2) The provisions of this Act apply to collective marks subject to the provisions of Schedule 1.

Certification marks

50   Certification marks

(1) A certification mark is a mark indicating that the goods or services in connection with which it is used are certified by the proprietor of the mark in respect of origin, material, mode of manufacture of goods or performance of services, quality, accuracy or other characteristics.

(2) The provisions of this Act apply to certification marks subject to the provisions of Schedule 2.

PART II

COMMUNITY TRADE MARKS AND INTERNATIONAL MATTERS

Community trade marks

51   Meaning of 'Community trade mark'

In this Act—

'Community trade mark' has the meaning given by Article 1(1) of the Community Trade Mark Regulation; and 'the Community Trade Mark Regulation' means Council Regulation (EC) No 40/94 of 20 December 1993 on the Community trade mark.

52 Power to make provision in connection with Community Trade Mark Regulation

(1) The Secretary of State may by regulations make such provision as he considers appropriate in connection with the operation of the Community Trade Mark Regulation.

(2) Provision may, in particular, be made with respect to—

   (a) the making of applications for Community trade marks by way of the Patent Office;

   (b) the procedures for determining *a posteriori* the invalidity, or liability to revocation, of the registration of a trade mark from which a Community trade mark claims seniority;

   (c) the conversion of a Community trade mark, or an application for a Community trade mark, into an application for registration under this Act;

   (d) the designation of courts in the United Kingdom having jurisdiction over proceedings arising out of the Community Trade Mark Regulation.

(3) Without prejudice to the generality of subsection (1), provision may be made by regulations under this section—

   (a) applying in relation to a Community trade mark the provisions of—

      (i)   section 21 (remedy for groundless threats of infringement proceedings);

      (ii)   sections 89 to 91 (importation of infringing goods, material or articles); and

      (iii) sections 92, 93, 95 and 96 (offences); and

   (b) making in relation to the list of professional representatives maintained in pursuance of Article 89 of the Community Trade Mark Regulation, and persons on that list, provision corresponding to that made by, or capable of being made under, sections 84 to 88 in relation to the register of trade mark agents and registered trade mark agents.

(4) Regulations under this section shall be made by statutory instrument which shall be subject to annulment in pursuance of a resolution of either House of Parliament.

The Madrid Protocol: international registration

53 The Madrid Protocol

In this Act—

   'the Madrid Protocol' means the Protocol relating to the Madrid Agreement concerning the International Registration of Marks, adopted at Madrid on 27 June 1989;

   'the International Bureau' has the meaning given by Article 2(1) of that Protocol; and

   'international trade mark (UK)' means a trade mark which is entitled to protection in the United Kingdom under that Protocol.

54 Power to make provision giving effect to Madrid Protocol

(1) The Secretary of State may by order make such provision as he thinks fit for giving effect in the United Kingdom to the provisions of the Madrid Protocol.

(2) Provision may, in particular, be made with respect to—

   (a) the making of applications for international registrations by way of the Patent Office as office of origin;

   (b) the procedures to be followed where the basic United Kingdom application or registration fails or ceases to be in force;

   (c) the procedures to be followed where the Patent Office receives from the International Bureau a request for extension of protection to the United Kingdom;

(d) the effects of a successful request for extension of protection to the United Kingdom;
(e) the transformation of an application for an international registration, or an international registration, into a national application for registration;
(f) the communication of information to the Information Bureau;
(g) the payment of fees and amounts prescribed in respect of applications for international registrations, extensions of protection and renewals.

(3) Without prejudice to the generality of subsection (1), provision may be made by regulations under this section applying in relation to an international trade mark (UK) the provisions of—

(a) section 21 (remedy for groundless threats of infringement proceedings);
(b) sections 89 to 91 (importation of infringing goods, material or articles); and
(c) sections 92, 93, 95 and 96 (offences).

(4) An order under this section shall be made by statutory instrument which shall be subject to annulment in pursuance of a resolution of either House of Parliament.

The Paris Convention: supplementary provisions

55   The Paris Convention

(1) In this Act—

(a) 'the Paris Convention' means the Paris Convention for the Protection of Industrial Property of March 20 1883, as revised or amended from time to time, and
(b) a 'Convention country' means a country, other than the United Kingdom, which is a party to that Convention.

(2) The Secretary of State may by order make such amendments of this Act, and rules made under this Act, as appear to him appropriate in consequence of any revision or amendment of the Paris Convention after the passing of this Act.

(3) Any such order shall be made by statutory instrument which shall be subject to annulment in pursuance of a resolution of either House of Parliament.

56   Protection of well-known trade marks: Article 6*bis*

(1) References in this Act to a trade mark which is entitled to protection under the Paris Convention as a well known trade mark are to a mark which is well-known in the United Kingdom as being the mark of a person who—

(a) is a national of a Convention country, or
(b) is domiciled in, or has a real and effective industrial or commercial establishment in, a Convention country,

whether or not that person carries on business, or has any goodwill, in the United Kingdom. References to the proprietor of such a mark shall be construed accordingly.

(2) The proprietor of a trade mark which is entitled to protection under the Paris Convention as a well known trade mark is entitled to restrain by injunction the use in the United Kingdom of a trade mark which, or the essential part of which, is identical or similar to his mark, in relation to identical or similar goods or services, where the use is likely to cause confusion.
This right is subject to section 48 (effect of acquiescence by proprietor of earlier trade mark).

(3) Nothing in subsection (2) affects the continuation of any *bona fide* use of a trade mark begun before the commencement of this section.

57   National emblems, etc. of Convention countries: Article 6*ter*

(1) A trade mark which consists of or contains the flag of a Convention country shall not be registered without the authorisation of the competent authorities of that country, unless it appears to the registrar that use of the flag in the manner proposed is permitted without such authorisation.

(2) A trade mark which consists of or contains the armorial bearings or any other state emblem of a Convention country which is protected under the Paris Convention shall not be registered without the authorisation of the competent authorities of that country.

(3) A trade mark which consists of or contains an official sign or hallmark adopted by a Convention country and indicating control and warranty shall not, where the sign or hallmark is protected under the Paris Convention, be registered in relation to goods or services of the same, or a similar kind, as those in relation to which it indicates control and warranty, without the authorisation of the competent authorities of the country concerned.

(4) The provisions of this section as to national flags and other state emblems, and official signs or hallmarks, apply equally to anything which from a heraldic point of view imitates any such flag or other emblem, or sign or hallmark.

(5) Nothing in this section prevents the registration of a trade mark on the application of a national of a country who is authorised to make use of a state emblem, or official sign or hallmark, of that country, notwithstanding that it is similar to that of another country.

(6) Where by virtue of this section the authorisation of the competent authorities of a Convention country is or would be required for the registration of a trade mark, those authorities are entitled to restrain by injunction any use of the mark in the United Kingdom without their authorisation.

58   Emblems, etc. of certain international organisations: Article 6*ter*

(1) This section applies to—

   (a)   the armorial bearings, flags or other emblems, and
   (b)   the abbreviations and names,

of international intergovernmental organisations of which one or more Convention countries are members.

(2) A trade mark which consists of or contains any such emblem, abbreviation or name which is protected under the Paris Convention shall not be registered without the authorisation of the international organisation concerned, unless it appears to the registrar that the use of the emblem, abbreviation or name in the manner proposed—

   (a)   is not such as to suggest to the public that a connection exists between the organisation and the trade mark, or
   (b)   is not likely to mislead the public as to the existence of a connection between the user and the organisation.

(3) The provisions of this section as to emblems of an international organisation apply equally to anything which from a heraldic point of view imitates any such emblem.

(4) Where by virtue of this section the authorisation of an international organisation is or would be required for the registration of a trade mark, that organisation is entitled to restrain by injunction any use of the mark in the United Kingdom without its authorisation.

(5) Nothing in this section affects the rights of a person whose *bona fide* use of the trade mark in

question began before 4 January 1962 (when the relevant provisions of the Paris Convention entered into force in relation to the United Kingdom).

59   Notification under Article 6*ter* of the Convention

(1) For the purposes of section 57 state emblems of a Convention country (other than the national flag), and official signs or hallmarks, shall be regarded as protected under the Paris Convention only if, or to the extent that—

(a) the country in question has notified the United Kingdom in accordance with Article 6*ter*(3) of the Convention that it desires to protect that emblem, sign or hallmark,

(b) the notification remains in force, and

(c) the United Kingdom has not objected to it in accordance with Article 6*ter*(4) or any such objection has been withdrawn.

(2) For the purposes of section 58 the emblems, abbreviations and names of an international organisation shall be regarded as protected under the Paris Convention only if, or to the extent that—

(a) the organisation in question has notified the United Kingdom in accordance with Article 6*ter*(3) of the Convention that it desires to protect that emblem, abbreviation or name,

(b) the notification remains in force, and

(c) the United Kingdom has not objected to it in accordance with Article 6*ter*(4) or any such objection has been withdrawn.

(3) Notification under Article 6*ter*(3) of the Paris Convention shall have effect only in relation to applications for registration made more than two months after the receipt of the notification.

(4) The registrar shall keep and make available for public inspection by any person, at all reasonable hours and free of charge, a list of—

(a) the state emblems and official signs or hallmarks, and

(b) the emblems, abbreviations and names of international organisations,

which are for the time being protected under the Paris Convention by virtue of notification under Article 6*ter*(3).

60   Acts of agent or representative: Article 6*septies*

(1) The following provisions apply where an application for registration of a trade mark is made by a person who is an agent or representative of a person who is the proprietor of the mark in a Convention country.

(2) If the proprietor opposes the application, registration shall be refused.

(3) If the application (not being so opposed) is granted, the proprietor may—

(a) apply for a declaration of the invalidity of the registration, or

(b) apply for the rectification of the register so as to substitute his name as the proprietor of the registered trade mark.

(4) The proprietor may (notwithstanding the rights conferred by this Act in relation to a registered trade mark) by injunction restrain any use of the trade mark in the United Kingdom which is not authorised by him.

(5) Subsections (2), (3) and (4) do not apply if, or to the extent that, the agent or representative justifies his action.

(6) An application under subsection (3)(a) or (b) must be made within three years of the

proprietor becoming aware of the registration; and no injunction shall be granted under subsection (4) in respect of a use in which the proprietor has acquiesced for a continuous period of three years or more.

Miscellaneous

61   Stamp duty

Stamp duty shall not be chargeable on an instrument relating to a Community trade mark or an international trade mark (UK), or an application for any such mark, by reason only of the fact that such a mark has legal effect in the United Kingdom.

PART III

ADMINISTRATIVE AND OTHER SUPPLEMENTARY PROVISIONS

The registrar

62   The registrar

In this Act 'the registrar' means the Comptroller-General of Patents, Designs and Trade Marks.

The register

63   The register

(1) The registrar shall maintain a register of trade marks.

References in this Act to 'the register' are to that register; and references to registration (in particular, in the expression 'registered trade mark') are, unless the context otherwise requires, to registration in that register.

(2) There shall be entered in the register in accordance with this Act—

  (a)   registered trade marks,
  (b)   such particulars as may be prescribed of registrable transactions affecting a registered trade mark, and
  (c)   such other matters relating to registered trade marks as may be prescribed.

(3) The register shall be kept in such manner as may be prescribed, and provision shall in particular be made for—

  (a)   public inspection of the register, and
  (b)   the supply of certified or uncertified copies, or extracts, of entries in the register.

64   Rectification or correction of the register

(1) Any person having a sufficient interest may apply for the rectification of an error or omission in the register:

  Provided that an application for rectification may not be made in respect of a matter affecting the validity of the registration of a trade mark.

(2) An application for rectification may be made either to the registrar or to the court, except that—

  (a)   if proceedings concerning the trade mark in question are pending in the court, the application must be made to the court; and
  (b)   if in any other case the application is made to the registrar, he may at any stage of the proceedings refer the application to the court.

(3) Except where the registrar or the court directs otherwise, the effect of rectification of the register is that the error or omission in question shall be deemed never to have been made.

(4) The registrar may, on request made in the prescribed manner by the proprietor of a registered trade mark, or a licensee, enter any change in his name or address as recorded in the register.

(5) The registrar may remove from the register matter appearing to him to have ceased to have effect.

65   Adaptation of entries to new classification

(1) Provision may be made by rules empowering the registrar to do such things as he considers necessary to implement any amended or substituted classification of goods or services for the purposes of the registration of trade marks.

(2) Provision may in particular be made for the amendment of existing entries on the register so as to accord with the new classification.

(3) Any such power of amendment shall not be exercised so as to extend the rights conferred by the registration, except where it appears to the registrar that compliance with this requirement would involve undue complexity and that any extension would not be substantial and would not adversely affect the rights of any person.

(4) The rules may empower the registrar—

  (a) to require the proprietor of a registered trade mark, within such time as may be prescribed, to file a proposal for amendment of the register, and
  (b) to cancel or refuse to renew the registration of the trade mark in the event of his failing to do so.

(5) Any such proposal shall be advertised, and may be opposed, in such manner as may be prescribed.

Powers and duties of the registrar

66   Power to require use of forms

(1) The registrar may require the use of such forms as he may direct for any purpose relating to the registration of a trade mark or any other proceeding before him under this Act.

(2) The forms, and any directions of the registrar with respect to their use, shall be published in the prescribed manner.

67   Information about applications and registered trade marks

(1) After publication of an application for registration of a trade mark, the registrar shall on request provide a person with such information and permit him to inspect such documents relating to the application, or to any registered trade mark resulting from it, as may be specified in the request, subject, however, to any prescribed restrictions.

  Any request must be made in the prescribed manner and be accompanied by the appropriate fee (if any).

(2) Before publication of an application for registration of a trade mark, documents or information constituting or relating to the application shall not be published by the registrar or communicated by him to any person except—

  (a) in such cases and to such extent as may be prescribed, or
  (b) with the consent of the applicant;

but subject as follows.

(3) Where a person has been notified that an application for registration of a trade mark has

been made, and that the applicant will if the application is granted bring proceedings against him in respect of acts done after publication of the application, he may make a request under subsection (1) notwithstanding that the application has not been published and that subsection shall apply accordingly.

68 Costs and security for costs

(1) Provision may be made by rules empowering the registrar, in any proceedings before him under this Act—

    (a) to award any party such costs as he may consider reasonable, and

    (b) to direct how and by what parties they are to be paid.

(2) Any such order of the registrar may be enforced—

    (a) in England and Wales or Northern Ireland, in the same way as an order of the High Court;

    (b) in Scotland, in the same way as a decree for expenses granted by the Court of Session.

(3) Provision may be made by rules empowering the registrar, in such cases as may be prescribed, to require a party to proceedings before him to give security for costs, in relation to those proceedings or to proceedings on appeal, and as to the consequences if security is not given.

69 Evidence before registrar

Provision may be made by rules—

    (a) as to the giving of evidence in proceedings before the registrar under this Act by affidavit or statutory declaration;

    (b) conferring on the registrar the powers of an official referee of the Supreme Court as regards the examination of witnesses on oath and the discovery and production of documents; and

    (c) applying in relation to the attendance of witnesses in proceedings before the registrar the rules applicable to the attendance of witnesses before such a referee.

70 Exclusion of liability in respect of official acts

(1) The registrar shall not be taken to warrant the validity of the registration of a trade mark under this Act or under any treaty, convention, arrangement or engagement to which the United Kingdom is a party.

(2) The registrar is not subject to any liability by reason of, or in connection with, any examination required or authorised by this Act, or any such treaty, convention, arrangement or engagement, or any report or other proceedings consequent on such examination.

(3) No proceedings lie against an officer of the registrar in respect of any matter for which, by virtue of this section, the registrar is not liable.

71 Registrar's annual report

(1) The Comptroller-General of Patents, Designs and Trade Marks shall in his annual report under section 121 of the Patents Act 1977, include a report on the execution of this Act, including the discharge of his functions under the Madrid Protocol.

(2) The report shall include an account of all money received and paid by him under or by virtue of this Act.

Legal proceedings and appeals

72 Registration to be *prima facie* evidence of validity

In all legal proceedings relating to a registered trade mark (including proceedings for rectification of the register) the registration of a person as proprietor of a trade mark shall be prima facie evidence of the validity of the original registration and of any subsequent assignment or other transmission of it.

73 Certificate of validity of contested registration

(1) If in proceedings before the court the validity of the registration of a trade mark is contested and it is found by the court that the trade mark is validly registered, the court may give a certificate to that effect.

(2) If the court gives such a certificate and in subsequent proceedings—

(a) the validity of the registration is again questioned, and
(b) the proprietor obtains a final order or judgment in his favour,

he is entitled to his costs as between solicitor and client unless the court directs otherwise.
    This subsection does not extend to the costs of an appeal in any such proceedings.

74 Registrar's appearance in proceedings involving the register

(1) In proceedings before the court involving an application for—

(a) the revocation of the registration of a trade mark,
(b) a declaration of the invalidity of the registration of a trade mark, or
(c) the rectification of the register,

the registrar is entitled to appear and be heard, and shall appear if so directed by the court.

(2) Unless otherwise directed by the court, the registrar may instead of appearing submit to the court a statement in writing signed by him, giving particulars of—

(a) any proceedings before him in relation to the matter in issue,
(b) the grounds of any decision given by him affecting it,
(c) the practice of the Patent Office in like cases, or
(d) such matters relevant to the issues and within his knowledge as registrar as he thinks fit;

and the statement shall be deemed to form part of the evidence in the proceedings.

(3) Anything which the registrar is or may be authorised or required to do under this section may be done on his behalf by a duly authorised officer.

75 The court

In this Act, unless the context otherwise requires, 'the court' means—

(a) in England and Wales and Northern Ireland, the Hight Court, and
(b) in Scotland, the Court of Session.

76 Appeals from the registrar

(1) An appeal lies from any decision of the registrar under this Act, except as otherwise expressly provided by rules.
    For this purpose 'decision' includes any act of the registrar in exercise of a discretion vested in him by or under this Act.

(2) Any such appeal may be brought either to an appointed person or to the court.

(3) Where an appeal is made to an appointed person, he may refer the appeal to the court if—

  (a) it appears to him that a point of general legal importance is involved,
  (b) the registrar requests that it be so referred, or
  (c) such a request is made by any party to the proceedings before the registrar in which the decision appealed against was made.

Before doing so the appointed person shall give the appellant and any other party to the appeal an opportunity to make representations as to whether the appeal should be referred to the court.

(4) Where an appeal is made to an appointed person and he does not refer it to the court, he shall hear and determine the appeal and his decision shall be final.

(5) The provisions of sections 68 and 69 (costs and security for costs; evidence) apply in relation to proceedings before an appointed person as in relation to proceedings before the registrar.

77   Persons appointed to hear and determine appeals

(1) For the purposes of section 76 an 'appointed person' means a person appointed by the Lord Chancellor to hear and decide appeals under this Act.

(2) A person is not eligible for such appointment unless—

  (a) he has a 7 year general qualification, within the meaning of section 71 of the Courts and Legal Services Act 1990;
  (b) he is an advocate or solicitor in Scotland of at least 7 years' standing;
  (c) he is a member of the Bar of Northern Ireland or solicitor of the Supreme Court of Northern Ireland of at least 7 years' standing; or
  (d) he has held judicial office.

(3) An appointed person shall hold and vacate office in accordance with his terms of appointment, subject to the following provisions—

  (a) there shall be paid to him such remuneration (whether by way of salary or fees), and such allowances, as the Secretary of State with the approval of the Treasury may determine;
  (b) he may resign his office by notice in writing to the Lord Chancellor;
  (c) the Lord Chancellor may by notice in writing remove him from office if—
     (i)   he has become bankrupt or made an arrangement with his creditors or, in Scotland, his estate has been sequestrated or he has executed a trust deed for his creditors or entered into a composition contract, or
     (ii) he is incapacitated by physical or mental illness, or if he is in the opinion of the Lord Chancellor otherwise unable or unfit to perform his duties as an appointed person.

(4) The Lord Chancellor shall consult the Lord Advocate before exercising his powers under this section.

Rules, fees, hours of business, etc.

78   Power of Secretary of State to make rules

(1) The Secretary of State may make rules—

  (a) for the purposes of any provision of this Act authorising the making of rules with respect to any matter, and
  (b) for prescribing anything authorised or required by any provision of this Act to be prescribed,

and generally for regulating practice and procedure under this Act.

(2) Provision may, in particular, be made—

    (a) as to the manner of filing of applications and other documents;

    (b) requiring and regulating the translation of documents and the filing and authentication of any translation;

    (c) as to the service of documents;

    (d) authorising the rectification of irregularities of procedure;

    (e) prescribing time limits for anything required to be done in connection with any proceeding under this Act;

    (f) providing for the extension of any time limit so prescribed, or specified by the registrar, whether or not it has already expired.

(3) Rules under this Act shall be made by statutory instrument which shall be subject to annulment in pursuance of a resolution of either House of Parliament.

79 Fees

(1) There shall be paid in respect of applications and registration and other matters under this Act such fees as may be prescribed.

(2) Provision may be made by rules as to—

    (a) the payment of a single fee in respect of two or more matters, and

    (b) the circumstances (if any) in which a fee may be repaid or remitted.

80 Hours of business and business days

(1) The registrar may give directions specifying the hours of business of the Patent Office for the purpose of the transaction by the public of business under this Act, and the days which are business days for that purpose.

(2) Business done on any day after the specified hours of business, or on a day which is not a business day, shall be deemed to have been done on the next business day; and where the time for doing anything under this Act expires on a day which is not a business day, that time shall be extended to the next business day.

(3) Directions under this section may make different provision for different classes of business and shall be published in the prescribed manner.

81 The trade marks journal

Provision shall be made by rules for the publication by the registrar of a journal containing particulars of any application for the registration of a trade mark (including a representation of the mark) and such other information relating to trade marks as the registrar thinks fit.

Trade mark agents

82 Recognition of agents

Except as otherwise provided by rules, any act required or authorised by this Act to be done by or to a person in connection with the registration of a trade mark, or any procedure relating to a registered trade mark, may be done by or to an agent authorised by that person orally or in writing.

83 The register of trade mark agents

(1) The Secretary of State may make rules requiring the keeping of a register of persons who act as agent for others for the purpose of applying for or obtaining the registration of trade marks;

and in this Act a 'registered trade mark agent' means a person whose name is entered in the register kept under this section.

(2) The rules may contain such provision as the Secretary of State thinks fit regulating the registration of persons, and may in particular—

  (a) require the payment of such fees as may be prescribed, and
  (b) authorise in prescribed cases the erasure from the register of the name of any person registered in it, or the suspension of a person's registration.

(3) The rules may delegate the keeping of the register to another person, and may confer on that person—

  (a) power to make regulations—
      (i)   with respect to the payment of fees, in the cases and subject to the limits prescribed by the rules, and
      (ii) with respect to any other matter which could be regulated by the rules, and
  (b) such other functions, including disciplinary functions, as may be prescribed by the rules.

84   Unregistered persons not to be described as registered trade mark agents

(1) An individual who is not a registered trade mark agent shall not—

  (a) carry on a business (otherwise than in partnership) under any name or other description which contains the words 'registered trade mark agent'; or
  (b) in the course of a business otherwise describe or hold himself out, or permit himself to be described or held out, as a registered trade mark agent.

(2) A partnership shall not—

  (a) carry on a business under any name or other description which contains the words 'registered trade mark agent'; or
  (b) in the course of a business otherwise describe or hold itself out, or permit itself to be described or held out, as a firm of registered trade mark agents,

unless all the partners are registered trade mark agents or the partnership satisfies such conditions as may be prescribed for the purposes of this section.

(3) A body corporate shall not—

  (a) carry on a business (otherwise than in partnership) under any name or other description which contains the words 'registered trade mark agent'; or
  (b) in the course of a business otherwise describe or hold itself out, or permit itself to be described or held out, as a registered trade mark agent,

unless all the directors of the body corporate are registered trade mark agents or the body satisfies such conditions as may be prescribed for the purposes of this section.

(4) A person who contravenes this section commits an offence and is liable on summary conviction to a fine not exceeding level 5 on the standard scale; and proceedings for such an offence may be begun at any time within a year from the date of the offence.

85   Power to prescribe conditions, etc. for mixed partnerships and bodies corporate

(1) The Secretary of State may make rules prescribing the conditions to be satisfied for the purposes of section 84 (persons entitled to be described as registered trade mark agents)—

  (a) in relation to a partnership where not all the partners are qualified persons, or

(b) in relation to a body corporate where not all the directors are qualified persons,

and imposing requirements to be complied with by such partnerships or bodies corporate.

(2) The rules may, in particular—

(a) prescribe conditions as to the number or proportion of partners or directors who must be qualified persons;
(b) impose requirements as to—
    (i) the identification of qualified and unqualified persons in professional advertisements, circulars or letters issued by or with the consent of the partnership or body corporate and which relate to its business, and
    (ii) the manner in which a partnership or body corporate is to organise its affairs so as to secure that qualified persons exercise a sufficient degree of control over the activities of unqualified persons.

(3) Contravention of a requirement imposed by the rules is an offence for which a person is liable on summary conviction to a fine not exceeding level 5 on the standard scale.

(4) In this section 'qualified person' means a registered trade mark agent.

86 Use of the term 'trade mark attorney'

(1) No offence is committed under the enactments restricting the use of certain expressions in reference to persons not qualified to act as solicitors by the use of the term 'trade mark attorney' in reference to a registered trade mark agent.

(2) The enactments referred to in subsection (1) are section 21 of the Solicitors Act 1974, section 31 of the Solicitors (Scotland) Act 1980 and Article 22 of the Solicitors (Northern Ireland) Order 1976.

87 Privilege for communications with registered trade mark agents

(1) This section applies to communications as to any matter relating to the protection of any design or trade mark, or as to any matter involving passing off.

(2) Any such communication—

(a) between a person and his trade mark agent, or
(b) for the purpose of obtaining, or in response to a request for, information which a person is seeking for the purpose of instructing his trade mark agent,

is privileged from, or in Scotland protected against, disclosure in legal proceedings in the same way as a communication between a person and his solicitor or, as the case may be, a communication for the purpose of obtaining, or in response to a request for, information which a person is seeking for the purpose of instructing his solicitor.

(3) In subsection (2) 'trade mark agent' means—

(a) a registered trade mark agent, or
(b) a partnership entitled to describe itself as a firm of registered trade mark agents, or
(c) a body corporate entitled to describe itself as a registered trade mark agent.

88 Power of registrar to refuse to deal with certain agents

(1) The Secretary of State may make rules authorising the registrar to refuse to recognise as agent in respect of any business under this Act—

(a) a person who has been convicted of an offence under section 84 (unregistered persons describing themselves as registered trade mark agents);

(b) an individual whose name has been erased from and not restored to, or who is suspended from, the register of trade mark agents on the ground of misconduct;

(c) a person who is found by the Secretary of State to have been guilty of such conduct as would, in the case of an individual registered in the register of trade mark agents, render him liable to have his name erased from the register on the ground of misconduct;

(d) a partnership or body corporate of which one of the partners or directors is a person whom the registrar could refuse to recognise under paragraph (a), (b) or (c) above.

(2) The rules may contain such incidental and supplementary provisions as appear to the Secretary of State to be appropriate and may, in particular, prescribe circumstances in which a person is or is not to be taken to have been guilty of misconduct.

Importation of infringing goods, material or articles

89   Infringing goods, material or articles may be treated as prohibited goods

(1) The proprietor of a registered trade mark, or a licensee, may give notice in writing to the Commissioners of Customs and Excise—

(a) that he is the proprietor or, as the case may be, a licensee of the registered trade mark,

(b) that, at a time and place specified in the notice, goods which are, in relation to that registered trade mark, infringing goods, material or articles are expected to arrive in the United Kingdom—
  (i)   from outside the European Economic Area, or
  (ii) from within that Area but not having been entered for free circulation, and

(c) that he requests the Commissioners to treat them as prohibited goods.

(2) When a notice is in force under this section the importation of the goods to which the notice relates, otherwise than by a person for his private and domestic use, is prohibited; but a person is not by reason of the prohibition liable to any penalty other than forfeiture of the goods.

(3) This section does not apply to goods entered, or expected to be entered, for free circulation in respect of which the proprietor of the registered trade mark, or a licensee, is entitled to lodge an application under Article 3(1) of Council Regulation (EEC) No 3842/86 laying down measures to prohibit the release for free circulation of counterfeit goods.

90   Power of Commissioners of Customs and Excise to make regulations

(1) The Commissioners of Customs and Excise may make regulations prescribing the form in which notice is to be given under section 89 and requiring a person giving notice—

(a) to furnish the Commissioners with such evidence as may be specified in the regulations, either on giving notice or when the goods are imported, or at both those times, and

(b) to comply with such other conditions as may be specified in the regulations.

(2) The regulations may, in particular, require a person giving such a notice—

(a) to pay such fees in respect of the notice as may be specified by the regulations;

(b) to give such security as may be so specified in respect of any liability or expense which the Commissioners may incur in consequence of the notice by reason of the detention of any goods or anything done to goods detained;

(c) to indemnify the Commissioners against any such liability or expense, whether security has been given or not.

(3) The regulations may make different provision as respects different classes of case to which they apply and may include such incidental and supplementary provisions as the Commissioners consider expedient.

(4) Regulations under this section shall be made by statutory instrument which shall be subject to annulment in pursuance of a resolution of either House of Parliament.

(5) Section 17 of the Customs and Excise Management Act 1979 (general provisions as to Commissioners' receipts) applies to fees paid in pursuance of regulations under this section as to receipts under the enactments relating to customs and excise.

91 Power of Commissioners of Customs and Excise to disclose information

Where information relating to infringing goods, material or articles has been obtained by the Commissioners of Customs and Excise for the purposes of, or in connection with, the exercise of their functions in relation to imported goods, the Commissioners may authorise the disclosure of that information for the purpose of facilitating the exercise by any person of any function in connection with the investigation or prosecution of an offence under section 92 below (unauthorised use of trade mark, etc. in relation to goods) or under the Trade Descriptions Act 1968.

Offences

92 Unauthorised use of trade mark, etc. in relation to goods

(1) A person commits an offence who with a view to gain for himself or another, or with intent to cause loss to another, and without the consent of the proprietor—

   (a) applies to goods or their packaging a sign identical to, or likely to be mistaken for, a registered trade mark, or
   (b) sells or lets for hire, offers or exposes for sale or hire or distributes goods which bear, or the packaging of which bears, such a sign, or
   (c) has in his possession, custody or control in the course of a business any such goods with a view to the doing of anything, by himself or another, which would be an offence under paragraph (b).

(2) A person commits an offence who with a view to gain for himself or another, or with intent to cause loss to another, and without the consent of the proprietor—

   (a) applies a sign identical to, or likely to be mistaken for, a registered trade mark to material intended to be used—
      (i) for labelling or packaging goods,
      (ii) as a business paper in relation to goods, or
      (iii) for advertising goods, or
   (b) uses in the course of a business material bearing such a sign for labelling or packaging goods, as a business paper in relation to goods, or for advertising goods, or
   (c) has in his possession, custody or control in the course of a business any such material with a view to the doing of anything, by himself or another, which would be an offence under paragraph (b).

(3) A person commits an offence who with a view to gain for himself or another, or with intent to cause loss to another, and without the consent of the proprietor—

   (a) makes an article specifically designed or adapted for making copies of a sign identical to, or likely to be mistaken for, a registered trade mark, or
   (b) has such an article in his possession, custody or control in the course of a business,

knowing or having reason to believe that it has been, or is to be, used to produce goods, or material for labelling or packaging goods, as a business paper in relation to goods, or for advertising goods.

(4) A person does not commit an offence under this section unless—

- (a) the goods are goods in respect of which the trade mark is registered, or
- (b) the trade mark has a reputation in the United Kingdom and the use of the sign takes or would take unfair advantage of, or is or would be detrimental to, the distinctive character or the repute of the trade mark.

(5) It is a defence for a person charged with an offence under this section to show that he believed on reasonable grounds that the use of the sign in the manner in which it was used, or was to be used, was not an infringement of the registered trade mark.

(6) A person guilty of an offence under this section is liable—

- (a) on summary conviction to imprisonment for a term not exceeding six months or a fine not exceeding the statutory maximum, or both;
- (b) on conviction on indictment to a fine or imprisonment for a term not exceeding ten years, or both.

93   Enforcement function of local weights and measures authority

(1) It is the duty of every local weights and measures authority to enforce within their area the provisions of section 92 (unauthorised use of trade mark, etc. in relation to goods).

(2) The following provisions of the Trade Descriptions Act 1968 apply in relation to the enforcement of that section as in relation to the enforcement of that Act—

section 27 (power to make test purchases),
section 28 (power to enter premises and inspect and seize goods and documents),
section 29 (obstruction of authorised officers), and
section 33 (compensation for loss, etc. of goods seized).

(3) Subsection (1) above does not apply in relation to the enforcement of section 92 in Northern Ireland, but it is the duty of the Department of Economic Development to enforce that section in Northern Ireland.

For that purpose the provisions of the Trade Descriptions Act 1968 specified in subsection (2) apply as if for the references to a local weights and measures authority and any officer of such an authority there were substituted references to that Department and any of its officers.

(4) Any enactment which authorises the disclosure of information for the purpose of facilitating the enforcement of the Trade Descriptions Act 1968 shall apply as if section 92 above were contained in that Act and as if the functions of any person in relation to the enforcement of that section were functions under that Act.

(5) Nothing in this section shall be construed as authorising a local weights and measures authority to bring proceedings in Scotland for an offence.

94   Falsification of register, etc.

(1) It is an offence for a person to make, or cause to be made, a false entry in the register of trade marks, knowing or having reason to believe that it is false.

(2) It is an offence for a person—

- (a) to make or cause to be made anything falsely purporting to be a copy of an entry in the register, or
- (b) to produce or tender or cause to be produced or tendered in evidence any such thing,

knowing or having reason to believe that it is false.

(3) A person guilty of an offence under this section is liable—

(a) on conviction on indictment, to imprisonment for a term not exceeding two years or a fine, or both;

(b) on summary conviction, to imprisonment for a term not exceeding six months or a fine not exceeding the statutory maximum, or both.

95 Falsely representing trade mark as registered

(1) It is an offence for a person—

(a) falsely to represent that a mark is a registered trade mark, or

(b) to make a false representation as to the goods or services for which a trade mark is registered

knowing or having reason to believe that the representation is false.

(2) For the purposes of this section, the use in the United Kingdom in relation to a trade mark—

(a) of the word 'registered', or

(b) of any other word or symbol importing a reference (express or implied) to registration,

shall be deemed to be a representation as to registration under this Act unless it is shown that the reference is to registration elsewhere than in the United Kingdom and that the trade mark is in fact so registered for the goods or services in question.

(3) A person guilty of an offence under this section is liable on summary conviction to a fine not exceeding level 3 on the standard scale.

96 Supplementary provisions as to summary proceedings in Scotland

(1) Notwithstanding anything in section 331 of the Criminal Procedure (Scotland) Act 1975, summary proceedings in Scotland for an offence under this Act may be begun at any time within six months after the date on which evidence sufficient in the Lord Advocate's opinion to justify the proceedings came to his knowledge.

For this purpose a certificate of the Lord Advocate as to the date on which such evidence came to his knowledge is conclusive evidence.

(2) For the purposes of subsection (1) and of any other provision of this Act as to the time within which summary proceedings for an offence may be brought, proceedings in Scotland shall be deemed to be begun on the date on which a warrant to apprehend or to cite the accused is granted, if such warrant is executed without undue delay.

Forfeiture of counterfeit goods, etc.

97 Forfeiture: England and Wales or Northern Ireland

(1) In England and Wales or Northern Ireland where there has come into the possession of any person in connection with the investigation or prosecution of a relevant offence—

(a) goods which, or the packaging of which, bears a sign identical to or likely to be mistaken for a registered trade mark,

(b) material bearing such a sign and intended to be used for labelling or packaging goods, as a business paper in relation to goods, or for advertising goods, or

(c) articles specifically designed or adapted for making copies of such a sign,

that person may apply under this section for an order for the forfeiture of the goods, material or articles.

(2) An application under this section may be made—

(a) where proceedings have been brought in any court for a relevant offence relating to some or all of the goods, material or articles, to that court;

(b) where no application for the forfeiture of the goods, material or articles has been made under paragraph (a), by way of complaint to a magistrates' court.

(3) On an application under this section the court shall make an order for the forfeiture of any goods, material or articles only if it is satisfied that a relevant offence has been committed in relation to the goods, material or articles.

(4) A court may infer for the purposes of this section that such an offence has been committed in relation to any goods, material or articles if it is satisfied that such an offence has been committed in relation to goods, material or articles which are representative of them (whether by reason of being of the same design or part of the same consignment or batch or otherwise).

(5) Any person aggrieved by an order made under this section by a magistrates' court, or by a decision of such a court not to make such an order, may appeal against that order or decision—

(a) in England and Wales, to the Crown Court;

(b) in Northern Ireland, to the county court;

and an order so made may contain such provision as appears to the court to be appropriate for delaying the coming into force of the order pending the making and determination of any appeal (including any application under section 111 of the Magistrates' Courts Act 1980 or Article 146 of the Magistrates' Courts (Northern Ireland) Order 1981 (statement of case)).

(6) Subject to subsection (7), where any goods, material or articles are forfeited under this section they shall be destroyed in accordance with such directions as the court may give.

(7) On making an order under this section the court may, if it considers it appropriate to do so, direct that the goods, material or articles to which the order relates shall (instead of being destroyed) be released, to such person as the court may specify, on condition that that person—

(a) causes the offending sign to be erased, removed or obliterated, and

(b) complies with any order to pay costs which has been made against him in the proceedings for the order for forfeiture.

(8) For the purposes of this section a 'relevant offence' means an offence under section 92 above (unauthorised use of trade mark, etc. in relation to goods) or under the Trade Descriptions Act 1968 or any offence involving dishonesty or deception.

98 Forfeiture: Scotland

(1) In Scotland the court may make an order for the forfeiture of any—

(a) goods which bear, or the packaging of which bears, a sign identical to or likely to be mistaken for a registered trade mark,

(b) material bearing such a sign and intended to be used for labelling or packaging goods, as a business paper in relation to goods, or for advertising goods, or

(c) articles specifically designed or adapted for making copies of such a sign.

(2) An order under this section may be made—

(a) on an application by the procurator-fiscal made in the manner specified in section 310 of the Criminal Procedure (Scotland) Act 1975, or

(b) where a person is convicted of a relevant offence, in addition to any other penalty which the court may impose.

(3) On an application under subsection (2)(a), the court shall make an order for the forfeiture of

any goods, material or articles only if it is satisfied that a relevant offence has been committed in relation to the goods, material or articles.

(4) The court may infer for the purposes of this section that such an offence has been committed in relation to any goods, material or articles if it is satisfied that such an offence has been committed in relation to goods, material or articles which are representative of them (whether by reason of being of the same design or part of the same consignment or batch or otherwise).

(5) The procurator-fiscal making the application under subsection (2)(a) shall serve on any person appearing to him to be the owner of, or otherwise to have an interest in, the goods, material or articles to which the application relates a copy of the application, together with a notice giving him the opportunity to appear at the hearing of the application to show cause why the goods, material or articles should not be forfeited.

(6) Service under subsection (5) shall be carried out, and such service may be proved, in the manner specified for citation of an accused in summary proceedings under the Criminal Procedure (Scotland) Act 1975.

(7) Any person upon whom notice is served under subsection (5) and any other person claiming to be the owner of, or otherwise to have an interest in, goods, material or articles to which an application under this section relates shall be entitled to appear at the hearing of the application to show cause why the goods, material or articles should not be forfeited.

(8) The court shall not make an order following an application under subsection (2)(a)—

  (a) if any person on whom notice is served under subsection (5) does not appear, unless service of the notice on that person is proved; or
  (b) if no notice under subsection (5) has been served, unless the court is satisfied that in the circumstances it was reasonable not to serve such notice.

(9) Where an order for the forfeiture of any goods, material or articles is made following an application under subsection (2)(a), any person who appeared, or was entitled to appear, to show cause why goods, material or articles should not be forfeited may, within 21 days of the making of the order, appeal to the High Court by Bill of Suspension; and section 452(4)(a) to (e) of the Criminal Procedure (Scotland) Act 1975 shall apply to an appeal under this subsection as it applies to a stated case under Part II of that Act.

(10) An order following an application under subsection (2)(a) shall not take effect—

  (a) until the end of the period of 21 days beginning with the day after the day on which the order is made; or
  (b) if an appeal is made under subsection (9) above within that period, until the appeal is determined or abandoned.

(11) An order under subsection (2)(b) shall not take effect—

  (a) until the end of the period within which an appeal against the order could be brought under the Criminal Procedure (Scotland) Act 1975; or
  (b) if an appeal is made within that period, until the appeal is determined or abandoned.

(12) Subject to subsection (13), goods, material or articles forfeited under this section shall be destroyed in accordance with such directions as the court may give.

(13) On making an order under this section the court may if it considers it appropriate to do so, direct that the goods, material or articles to which the order relates shall (instead of being destroyed) be released, to such person as the court may specify, on condition that that person causes the offending sign to be erased, removed or obliterated.

(14) For the purposes of this section—

'relevant offence' means an offence under section 92 (unauthorised use of trade mark, etc. in relation to goods) or under the Trade Descriptions Act 1968 or any offence involving dishonesty or deception,

'the court' means—

   (a) in relation to an order made on an application under subsection (2)(a), the sheriff, and

   (b) in relation to an order made under subsection (2)(b), the court which imposed the penalty.

PART IV

MISCELLANEOUS AND GENERAL PROVISIONS

Miscellaneous

99 Unauthorised use of Royal arms, etc.

(1) A person shall not without the authority of Her Majesty use in connection with any business the Royal arms (or arms so closely resembling the Royal arms as to be calculated to deceive) in such manner as to be calculated to lead to the belief that he is duly authorised to use the Royal arms.

(2) A person shall not without the authority of Her Majesty or of a member of the Royal family use in connection with any business any device, emblem or title in such a manner as to be calculated to lead to the belief that he is employed by, or supplies goods or services to, Her Majesty or that member of the Royal family.

(3) A person who contravenes subsection (1) commits an offence and is liable on summary conviction to a fine not exceeding level 2 on the standard scale.

(4) Contravention of subsection (1) or (2) may be restrained by injunction in proceedings brought by—

   (a) any person who is authorised to use the arms, device, emblem or title in question, or

   (b) any person authorised by the Lord Chamberlain to take such proceedings.

(5) Nothing in this section affects any right of the proprietor of a trade mark containing any such arms, device, emblem or title to use that trade mark.

100 Burden of proving use of trade mark

If in any civil proceedings under this Act a question arises as to the use to which a registered trade mark has been put, it is for the proprietor to show what use has been made of it.

101 Offences committed by partnerships and bodies corporate

(1) Proceedings for an offence under this Act alleged to have been committed by a partnership shall be brought against the partnership in the name of the firm and not in that of the partners; but without prejudice to any liability of the partners under subsection (4) below.

(2) The following provisions apply for the purposes of such proceedings as in relation to a body corporate—

   (a) any rules of court relating to the service of documents;

   (b) in England and Wales or Northern Ireland, Schedule 3 to the Magistrates' Courts Act

1980 or Schedule 4 to the Magistrates' Courts (Northern Ireland) Order 1981 (procedure on charge of offence).

(3) A fine imposed on a partnership on its conviction in such proceedings shall be paid out of the partnership assets.

(4) Where a partnership is guilty of an offence under this Act, every partner, other than a partner who is proved to have been ignorant of or to have attempted to prevent the commission of the offence, is also guilty of the offence and liable to be proceeded against and punished accordingly.

(5) Where an offence under this Act committed by a body corporate is proved to have been committed with the consent or connivance of a director, manager, secretary or other similar officer of the body, or a person purporting to act in any such capacity, he as well as the body corporate is guilty of the offence and liable to be proceeded against and punished accordingly.

Interpretation

102 Adaptation of expressions for Scotland
In the application of this Act to Scotland—

'account of profits' means accounting and payment of profits;
'accounts' means count, reckoning and payment;
'assignment' means assignation;
'costs' means expenses;
'declaration' means declarator;
'defendant' means defender;
'delivery up' means delivery;
'injunction' means interdict;
'interlocutory relief' means interim remedy; and
'plaintiff' means pursuer.

103 Minor definitions
(1) In this Act—

'business' includes a trade or profession;
'director', in relation to a body corporate whose affairs are managed by its members, means any member of the body;
'infringement proceedings', in relation to a registered trade mark, includes proceedings under section 16 (order for delivery up of infringing goods, etc.);
'publish' means make available to the public, and references to publication—

(a) in relation to an application for registration, are to publication under section 38(1), and

(b) in relation to registration, are to publication under section 40(4);

'statutory provisions' includes provisions of subordinate legislation within the meaning of the Interpretation Act 1978;
'trade' includes any business or profession.

(2) References in this Act to use (or any particular description of use) of a trade mark, or of a sign identical with, similar to, or likely to be mistaken for a trade mark, include use (or that description of use) otherwise than by means of a graphic representation.

(3) References in this Act to a Community instrument include references to any instrument amending or replacing that instrument.

104 Index of defined expressions

In this Act the expressions listed below are defined by or otherwise fall to be construed in accordance with the provisions indicated—

account of profits and accounts (in Scotland)	section 102
appointed person (for purposes of section 76)	section 77
assignment (in Scotland)	section 102
business	section 103(1)
certification mark	section 50(1)
collective mark	section 49(1)
commencement (of this Act)	section 109(2)
Community trade mark	section 51
Community Trade Mark Regulation	section 51
Convention country	section 55(1)(b)
costs (in Scotland)	section 102
the court	section 75
date of application	section 33(2)
date of filing	section 33(1)
date of registration	section 40(3)
defendant (in Scotland)	section 102
delivery up (in Scotland)	section 102
director	section 103(1)
earlier right	section 5(4)
earlier trade mark	section 6
exclusive licence and licensee	section 29(1)
infringement (of registered trade mark)	sections 9(1) and (2) and 10
infringement proceedings	section 103(1)
infringing articles	section 17
infringing goods	section 17
infringing material	section 17
injunction (in Scotland)	section 102
interlocutory relief (in Scotland)	section 102
the International Bureau	section 53
international trade mark (UK)	section 53
Madrid Protocol	section 53
Paris Convention	section 55(1)(a)
plaintiff (in Scotland)	section 102
prescribed	section 78(1)(b)
protected under the Paris Convention	
—well-known trade marks	section 56(1)
—state emblems and official signs or hallmarks	section 57(1)
—emblems, etc. of international organisations	section 58(2)
publish and references to publication	section 103(1)
register, registered (and related expressions)	section 63(1)
registered trade mark agent	section 83(1)
registrable transaction	section 25(2)
the registrar	section 62
rules	section 78
statutory provisions	section 103(1)
trade	section 103(1)

trade mark
   —generally   section 1(1)
   —includes collective mark or certification mark   section 1(2)
United Kingdom (references include Isle of Man)   section 108(2)
use (of trade mark or sign)   section 103(2)
well-known trade mark (under Paris Convention)   section 56(1)

Other general provisions

105 Transitional provisions

The provisions of Schedule 3 have effect with respect to transitional matters, including the treatment of marks registered under the Trade Marks Act 1938, and applications for registration and other proceedings pending under that Act, on the commencement of this Act.

106 Consequential amendments and repeals

(1) The enactments specified in Schedule 4 are amended in accordance with that Schedule, the amendments being consequential on the provisions of this Act.

(2) The enactments specified in Schedule 5 are repealed to the extent specified.

107 Territorial waters and the continental shelf

(1) For the purposes of this Act the territorial waters of the United Kingdom shall be treated as part of the United Kingdom.

(2) This Act applies to things done in the United Kingdom sector of the continental shelf on a structure or vessel which is present there for purposes directly connected with the exploration of the sea bed or subsoil or the exploitation of their natural resources as it applies to things done in the United Kingdom.

(3) The United Kingdom sector of the continental shelf means the areas designated by order under section 1(7) of the Continental Shelf Act 1964.

108 Extent

(1) This Act extends to England and Wales, Scotland and Northern Ireland.

(2) This Act also extends to the Isle of Man, subject to such exceptions and modifications as Her Majesty may specify by Order in Council; and subject to any such Order references in this Act to the United Kingdom shall be construed as including the Isle of Man.

109 Commencement

(1) The provisions of this Act come into force on such day as the Secretary of State may appoint by order made by statutory instrument.

    Different days may be appointed for different provisions and different purposes.

(2) The references to the commencement of this Act in Schedules 3 and 4 (transitional provisions and consequential amendments) are to the commencement of the main substantive provisions of Parts I and III of this Act and the consequential repeal of the Trade Marks Act 1938.

    Provision may be made by order under this section identifying the date of that commencement.

110 Short title

This Act may be cited as the Trade Marks Act 1994.

SCHEDULES

SCHEDULE 1
COLLECTIVE MARKS

Section 49

General

1 The provisions of this Act apply to collective marks subject to the following provisions.

Signs of which a collective mark may consist

2 In relation to a collective mark the reference in section 1(1) (signs of which a trade mark may consist) to distinguishing goods or services of one undertaking from those of other undertakings shall be construed as a reference to distinguishing goods or services of members of the association which is the proprietor of the mark from those of other undertakings.

Indication of geographical origin

3 (1) Notwithstanding section 3(1)(c), a collective mark may be registered which consists of signs or indications which may serve, in trade, to designate the geographical origin of the goods or services.

(2) However, the proprietor of such a mark is not entitled to prohibit the use of the signs or indications in accordance with honest practices in industrial or commercial matters (in particular, by a person who is entitled to use a geographical name).

Mark not to be misleading as to character or significance

4 (1) A collective mark shall not be registered if the public is liable to be misled as regards the character or significance of the mark, in particular if it is likely to be taken to be something other than a collective mark.

(2) The registrar may accordingly require that a mark in respect of which application is made for registration include some indication that it is a collective mark.

Notwithstanding section 39(2), an application may be amended so as to comply with any such requirement.

Regulations governing use of collective mark

5 (1) An applicant for registration of a collective mark must file with the registrar regulations governing the use of the mark.

(2) The regulations must specify the persons authorised to use the mark, the conditions of membership of the association and, where they exist, the conditions of use of the mark, including any sanctions against misuse.

Further requirements with which the regulations have to comply may be imposed by rules.

Approval of regulations by registrar

6 (1) A collective mark shall not be registered unless the regulations governing the use of the mark—

(a) comply with paragraph 5(2) and any further requirements imposed by rules, and

(b) are not contrary to public policy or to accepted principles of morality.

(2) Before the end of the prescribed period after the date of the application for registration of a collective mark, the applicant must file the regulations with the registrar and pay the prescribed fee.

If he does not do so, the application shall be deemed to be withdrawn.

7 (1) The registrar shall consider whether the requirements mentioned in paragraph 6(1) are met.

(2) If it appears to the registrar that those requirements are not met, he shall inform the applicant and give him an opportunity, within such period as the registrar may specify, to make representations or to file amended regulations.

(3) If the applicant fails to satisfy the registrar that those requirements are met, or to file regulations amended so as to meet them, or fails to respond before the end of the specified period, the registrar shall refuse the application.

(4) If it appears to the registrar that those requirements, and the other requirements for registration, are met, he shall accept the application and shall proceed in accordance with section 38 (publication, opposition proceedings and observations).

8 The regulations shall be published and notice of opposition may be given, and observations may be made, relating to the matters mentioned in paragraph 6(1).

This is in addition to any other grounds on which the application may be opposed or observations made.

Regulations to be open to inspection

9 The regulations governing the use of a registered collective mark shall be open to public inspection in the same way as the register.

Amendment of regulations

10 (1) An amendment of the regulations governing the use of a registered collective mark is not effective unless and until the amended regulations are filed with the registrar and accepted by him.

(2) Before accepting any amended regulations the registrar may in any case where it appears to him expedient to do so cause them to be published.

(3) If he does so, notice of opposition may be given, and observations may be made, relating to the matters mentioned in paragraph 6(1).

Infringement: rights of authorised users

11 The following provisions apply in relation to an authorised user of a registered collective mark as in relation to a licensee of a trade mark—

(a) section 10(5) (definition of infringement: unauthorised application of mark to certain material);

(b) section 19(2) (order as to disposal of infringing goods, material or articles: adequacy of other remedies);

(c) section 89 (prohibition of importation of infringing goods, material or articles: request to Commissioners of Customs and Excise).

12   (1) The following provisions (which correspond to the provisions of section 30 (general provisions as to rights of licensees in case of infringement)) have effect as regards the rights of an authorised user in relation to infringement of a registered collective mark.

(2) An authorised user is entitled, subject to any agreement to the contrary between him and the proprietor, to call on the proprietor to take infringement proceedings in respect of any matter which affects his interests.

(3) If the proprietor—

(a)   refuses to do so, or
(b)   fails to do so within two months after being called upon,

the authorised user may bring the proceedings in his own name as if he were the proprietor.

(4) Where infringement proceedings are brought by virtue of this paragraph, the authorised user may not, without the leave of the court, proceed with the action unless the proprietor is either joined as a plaintiff or added as a defendant.

This does not affect the granting of interlocutory relief on an application by an authorised user alone.

(5) A proprietor who is added as a defendant as mentioned in sub-paragraph (4) shall not be made liable for any costs in the action unless he takes part in the proceedings.

(6) In infringement proceedings brought by the proprietor of a registered collective mark any loss suffered or likely to be suffered by authorised users shall be taken into account; and the court may give such directions as it thinks fit as to the extent to which the plaintiff is to hold the proceeds of any pecuniary remedy on behalf of such users.

Grounds for revocation of registration

13   Apart from the grounds of revocation provided for in section 46, the registration of a collective mark may be revoked on the ground—

(a)   that the manner in which the mark has been used by the proprietor has caused it to become liable to mislead the public in the manner referred to in paragraph 4(1), or
(b)   that the proprietor has failed to observe, or to secure the observance of, the regulations governing the use of the mark, or
(c)   that an amendment of the regulations has been made so that the regulations—
    (i)   no longer comply with paragraph 5(2) and any further conditions imposed by rules, or
    (ii)   are contrary to public policy or to accepted principles of morality.

Grounds for invalidity of registration

14   Apart from the grounds of invalidity provided for in section 47, the registration of a collective mark may be declared invalid on the ground that the mark was registered in breach of the provisions of paragraph 4(1) or 6(1).

SCHEDULE 2

CERTIFICATION MARKS

Section 50

General

1 The provisions of this Act apply to certification marks subject to the following provisions.

Signs of which a certification mark may consist

2 In relation to a certification mark the reference in section 1(1) (signs of which a trade mark may consist) to distinguishing goods or services of one undertaking from those of other undertakings shall be construed as a reference to distinguishing goods or services which are certified from those which are not.

Indication of geographical origin

3 (1) Notwithstanding section 3(1)(c), a certification mark may be registered which consists of signs or indications which may serve, in trade, to designate the geographical origin of the goods or services.

(2) However, the proprietor of such a mark is not entitled to prohibit the use of the signs or indications in accordance with honest practices in industrial or commercial matters (in particular, by a person who is entitled to use a geographical name).

Nature of proprietor's business

4 A certification mark shall not be registered if the proprietor carries on a business involving the supply of goods or services of the kind certified.

Mark not to be misleading as to character or significance

5 (1) A certification mark shall not be registered if the public is liable to be misled as regards the character or significance of the mark, in particular if it is likely to be taken to be something other than a certification mark.

(2) The registrar may accordingly require that a mark in respect of which application is made for registration include some indication that it is a certification mark.

Notwithstanding section 39(2), an application may be amended so as to comply with any such requirement.

Regulations governing use of certification mark

6 (1) An applicant for registration of a certification mark must file with the registrar regulations governing the use of the mark.

(2) The regulations must indicate who is authorised to use the mark, the characteristics to be certified by the mark, how the certifying body is to test those characteristics and to supervise the use of the mark, the fees (if any) to be paid in connection with the operation of the mark and the procedures for resolving disputes.

Further requirements with which the regulations have to comply may be imposed by rules.

7   (1) A certification mark shall not be registered unless—

(a)   the regulations governing the use of the mark—
    (i)   comply with paragraph 6(2) and any further requirements imposed by rules, and
    (ii)   are not contrary to public policy or to accepted principles of morality, and
(b)   the applicant is competent to certify the goods or services for which the mark is to be registered.

(2) Before the end of the prescribed period after the date of the application for registration of a certification mark, the applicant must file the regulations with the registrar and pay the prescribed fee.

If he does not do so, the application shall be deemed to be withdrawn.

8   (1) The registrar shall consider whether requirements mentioned in paragraph 7(1) are met.

(2) If it appears to the registrar that those requirements are not met, he shall inform the applicant and give him an opportunity, within such period as the registrar may specify, to make representations or to file amended regulations.

(3) If the applicant fails to satisfy the registrar that those requirements are met, or to file regulations amended so as to meet them, or fails to respond before the end of the specified period, the registrar shall refuse the application.

(4) If it appears to the registrar that those requirements, and the other requirements for registration, are met, he shall accept the application and shall proceed in accordance with section 38 (publication, opposition proceedings and observations).

9   The regulations shall be published and notice of opposition may be given, and observations may be made, relating to the matters mentioned in paragraph 7(1).

This is in addition to any other grounds on which the application may be opposed or observations made.

10   The regulations governing the use of a registered certification mark shall be open to public inspection in the same way as the register.

11   (1) An amendment of the regulations governing the use of a registered certification mark is not effective unless and until the amended regulations are filed with the registrar and accepted by him.

(2) Before accepting any amended regulations the registrar may in any case where it appears to him expedient to do so cause them to be published.

(3) If he does so, notice of opposition may be given, and observations may be made, relating to the matters mentioned in paragraph 7(1).

12   The assignment or other transmission of a registered certification mark is not effective without the consent of the registrar.

Infringement: rights of authorised users

13 The following provisions apply in relation to an authorised user of a registered certification mark as in relation to a licensee of a trade mark—

(a) section 10(5) (definition of infringement: unauthorised application of mark to certain material);

(b) section 19(2) (order as to disposal of infringing goods, material or articles: adequacy of other remedies);

(c) section 89 (prohibition of importation of infringing goods, material or articles: request to Commissioners of Customs and Excise).

14 In infringement proceedings brought by the proprietor of a registered certification mark any loss suffered or likely to be suffered by authorised users shall be taken into account; and the court may give such directions as it thinks fit as to the extent to which the plaintiff is to hold the proceeds of any pecuniary remedy on behalf of such users.

Grounds for revocation of registration

15 Apart from the grounds of revocation provided for in section 46, the registration of a certification mark may be revoked on the ground—

(a) that the proprietor has begun to carry on such a business as is mentioned in paragraph 4,

(b) that the manner in which the mark has been used by the proprietor has caused it to become liable to mislead the public in the manner referred to in paragraph 5(1),

(c) that the proprietor has failed to observe, or to secure the observance of, the regulations governing the use of the mark,

(d) that an amendment of the regulations has been made so that the regulations—

  (i) no longer comply with paragraph 6(2) and any further conditions imposed by rules, or

  (ii) are contrary to public policy or to accepted principles of morality, or

(e) that the proprietor is no longer competent to certify the goods or services for which the mark is registered.

Grounds for invalidity of registration

16 Apart from the grounds of invalidity provided for in section 47, the registration of a certification mark may be declared invalid on the ground that the mark was registered in breach of the provisions of paragraph 4, 5(1) or 7(1).

SCHEDULE 3

TRANSITIONAL PROVISIONS

Section 105

Introductory

1 (1) In this Schedule—

'existing registered mark' means a trade mark, certification trade mark or service mark registered under the 1938 Act immediately before the commencement of this Act;

'the 1938 Act' means the Trade Marks Act 1938; and

'the old law' means that Act and any other enactment or rule of law applying to existing registered marks immediately before the commencement of this Act.

(2) For the purposes of this Schedule—

    (a) an application shall be treated as pending on the commencement of this Act if it was made but not finally determined before commencement, and

    (b) the date on which it was made shall be taken to be the date of filing under the 1938 Act.

Existing registered marks

2 (1) Existing registered marks (whether registered in Part A or B of the register kept under the 1938 Act) shall be transferred on the commencement of this Act to the register kept under this Act and have effect, subject to the provisions of this Schedule, as if registered under this Act.

(2) Existing registered marks registered as a series under section 21(2) of the 1938 Act shall be similarly registered in the new register.

Provision may be made by rules for putting such entries in the same form as is required for entries under this Act.

(3) In any other case notes indicating that existing registered marks are associated with other marks shall cease to have effect on the commencement of this Act.

3 (1) A condition entered on the former register in relation to an existing registered mark immediately before the commencement of this Act shall cease to have effect on commencement.

Proceedings under section 33 of the 1938 Act (application to expunge or vary registration for breach of condition) which are pending on the commencement of this Act shall be dealt with under the old law and any necessary alteration made to the new register.

(2) A disclaimer or limitation entered on the former register in relation to an existing registered mark immediately before the commencement of this Act shall be transferred to the new register and have effect as if entered on the register in pursuance of section 13 of this Act.

Effects of registration: infringement

4 (1) Sections 9 to 12 of this Act (effects of registration) apply in relation to an existing registered mark as from the commencement of this Act and section 14 of this Act (action for infringement) applies in relation to infringement of an existing registered mark committed after the commencement of this Act, subject to sub-paragraph (2) below.

The old law continues to apply in relation to infringements committed before commencement.

(2) It is not an infringement of—

    (a) an existing registered mark, or

    (b) a registered trade mark of which the distinctive elements are the same or substantially the same as those of an existing registered mark and which is registered for the same goods or services,

to continue after commencement any use which did not amount to infringement of the existing registered mark under the old law.

Infringing goods, material or articles

5 Section 16 of this Act (order for delivery up of infringing goods, material or articles) applies to infringing goods, material or articles whether made before or after the commencement of this Act.

Rights and remedies of licensee or authorised user

6 (1) Section 30 (general provisions as to rights of licensees in case of infringement) of this Act applies to licences granted before the commencement of this Act, but only in relation to infringements committed after commencement.

(2) Paragraph 14 of Schedule 2 of this Act (court to take into account loss suffered by authorised users, etc.) applies only in relation to infringements committed after commencement.

Co-ownership of registered mark

7 The provisions of section 23 of this Act (co-ownership of registered mark) apply as from the commencement of this Act to an existing registered mark of which two or more persons were immediately before commencement registered as joint proprietors.

But so long as the relations between the joint proprietors remains such as are described in section 63 of the 1938 Act (joint ownership) there shall be taken to be an agreement to exclude the operation of subsections (1) and (3) of section 23 of this Act (ownership in undivided shares and right of co-proprietor to make separate use of the mark).

Assignment, etc. of registered mark

8 (1) Section 24 of this Act (assignment or other transmission of registered mark) applies to transactions and events occurring after the commencement of this Act in relation to an existing registered mark; and the old law continues to apply in relation to transactions and events occurring before commencement.

(2) Existing entries under section 25 of the 1938 Act (registration of assignments and transmissions) shall be transferred on the commencement of this Act to the register kept under this Act and have effect as if made under section 25 of this Act.

Provision may be made by rules for putting such entries in the same form as is required for entries made under this Act.

(3) An application for registration under section 25 of the 1938 Act which is pending before the registrar on the commencement of this Act shall be treated as an application for registration under section 25 of this Act and shall proceed accordingly.

The registrar may require the applicant to amend his application so as to conform with the requirements of this Act.

(4) An application for registration under section 25 of the 1938 Act which has been determined by the registrar but not finally determined before the commencement of this Act shall be dealt with under the old law; and sub-paragraph (2) above shall apply in relation to any resulting entry in the register.

(5) Where before the commencement of this Act a person has become entitled by assignment or transmission to an existing registered mark but has not registered his title, any application for registration after commencement shall be made under section 25 of this Act.

(6) In cases to which sub-paragraph (3) or (5) applies section 25(3) of the 1938 Act continues to apply (and section 25(3) and (4) of this Act do not apply) as regards the consequences of failing to register.

Licensing of registered mark

9 (1) Sections 28 and 29(2) of this Act (licensing of registered trade mark; rights of exclusive licensee against grantor's successor in title) apply only in relation to licences granted after the commencement of this Act; and the old law continues to apply in relation to licences granted before commencement.

(2) Existing entries under section 28 of the 1938 Act (registered users) shall be transferred on the commencement of this Act to the register kept under this Act and have effect as if made under section 25 of this Act.

Provision may be made by rules for putting such entries in the same form as is required for entries made under this Act.

(3) An application for registration as a registered user which is pending before the registrar on the commencement of this Act shall be treated as an application for registration of a licence under section 25(1) of this Act and shall proceed accordingly.

The registrar may require the applicant to amend his application so as to conform with the requirements of this Act.

(4) An application for registration as a registered user which has been determined by the registrar but not finally determined before the commencement of this Act shall be dealt with under the old law; and sub-paragraph (2) above shall apply in relation to any resulting entry in the register.

(5) Any proceedings pending on the commencement of this Act under section 28(8) or (10) of the 1938 Act (variation or cancellation of registration of registered user) shall be dealt with under the old law and any necessary alteration made to the new register.

Pending applications for registration

10   (1) An application for registration of a mark under the 1938 Act which is pending on the commencement of this Act shall be dealt with under the old law, subject as mentioned below, and if registered the mark shall be treated for the purposes of this Schedule as an existing registered mark.

(2) The power of the Secretary of State under section 78 of this Act to make rules regulating practice and procedure, and as to the matters mentioned in subsection (2) of that section, is exercisable in relation to such an application; and different provision may be made for such applications from that made for other applications.

(3) Section 23 of the 1938 Act (provisions as to associated trade marks) shall be disregarded in dealing after the commencement of this Act with an application for registration.

Conversion of pending application

11   (1) In the case of a pending application for registration which has not been advertised under section 18 of the 1938 Act before the commencement of this Act, the applicant may give notice to the registrar claiming to have the registrability of the mark determined in accordance with the provisions of this Act.

(2) The notice must be in the prescribed form, be accompanied by the appropriate fee and be given no later than six months after the commencement of this Act.

(3) Notice duly given is irrevocable and has the effect that the application shall be treated as if made immediately after the commencement of this Act.

Trade marks registered according to old classification

12   The registrar may exercise the powers conferred by rules under section 65 of this Act (adaptation of entries to new classification) to secure that any existing registered marks which do not conform to the system of classification prescribed under section 34 of this Act are brought into conformity with that system.

This applies, in particular, to existing registered marks classified according to the pre-1938 classification set out in Schedule 3 to the Trade Marks Rules 1986.

Claim to priority from overseas application

13 Section 35 of this Act (claim to priority of Convention application) applies to an application for registration under this Act made after the commencement of this Act notwithstanding that the Convention application was made before commencement.

14 (1) Where before the commencement of this Act a person has duly filed an application for protection of a trade mark in a relevant country within the meaning of section 39A of the 1938 Act which is not a Convention country (a 'relevant overseas application'), he, or his successor in title, has a right to priority, for the purposes of registering the same trade mark under this Act for some or all of the same goods or services, for a period of six months from the date of filing of the relevant overseas application.

(2) If the application for registration under this Act is made within that six-month period—

(a) the relevant date for the purposes of establishing which rights take precedence shall be the date of filing of the relevant overseas application, and

(b) the registrability of the trade mark shall not be affected by any use of the mark in the United Kingdom in the period between that date and the date of the application under this Act.

(3) Any filing which in a relevant country is equivalent to a regular national filing, under its domestic legislation or an international agreement, shall be treated as giving rise to the right of priority.

A 'regular national filing' means a filing which is adequate to establish the date on which the application was filed in that country, whatever may be the subsequent fate of the application.

(4) A subsequent application concerning the same subject as the relevant overseas application, filed in the same country, shall be considered the relevant overseas application (of which the filing date is the starting date of the period of priority), if at the time of the subsequent application—

(a) the previous application has been withdrawn, abandoned or refused, without having been laid open to public inspection and without leaving any rights outstanding, and

(b) it has not yet served as a basis for claiming a right of priority.

The previous application may not thereafter serve as a basis for claiming a right of priority.

(5) Provision may be made by rules as to the manner of claiming a right to priority on the basis of a relevant overseas application.

(6) A right to priority arising as a result of a relevant overseas application may be assigned or otherwise transmitted, either with the application or independently.

The reference in sub-paragraph (1) to the applicant's 'successor in title' shall be construed accordingly.

(7) Nothing in this paragraph affects proceedings on an application for registration under the 1938 Act made before the commencement of this Act (see paragraph 10 above).

Duration and renewal of registration

15   (1) Section 42(1) of this Act (duration of original period of registration) applies in relation to the registration of a mark in pursuance of an application made after the commencement of this Act; and the old law applies in any other case.

(2) Sections 42(2) and 43 of this Act (renewal) apply where the renewal falls due on or after the commencement of this Act; and the old law continues to apply in any other case.

(3) In either case it is immaterial when the fee is paid.

Pending application for alteration of registered mark

16   An application under section 35 of the 1938 Act (alteration of registered trade mark) which is pending on the commencement of this Act shall be dealt with under the old law and any necessary alteration made to the new register.

Revocation for non-use

17   (1) An application under section 26 of the 1938 Act (removal from register or imposition of limitation on ground of non-use) which is pending on the commencement of this Act shall be dealt with under the old law and any necessary alteration made to the new register.

(2) An application under section 46(1)(a) or (b) of this Act (revocation for non-use) may be made in relation to an existing registered mark at any time after the commencement of this Act.

Provided that no such application for the revocation of the registration of an existing registered mark registered by virtue of section 27 of the 1938 Act (defensive registration of well-known trade marks) may be made until more than five years after the commencement of this Act.

Application for rectification, etc.

18   (1) An application under section 32 or 34 of the 1938 Act (rectification or correction of the register) which is pending on the commencement of this Act shall be dealt with under the old law and any necessary alteration made to the new register.

(2) For the purposes of proceedings under section 47 of this Act (grounds for invalidity of registration) as it applies in relation to an existing registered mark, the provisions of this Act shall be deemed to have been in force at all material times.

Provided that no objection to the validity of the registration of an existing registered mark may be taken on the ground specified in subsection (3) of section 5 of this Act (relative grounds for refusal of registration: conflict with earlier mark registered for different goods or services).

Regulations as to use of certification mark

19   (1) Regulations governing the use of an existing registered certification mark deposited at the Patent Office in pursuance of section 37 of the 1938 Act shall be treated after the commencement of this Act as if filed under paragraph 6 of Schedule 2 to this Act.

(2) Any request for amendment of the regulations which was pending on the commencement of this Act shall be dealt with under the old law.

Sheffield marks

20   (1) For the purposes of this Schedule the Sheffield register kept under Schedule 2 to the 1938 Act shall be treated as part of the register of trade marks kept under that Act.

(2) Applications made to the Cutlers' Company in accordance with that Schedule which are pending on the commencement of this Act shall proceed after commencement as if they had been made to the registrar.

Certificate of validity of contested registration

21 A certificate given before the commencement of this Act under section 47 of the 1938 Act (certificate of validity of contested registration) shall have effect as if given under section 73(1) of this Act.

Trade mark agents

22 (1) Rules in force immediately before the commencement of this Act under section 282 or 283 of the Copyright, Designs and Patents Act 1988 (register of trade mark agents; persons entitled to describe themselves as registered) shall continue in force and have effect as if made under section 83 or 85 of this Act.

(2) Rules in force immediately before the commencement of this Act under section 40 of the 1938 Act as to the persons whom the registrar may refuse to recognise as agents for the purposes of business under that Act shall continue in force and have effect as if made under section 88 of this Act.

(3) Rules continued in force under this paragraph may be varied or revoked by further rules made under the relevant provisions of this Act.

SCHEDULE 4

CONSEQUENTIAL AMENDMENTS

Section 106(1)

General adaptation of existing references

1 (1) References in statutory provisions passed or made before the commencement of this Act to trade marks or registered trade marks within the meaning of the Trade Marks Act 1938 shall, unless the context otherwise requires, be construed after the commencement of this Act as references to trade marks or registered trade marks within the meaning of this Act.

(2) Sub-paragraph (1) applies, in particular, to the references in the following provisions—

Industrial Organisation and Development Act 1947	Schedule 1, paragraph 7
Crown Proceedings Act 1947	section 3(1)(b)
Horticulture Act 1960	section 15(1)(b)
Printer's Imprint Act 1961	section 1(1)(b)
Plant Varieties and Seeds Act 1964	section 5A(4)
Northern Ireland Constitution Act 1973	Schedule 3, paragraph 17
Patents Act 1977	section 19(2)
	section 27(4)
	section 123(7)
Unfair Contract Terms Act 1977	Schedule 1, paragraph 1(c)
Judicature (Northern Ireland) Act 1978	section 94A(5)
State Immunity Act 1978	section 7(a) and (b)
Supreme Court Act 1981	section 72(5)
	Schedule 1, paragraph 1(i)

Civil Jurisdiction and Judgments Act 1982	Schedule 5, paragraph 2 Schedule 8, paragraph 2(14) and 4(2)
Value Added Tax Act 1983	Schedule 3, paragraph 1
Companies Act 1985	section 396(3A)(a) or (as substituted by the Companies Act 1989) section 396(2)(d)(i) section 410(4)(c)(v) Schedule 4, Part I, Balance Sheet Formats 1 and 2 and Note (2) Schedule 9, Part I, paragraphs 5(2)(d) and 10(2)
Law Reform (Miscellaneous Provisions) (Scotland) Act 1985	section 15(5)
Atomic Energy Authority Act 1986	section 8(2)
Companies (Northern Ireland) Order 1986	article 403(3A)(a) or (as substituted by the Companies (No.2) (Northern Ireland) Order 1990) article 403(2)(d)(i) Schedule 4, Part I, Balance Sheet Formats 1 and 2 and Note (2) Schedule 9, Part I, paragraphs 5(2)(d) and 10(2)
Consumer Protection Act 1987	section 2(2)(b)
Consumer Protection (Northern Ireland) Order 1987	article 5(2)(b)
Income and Corporation Taxes Act 1988	section 83(a)
Taxation of Chargeable Gains Act 1992	section 275(h)
Tribunals and Inquiries Act 1992	Schedule 1, paragraph 34.

Patents and Designs Act 1907 (c.29)

2   (1) The Patents and Designs Act 1907 is amended as follows.

(2) In section 62 (the Patent Office)—

  (a)   in subsection (1) for 'this Act and the Trade Marks Act 1905' substitute 'the Patents Act 1977, the Registered Designs Act 1949 and the Trade Marks Act 1994'; and

  (b)   in subsections (2) and (3) for 'the Board of Trade' substitute 'the Secretary of State'.

(3) In section 63 (officers and clerks of the Patents Office)—

  (a)   for 'the Board of Trade' in each place where it occurs substitute 'the Secretary of State'; and

  (b)   in subsection (2) omit the words from 'and those salaries' to the end.

(4) The repeal by the Patents Act 1949 and the Registered Designs Act 1949 of the whole of the 1907 Act, except certain provisions, shall be deemed not to have extended to the long title, date of enactment or enacting words or to so much of section 99 as provides the Act with its short title.

Patents, Designs, Copyright and Trade Marks (Emergency) Act 1939 (c. 107)

3   (1) The Patents, Designs, Copyright and Trade Marks (Emergency) Act 1939 is amended as follows.

(2) For section 3 (power of comptroller to suspend rights of enemy or enemy subject) substitute—

'**3** Power of comptroller to suspend trade mark rights of enemy or enemy subject
(1) Where on application made by a person proposing to supply goods or services of any description it is made to appear to the comptroller—

    (a) that it is difficult or impracticable to describe or refer to the goods or services without the use of a registered trade mark, and

    (b) that the proprietor of the registered trade mark (whether alone or jointly with another) is an enemy or an enemy subject,

the comptroller may make an order suspending the rights given by the registered trade mark.

(2) An order under this section shall suspend those rights as regards the use of the trade mark—

    (a) by the applicant, and

    (b) by any person authorised by the applicant to do, for the purposes of or in connection with the supply by the applicant of the goods or services, things which would otherwise infringe the registered trade mark,

to such extent and for such period as the comptroller considers necessary to enable the applicant to render well-known and established some other means of describing or referring to the goods or services in question which does not involve the use of the trade mark.

(3) Where an order has been made under this section, no action for passing off lies on the part of any person interested in the registered trade mark in respect of any use of it which by virtue of the order is not an infringement of the right conferred by it.

(4) An order under this section may be varied or revoked by a subsequent order made by the comptroller.'

(3) In each of the following provisions—

    (a) section 4(1)(c) (effect of war on registration of trade marks),

    (b) section 6(1) (power of comptroller to extend time limits),

    (c) section 7(1)(a) (evidence as to nationality, etc.), and

    (d) the definition of 'the comptroller' in section 10(1) (interpretation),

for 'the Trade Marks Act 1938' substitute 'the Trade Marks Act 1994'.

Trade Descriptions Act 1968 (c.29)

4 In the Trade Descriptions Act 1968, in section 34 (exemption of trade description contained in pre-1968 trade mark)—

    (a) in the opening words, omit 'within the meaning of the Trade Marks Act 1938'; and

    (b) in paragraph (c), for 'a person registered under section 28 of the Trade Marks Act 1938 as a registered user of the trade mark' substitute ', in the case of a registered trade mark, a person licensed to use it'.

Solicitors Act 1974 (c.47)

5 (1) Section 22 of the Solicitors Act 1974 (preparation of instruments by unqualified persons) is amended as follows.

(2) In subsection (2)(aa) and (ab) (instruments which may be prepared by registered trade mark agent or registered patent agent) for ', trade mark or service mark' substitute 'or trade mark'.

(3) In subsection (3A) (interpretation)—

(a) in the definition of 'registered trade mark agent' for 'section 282(1) of the Copyright, Designs and Patents Act 1988' substitute 'the Trade Marks Act 1994'; and

(b) in the definition of 'registered patent agent' for 'of that Act' substitute 'of the Copyright, Designs and Patents Act 1988'.

House of Commons Disqualification Act 1975 (c.24)

6   In Part III of Schedule 1 to the House of Commons Disqualification Act 1975 (other disqualifying offices), for the entry relating to persons appointed to hear and determine appeals under the Trade Marks Act 1938 substitute—

'Person appointed to hear and determine appeals under the Trade Marks Act 1994.'.

Restrictive Trade Practices Act 1976 (c.34)

7   In Schedule 3 to the Restrictive Trade Practices Act 1976 (excepted agreements), for paragraph 4 (agreements relating to trade marks) substitute—

'**4**   (1) This Act does not apply to an agreement authorising the use of a registered trade mark (other than a collective mark or certification mark) if no such restrictions as are described in section 6(1) or 11(2) above are accepted, and no such information provisions as are described in section 7(1) or 12(2) above are made, except in respect of—

(a) the descriptions of goods bearing the mark which are to be produced or supplied, or the processes of manufacture to be applied to such goods or to goods to which the mark is to be applied, or

(b) the kinds of services in relation to which the mark is to be used which are to be made available or supplied, or the form or manner in which such services are to be made available or supplied, or

(c) the descriptions of goods which are to be produced or supplied in connection with the supply of services in relation to which the mark is to be used, or the process of manufacture to be applied to such goods.

(2) This Act does not apply to an agreement authorising the use of a registered collective mark or certification mark if—

(a) the agreement is made in accordance with regulations approved by the registrar under Schedule 1 or 2 to the Trade Marks Act 1994, and

(b) no such restrictions as are described in section 6(1) or 11(2) above are accepted, and no such information provisions as are described in section 7(1) or 12(2) above are made, except as permitted by those regulations.'.

Copyright, Designs and Patents Act 1988 (c.48)

8   (1) The Copyright, Designs and Patents Act 1988 is amended as follows.

(2) In sections 114(6), 204(6) and 231(6) (persons regarded as having an interest in infringing copies, etc.), for 'section 58C of the Trade Marks Act 1938' substitute 'section 19 of the Trade Marks Act 1944'.

(3) In section 280(1) (privilege for communications with patent agents), for 'trade mark or service mark' substitute 'or trade mark'.

9 In Part I of Schedule 1 to the Tribunals and Inquiries Act 1992 (tribunals under direct supervision of Council on Tribunals), for 'Patents, designs, trade marks and service marks' substitute 'Patents, designs and trade marks'.

SCHEDULE 5

REPEALS AND REVOCATIONS

Section 106(2)

Chapter or number	Short title	Extent of repeal or revocation
1891 c. 50.	Commissioners for Oaths Act 1891.	In section 1, the words 'or the Patents, Designs and Trade Marks Acts, 1883 to 1888,'.
1907 c. 29.	Patents and Designs Act 1907.	In section 63(2), the words from 'and those salaries' to the end.
1938 c. 22.	Trade Marks Act 1938.	The whole Act.
1947 c. 44.	Crown Proceedings Act 1947.	In section 3(1)(b), the words 'or registered service mark'.
1949 c. 87	Patents Act 1949.	Section 92(2).
1964 c. 14.	Plant Varieties and Seeds Act 1964.	In section 5A(4), the words 'under the Trade Marks Act 1938'.
1967 c. 80	Criminal Justice Act 1967.	In Schedule 3, in Parts I and IV, the entries relating to the Trade Marks Act 1938.
1978 c. 23.	Judicature (Northern Ireland) Act 1978.	In Schedule 5, in Part II, the paragraphs amending the Trade Marks Act 1938.
1984 c. 19.	Trade Marks (Amendment) Act 1984.	The whole Act.
1985 c. 6.	Companies Act 1985.	In section 396— (a) in subsection (3A)(a), and (b) in subsection (2)(d)(i) as inserted by the Companies Act 1989, the words 'service mark,'.
1986 c. 12.	Statute Law (Repeals) Act 1986.	In Schedule 2, paragraph 2.
1986 c. 39.	Patents, Designs and Marks Act 1986	Section 2. Section 4(4). In Schedule 1, paragraphs 1 and 2. Schedule 2.
S.I. 1986/1032 (N.I. 6).	Companies (Northern Ireland) Order 1986.	In article 403— (a) in paragraph (3A)(a), and

Chapter or number	*Short title*	*Extent of repeal or revocation*
		(b) in paragraph (2)(d)(i) as inserted by the Companies (No.2) (Northern Ireland) Order 1990, the words 'service mark,'.
1987 c. 43.	Consumer Protection Act 1987.	In Section 45— (a) in subsection (1), the definition of 'mark' and 'trade mark'; (b) subsection (4).
S.I. 1987/2049.	Consumer Protection (Northern Ireland) Order 1987.	In article 2— (a) in paragraph (2), the definitions of 'mark' and 'trade mark'; (b) paragraph (3).
1988 c. 1.	Income and Corporation Taxes Act 1988.	In section 83, the words from 'References in this section' to the end.
1988 c. 48.	Copyright, Designs and Patents Act 1988.	Sections 282 to 284. In section 286, the definition of 'registered trade mark agent'. Section 300.
1992 c. 12.	Taxation of Chargeable Gains Act 1992.	In section 275(h), the words 'service marks' and 'service mark'.

APPENDIX 2

The Trade Marks Rules 1994
(SI 1994/2583)

ARRANGEMENT OF RULES

Preliminary

		Page
1	Citation and commencement	205
2	Interpretation	206
3	Forms and directions of the registrar under s 66	206
4	Requirement as to fees	206

Application for registration

5	Application for registration; s 32	206
6	Claim to priority; ss 35 & 36	206
7	Classification of goods and services; s 34	207
8	Application may relate to more than one class and shall specify the class	207
9	Prohibition on registration of mark consisting of arms; s 4	207
10	Address for service	207
11	Deficiencies in application: s 32	208

Publication, observations, opposition and registration

12	Publication of application for registration; s 38(1)	208
13	Opposition proceedings; s 38(2)	208
14	Decision of registrar in opposition proceedings	209
15	Observations on application to be sent to applicant; s 38(3)	209
16	Publication of registration; s 40	209

Amendment of application

17	Amendment of application; s 39	209
18	Amendment of application; s 39	209

Division, merger and series of marks

19	Division of application; s 41	210
20	Merger of separate applications or registrations; s 41	210
21	Registration of a series of trade marks; s 41	211

Collective and certification marks

22 Filing of regulations for collective and certification marks; Schs 1 & 2   211
23 Amendment of regulations of collective and certification marks; Sch 1 para 10 &
   Sch 2 para 11   211

Disclaimers, limitations and alteration or surrender of registered trade mark

24 Registration subject to disclaimer or limitation; s 13   212
25 Alteration of registered trade mark; s 44   212
26 Surrender of registered trade mark; s 45   212

Renewal and restoration

27 Reminder of renewal of registration; s 43   212
28 Renewal of registration; s 43   213
29 Delayed renewal and removal of registration; s 43   213
30 Restoration of registration; s 43   213

Revocation, invalidation and rectification

31 Procedure on application for revocation, declaration of invalidity and rectification
   of the register; ss 46, 47 & 64   213

The register

32 Form of register; s 63(3)   214
33 Entry in register of particulars of registered trade marks; s 63   214
34 Entry in register of particulars of registrable transactions; s 25   215
35 Application to register or give notice of transaction; ss 25 & 27(3)   215
36 Public inspection of register; s 63(3)   216
37 Supply of certified copies, etc; s 63(3)   216
38 Request for change of name or address in register; s 64(4)   216
39 Removal of matter from register; s 64(5)   216

Change of classification

40 Change of classification; ss 65(2) & 76(1)   217
41 Opposition to proposals; ss 65(3) & 76(1)   217

Request for information, inspection of documents and confidentiality

42 Request for information; s 67(1)   218
43 Information available before publication; s 67(2)   218
44 Inspection of documents; ss 67 & 76(1)   218
45 Confidential documents   218

Agents

46 Proof of authorisation of agent may be required; s 82   219
47 Registrar may refuse to deal with certain agents; s 88   219

Decision of registrar, evidence and costs

48 Decisions of registrar to be taken after hearing   219
49 Evidence in proceedings before registrar; s 69   220

50 Making and subscription of statutory declaration or affidavit   220
51 Registrar's power to require documents, information or evidence   220
52 Registrar to have power of an official referee; s 69   220
53 Hearings before registrar to be in public   220
54 Costs of proceedings; s 68   220
55 Security for costs; s 68   221
56 Decision of registrar   221

Appeals

57 Appeal to person appointed; s 76   221
58 Determination whether appeal be referred to Court; s 76(3)   221
59 Hearing of appeal; s 76(4)   222

Correction of irregularities, calculation and extension of time

60 Correction of irregularities of procedure   222
61 Calculation of times and periods   222
62 Alteration of time limits   223

Filing of documents, hours of business, Trade Marks Journal and translations

63 Filing of documents by electronic means   223
64 Directions on hours of business; s 80   224
65 Trade Marks Journal; s 81   224
66 Translations   224

Transitional provisions and revocations

67 Pending applications for registration; Sch 3, para 10(2)   224
68 Form for conversion of pending application; Sch 3, para 11(2)   224
69 Revocation of previous Rules   224

Schedules

Schedule 1—Revocations   225
Schedule 2—Form of Notice under Sch 3, para 11   225
Schedule 3—Classification of goods (pre-1938)   226
Schedule 4—Classification of goods and services   228

The Secretary of State, in exercise of the powers conferred upon him by sections 4(4), 13(2), 25(1), (5) and (6), 34(1), 35(5), 38(1) and (2), 39(3), 40(4), 41(1) and (3), 43(2), (3), (5) and (6), 44(3), 45(2), 63(2) and (3), 64(4), 65, 66(2), 67(1) and (2), 68(1) and (3), 69, 76(1), 78, 80(3), 81, 82 and 88 of, paragraph 6(2) of Schedule 1 to, paragraph 7(2) of Schedule 2 to, and paragraphs 10(2), 11(2), 12 and 14(5) of Schedule 3 to, the Trade Marks Act 1994, after consultation with the Council on Tribunals pursuant to section 8(1) of the Tribunals and Inquiries Act 1992, hereby makes the following Rules:—

Preliminary

1   Citation and commencement

These Rules may be cited as the Trade Marks Rules 1994 and shall come into force on 31 October 1994.

2 Interpretation
(1) In these Rules, unless the context otherwise requires—

'the Act' means the Trade Marks Act 1994;
'the Journal' means the Trade Marks Journal published in accordance with rule 65 below;
'the Office' means the Patent Office;
'old law' means the Trade Marks Act 1938 (as amended) and any rules made thereunder existing immediately before the commencement of the Act;
'proprietor' means the person registered as the proprietor of the trade mark;
'publish' means publish in the Journal;
'send' includes give;
'specification' means the statement of goods or services in respect of which a trade mark is registered or proposed to be registered;
'United Kingdom' includes the Isle of Man.

(2) In these Rules, except where otherwise indicated, a reference to a section is a reference to that section in the Act, a reference to a rule is a reference to that rule in these Rules, a reference to a Schedule is a reference to that Schedule to these Rules and a reference to a form is a reference to that form as published by the registrar under rule 3 below.

(3) In these Rules references to the filing of any application, notice or other document are to be construed as references to its being sent or delivered to the registrar at the Office.

3 Forms and directions of the registrar under s 66
(1) Any forms required by the registrar to be used for the purpose of registration of a trade mark or any other proceedings before him under the Act pursuant to section 66 and any directions with respect to their use shall be published and any amendment or modification of a form or of the directions with respect to its use shall be published.

(2) A requirement under this rule to use a form as published is satisfied by the use either of a replica of that form or of a form which is acceptable to the registrar and contains the information required by the form as published and complies with any directions as to the use of such a form.

4 Requirement as to fees
(1) The fees to be paid in respect of any application, registration or any other matter under the Act and these Rules shall be those (if any) prescribed in relation to such matter by rules under section 79 (fees).

(2) Any form required to be filed with the registrar in respect of any specified matter shall be subject to the payment of the fee (if any) prescribed in respect of that matter by those rules.

Application for registration

5 Applications for registration; s 32
An application for the registration of a trade mark shall be filed on Form TM3 and shall be subject to the payment of the application fee and such class fees as may be appropriate.

6 Claim to priority; ss 35 & 36
(1) Where a right to priority is claimed by reason of an application for protection of a trade mark duly filed in a Convention country under section 35 or in another country or territory in respect of which provision corresponding to that made by section 35 is made under section 36, particulars of that claim shall be included in the application for registration under rule 5 above

and, where no certificate as is referred to in paragraph (2) below is filed with the application, such particulars shall include the country or countries and the date or dates of filing.

(2) Unless it has been filed at the time of the filing of the application for registration, there shall be filed, within three months of the filing of the application under rule 5, a certificate by the registering or other competent authority of that country certifying, or verifying to the satisfaction of the registrar, the date of the filing of the application, the country or registering or competent authority, the representation of the mark, and the goods or services covered by the application.

7 Classification of goods and services; s 34
(1) For the purposes of trade mark registrations in respect of goods dated before 27 July 1938, goods are classified in accordance with Schedule 3 to these Rules, except where a specification has been converted, whether under the old law or under rule 40 below, to Schedule 4.

(2) For the purposes of trade mark registrations in respect of goods dated on or after 27 July 1938 and for the purposes of any registrations dated before that date in respect of which the specifications were converted under the old law, and for the purposes of trade mark registrations in respect of services, goods and services are classified in accordance with Schedule 4, which sets out the current version of the classes of the International Classification of Goods and Services.

8 Application may relate to more than one class and shall specify the class
(1) An application may be made for registration in more than one class of Schedule 4.

(2) Every application shall specify the class in Schedule 4 to which it relates; and if the application relates to more than one class in that Schedule the specification contained in it shall set out the classes in consecutive numerical order and list under each class the goods or services appropriate to that class.

(3) If the specification contained in the application lists items by reference to a class in Schedule 4 in which they do not fall, the applicant may request, by filing Form TM3A, that his application be amended to include the appropriate class for those items, and upon the payment of such class fee as may be appropriate the registrar shall amend his application accordingly.

9 Prohibition on registration of mark consisting of arms; s 4
Where a representation of any arms or insignia as is referred to in section 4(4) appears on a mark, the registrar shall refuse to accept an application for the registration of the mark unless satisfied that the consent of the person entitled to the arms has been obtained.

10 Address for service
(1) For the purposes of any proceedings before the registrar under these Rules or any appeal from a decision of the registrar under the Act or these Rules, an address for service in the United Kingdom shall be filed by—

(a) every applicant for the registration of a trade mark;
(b) every person opposing an application for registration of a trade mark;
(c) every applicant applying to the registrar under section 46 for the revocation of the registration of a trade mark, under section 47 for the invalidation of the registration of a trade mark, or under section 64 for the rectification of the register;
(d) every person granted leave to intervene under rule 31(5) (the intervener); and
(e) every proprietor of a registered trade mark which is the subject of an application to the registrar for the revocation, invalidation or rectification of the registration of the mark.

(2) The address for service of an applicant for registration of a trade mark shall upon registration

of the mark be deemed to be the address for service or the registered proprietor, subject to any filing to the contrary under paragraph (1) above or rule 38(2) below.

(3) In any case in which an address for service is filed at the same time as the filing of a form required by the registrar under rule 3 which requires the furnishing of an address for service, the address shall be filed on that form and in any other case it shall be filed on Form TM33.

(4) Anything sent to any applicant, opponent, intervener or registered proprietor at his address for service shall be deemed to be properly sent; and the registrar may, where no address for service is filed, treat as the address for service of the person concerned his trade or business address in the United Kingdom, if any.

(5) An address for service in the United Kingdom may be filed at any time by the proprietor of a registered trade mark and by any person having an interest in or charge on a registered trade mark which has been registered under rule 34.

(6) Where an address for service is not filed as required by paragraph (1) above, the registrar shall send the person concerned notice to file an address for service within two months of the date of the notice and if that person fails to do so—

(a) in the case of an applicant as is referred to in sub-paragraph (a) or (c), the application shall be treated as abandoned;
(b) in the case of a person as is referred to in sub-paragraph (b) or (d), he shall be deemed to have withdrawn from the proceedings; and
(c) in the case of the proprietor referred to in sub-paragraph (e), he shall not be permitted to take part in any proceedings.

11   Deficiencies in application: s 32

Where an application for registration of a trade mark does not satisfy the requirements of section 32(2), (3) or (4) or rule 5 or 8(2), the registrar shall send notice thereof to the applicant to remedy the deficiencies or, in the case of section 32(4), the default of payment and if within two months of the date of the notice the applicant—

(a) fails to remedy any deficiency notified to him in respect of section 32(2), the application shall be deemed never to have been made; or
(b) fails to remedy any deficiency notified to him in respect of section 32(3) or rule 5 or 8(2) or fails to make payment as required by section 32(4), the application shall be treated as abandoned.

Publication, observations, oppositions and registration

12   Publication of application for registration; s 38(1)

An application which has been accepted for registration shall be published.

13   Opposition proceedings; s 38(2)

(1) Notice of opposition to the registration of a trade mark shall be sent to the registrar on Form TM7 within three months of the date on which the application was published under rule 12, and shall include a statement of the grounds of opposition; the registrar shall send a copy of the notice and the statement to the applicant.

(2) Within three months of the date on which a copy of the statement is sent by the registrar to the applicant the applicant may file, in conjunction with notice of the same on Form TM8, a counter-statement; the registrar shall send a copy of the Form TM8 and the counter-statement to the person opposing the application.

(3) Within three months of the date on which a copy of the counter-statement is sent by the registrar to the person opposing the registration, that person shall file such evidence by way of statutory declaration or affidavit as he may consider necessary to adduce in support of his opposition and shall send a copy thereof to the applicant.

(4) If the person opposing the registration files no evidence under paragraph (3) above, he shall, unless the registrar otherwise directs, be deemed to have abandoned his opposition.

(5) If the person opposing the registration files evidence under paragraph (3) above or the registrar otherwise directs under paragraph (4) above, the applicant shall, within three months of the date on which either a copy of the evidence or a copy of the direction is sent to the applicant, file such evidence by way of statutory declaration or affidavit as he may consider necessary to adduce in support of his application, and shall send a copy thereof to the person opposing the application.

(6) Within three months of the date on which a copy of the applicant's evidence is sent to him, the person opposing the application may file evidence in reply by statutory declaration or affidavit which shall be confined to matters strictly in reply to the applicant's evidence, and shall send a copy thereof to the applicant.

(7) No further evidence may be filed, except that, in relation to any proceedings before him, the registrar may at any time if he thinks fit give leave to either party to file evidence upon such terms as he may think fit.

(8) Upon completion of the evidence the registrar shall, if a hearing is requested by any party to the proceedings, send to the parties notice of a date for the hearing.

14 Decision of registrar in opposition proceedings
(1) When the registrar has made a decision on the acceptability of an application for registration following the procedure under rule 13, he shall send the applicant and the person opposing the application written notice of it, stating the reasons for his decision.

(2) For the purpose of any appeal against the registrar's decision the date of the decision shall be the date when notice of the decision is sent under paragraph (1) above.

15 Observations on application to be sent to applicant; s 38(3)
The registrar shall send to the applicant a copy of any documents containing observations made under section 38(3).

16 Publication of registration; s 40
On the registration of the trade mark the registrar shall publish the registration, specifying the date upon which the trade mark was entered in the register.

Amendment of application

17 Amendment of application; s 39
A request for an amendment of an application to correct an error or to change the name or address of the applicant or in respect of any amendment requested after publication of the application shall be made on Form TM21.

18 Amendment of application after publication; s 39
(1) Where, pursuant to section 39, a request is made for amendment of an application which has been published and the amendment affects the representation of the trade mark or the goods or services covered by the application, the amendment or a statement of the effect of the amendment shall also be published.

(2) Notice of opposition to the amendment shall be sent to the registrar on Form TM7 within one month of the date on which the application as amended was published under paragraph (1) above, and shall include a statement of the grounds of objection and, in particular, how the amendments would be contrary to section 39(2).

(3) The provisions of rule 13 shall apply to proceedings relating to the opposition to the amendment of the application as they apply to proceedings relating to opposition to the registration of a trade mark.

Division, merger and series of marks

19　Division of application; s 41

(1) At any time before registration an applicant may send to the registrar a request on Form TM12 for a division of his application for registration (the original application) into two or more separate applications (divisional applications), indicating for each division the specification of goods or services; each divisional application shall be treated as a separate application for registration with the same filing date as the original application.

(2) Where the request to divide an application is sent after publication of the application, any objections in respect of, or opposition to, the original application shall be taken to apply to each divisional application and shall be proceeded with accordingly.

(3) Upon division of an original application in respect of which notice has been given to the registrar of particulars relating to the grant of a licence, or a security interest or any right in or under it, the notice and the particulars shall be deemed to apply in relation to each of the applications into which the original application has been divided.

20　Merger of separate applications or registrations; s 41

(1) An applicant who has made separate applications for registration of a mark may, at any time before preparations for the publication of any of the applications have been completed by the Office, request the registrar on Form TM17 to merge the separate applications into a single application.

(2) The registrar shall, if satisfied that all the applications which are the subject of the request for merger—

    (a)　are in respect of the same trade mark,
    (b)　bear the same date of application, and
    (c)　are, at the time of the request, in the name of the same person,

merge them into a single application.

(3) The proprietor of two or more registrations of a trade mark may request the registrar on Form TM17 to merge them into a single registration; and the registrar shall, if satisfied that the registrations are in respect of the same trade mark, merge them into a single registration.

(4) Where any registration of a trade mark to be merged under paragraph (3) above is subject to a disclaimer or limitation, the merged registration shall also be restricted accordingly.

(5) Where any registration of a trade mark to be merged under paragraph (3) above has had registered in relation to it particulars relating to the grant of a licence or a security interest or any right in or under it, or of any memorandum or statement of the effect of a memorandum, the registrar shall enter in the register the same particulars in relation to the merged registration.

(6) The date of registration of the merged registration shall, where the separate registrations bear different dates, be the latest of those dates.

21 Registration of a series of trade marks; s 41

(1) The proprietor of a series of trade marks may apply to the registrar on Form TM3 for their registration as a series in a single registration and there shall be included in such application a representation of each mark claimed to be in the series; and the registrar shall, if satisfied that the marks constitute a series, accept the application.

(2) At any time before preparations of publication of the application have been completed by the Office, the applicant under paragraph (1) above may request on Form TM12 the division of the application into separate applications in respect of one or more marks in that series and the registrar shall, if he is satisfied that the division requested conforms with section 41(2), divide the application accordingly.

(3) At any time the applicant for registration of a series of trade marks or the proprietor of a registered series of trade marks may request the deletion of a mark in that series, and the registrar shall delete the mark accordingly.

(4) The division of an application into one or more applications under paragraph (2) above shall be subject to the payment of a divisional fee and such application and class fees as are appropriate.

Collective and certification marks

22 Filing of regulations for collective and certification marks; Schs 1 & 2

Within nine months of the date of the application for the registration of a collective or certification mark, the applicant shall file Form TM35 accompanied by a copy of the regulations governing the use of the mark.

23 Amendment of regulations of collective and certification marks; Sch 1 para 10 and Sch 2 para 11

(1) An application for the amendment of the regulations governing the use of a registered collective or certification mark shall be filed on Form TM36.

(2) Where it appears expedient to the registrar that the amended regulations should be made available to the public he shall publish a notice indicating where copies of the amended regulations may be inspected.

(3) Any person may, within three months of the date of publication of the notice under paragraph (2) above, make observations to the registrar on the amendments relating to the matters referred to in paragraph 6(1) of Schedule 1 in relation to a collective mark, or, paragraph 7(1) of Schedule 2 in relation to a certification mark; the registrar shall send a copy thereof to the proprietor.

(4) Any person may, within three months of the date of publication of the notice, file notice on Form TM7 to the registrar of opposition to the amendment, accompanied by a statement of the grounds of opposition, indicating why the amended regulations do not comply with the requirements of paragraph 6(1) of Schedule 1 or, as the case may be, paragraph 7(1) of Schedule 2.

(5) The registrar shall send a copy of the notice and the statement to the proprietor and thereafter the procedure in rule 13(2)–(8) shall apply to the proceedings as they apply to proceedings relating to opposition to an application for registration.

Disclaimers, limitations and alteration or surrender of registered trade mark

24   Registration subject to disclaimer or limitation; s 13

Where the applicant for registration of a trade mark or the proprietor by notice in writing sent to the registrar—

(a)   disclaims any right to the exclusive use of any specified element of the trade mark, or
(b)   agrees that the rights conferred by the registration shall be subject to a specified territorial or other limitation,

the registrar shall make the appropriate entry in the register and publish such disclaimer or limitation.

25   Alteration of registered trade marks; s 44

(1) The proprietor may request the registrar on Form TM25 for such alteration of his registered mark as is permitted under section 44; and the registrar may require such evidence by statutory declaration or otherwise as to the circumstances in which the application is made.

(2) Where, upon the request of the proprietor, the registrar proposes to allow such alteration, he shall publish the mark as altered.

(3) Any person claiming to be affected by the alteration may within three months of the date of publication of the alteration under paragraph (2) send a notice on Form TM7 to the registrar of opposition to the alteration and shall include a statement of the grounds of opposition; the registrar shall send a copy of the notice and the statement of the proprietor and thereafter the procedure in rule 13(2)–(8) shall apply to the proceedings as they apply to proceedings relating to opposition to an application for registration.

26   Surrender of registered trade mark; s 45

(1) Subject to paragraph (2) below, the proprietor may surrender a registered trade mark, by sending notice to the registrar—

(a)   on Form TM22 in respect of all the goods or services for which it is registered; or
(b)   on Form TM23, in respect only of those goods or services specified by him in the notice.

(2) A notice under paragraph (1) above shall be of no effect unless the proprietor in that notice—

(a)   gives the name and address of any person having a registered interest in the mark, and
(b)   certifies that any such person—
    (i)   has been sent not less than three months' notice of the proprietor's intention to surrender the mark, or
    (ii)   is not affected or if affected consents thereto.

(3) The registrar shall, upon the surrender taking effect, make the appropriate entry in the register and publish the same.

Renewal and restoration

27   Reminder of renewal of registration; s 43

At any time not earlier than six months nor later than one month before the expiration of the last registration of a trade mark, the registrar shall (except where renewal has already been effected under rule 28 below) send to the registered proprietor notice of the approaching expiration and inform him at the same time that the registration may be renewed in the manner described in rule 28 below.

28 Renewal of registration; s 43

Renewal of registration shall be effected by filing a request for renewal on Form TM11 at any time within the period of six months ending on the date of the expiration of the registration.

29 Delayed renewal and removal of registration; s 43

(1) If on the expiration of the last registration of a trade mark, the renewal fee has not been paid, the registrar shall publish that fact; and if, within six months from the date of the expiration of the last registration, the request for renewal is filed on Form TM11 accompanied by the appropriate renewal fee and additional renewal fee, the registrar shall renew the registration without removing the mark from the register.

(2) Where no request for renewal is filed as aforesaid, the registrar shall, subject to rule 30 below, remove the mark from the register.

(3) Where, in the case of a mark the registration of which (by reference to the date of application for registration) becomes due for renewal, the mark is registered at any time within six months before the date on which renewal is due, the registration may be renewed by the payment of—

(a) the renewal fee within six months after the actual date of registration; or
(b) the renewal fee and additional renewal fee within the period commencing on the date six months after the actual date of registration (that is to say, at the end of the period referred to in paragraph (a)) and ending on the date six months after the due date of renewal;

and, where the fees referred to in paragraph (b) are not paid within the period specified in that paragraph the register shall, subject to rule 30 below, remove the mark from the register.

(4) Where, in the case of a mark the registration of which (by reference to the date of application for registration) becomes due for renewal, the mark is registered after the date of renewal, the registration may be renewed by the payment of the renewal fee within six months of the actual date of registration; and where the renewal fee is not paid within that period the registrar shall, subject to rule 30 below, remove the mark from the register.

(5) The removal of the registration of a trade mark shall be published.

30 Restoration of registration; s 43

(1) Where the registrar has removed the mark from the register for failure to renew its registration in accordance with rule 29 above, he may, upon a request filed on Form TM13 within six months of the date of the removal of the mark accompanied by the appropriate renewal fee and appropriate restoration fee, restore the mark to the register and renew its registration if, having regard to the circumstances of the failure to renew, he is satisfied that it is just to do so.

(2) The restoration of the registration shall be published, with the date of restoration shown.

Revocation, invalidation and rectification

31 Procedure on application for revocation, declaration of invalidity and rectification of the register; ss 46, 47 & 64

(1) An application to the registrar for revocation under section 46 or declaration of invalidity under section 47 of the registration of a trade mark or for the rectification of an error or

omission in the register under section 64 shall be made on Form TM26 together with a statement of the grounds on which the application is made.

(2) Where any application is made under paragraph (1) by a person other than the proprietor of the registered trade mark, the registrar shall send a copy of the application and the statement to the proprietor.

(3) Within three months of the date on which the registrar sends a copy of the application and the statement to the proprietor, the proprietor may file a counter-statement together with Form TM8 and the registrar shall send a copy thereof to the applicant:

Provided that where an application for revocation is based on the ground of non-use under section 46(1)(a) or (b), the proprietor shall file (within the period allowed for the filing of any counter-statement) evidence of the use by him of the mark; and if he fails so to file evidence the registrar may treat his opposition to the application as having been withdrawn.

(4) Subject to paragraph (2) above and paragraphs (6) and (7) below, the provisions of rule 13 shall apply to proceedings relating to the application as they apply to opposition proceedings for the registration of a trade mark, save that, in the case of an application for revocation on the grounds of non-use under section 46(1)(a) or (b), the application shall be granted where no counter-statement is filed.

(5) Any person, other than the registered proprietor, claiming to have an interest in proceedings on an application under this rule may file an application to the registrar on Form TM27 for leave to intervene, stating the nature of his interest and the registrar may, after hearing the parties concerned if so required, refuse such leave or grant leave upon such terms or conditions (including any undertaking as to costs) as he thinks fit.

(6) Any person granted leave to intervene (the intervener) shall, subject to the terms and conditions imposed in respect of the intervention, be treated as a party for the purposes of the application of the provisions of rule 13 to the proceedings on an application under this rule.

(7) When the registrar has made a decision on the application following any opposition, intervention or proceedings held in accordance with this rule, he shall send the applicant, the person opposing the application and the intervener (if any) written notice of it, stating the reasons for his decision; and for the purposes of any appeal against the registrar's decision the date when the notice of the decision is sent shall be taken to be the date of the decision.

The register

32   Form of register; s 63(1)
The register required to be maintained by the registrar under section 63(1) need not be kept in documentary form.

33   Entry in register of particulars of registered trade marks; s 63(2)
In addition to the entries in the register of registered trade marks required to be made by section 63(2)(a), there shall be entered in the register in respect of each trade mark registered therein the following particulars—

    (a) the date of registration as determined in accordance with section 40(3) (that is to say, the date of the filing of the application for registration);

    (b) the actual date of registration (that is to say, the date of the entry in the register);

    (c) the priority date (if any) to be accorded pursuant to a claim to a right to priority made under section 35 or 36;

    (d) the name and address of the proprietor;

(e) the address for service (if any) as furnished pursuant to rule 10 above;
(f) any disclaimer or limitation of rights under section 13(1)(a) or (b);
(g) any memorandum or statement of the effect of any memorandum relating to a trade mark of which the registrar has been notified on Form TM24;
(h) the goods or services in respect of which the mark is registered;
(i) where the mark is a collective or certification mark, that fact; and
(j) where the mark is registered pursuant to section 5(5) with the consent of the proprietor of an earlier trade mark or other earlier right, that fact.

34 Entry in register of particulars of registrable transactions; s 25
Upon application made to the registrar by such person as is mentioned in section 25(1)(a) or (b) there shall be entered in the register the following particulars of registrable transactions, that is to say—

(a) in the case of an assignment of a registered trade mark or any right in it—
  (i) the name and address of the assignee,
  (ii) the date of the assignment, and
  (iii) where the assignment is in respect of any right in the mark, a description of the right assigned;
(b) in the case of the grant of a licence under a registered trade mark—
  (i) the name and address of the licensee,
  (ii) where the licence is an exclusive licence, that fact,
  (iii) where the licence is limited, a description of the limitation, and
  (iv) the duration of the licence if the same is or is ascertainable as a definite period;
(c) in the case of the grant of any security interest over a registered trade mark or any right in or under it—
  (i) the name and address of the grantee,
  (ii) the nature of the interest (whether fixed or floating), and
  (iii) the extent of the security and the right in or under the mark secured;
(d) in the case of the making by personal representatives of an assent in relation to a registered trade mark or any right in or under it—
  (i) the name and address of the person in whom the mark or any right in or under it vests by virtue of the assent, and
  (ii) the date of the assent; and
(e) in the case of a court or other competent authority transferring a registered trade mark or any right in or under it—
  (i) the name and address of the transferee,
  (ii) the date of the order, and
  (iii) where the transfer is in respect of a right in the mark, a description of the right transferred;
and, in each case, there shall be entered the date on which the entry is made.

35 Application to register or give notice of transaction; ss 25 & 27(3)
(1) An application to register particulars of a transaction to which section 25 applies or to give notice to the registrar of particulars of a transaction to which section 27(3) applies shall be made, subject to paragraph (2) below,

(a) relating to an assignment or transaction other than a transaction referred to in sub-paragraphs (b) to (d) below, on Form TM16;
(b) relating to a grant of a licence, on Form TM50;

(c) relating to an amendment to, or termination of a licence, on Form TM51;

(d) relating to the grant, amendment or termination of any security interest, on Form TM24; and

(e) relating to the making by personal representatives of an assent or to an order of a court or other competent authority, on Form TM24.

(2) An application under paragraph (1) above shall—

(a) where the transaction is an assignment, be signed by or on behalf of the parties to the assignment;

(b) where the transaction falls within sub-paragraphs (b), (c) or (d) of paragraph (1) above, be signed by or on behalf of the grantor of the licence or security interest;

or be accompanied by such documentary evidence as suffices to establish the transaction.

(3) Where the transaction is effected by an instrument chargeable with duty, the application shall be subject to the registrar being satisfied that the instrument has been duly stamped.

(4) Where an application to give notice to the registrar has been made of particulars relating to an application for registration of a trade mark, upon registration of the trade mark, the registrar shall enter those particulars in the register.

36 Public inspection of register; s 63(3)
(1) The register shall be open for public inspection at the Office during the hours of business of the Office as published in accordance with rule 64 below.

(2) Where any portion of the register is kept otherwise than in documentary form, the right of inspection is a right to inspect the material on the register.

37 Supply of certified copies etc; s 63(3)
The registrar shall supply a certified copy or extract or uncertified copy or extract, as requested on Form TM31R, of any entry in the register.

38 Request for change of name or address in register; s 64(4)
(1) The registrar shall, on a request made on Form TM21 by the proprietor of a registered trade mark or a licensee or any person having an interest in or charge on a registered trade mark which has been registered under rule 34, enter any change in his name or address as recorded in the register.

(2) The registrar may at any time, on a request made on Form TM33 by any person who has furnished an address for service under rule 10 above, if the address is recorded in the register, change it.

39 Removal of matter from register; s 64(5)
(1) Where it appears to the registrar that any matter in the register has ceased to have effect, before removing it from the register—

(a) he may, where he considers it appropriate, publish his intention to remove that matter, and

(b) where any person appears to him to be affected by the removal, he shall send notice of his intention to that person.

(2) Within three months of the date on which his intention to remove the matter is published, or notice of his intention is sent, as the case may be—

(a) any person may file notice of opposition to the removal on form TM7; and

(b) the person to whom a notice is sent under paragraph (1)(b) above may file, in writing—
  (i) his objections, if any, to the removal, or
  (ii) a request to have his objections heard orally;

and where such opposition or objections are made, rule 47 shall apply.

(3) If the registrar is satisfied after considering any objections or opposition to the removal that the matter has not ceased to have effect, he shall not remove it.

(4) Where there has been no response to the registrar's notice he may remove the matter; where representations objecting to the removal of the entry have been made (whether in writing or orally) the registrar may, if he is of the view after considering the objections that the entry of any part thereof has ceased to have effect, remove it or, as appropriate, the part thereof.

Change of classification

40   Change of classification; ss 65(2) & 76(1)
(1) Subject to section 65(3), the registrar may—

  (a) in order to reclassify the specification of a registered trade mark founded on Schedule 3 to one founded on Schedule 4, or
  (b) consequent upon an amendment of the International Classification of Goods and Services referred to in rule 7(2) above,

make such amendments to entries on the register as he considers necessary for the purposes of reclassifying the specification of the registered trade mark.

(2) Before making any amendment to the register under paragraph (1) above the registrar shall give the proprietor of the mark written notice of his proposals for amendment and shall at the same time advise him that—

  (a) he may make written objections to the proposals, within three months of the date of the notice, stating the grounds of his objections, and
  (b) if no written objections are received within the period specified the registrar will publish the proposals and he will not be entitled to make any objections thereto upon such publication.

(3) If the proprietor makes no written objections within the period specified in paragraph (2)(a) above or at any time before the expiration of that period gives the registrar written notice of his intention not to make any objections, the registrar shall as soon as practicable after the expiration of that period or upon receipt of the notice publish the proposals.

(4) Where the proprietor makes written objections within the period specified in paragraph (2)(a) above, the registrar shall, as soon as practicable after he has considered the objections, publish the proposals or, where he has amended the proposals, publish the proposals as amended; and his decision shall be final and not subject to appeal.

41   Opposition to proposals; ss 65(3) & 76(1)
(1) Notice of any opposition shall be filed on Form TM7 within three months of the date of publication of the proposals under rule 40 above and there shall be stated in the notice the grounds of opposition and, in particular, how the proposed amendments would be contrary to section 65(3).

(2) The registrar may require or admit evidence directed to the questions in issue and if so requested by any person opposing the proposal give that person the opportunity to be heard thereon before deciding the matter.

(3) If no notice of opposition under paragraph (1) above is filed within the time specified, or where any opposition has been determined, the registrar shall make the amendments as proposed and shall enter in the register the date when they were made; and his decision shall be final and not subject to appeal.

Request for information, inspection of documents and confidentiality

42 Request for information; s 67(1)
A request for information relating to an application for registration or to a registered trade mark shall be made on Form TM31C.

43 Information available before publication; s 67(2)
Before publication of an application for registration the registrar shall make available for inspection by the public the application and any amendments made to it and any particulars contained in a notice given to the registrar under rule 35.

44 Inspection of documents; ss 67 & 76(1)
(1) Subject to paragraphs (2) and (3) below, the registrar shall permit all documents filed or kept at the Office in relation to a registered mark or, where an application for the registration of a trade mark has been published, in relation to that application, to be inspected.

(2) The registrar shall not be obliged to permit the inspection of any such document as is mentioned in paragraph (1) above until he has completed any procedure, or the stage in the procedure which is relevant to the document in question, which he is required or permitted to carry out under the Act or these Rules.

(3) The right of inspection under paragraph (1) above does not apply to—

    (a) any document until fourteen days after it has been filed at the Office;
    (b) any document prepared in the Office solely for use therein;
    (c) any document sent to the Office, whether at its request or otherwise, for inspection and subsequent return to the sender;
    (d) any request for information under rule 42 above;
    (e) any document issued by the Office which the registrar considers should be treated as confidential;
    (f) any document in respect of which the registrar issues directions under rule 45 below that it be treated as confidential.

(4) Nothing in paragraph (1) shall be construed as imposing on the registrar any duty of making available for public inspection—

    (a) any document or part of a document which in his opinion disparages any person in a way likely to damage him; or
    (b) any document filed with or sent to the Office before 31 October 1994.

(5) No appeal shall lie from a decision of the registrar under paragraph (4) above not to make any document or part of a document available for public inspection.

45 Confidential documents
(1) Where a document other than a form required by the registrar and published in accordance with rule 3 above is filed at the Office and the person filing it requests, at the time of filing or within fourteen days of the filing, that it or a specified part of it be treated as confidential, giving his reasons, the registrar may direct that it or part of it, as the case may be, be treated as confidential, and the document shall not be open to public inspection while the matter is being determined by the registrar.

(2) Where such direction has been given and not withdrawn, nothing in this rule shall be taken to authorise or require any person to be allowed to inspect the document or part of it to which the direction relates except by leave of the registrar.

(3) The registrar shall not withdraw any direction given under this rule without prior consultation with the person at whose request the direction was given, unless the registrar is satisfied that such prior consultation is not reasonably practical.

(4) The registrar may where he considers that any document issued by the Office should be treated as confidential so direct, and upon such direction that document shall not be open to public inspection except by leave of the registrar.

(5) Where a direction is given under this rule for a document to be treated as confidential a record of the fact shall be filed with the document.

Agents

46 Proof of authorisation of agent may be required; s 82

(1) Where an agent has been authorised under section 82, the registrar may in any particular case require the personal signature or presence of the agent or the person authorising him to act as agent.

(2) Where after a person has become a party to proceedings before the registrar, he appoints an agent for the first time or appoints one agent in substitution for another, the newly appointed agent shall file Form TM33, and any act required or authorised by the Act in connection with the registration of a trade mark or any procedure relating to a trade mark may not be done by or to the newly appointed agent until on or after the date on which he files that form.

(3) The registrar may by notice in writing sent to an agent require him to produce evidence of his authority.

47 Registrar may refuse to deal with certain agents; s 88

The registrar may refuse to recognise as agent in respect of any business under the Act—

(a) a person who has been convicted of an offence under section 84;

(b) an individual whose name has been erased from and not restored to, or who is suspended from, the register of trade mark agents on the ground of misconduct;

(c) a person who is found by the Secretary of State to have been guilty of such conduct as would, in the case of an individual registered in that register, render him liable to have his name erased from it on the ground of misconduct;

(d) a partnership or body corporate of which one of the partners or directors is a person whom the registrar could refuse to recognise under paragraph (a), (b) or (c) above.

Decision of registrar, evidence and costs

48 Decisions of registrar to be taken after hearing

(1) Without prejudice to any provisions of the Act or these Rules requiring the registrar to hear any party to proceedings under the Act or these Rules, or to give such party an opportunity to be heard, the registrar shall, before taking any decision on any matter under the Act or these Rules which is or may be adverse to any party to any proceedings before him, give that party an opportunity to be heard.

(2) The registrar shall give that party at least fourteen days' notice of the time when he may be heard unless that party consents to shorter notice.

49 Evidence in proceedings before registrar; s 69
(1) Where under these Rules evidence may be admitted by the registrar in any proceedings before him, it shall be by the filing of a statutory declaration or affidavit.

(2) The registrar may in any particular case take oral evidence in lieu of or in addition to such evidence and shall, unless he otherwise directs, allow any witness to be cross-examined on his statutory declaration, affidavit or oral evidence.

50 Making and subscription of statutory declaration or affidavit
(1) Any statutory declaration or affidavit filed under the Act or these Rules shall be made and subscribed as follows—

    (a) in the United Kingdom, before any justice of the peace or any commissioner or other officer authorised by law in any part of the United Kingdom to administer an oath for the purpose of any legal proceedings;

    (b) in any other part of Her Majesty's dominions or in the Republic of Ireland, before any court, judge, justice of the peace or any officer authorised by law to administer an oath there for the purpose of any legal proceedings; and

    (c) elsewhere, before a commissioner for oaths, notary public, judge or magistrate.

(2) Any document purporting to have affixed, impressed or subscribed thereto or thereon the seal or signature of any person authorised by paragraph (1) above to take a declaration may be admitted by the registrar without proof of the genuineness of the seal or signature, or of the official character of the person or his authority to take the declaration.

51 Registrar's power to require documents, information or evidence
At any stage of any proceedings before the registrar, he may direct that such documents, information or evidence as he may reasonably require shall be filed within such period as he may specify.

52 Registrar to have power of an official referee; s 69
(1) The registrar shall in relation to the examination of witnesses on oath and the discovery and production of documents have all the powers of an official referee of the Supreme Court.

(2) The rules applicable to the attendance of witnesses before such a referee shall apply in relation to the attendance of witnesses in proceedings before the registrar.

53 Hearings before registrar to be in public
(1) The hearing before the registrar of any dispute between two or more parties relating to any matter in connection with an application for the registration of a mark or a registered mark shall be in public unless the registrar, after consultation with those parties who appear in person or are represented at the hearing, otherwise directs.

(2) Nothing in this rule shall prevent a member of the Council on Tribunals or of its Scottish Committee from attending a hearing in his capacity as such.

54 Costs of proceedings; s 68
The registrar may, in any proceedings before him under the Act or these Rules, by order award to any party such costs as he may consider reasonable, and direct how and by what parties they are to be paid.

55 Security for costs; s 68

(1) The registrar may require any person who is a party in any proceedings before him under the Act or these Rules to give security for costs in relation to those proceedings; and he may require security for the costs of any appeal from his decision.

(2) In default of such security being given, the registrar, in the case of the proceedings before him, or, in the case of an appeal, the person appointed under section 76 may treat the party in default as having withdrawn his application, opposition, objection or intervention, as the case may be.

56 Decision of registrar

(1) When, in any proceedings before him, the registrar has made a decision following a hearing or, if a hearing has not been requested, after considering any submission in writing, he shall send notice of his decision in writing to each party to the proceedings, and for the purpose of any appeal against the registrar's decision, subject to paragraph (2) below, the date of the decision shall be the date when the notice is sent.

(2) Where a statement of the reasons for the decision is not included in the notice sent under paragraph (1) above, any party may, within one month of the date on which the notice was sent to him, request the registrar on form TM5 to send him a statement of the reasons for the decision and upon such request the registrar shall send such a statement; and the date on which that statement is sent shall be deemed to be the date of the registrar's decision for the purpose of any appeal against it.

Appeals

57 Appeal to person appointed; s 76

(1) Notice of appeal to the person appointed under section 76 shall be sent to the registrar within one month of the date of the registrar's decision which is the subject of the appeal accompanied by a statement in writing of the appellant's grounds of appeal and of his case in support of the appeal.

(2) The registrar shall send the notice and the statement to the person appointed.

(3) Where any person other than the appellant was a party to the proceedings before the registrar in which the decision appealed against was made, the registrar shall send to that person a copy of the notice and the statement.

58 Determination whether appeal should be referred to court; s 76(3)

(1) Within one month of the date on which the notice of appeal is sent by the registrar under rule 57(3) above;

  (a) the registrar, or
  (b) any person who was a party to the proceedings in which the decision appealed against was made,

may request that the person appointed refer the appeal to the court.

(2) Where the registrar requests that the appeal be referred to the court, he shall send a copy of the request to each party to the proceedings.

(3) A request under paragraph (1)(b) above shall be sent to the registrar; the registrar shall send it to the person appointed and shall send a copy of the request to any other party to the proceedings.

(4) Within one month of the date on which a copy of a request is sent by the registrar under

paragraph (2) or (3) above, the person to whom it is sent may make representations as to whether the appeal should be referred to the court.

(5) In any case where, it appears to the person appointed that a point of general legal importance is involved in the appeal, he shall send to the registrar and to every party to the proceedings in which the decision appealed against was made, notice thereof.

(6) Within one month of the date on which a notice is sent under paragraph (5) above, the person to whom it was sent may make representations as to whether the appeal should be referred to the court.

59   Hearing of appeal; s 76(4)

(1) Where the person appointed does not refer the appeal to the court, he shall send notice of the time and place appointed for the hearing of the appeal—

(a) where no person other than the appellant was a party to the proceedings in which the decision appealed against was made, to the registrar and to the appellant, and
(b) in any other case, to the registrar and to each person who was a party to those proceedings.

(2) The provisions of rule 48(2) and rules 49 to 55 shall apply to the person appointed and to proceedings before the person appointed as they apply to the registrar and to proceedings before the registrar.

(3) The person appointed shall send a copy of his decision, with a statement of his reasons therefor, to the registrar and to each person who was a party to the proceedings before him.

Correction of irregularities, calculation and extension of time

60   Correction of irregularities of procedure

(1) Any irregularity in procedure in or before the Office or the registrar may be rectified, subject to paragraph (2) below, on such terms as he may direct.

(2) In the case of an irregularity or prospective irregularity—

(a) which consists of a failure to comply with any limitation as to times or periods specified in the Act, these Rules or the old law as that law continues to apply and which has occurred or appears to the registrar as likely to occur in the absence of a direction under this rule, and
(b) which is attributable wholly or in part to an error, default or omission on the part of the Office or the registrar and which it appears to him should be rectified,

he may direct that the time or period in question shall be altered in such manner as he may specify.

(3) Paragraph (2) above is without prejudice to the registrar's power to extend any time or periods under rule 62 below.

61   Calculation of times and periods

(1) Where, on any day, there is—

(a) a general interruption or subsequent dislocation in the postal services of the United Kingdom, or
(b) an event or circumstances causing an interruption in the normal operation of the Office,

the registrar may certify the day as being one on which there is an 'interruption' and, where any period of time specified in the Act or these Rules for the giving, making or filing of any notice, application or other document expires on a day so certified the period shall be extended to the first day next following (not being an excluded day) which is not so certified.

(2) Any certificate of the registrar given pursuant to this rule shall be posed in the Office.

(3) If in any particular case the registrar is satisfied that the failure to give, make or file any notice, application or other document within any period of time specified in the Act or these Rules for such giving, making or filing was wholly or mainly attributable to a failure or undue delay in the postal services in the United Kingdom, the registrar may, if he thinks fit, extend the period so that it ends on the day of the receipt by the addressee of the notice, application or other document (or, if the day of such receipt is an excluded day, on the first following day which is not an excluded day), upon such notice to other parties and upon such terms as he may direct.

(4) In this rule 'excluded day' means a day which is not a business day of the Office under the registrar's direction pursuant to section 80, as published in accordance with rule 64 below.

62 Alteration of time limits

(1) The time or periods—

(a) prescribed by these Rules, other than the times or periods prescribed by the rules mentioned in paragraph (3) below, or

(b) specified by the registrar for doing any act or taking any proceedings,

may, at the request of the person or party concerned, be extended by the registrar as he thinks fit, upon such notice to any other person or partly affected and upon such terms as he may direct.

(2) A request for the extension of a period prescribed by these Rules which is filed after the application has been published under rule 12 above shall be on Form TM9 and shall in any other case be on that form if the registrar so directs.

(3) The rules excepted from paragraph (1) above are rule 10(6) (failure to file address for service), rule 11 (deficiencies in application), rule 13(1) (time for filing opposition), rule 13(2) (time for filing counter-statement), rule 29 (delayed renewal) and rule 30 (restoration of registration).

(4) Subject to paragraph (5) below, a request for extension under paragraph (1) above shall be made before the time or period in question has expired.

(5) Where the request for extension is made after the time or period has expired, the registrar may, at his discretion, extend the period or time if he is satisfied with the explanation for the delay in requesting the extension and it appears to him that any extension would not disadvantage any other person or party affected by it.

(6) Where the period within which any party to any proceedings before the registrar may file evidence under these Rules is to begin upon the expiry of any period in which any other party may file evidence and that other party notifies the registrar that he does not wish to file any, or any further, evidence the registrar may direct that the period within which the first mentioned party may file evidence shall begin on such date as may be specified in the direction and shall notify all parties to the dispute of that date.

Filing of documents, hours of business, Trade Marks Journal and translations

63 Filing of documents by electronic means

The registrar may, at his discretion, permit as an alternative to the sending by post or delivery of the application, notice or other document in legible form the filing of the application, notice or other document by electronic means subject to such terms or conditions as he may specify either generally by published notice or in any particular case by written notice to the person desiring to file any such documents by such means.

64 Directions on hours of business; s 80

Any directions given by the registrar under section 80 specifying the hours of business of the Office and business days of the Office shall be published and posted in the Office.

65 Trade Marks Journal; s 81

The registrar shall publish a journal, entitled 'The Trade Marks Journal', containing particulars of any application for the registration of a trade mark (including a representation of the mark), such information as is required to be published under these Rules and such other information as the registrar thinks fit.

66 Translations

(1) Where any document or part thereof which is in a language other than English is filed or sent to the registrar in pursuance of the Act or these Rules, the registrar may require that there be furnished a translation into English of the document or that part, verified to the satisfaction of the registrar as corresponding to the original text.

(2) The registrar may refuse to accept any translation which is in his opinion inaccurate and thereupon another translation of the document in question verified as aforesaid shall be furnished.

Transitional provisions and revocations

67 Pending applications for registration; Sch 3 para 10(2)

Where an application for registration of a mark made under the old law is advertised on or after 31 October 1994, the period within which notice of opposition may be filed shall be three months from the date of advertisement, and such period shall not be extendible.

68 Form for conversions of pending application; Sch 3, para 11(2)

A notice to the registrar under paragraph 11(2) of Schedule 3 to the Act, claiming to have the registrability of the mark determined in accordance with the provisions of the Act, shall be in the form set out in Schedule 2 to these Rules.

69 Revocation of previous Rules

(1) The rules specified in Schedule 1 are hereby revoked.

(2) Except as provided by rule 67 above, where—

    (a) immediately before these Rules come into force, any time or period prescribed by the Rules hereby revoked has effect in relation to any act or proceeding and has not expired, and

    (b) the corresponding time or period prescribed by these Rules would have expired or would expire earlier,

the time or period prescribed by those Rules and not by these Rules shall apply to that act or proceeding.

SCHEDULE 1

Revocations

Rule 69

Rules revoked	Reference
The Trade Marks and Service Marks Rules 1986	SI 1986/1319
The Trade Marks and Service Marks (Amendment) Rules 1988	SI 1988/1112
The Trade Marks and Service Marks (Amendment) Rules 1989	SI 1989/1117
The Trade Marks and Service Marks (Amendment) Rules 1990	SI 1990/1459
The Trade Marks and Service Marks (Amendment) (No 2) Rules 1990	SI 1990/1799
The Trade Marks and Service Marks (Amendment) Rules 1991	SI 1991/1431
The Trade Marks and Service Marks (Amendment) Rules 1994	SI 1994/2549

SCHEDULE 2

Rule 68

Form TM15

Notice under Schedule 3, paragraph 11 of the Act: Claim to have registrability of a mark applied for before 31 October 1994 determined under the Act (Conversion of application)

1   Your reference

2   Give details of the application you made under the
Trade Marks Act 1938   Number   Class

3   Full name, address and postcode of the applicant

Trade Marks ADP number (if you know it)

4   Name of agent (if appropriate) address for service in the United Kingdom which all correspondence should be sent to (including postcode)

Trade Marks ADP number (if you know it)

I claim to have the registrability of the mark determined in accordance with the provisions of the Trade Marks Act 1994. I acknowledge that this notice is irrevocable.

Signature

Name (block capitals)

Date

Name and daytime telephone number of person we should contact

State the number of any sheets attached to this form

Reminder
You cannot amend a mark under the 1994 Act. If you want to amend the mark you must file form TM21 before or with this form.

The new filing date of your converted application will be the 31st October 1994, which is the commencement date of the 1994 Act.

SCHEDULE 3

Classification of goods (pre-1938)

Rule 7(1)

Class 1 Chemical substances used in manufactures, photography, or philosophical research, and anti-corrosives.

Class 2 Chemical substances used for agricultural, horticultural, veterinary and sanitary purposes.

Class 3 Chemical substances prepared for use in medicine and pharmacy.

Class 4 Raw, or partly prepared, vegetable, animal, and mineral substances used in manufactures, not included in other Classes.

Class 5 Unwrought and partly wrought metals used in manufacture.

Class 6 Machinery of all kinds, and parts of machinery, except agricultural and horticultural machines and their parts included in Class 7.

Class 7 Agricultural and horticultural machinery, and parts of such machinery.

Class 8 Philosophical instruments, scientific instruments, and apparatus for useful purposes; instruments and apparatus for teaching.

Class 9 Musical instruments.

Class 10 Horological instruments.

Class 11 Instruments, apparatus, and contrivances, not medicated, for surgical or curative purposes, or in relation to the health of men or animals.

Class 12 Cutlery and edge tools.

Class 13 Metal goods, not included in other Classes.

Class 14 Goods of precious metals and jewellery, and imitations of such goods and jewellery.

Class 15 Glass.

Class 16 Porcelain and earthenware.

Class 17 Manufactures from mineral and other substances for building or decoration.

Class 18 Engineering, architectural, and building contrivances.

Class 19 Arms, ammunition, and stores, not included in Class 20.

Class 20 Explosive substances.

Class 21 Naval architectural contrivances and naval equipments not included in other Classes.

Class 22 Carriages.

Class 23 (a) Cotton yarn; (b) Sewing cotton.

Class 24 Cotton piece goods.

Class 25 Cotton goods not included in other Classes.

Class 26 Linen and hemp yarn and thread.

Class 27 Linen and hemp piece goods.

Class 28 Linen and hemp goods not included in other Classes.

Class 29 Jute yarns and tissues, and other articles made of jute, not included in other Classes.

Class 30 Silk, spun, thrown, or sewing.

Class 31 Silk piece goods.

Class 32 Silk goods not included in other Classes.

Class 33 Yarns of wool, worsted, or hair.

Class 34 Cloths and stuffs of wool, worsted, or hair.

Class 35 Woollen and worsted and hair goods, not included in other Classes.

Class 36 Carpets, floor-cloth, and oil-cloth.

Class 37 Leather, skins unwrought and wrought, and articles made of leather not included in other Classes.

Class 38 Articles of clothing.

Class 39 Paper (except paper hangings), stationery, and bookbinding.

Class 40 Goods manufactured from india-rubber and gutta-percha not included in other Classes.

Class 41 Furniture and upholstery.

Class 42 Substances used as food or as ingredients in food.

Class 43 Fermented liquors and spirits.

Class 44 Mineral and aerated waters, natural and artificial, including ginger beer.

Class 45 Tobacco, whether manufactured or unmanufactured.

Class 46 Seeds for agricultural and horticultural purposes.

Class 47 Candles, common soap, detergents; illuminating, heating, or lubricating oils; matches; and starch, blue, and other preparations for laundry purposes.

Class 48 Perfumery (including toilet articles, preparations for the teeth and hair, and perfumed soap).

Class 49 Games of all kinds and sporting articles not included in other Classes.

Class 50 Miscellaneous:—
  (1) Goods manufactured from ivory, bone or wood, not included in other Classes.
  (2) Goods manufactured from straw or grass, not included in other Classes.
  (3) Goods manufactured from animal and vegetable substances, not included in other Classes.
  (4) Tobacco pipes.
  (5) Umbrellas, walking sticks, brushes and combs for the hair.
  (6) Furniture cream, plate powder.
  (7) Tarpaulins, tents, rick-cloths, rope (jute or hemp), twine.
  (8) Buttons of all kinds other than of precious metal or imitations thereof.
  (9) Packing and hose.
  (10) Other goods not included in the foregoing Classes.

SCHEDULE 4

CLASSIFICATION OF GOODS AND SERVICES

Rule 7(2)

Goods

Class 1 Chemicals used in industry, science and photography, as well as in agriculture, horticulture and forestry; unprocessed artificial resins, unprocessed plastics; manures; fire extinguishing compositions; tempering and soldering preparations; chemical substances for preserving foodstuffs; tanning substances; adhesives used in industry.

Class 2 Paints, varnishes, lacquers; preservatives against rust and against deterioration of wood; colorants; mordants; raw natural resins; metals in foil and powder form for painters, decorators, printers and artists.

Class 3 Bleaching preparations and other substances for laundry use; cleaning, polishing, scouring and abrasive preparations; soaps; perfumery, essential oils, cosmetics, hair lotions; dentifrices.

Class 4 Industrial oils and greases; lubricants; dust absorbing, wetting and binding compositions; fuels (including motor spirit) and illuminants; candles, wicks.

Class 5 Pharmaceutical, veterinary and sanitary preparations; dietetic substances adapted for medical use, food for babies; plasters, materials for dressings; material for stopping teeth, dental wax; disinfectants; preparations for destroying vermin; fungicides, herbicides.

Class 6 Common metals and their alloys; metal building materials; transportable buildings of metal; materials of metal for railway tracks; non-electric cables and wires of common metal; ironmongery, small items of metal hardware; pipes and tubes of metal; safes; goods of common metal not included in other classes; ores.

Class 7 Machines and machine tools; motors and engines (except for land vehicles); machine coupling and transmission components (except for land vehicles); agricultural implements; incubators for eggs.

Class 8 Hand tools and implements (hand operated); cutlery; side arms; razors.

Class 9 Scientific, nautical, surveying, electric, photographic, cinematographic, optical, weighing, measuring, signalling, checking (supervision), life-saving and teaching apparatus and instruments; apparatus for recording, transmission or reproduction of sound or images; magnetic data carriers, recording discs; automatic vending machines and mechanisms for coin-operated apparatus; cash registers, calculating machines, data processing equipment and computers; fire-extinguishing apparatus.

Class 10 Surgical, medical, dental and veterinary apparatus and instruments, artificial limbs, eyes and teeth; orthopaedic articles; suture materials.

Class 11 Apparatus for lighting, heating, steam generating, cooking, refrigerating, drying, ventilating, water supply and sanitary purposes.

Class 12 Vehicles; apparatus for locomotion by land, air or water.

Class 13 Firearms; ammunition and projectiles; explosives; fireworks.

Class 14 Precious metals and their alloys and goods in precious metals or coated therewith, not included in other classes; jewellery, precious stones; horological and chronometric instruments.

Class 15 Musical instruments.

Class 16 Paper, cardboard and goods made from these materials, not included in other classes; printed matter; bookbinding material; photographs; stationery; adhesives for stationery or household purposes; artists' materials; paint brushes; typewriters and office requisites (except furniture); instructional and teaching material (except apparatus); plastic materials for packaging (not included in other classes); playing cards; printers' type; printing blocks.

Class 17 Rubber, gutta-percha, gum, asbestos, mica and goods made from these materials and not included in other classes; plastics in extruded form for use in manufacture; packing, stopping and insulating materials; flexible pipes, not of metal.

Class 18 Leather and imitations of leather, and goods made of these materials and not included in other classes; animal skins, hides; trunks and travelling bags; umbrellas, parasols and walking sticks; whips, harness and saddlery.

Class 19 Building materials (non-metallic); non-metallic rigid pipes for building; asphalt, pitch and bitumen; non-metallic transportable buildings; monuments, not of metal.

Class 20 Furniture, mirrors, picture frames; goods (not included in other classes) of wood, cork, reed, cane, wicker, horn, bone ivory, whalebone, shell, amber, mother-of-pearl, meerschaum and substitutes for all these materials, or of plastics.

Class 21 Household or kitchen utensils and containers (not of precious metal or coated therewith); combs and sponges; brushes (except paint brushes); brush-making materials; articles for cleaning purposes; steelwool; unworked or semi-worked glass (except glass used in building); glassware, porcelain and earthenware not included in other classes.

Class 22 Ropes, string, nets, tents, awnings, tarpaulins, sails, sacks and bags (not included in other classes); padding and stuffing materials (except of rubber or plastics); raw fibrous textile materials.

Class 23 Yarns and threads, for textile use.

Class 24 Textiles and textile goods, not included in other classes; bed and table covers.

Class 25 Clothing, footwear, headgear.

Class 26 Lace and embroidery, ribbons and braid; buttons, hooks and eyes, pins and needles; artificial flowers.

Class 27 Carpets, rugs, mats and matting, linoleum and other materials for covering existing floors; wall hangings (non-textile).

Class 28 Games and playthings; gymnastic and sporting articles not included in other classes; decorations for Christmas trees.

Class 29 Meat, fish, poultry and game; meat extracts; preserved, dried and cooked fruits and vegetables; jellies, jams, fruit sauces; eggs, milk and milk products; edible oils and fats.

Class 30 Coffee, tea, cocoa, sugar, rice, tapioca, sago, artificial coffee; flour and preparations made from cereals, bread, pastry and confectionery, ices; honey, treacle; yeast, baking-powder; salt, mustard; vinegar, sauces (condiments); spices; ice.

Class 31 Agricultural, horticultural and forestry products and grains not included in other classes; live animals; fresh fruits and vegetables; seeds, natural plants and flowers; foodstuffs for animals, malt.

Class 32 Beers; mineral and aerated waters and other non-alcoholic drinks; fruit drinks and fruit juices; syrups and other preparations for making beverages.

Class 33 Alcoholic beverages (except beers).

Class 34 Tobacco; smokers' articles; matches.

Services

Class 35 Advertising; business management; business administration; office functions.

Class 36 Insurance; financial affairs; monetary affairs; real estate affairs.

Class 37 Building construction; repair; installation services.

Class 38 Telecommunications.

Class 39 Transport; packaging and storage of goods; travel arrangement.

Class 40 Treatment of materials.

Class 41 Education; providing of training; entertainment; sporting and cultural activities.

Class 42 Providing of food and drink; temporary accommodation; medical, hygienic and beauty care; veterinary and agricultural services; legal services; scientific and industrial research; computer programming; services that cannot be placed in other classes.

Author's note
The addresses for the filing of documents at the Patent Office are:

Cardiff Road
Newport
Gwent NP9 1RH

and

25 Southampton Buildings
London WC2A 1AY

For the Trade and Service Marks Enquiry desk, telephone 01633 814706/9.

APPENDIX 3

First Council Directive of 21 December 1988 to approximate the laws of the Member States relating to trade marks (89/104/EEC)

THE COUNCIL OF THE EUROPEAN COMMUNITIES,

Having regard to the Treaty establishing the European Economic Community, and in particular Article 100a thereof,

Having regard to the proposal from the Commission,

In co-operation with the European Parliament,

Having regard to the opinion of the Economic and Social Committee,

Whereas the trade mark laws at present applicable in the Member States contain disparities which may impede the free movement of goods and freedom to provide services and may distort competition within the common market; whereas it is therefore necessary, in view of the establishment and functioning of the internal market, to approximate the laws of Member States;

Whereas it is important not to disregard the solutions and advantages which the Community trade mark system may afford to undertakings wishing to acquire trade marks;

Whereas it does not appear to be necessary at present to undertake full-scale approximation of the trade mark laws of the Member States and it will be sufficient if approximation is limited to those national provisions of law which most directly affect the functioning of the internal market;

Whereas the Directive does not deprive the Member States of the right to continue to protect trade marks acquired through use but takes them into account only in regard to the relationship between them and trade marks acquired by registration;

Whereas Member States also remain free to fix the provisions of procedure concerning the registration, the revocation and the invalidity of trade marks acquired by registration; whereas they can, for example, determine the form of trade mark registration and invalidity procedures, decide whether earlier rights should be invoked either in the registration procedure or in the invalidity procedure or in both and, if they allow earlier rights to be invoked in the registration procedure, have an opposition procedure or an *ex officio* examination procedure or both; whereas Member States remain free to determine the effects of revocation or invalidity of trade marks;

Whereas this Directive does not exclude the application to trade marks of provisions of law of the Member States other than trade mark law, such as the provisions relating to unfair competition, civil liability or consumer protection;

Whereas attainment of the objectives at which this approximation of laws is aiming requires that the conditions for obtaining and continuing to hold a registered trade mark are, in general, identical in all Member States; whereas, to this end, it is necessary to list examples of signs which may constitute a trade mark, provided that such signs are capable of distinguishing the goods or services of one undertaking from those of other undertakings; whereas the grounds for refusal or invalidity concerning the trade mark itself, for example, the absence of any distinctive character, or concerning conflicts between the trade mark and earlier rights, are to be listed in an exhaustive manner, even if some of these grounds are listed as an option for the Member States which will therefore be able to maintain or introduce those grounds in their legislation; whereas Member States will be able to maintain or introduce into their legislation grounds of refusal or invalidity linked to conditions for obtaining and continuing to hold a trade mark for which there is no provision of approximation, concerning, for example, the eligibility for the grant of a trade mark, the renewal of the trade mark or rules on fees, or related to the non-compliance with procedural rules;

Whereas in order to reduce the total number of trade marks registered and protected in the Community and, consequently, the number of conflicts which arise between them, it is essential to require that registered trade marks must actually be used or, if not used, be subject to revocation; whereas it is necessary to provide that a trade mark cannot be invalidated on the basis of the existence of a non-used earlier trade mark, while the Member States remain free to apply the same principle in respect of the registration of a trade mark or to provide that a trade mark may not be successfully invoked in infringement proceedings if it is established as a result of a plea that the trade mark could be revoked; whereas in all these cases it is up to the Member States to establish the applicable rules of procedure;

Whereas it is fundamental, in order to facilitate the free circulation of goods and services, to ensure that henceforth registered trade marks enjoy the same protection under the legal systems of all the Member States; whereas this should however not prevent the Member States from granting at their option extensive protection to those trade marks which have a reputation;

Whereas the protection afforded by the registered trade mark, the function of which is in particular to guarantee the trade mark as an indication of origin, is absolute in the case of identity between the mark and the sign and goods or services; whereas the protection applies also in case of similarity between the mark and the sign and the goods or services; whereas it is indispensable to give an interpretation of the concept of similarity in relation to the likelihood of confusion; whereas the likelihood of confusion, the appreciation of which depends on numerous elements and, in particular, on the recognition of the trade mark on the market, of the association which can be made with the used or registered sign, of the degree of similarity between the trade mark and the sign and between the goods or services identified, constitutes the specific condition for such protection; whereas the ways in which likelihood of confusion may be established, and in particular the onus of proof, are a matter for national procedural rules which are not prejudiced by the Directive;

Whereas it is important, for reasons of legal certainty and without inequitably prejudicing the interests of a proprietor of an earlier trade mark, to provide that the latter may no longer request a declaration of invalidity nor may he oppose the use of a trade mark subsequent to his own of which he has knowingly tolerated the use for a substantial length of time, unless the application for the subsequent trade mark was made in bad faith;

Whereas all Member States of the Community are bound by the Paris Convention for the Protection of Industrial Property; whereas it is necessary that the provisions of this Directive are entirely consistent with those of the Paris Convention; whereas the obligations of the Member

States resulting from this Convention are not affected by this Directive; whereas, where appropriate, the second subparagraph of Article 234 of the Treaty is applicable.

HAS ADOPTED THIS DIRECTIVE:

Article 1

Scope

This Directive shall apply to every trade mark in respect of goods or services which is the subject of registration or of an application in a Member State for registration as an individual trade mark, a collective mark or a guarantee or certification mark, or which is the subject of a registration or an application for registration in the Benelux Trade Mark Office or of an international registration having effect in a Member State.

Article 2

Signs of which a trade mark may consist

A trade mark may consist of any sign capable of being represented graphically, particularly words, including personal names, designs, letters, numerals, the shape of goods or of their packaging, provided that such signs are capable of distinguishing the goods or services of one undertaking from those of other undertakings.

Article 3

Grounds for refusal or invalidity

1   The following shall not be registered or if registered shall be liable to be declared invalid:

(a) signs which cannot constitute a trade mark;

(b) trade marks which are devoid of any distinctive character;

(c) trade marks which consist exclusively of signs or indications which may serve, in trade, to designate the kind, quality, quantity, intended purpose, value, geographical origin, or the time of production of the goods or of rendering of the service, or other characteristics of the goods or service;

(d) trade marks which consist exclusively of signs or indications which have become customary in the current language or in the *bona fide* and established practices of the trade;

(e) signs which consist exclusively of:
   — the shape which results from the nature of the goods themselves, or
   — the shape of goods which is necessary to obtain a technical result, or
   — the shape which gives substantial value to the goods;

(f) trade marks which are contrary to public policy or to accepted principles of morality;

(g) trade marks which are of such a nature as to deceive the public, for instance as to the nature, quality or geographical origin of the goods or service;

(h) trade marks which have not been authorised by the competent authorities and are to be refused or invalidated pursuant to Article 6 *ter* of the Paris Convention for the Protection of Industrial Property, hereinafter referred to as the 'Paris Convention'.

2   Any Member State may provide that a trade mark shall not be registered or, if registered, shall be liable to be declared invalid where and to the extent that:

(a) the use of that trade mark may be prohibited pursuant to provisions of law other than trade mark law of the Member State concerned or of the Community;

(b) the trade mark covers a sign of high symbolic value, in particular a religious symbol;

    (c) the trade mark includes badges, emblems and escutcheons other than those covered by Article 6 *ter* of the Paris Convention and which are of public interest, unless the consent of the appropriate authorities to its registration has been given in conformity with the legislation of the Member State;

    (d) the application for registration of the trade mark was made in bad faith by the applicant.

3   A trade mark shall not be refused registration or be declared invalid in accordance with paragraph 1 (b), (c) or (d) if, before the date of application for registration and following the use which has been made of it, it has acquired a distinctive character. Any Member State may in addition provide that this provision shall also apply where the distinctive character was acquired after the date of application for registration or after the date of registration.

4   Any Member State may provide that, by derogation from the preceding paragraphs, the grounds of refusal of registration or invalidity in force in that State prior to the date on which the provisions necessary to comply with this Directive enter into force, shall apply to trade marks for which application has been made prior to that date.

Article 4

Further grounds for refusal or invalidity concerning conflicts with earlier rights

1   A trade mark shall not be registered or, if registered, shall be liable to be declared invalid:

    (a) if it is identical with an earlier trade mark, and the goods or services for which the trade mark is applied for or is registered are identical with the goods or services for which the earlier trade mark is protected;

    (b) if because of its identity with, or similarity to, the earlier trade mark and the identity or similarity of the goods or services covered by the trade marks, there exists a likelihood of confusion on the part of the public, which includes the likelihood of association with the earlier trade mark.

2   'Earlier trade marks' within the meaning of paragraph 1 means:

    (a) trade marks of the following kinds with a date of application for registration which is earlier than the date of application for registration of the trade mark, taking account, where appropriate, of the priorities claimed in respect of those trade marks:
        (i)   Community trade marks;
        (ii) trade marks registered in the Member State or, in the case of Belgium, Luxembourg or the Netherlands, at the Benelux Trade Mark Office;
        (iii) trade marks registered under international arrangements which have effect in the Member State;

    (b) Community trade marks which validly claim seniority, in accordance with the Regulation on the Community trade mark, from a trade mark referred to in (a)(ii) and (iii), even when the latter trade mark has been surrendered or allowed to lapse;

    (c) applications for the trade marks referred to in (a) and (b), subject to their registration;

    (d) trade marks which, on the date of application for registration of the trade mark, or, where appropriate, of the priority claimed in respect of the application for registration of the trade mark, are well known in a Member State, in the sense in which the words 'well known' are used in Article 6 *bis* of the Paris Convention;

3   A trade mark shall furthermore not be registered or, if registered, shall be liable to be declared invalid if it is identical with, or similar to, an earlier Community trade mark within the meaning of paragraph 2 and is to be, or has been, registered for goods or services which are not similar to those for which the earlier Community trade mark is registered, where the earlier Community trade mark has a reputation in the Community and where the use of the later trade

mark without due cause would take unfair advantage of, or be detrimental to, the distinctive character or the repute of the earlier Community trade mark.

4   Any Member State may furthermore provide that a trade mark shall not be registered or, if registered, shall be liable to be declared invalid where, and to the extent that:

(a) the trade mark is identical with, or similar to, an earlier national trade mark within the meaning of paragraph 2 and is to be, or has been, registered for goods or services which are not similar to those for which the earlier trade mark is registered, where the earlier trade mark has a reputation in the Member State concerned and where the use of the later trade mark without due cause would take unfair advantage of, or be detrimental to, the distinctive character or the repute of the earlier trade mark;

(b) rights to a non-registered trade mark or to another sign used in the course of trade were acquired prior to the date of application for registration of the subsequent trade mark, or the date of the priority claimed for the application for registration of the subsequent trade mark and that non-registered trade mark or other sign confers on its proprietor the right to prohibit the use of a subsequent trade mark;

(c) the use of the trade mark may be prohibited by virtue of an earlier right other than the rights referred to in paragraphs 2 and 4 (b) and in particular:
   (i)   a right to a name;
   (ii) a right of personal portrayal;
   (iii) a copyright;
   (iv) an individual property right;

(d) the trade mark is identical with, or similar to, an earlier collective trade mark conferring a right which expired within a period of a maximum of three years preceding application;

(e) the trade mark is identical with, or similar to, an earlier guarantee or certification mark conferring a right which expired within a period preceding application the length of which is fixed by the Member State;

(f) the trade mark is identical with, or similar to, an earlier trade mark which was registered for identical or similar goods or services and conferred on them a right which has expired for failure to renew within a period of a maximum of two years preceding application, unless the proprietor of the earlier trade mark gave his agreement for the registration of the later mark or did not use his trade mark;

(g) the trade mark is liable to be confused with a mark which was in use abroad on the filing date of the application and which is still in use there, provided that at the date of the application the applicant was acting in bad faith.

5   The Member States may permit that in appropriate circumstances registration need not be refused or the trade mark need not be declared invalid where the proprietor of the earlier trade mark or other earlier right consents to the registration of the later trade mark.

6   Any Member State may provide that, by derogation from paragraphs 1 to 5, the grounds for refusal of registration or invalidity in force in that State prior to the date on which the provisions necessary to comply with this Directive enter into force, shall apply to trade marks for which application has been made prior to that date.

Article 5

Rights conferred by a trade mark
1   The registered trade mark shall confer on the proprietor exclusive rights therein. The proprietor shall be entitled to prevent all third parties not having his consent from using in the course of trade:

(a) any sign which is identical with the trade mark in relation to goods or services which are identical with those for which the trade mark is registered;
(b) any sign where, because of its identity with, or similarity to, the trade mark and the identity or similarity of the goods or services covered by the trade mark and the sign, there exists a likelihood of confusion on the part of the public, which includes the likelihood of association between the sign and the trade mark.

2   Any Member State may also provide that the proprietor shall be entitled to prevent all third parties not having his consent from using in the course of trade any sign which is identical with, or similar to, the trade mark in relation to goods or services which are not similar to those for which the trade mark is registered, where the latter has a reputation in the Member State and where use of that sign without due cause takes unfair advantage of, or is detrimental to, the distinctive character or the repute of the trade mark.

3   The following, *inter alia*, may be prohibited under paragraphs 1 and 2:

(a) affixing the sign to the goods or to the packaging thereof;
(b) offering the goods, or putting them on the market or stocking them for these purposes under that sign, or offering or supplying services thereunder;
(c) importing or exporting the goods under the sign;
(d) using the sign on business papers and in advertising.

4   Where, under the law of the Member State, the use of a sign under the conditions referred to in 1 (b) or 2 could not be prohibited before the date on which the provisions necessary to comply with this Directive entered into force in the Member State concerned, the rights conferred by the trade mark may not be relied on to prevent the continued use of the sign.

5   Paragraphs 1 to 4 shall not affect provisions in any Member State relating to the protection against the use of a sign other than for the purposes of distinguishing goods or services, where use of that sign without due cause takes unfair advantage of, or is detrimental to, the distinctive character or the repute of the trade mark.

Article 6

Limitation of the effects of a trade mark
1   The trade mark shall not entitle the proprietor to prohibit a third party from using, in the course of trade,

(a) his own name or address;
(b) indications concerning the kind, quality, quantity, intended purpose, value, geographical origin, the time of production of goods or of rendering of the service, or other characteristics of goods or services;
(c) the trade mark where it is necessary to indicate the intended purpose of a product or service, in particular as accessories or spare parts;

provided he uses them in accordance with honest practices in industrial or commercial matters.

2   The trade mark shall not entitle the proprietor to prohibit a third party from using, in the course of trade, an earlier right which only applies in a particular locality if that right is recognised by the laws of the Member State in question and within the limits of the territory in which it is recognised.

Article 7

Exhaustion of the rights conferred by a trade mark

1   The trade mark shall not entitle the proprietor to prohibit its use in relation to goods which have been put on the market in the Community under that trade mark by the proprietor or with his consent.

2   Paragraph 1 shall not apply where there exist legitimate reasons for the proprietor to oppose further commercialisation of the goods, especially where the condition of the goods is changed or impaired after they have been put on the market.

Article 8

Licensing

1   A trade mark may be licensed for some or all of the goods or services for which it is registered and for the whole or part of the Member State concerned. A licence may be exclusive or non-exclusive.

2   The proprietor of a trade mark may invoke the rights conferred by that trade mark against a licensee who contravenes any provision in his licensing contract with regard to its duration, the form covered by the registration in which the trade mark may be used, the scope of the goods or services for which the licence is granted, the territory in which the trade mark may be affixed, or the quality of the goods manufactured or of the services provided by the licensee.

Article 9

Limitation in consequence of acquiescence

1   Where, in a Member State, the proprietor of an earlier trade mark as referred to in Article 4(2) has acquiesced, for a period of five successive years, in the use of a later trade mark registered in that Member State while being aware of such use, he shall no longer be entitled on the basis of the earlier trade mark either to apply for a declaration that the later trade mark is invalid or to oppose the use of the later trade mark in respect of the goods or services for which the later trade mark has been used, unless registration of the later trade mark was applied for in bad faith.

2   Any Member State may provide that paragraph 1 shall apply *mutatis mutandis* to the proprietor of an earlier trade mark referred to in Article 4(4)(a) or another earlier right referred to in Article 4(4)(b) or (c).

3   In the cases referred to in paragraphs 1 and 2, the proprietor of a later registered trade mark shall not be entitled to oppose the use of the earlier right, even though that right may no longer be invoked against the later trade mark.

Article 10

Use of trade marks

1   If, within a period of five years following the date of the completion of the registration procedure, the proprietor has not put the trade mark to genuine use in the Member State in connection with the goods or services in respect of which it is registered, or if such use has been suspended during an uninterrupted period of five years, the trade mark shall be subject to the sanctions provided for in this Directive, unless there are proper reasons for non-use.

2   The following shall also constitute use within the meaning of paragraph 1:

(a) use of the trade mark in a form differing in elements which do not alter the distinctive character of the mark in the form in which it was registered;

(b) affixing of the trade mark to goods or to the packaging thereof in the Member State concerned solely for export purposes.

3   Use of the trade mark with the consent of the proprietor or by any person who has authority to use a collective mark or a guarantee or certification mark shall be deemed to constitute use by the proprietor.

4   In relation to trade marks registered before the date on which the provisions necessary to comply with this Directive enter into force in the Member State concerned:

(a) where a provision in force prior to that date attaches sanctions to non-use of a trade mark during an uninterrupted period, the relevant period of five years mentioned in paragraph 1 shall be deemed to have begun to run at the same time as any period of non-use which is already running at that date;

(b) where there is no-use provision in force prior to that date, the periods of five years mentioned in paragraph 1 shall be deemed to run from that date at the earliest.

Article 11

Sanctions for non-use of a trade mark in legal or administrative proceedings

1   A trade mark may not be declared invalid on the ground that there is an earlier conflicting trade mark if the latter does not fulfil the requirements of use set out in Article 10(1), (2) and (3) or in Article 10(4), as the case may be.

2   Any Member State may provide that registration of a trade mark may not be refused on the ground that there is an earlier conflicting trade mark if the latter does not fulfil the requirements of use set out in Article 10(1), (2) and (3) or in Article 10(4), as the case may be.

3   Without prejudice to the application of Article 12, where a counter-claim for revocation is made, any Member State may provide that a trade mark may not be successfully invoked in infringement proceedings if it is established as a result of a plea that the trade mark could be revoked pursuant to Article 12(1).

4   If the earlier trade mark has been used in relation to part only of the goods or services for which it is registered, it shall, for purposes of applying paragraphs 1, 2 and 3, be deemed to be registered in respect only of that part of the goods or services.

Article 12

Grounds for revocation

1   A trade mark shall be liable to revocation if, within a continuous period of five years, it has not been put to genuine use in the Member State in connection with the goods or services in respect of which it is registered, and there are no proper reasons for non-use; however, no person may claim that the proprietor's rights in a trade mark should be revoked where, during the interval between expiry of the five-year period and filing of the application for revocation, genuine use of the trade mark has been started or resumed; the commencement or resumption of use within a period of three months preceding the filing of the application for revocation which began at the earliest on expiry of the continuous period of five years of non-use, shall, however, be disregarded where preparations for the commencement or resumption occur only after the proprietor becomes aware that the application for revocation may be filed.

2   A trade mark shall also be liable to revocation if, after the date on which it was registered,

(a) in consequence of acts or inactivity of the proprietor, it has become the common name in the trade for a product or service in respect of which it is registered;

(b) in consequence of the use made of it by the proprietor of the trade mark or with his consent in respect of the goods or services for which it is registered, it is liable to mislead the public, particularly as to the nature, quality or geographical origin of those goods or services.

Article 13

Grounds for refusal or revocation or invalidity relating to only some of the goods or services
Where grounds for refusal of registration or for revocation or invalidity of a trade mark exist in respect of only some of the goods or services for which that trade mark has been applied for or registered, refusal of registration or revocation or invalidity shall cover those goods or services only.

Article 14

Establishment *a posteriori* of invalidity or revocation of a trade mark
Where the seniority of an earlier trade mark which has been surrendered or allowed to lapse, is claimed for a Community trade mark, the invalidity or revocation of the earlier trade mark may be established *a posteriori*.

Article 15

Special provisions in respect of collective marks, guarantee marks and certification marks
1   Without prejudice to Article 4, Member States whose laws authorise the registration of collective marks or of guarantee or certification marks may provide that such marks shall not be registered, or shall be revoked or declared invalid, on grounds additional to those specified in Articles 3 and 12 where the function of those marks so requires.

2   By way of derogation from Article 3(1)(c), Member States may provide that signs or indications which may serve, in trade, to designate the geographical origin of the goods or services may constitute collective, guarantee or certification marks. Such a mark does not entitle the proprietor to prohibit a third party from using in the course of trade such signs or indications, provided he uses them in accordance with honest practices in industrial or commercial matters; in particular, such a mark may not be invoked against a third party who is entitled to use a geographical name.

Article 16

National provisions to be adopted pursuant to this Directive
1   The Member States shall bring into force the laws, regulations and administrative provisions necessary to comply with this Directive not later than 28 December 1991. They shall immediately inform the Commission thereof.

2   Acting on a proposal from the Commission, the Council, acting by qualified majority, may defer the date referred to in paragraph 1 until 31 December 1992 at the latest.

3   Member States shall communicate to the Commission the text of the main provisions of national law which they adopt in the field governed by this Directive.

Article 17

Addressees

This Directive is addressed to the Member States.

Done at Brussels, 21 December 1988.

INDEX

References are to paragraph numbers.

Abroad   1.34
  see also European Community; Foreign
    International matters
  business carried on outside UK   4.8
  exhaustion principle   4.12
  infringing activities   4.8, 4.9, 4.10
  jurisdictional limits   4.8–4.10
  movement of goods, control of   4.12
  parallel rights   4.10
  Paris Convention countries, see Paris
    Convention; Well-known
    mark
  use of sign, and acquisition of
    distinctiveness   2.24, 5.12
Accessories   8.11
Account of profits   7.40, 11.13
Acquiescence
  concurrent user of mark, by, and
    registration   5.25, 8.11
  passing off action defence   3.19
Additional indicia, use of   6.3, 7.21
Address
  service, for, and registration   5.1
  use of own   4.7, 8.11
Advertising   1.30, 1.31
  comparison, use for   1.31, 7.13–7.15,
    see also Comparative advertising
  distinctive feature, of, and whether trade
    mark   2.16
  function of mark, as   1.11, 1.12
  influence on interpretation of mark
    1.7
  misleading   7.13, 7.15
  printer's liability for infringement
    7.34, 7.35
  subliminal   2.5
  suitability for   2.17
  technique for, maturing into trade mark
    2.18
  use of mark in   1.30, 1.31
Advocaat case   3.7, 3.10
Agencies, enforcement   1.16
Agent   1.8, 3.28
  communications with privileged   3.28

employment by solicitor   3.29
local, for international marks   14.6
mark wrongly registered with, restraint
  of use of   7.39
registered trade mark agent, unjustified
  representation as, offence   3.29
Agreement
  see Licence, assignment
  restricting trade mark use   4.14, 4.15,
    see also Restraint of trade
Amendment of mark during application
  5.20, 12.7
Anton Piller order   7.41
Appeal
  refusal to register, against   5.42
  revocation, against   9.19
Appearance, see Packaging; Shape
Appellations of origin
  see Geographical origin; Certification
    mark
Application for registration, see
  Registration
Arbitration   7.2, 14.22
Assignment   1.30, 3.24, 5.27,
  11.1–11.23
  advertisement of   11.7, 11.8
  application to register, of   11.3
  assignee, position of   11.11, 11.12
  certification mark, of   11.20, 12.13
  collective mark, of   11.19
  common law, at   3.24, 11.1
  Community trade mark, of
    13.14–13.17
  defects in title, and   11.8, 11.11
  equitable interests in mark, and
    11.11
  form for   11.15
  formalities   11.10–11.13
  goodwill, of
    effect   11.1, 11.5
    mark with   3.24, 11.1, 11.5, 11.6
    mark without   3.24, 11.7–11.9
    part only   11.6
  'in gross', effect   11.1
  jointly owned marks   11.17, 11.18
  registered mark   11.1–11.23

Assignment – (*contd.*)
  registered mark – (*contd.*)
    goodwill, with   3.24, 11.1, 11.5,
      11.6
    goodwill, without   3.24, 11.7–11.9
    registration   11.13
    retained marks   11.5
    right of priority, of   11.21
    stamping   11.12
    territory   11.8, 11.10
    transitional provisions   11.23
    unregistered mark   11.1, 11.5, 11.9
    writing, requirement for   11.4
Association, likelihood of   5.28, 5.33,
    5.19
  see also Confusion
  Benelux law, concept stemming from
    7.24, 7.26
  distinguished from confusion
    7.24–7.26
Association (organisation)
  retailers, of   1.33, 4.14, *see also*
    Collective mark
Attorney, trade mark   3.28
Australia   14.18

Bad faith
  cancellation for   9.4
  Community trade mark, and   13.6
  concurrent use, and   5.25
  registration application made in   5.1,
    5.9, 9.10
  well-known mark used in   12.25
Benelux countries
  confusion concept, from law in   7.24,
    7.26
  mark registered in, as 'earlier trade
    mark'   13.6
  registration method   14.2
Bona fide   5.1, *see also* Bad faith; Honest
    practices
Brand name   1.1, 1.8
British Standards   1.32, 4.14, 10.17,
    12.7, 12.8
Business
  see also Goodwill; Trade connection
  cessation of   3.12
  format franchise   12.8
  non-business use   1.35

severance, on assignment of part of
    goodwill   11.6
  use in course of   4.2, 4.3, 7.6
Business name   1.21–1.24

Cablecasting   2.17
Canada   14.18
Cancellation of registration   9.1–9.20,
    see also Invalidity, declaration of;
    Revocation
Categorisation of marks   2.36
Certification mark   1.25, 1.32,
    12.1–12.4, 12.7–12.18
  assignment   11.20, 12.13
  fees   12.11
  general criteria applying   12.9
  geographical origin, indicating   12.3
  infringement   12.14
    breach of statutory duty, misuse as
      12.18
    user's loss   12.15
    who can sue   12.15
  invalidity   12.17
  meaning   12.2
  passing off action to protect   12.4
  proprietor not to supply goods   12.10
  publication and opposition   12.12
  quality indicated   12.8
  registration of   1.32, 5.50, 12.4, 12.12
    refusal of   12.9
  revocation, grounds for   12.16
  special conditions for   12.9
  transfer or transmission of   11.20
  transmission   12.13
  use of, authorised   10.1, 12.10, 12.15
    regulations governing use   12.10,
      12.12
Channel Islands   5.3
Character merchandising   10.4
Charge on mark   11.22
Chartered Institute of Patent Agents
    3.28
Choice of mark   2.36
Chose in action   11.4
Classification of goods and services
    1.17, 1.19, 5.2
Coca-Cola
  bottle shape
    not registrable under 1938 Act
      2.7, 2.8, 2.15
    passing off action   3.9

Coined mark   2.36
Collective mark   1.32, 1.33, 12.1–12.5,
    12.19–12.23
  amendment during registration process
    12.20, 12.22
  assignment   11.19
  Community   12.2
  competition law, compliance with
    12.23
  definition   12.19
  fees   12.22
  infringement, right to sue for   12.24
  misuse   12.21
  origin, indicating   12.1, 12.3, 12.20
  Paris Union, and   12.5
  prohibitions applying   12.20
  publication and opposition   12.22
  quality standards   12.1
  registration of   1.33, 5.50, 12.1,
    12.19, 12.22
    mode of   12.21
    trading, and   12.20
  transfer of   11.19
  use of, authorised   10.1, 12.21
    amendment to regulations   12.22
    regulations for use   12.21, 12.22
Collective purchasing organisation
    12.1
Colour   2.2, 2.3, 2.9
  colour depletion theory (US)   2.9
  passing off action   3.9
Commencement, *see* Transitional
    provisions
Common use, sign in   4.5
  common to trade   5.12
Community trade mark   5.35, 5.40,
    13.5–13.17
  appeal   13.11
  applicant for
    choice of route   13.17
    who may be   13.6
  application   13.7–13.10
  assignment   13.14–13.17
    registration of   13.14, 13.16
  bankruptcy proceedings, effect on
    13.15
  collective mark   12.2, 13.6
  comparative advertising, and   7.15

conversion into national trade mark
    application   13.6
courts for   13.12
dictionary use   13.6
differences from Directive   13.6
evidence   13.10
fees   13.7, 13.17
history of   13.1
interaction with national filing
    13.8
invalidity ground   13.6
jointly owned   13.15
language for application   13.7,
    13.17
licences   13.13–13.17
  exclusive or non-exclusive   13.13
  grant of   13.13
  registration of   13.16
nature of   13.6, 13.15
non-use, and   9.13
Office for Harmonisation in the Internal
    Market   13.5, 13.7–13.11
opposition to   13.6, 13.9
priority, claiming   13.8
proprietor's right when uses agent
    13.6
proprietary status and location of
    13.15
refusal of registration, grounds   13.6,
    13.10
register search   13.9
registration, block to   13.6
scope of Regulation   13.5
transfer of undertaking, and   13.14
Community trade mark courts   13.12
Company
  corporate veil   4.12
Company name   1.21, 1.22, 1.24
  trade mark as part of   1.24
  use of, defence to infringement   6.10,
    8.11
Company officer, liability of   7.53
Comparative advertising   1.31,
    7.13–7.15
  justification   7.14
  use in relation to proprietor's goods
    7.36, 7.37, 8.11
  use other than honest, restraining
    1.37

Comparison
  Registry, by
    for infringement   7.18–7.26, *see also*
      Infringement
    for registration   5.28–5.34, *see also*
      Registration of mark
Compensation   7.51, *see also* Damages
Competition
  European restrictions   4.11, 4.15,
    8.13, 13.20–13.25
    block exemptions   10.19
    licence, effect on   10.19
    see also Free movement of goods
  licence, impact of laws on
    10.19–10.21
  national law, and exploitation of rights
    4.11
  restraint of trade doctrine, and   4.13,
    see also Restraint of trade
  unfair   3.22
Competitor   1.8, 1.13, *see also*
    Competition; Comparative
    advertising
Compound or composite mark   2.14,
  5.23
Computer
  register kept on   2.19
Concurrent right to use mark
  passing off, and   3.18, 4.5
  registration of mark, and   5.25, 5.26
    bad faith   5.25
    concurrent registration   8.11
    criteria for   5.26
Conditions   5.23
Confidentiality
  see also Privilege
  documents filed, of   5.15
Confusion
  evidence of   5.14
  infringement of registered trade mark
    3.23, 7.18–7.26
  passing off action   3.5, 3.6, 3.14
  registration of mark
    concurrent user, and   5.26
    similar mark, test of   5.28–5.31
    similar mark and product, interaction
      5.32, 5.33
  similarity of marks and products,
    interaction of   7.22
  survey, use of to find   5.13, 5.14, 7.23

  test of, for infringement   7.22–7.26
    relevant public for   7.23
    well-known mark, infringing use of, and
      7.32
Connection with trade, indication of
  1.4–1.7, 1.26
Consent
  earlier mark's proprietor, of, to use
    5.26
  proprietor's, and use of mark   6.6,
    7.6
    goods marketed in EEA   8.11
    lack of   6.6, 7.6, *see also*
      Infringement
    movement of goods, and   4.12
    see also Licence
Consumer
  chain of commercial transaction, in
    1.8
  confusion of, *see* Confusion
  education of, need for   6.13,
    6.14
  effect on   1.9, 1.12
  protection of   1.16, 2.33
Consumers' Association   1.14
Containers, *see* Packaging; Shape
Convention country
  see also Paris Convention; Well-known
    mark
  meaning   7.32
Copy
  'brand'   7.48
Counterfeit goods   7.51, 13.26
  EC measures to restrain   13.26
Country of manufacture, *see* Abroad;
  Origin
Court for proceedings   3.26, 7.1
  Community trade mark courts   13.12
Criminal offences   3.27, 7.46–7.53
  use of mark in relation to goods for
    which registered   7.46–7.48
    defence   7.47, 7.48
    elements of offences   7.47
    liability   7.50–7.52
    penalties   7.50
    triable either way   7.50
Customer
  see also Consumer
  sharing agreement   10.21
Customs and Excise, HM   7.45, 7.49

Damage
  infringement, arising from   4.4
Damages
  infringement, for   7.40
Deceit, tort of   3.5, *see also* Deceptive
    use of mark
Deceptive use of mark
  confusion with other mark leading to
    2.33, *see also* Confusion
  connection with Royal Family, etc,
    suggested   2.34
  history of control of   3.1–3.4
  guarding against   6.12
  objection to registration, as, overcoming
    5.11, 5.19
  revocation for   6.2, 9.5, 9.17
  quality not controlled, where   10.15,
    10.16, *see also* Quality
Declaration of invalidity, *see* Invalidity,
    declaration of
Defective goods   3.25, 10.1
Defence
  infringement, to   4.7, 8.1–8.13
    concurrent user   8.11
    confusion not caused, proving   8.9,
      see also Confusion
    deceptiveness   8.9, *see also*
      Deceptive use of mark
    disclaimer, coming within   8.11
    generic sign   8.9, *see also* Generic
      use
    genuine goods or services   8.11
    innocence, effect of   8.11
    invalidity of mark   8.12, *see also*
      Invalidity, declaration of;
      Revocation
    licensee, claim by, whether has
      standing   8.9
    local right   8.11
    non-trade mark use   8.11, *see also*
      Non-trade mark use
    non-use   8.9, *see also* Non-use
    parallel imports   8.11
    registration, attack on   8.9
    settlement   8.13
Defensive registration   12.30
Definition   2.1
Delivery up and destruction of goods
    3.26, 7.2, 7.42, 7.43
  limitation period   7.44

Description
  false, trade   5.37
  same, confusion over   5.30, 5.31
  use of registered mark on goods of same
    6.4
Descriptive mark   2.36
  debarred from registration
    2.26–2.29, 4.5, *see also* Non-
    distinctive sign
Design   2.2
Destruction, *see* Delivery up and
    destruction
Detriment to mark, use which is   7.30,
    7.36, 7.37
  criminal offence   7.46
Development of mark   1.10, 6.3
Device   2.20, 2.27
  passing off action   3.9
Dictionary, reproduction in   2.31, 6.12,
    7.17
Dilution, concept of   5.45, 7.10–7.12
  meaning   7.10
  prejudice to reputation, similar to
    7.30
  US laws   7.11, 7.12, 9.15
Disclaimer   2.13, 2.14, 5.23
  'brand copy', as to   7.48
  defence that activities fall within   8.11
Distinctive nature   1.6, 1.14, 2.22–2.34
  see also Non-distinctive sign
  attrition of, *see* Dilution, concept of
  distinctiveness acquired through use
    2.24, 5.11
    invalidity application, countering
      9.6
  evidence of   5.11–5.15
  losing   6.2, 9.16
  non-distinctive, categories of
    2.23–2.34
Document
  see also Evidence; Forms
  confidentiality   5.15
  records of use of registered mark   6.5
Duration of registration   5.44

Earlier trade mark   5.35–5.38
Effect of mark
  factors influencing   1.7, 1.10, *see also*
    Functions of mark

Emblem   5.4, 7.39
  invalidity declaration   9.9
Entry on Register, *see* Application
Erasure   7.2, 7.42
Esso, extension of range under mark
    5.18
European Commission   1.12, 1.18, 1.36
  Explanatory Memo on the Community
    trade mark   2.3
European Community   13.1–13.26
  see also Community trade mark
  abuse of monopoly   4.11
  attitude to national trade marks
    13.18–13.25, *see also* Free
    movement of goods
  Directive, First Council, on trade marks
    harmonisation   1.2, 1.36, 3.3,
    4.6, App 3
    implementation   13.3
    proposals for and history of   13.1
    scope   13.2
    use under licence   10.1, *see also*
      Licence
  'earlier mark', as   5.35
  enforcement of rights in   13.3
  free movement of goods, *see* Free
    movement of goods
  languages, official, of Office   13.5
  mark registered in member State, and
    Community trade mark
    registration   13.6
  restrictive trade practices   4.11, 4.15,
    8.13
  unitary system of protection   1.2
European Court of Justice   13.3, 13.5,
    14.21
European Economic Area
  see also European Community
  free movement provisions extend to
    13.25
  goods arriving from outside, etc   7.45
  parallel imports from   8.11
European Union
  see also European Community
  role in GATT and TRIPS   14.21
  unfair competition law   3.22
Evidence
  opposition to registration, by opponent
    and applicant   5.40
  registration hearing, at   5.9,

    5.10–5.16, *see also* Objection to
      registration, countering
Exploitation of registered mark by use
    6.1–6.14
  additional indicia, use with   6.3, 7.21
  adjectival use   6.14
  basic rules for use   6.14
  consent of proprietor to use   6.6
  development, new registration
    application required   6.3
  education of consumers and customers,
    need for   6.13
  failure to use on goods and services
    6.4
  'genuine commercial use'   6.9, 9.12
  generic use, avoiding   6.10, 6.12
  goods and services, scope of use on
    6.4, 6.8
  licensor's consent to sub-licence   6.6
  non-use, *see* Non-use
  problems arising   6.11, 6.12
  records, need for   6.5
  significance of proper use   6.2
  single instance of use   6.9
  trade mark, need for use as   6.10
  'use', meaning   6.7, 6.8
  use as registered, need for   6.3
Export of goods   4.12, 6.7, 13.23
  see also Free movement of goods
  infringing use, may be   7.33

False trade description   5.37, 7.51, 10.1
  certification mark, and   12.18
Falsehood, injurious or malicious   3.20,
    3.21, 7.11
  malice, meaning of   3.21
  protection of earlier unregistered mark
    by   5.37
Falsification of the Register   7.52
Fanciful mark   2.36
Faulty goods   1.8
Fictional character
  association with   1.9
  merchandising of   10.4
First-to-file versus first-to-use   14.2
Flag, use of   2.34, 7.39
Foreign plaintiff   4.8, 5.12, 12.6, *see also*
    Abroad
Foreign word, use of   2.27, 2.29, 5.7

Forfeiture order   3.27, 7.51
Form
    mark, of, use of   7.33, *see also* Shape
Forms
    assignment   11.15
    invalidity application, for   9.19
    licence registration, agreement for
        10.18
    registration   5.1, 5.40, 5.49
    revocation, for   9.19
    surrender, for   9.18
    transmission, for   11.15
France   13.3, 14.2
Franchise agreement   4.15, 10.4, 10.5
    business format franchise   12.8
Free movement of goods   4.11, 13.1,
        13.18–13.25
    counterfeit goods, and   13.26
    cross supplies   13.21
    EEA, in   7.45, 13.25
    European Community competition
        rules, and   13.18–13.25
        dominant position, forms of abuse of
            13.22
        restrictive trade practices, decisions
            on   13.20, 13.21
    field-of-use restrictions   13.21
    import and export restrictions   13.23
    national trade mark
        effect of rights, ECJ ruling   13.20
        use to prevent   13.19
    opposition procedure used oppressively,
        effect   13.22
    repackaging bans   13.21
Freedom of trade   4.1, 4.11–4.15, *see
        also* Restraint of trade
Functions of mark   1.4, 1.11–1.16
    categories of   1.11
    EC Commission's reference to   1.12
    origin, *see* Origin
    protection of   1.15, 1.16
    publicity, *see* Advertising
    quality, *see* Quality

GATT   14.21, 14.22
Generic use   1.7, 2.31
    avoiding   6.10, 6.12
    non-trade mark use as   7.17
    revocation of registration for   9.15
Geneva   14.11

'Genuine' use   6.9, 9.12
Geographical limits   4.8–4.10
    defence where local right to use   8.11
    registration, in   5.24
Geographical origin   1.25, 1.32
    certification mark indicating   12.2
    word descriptive of   2.26
        acquiring significance through
            changes   9.8
Germany   4.10, 12.31, 13.3, *see also*
        European Community
Get-up   3.9, *see also* Passing off action
Goods
    classes of   1.17, 5.2
    registration of mark for   1.17, 1.18
Goodwill
    build up of   1.10
    damage to   3.6, *see also* Passing off
        action
    geographical limits   4.8
    transfer of   11.1, 11.5, *see also*
        Assignment
Graphic representation
    need for   2.1, 2.4, 2.19, 5.1
    non-graphic use   6.7, 7.33
    size of   2.20, 5.1
    use of sign otherwise than as   6.7,
        7.33
Groundless threats of infringement
    proceedings   3.25, 8.3–8.8
Guarantee function   1.13, 1.25, 1.26, *see
        also* Origin
Guarantee mark   1.32, 12.2, *see also*
        Certification mark
Guild system   3.1, 3.4

Hearing   5.9, 5.40
Hearing officer   5.40
High Court
    infringement proceedings in   3.26,
        7.1
Honest practices   7.36, 8.11
    use of mark in comparative advertising,
        and need for   1.37

Identical mark
    phonetically identical   7.20
    registration, refusal of
        absolute objection   5.28
        relative objection   5.27, 7.18
    use of   7.20, *see also* Infringement

Imitations   7.14, *see also* Similar mark
Imports   6.7, 7.45, 13.23
  see also Free movement of goods
  infringing use, may be   7.33
  parallel   8.11
  prevention of by exercise of trade mark
    rights
    cases when not permissible   13.23
    cases when permissible   13.24
Inappropriate sign   2.35
Information, mark as   1.1, 1.7
Infringement   3.23, 7.1 *et seq*
  action for, combined with other action
    7.38
  acts which amount to   4.3, 6.7, 7.6,
    7.33
  additional indicia, use of   7.21
  avoiding by search of register   3.25
  civil proceedings for   3.26
  collective mark, of   12.24
  commencement of new provisions
    5.46, 7.3
  comparison, tests for   7.18–7.26
    confusion and association
      distinguished   7.24–7.26
    Table   7.19
  confusion, *see* Confusion
  consent of proprietor, act done without
    6.6, 7.6
  criminal sanctions   7.46–7.53, *see also*
    Criminal offences
  damage
    causing   4.4
    proof not required   7.1, 7.20
  defending proceedings   4.7, 8.1–8.13
    challenge to registration   8.9
    settlement   8.13
    substantive defences   8.11
    see also Defence
  exemption where proprietor's goods or
    services   7.36, 8.11
  identical mark   7.20
  injunction for   4.4, 7.41
  licensing, and, *see* Licensee
  limitation period   8.11
  manner of   7.33–7.35
  non-visual use   7.33
  old law on   7.3–7.5, 7.10
  printing of labels, stationery, etc
    7.34, 7.35

remedies   7.40–7.45
reputation, of mark with   7.27–7.30
  detriment to distinctive character or
    repute of mark   7.30
  unfair advantage to defendant
    7.29
  use 'without due cause'   7.28
similar mark   7.22
trade, in the course of   7.6–7.8, 7.20
  use in other trade   7.7, 7.8
transitional provisions   7.54, 7.55
unjustified threat of proceedings
    3.25, 8.3–8.8
  notification of registration   8.7, 8.8
  remedy   8.3
  when action not available   8.5
use for which mark registered   7.7,
    7.8, 7.18
well-known mark in UK, of   7.31,
    7.32
Injunction
  actions for   7.38, 7.39
  infringement of registered trade mark,
    for   4.4, 7.41
  passing off, for   3.18, 3.19, 4.9
  qualified   4.7
  unjustified threat of proceedings, to
    restrain   8.3
Injurious falsehood, *see* Falsehood,
    injurious or malicious
Insolvency
  assignment, effect on   11.15
  licensee, of   10.18
Institute of Trade Mark Agents   3.28,
    see also Agent
Integral mark   2.7
Intellectual property law
  influence of EC law   13.1, *see also*
    European Community
Interference with contract   3.23
Interlocutory injunction   7.41
  licensee seeking   10.9
  tactics for defendant   8.10
International matters   14.1 *et seq*
  agent, use of   14.6
  classification of marks   14.2
  direct registration   14.7
  elements of registration systems   14.4
  exhaustion principle   4.12
  protection internationally   14.7
  recognition of mark   1.34

regional systems   14.7
registration internationally   14.7,
   14.10, 14.17, *see also* Madrid
   Arrangement; Madrid Protocol
International symbol
connection with, suggestion of   2.34
Invalidity, declaration of   5.27, 7.39,
   9.4, 9.6–9.11
   certification mark, for   12.17
   effect of   9.4, 9.20
   form for   9.19
   grounds of   9.6
      deceptive at date of application
         9.7
      incapable of graphic representation
         9.6
      legal prohibition on use   9.7
      not distinctive   9.6
      prohibited shape   9.7
      public order or morality   9.7, 9.8
      similarity, etc, with earlier mark
         9.11
      use on some goods for which
         registered only   9.14
   procedure   9.19
Ireland, delay in implementing Directive
   13.3
Italy   13.3

Japan   12.31, 14.18
Jingle   2.4
Jif lemon case   3.7–3.9, *see also* Passing
   off action
Jointly owned mark   11.17, 11.18
   Community trade mark   13.15
Jurisdictional limits   4.1, 4.8–4.10
   Community trade mark courts   13.12
   'double actionability' rule   4.8
   exclusive jurisdiction of UK courts,
      circumstances   4.10

Kite mark   1.32, 12.7

Label
   printer as party to infringement   7.35
Language
   official

Community trade mark application,
   for   13.7, 13.17
Madrid Arrangement, for application
   under   14.11
Madrid Protocol, for application
   under   14.17
Laudatory word(s)   2.26
Legislation, history of   3.1–3.3, 3.6
   Table   3.3
Letters   2.2, 2.25; *see also* Threats
Liability
   civil, *see* Infringement
   criminal, *see* Criminal offences
Licence
   breach of   10.6, 10.8, 10.18, *see also*
      Licensee
   categories   10.4
   character merchandising   10.4
   common law, effect at   10.2, 10.3
   Community trade mark, of
      13.13–13.17
   competition laws, and   10.19–10.21
   compromise of litigation, reached in
      10.19
   consideration   10.18
   customer sharing restrictions   10.21
   duration   10.18
   exclusive   10.8
   field-of-use restrictions   10.21
   form of   10.7
   franchise, as   10.4, 10.5
   general   10.11
   grant of   10.1–10.21
   insolvency   10.18
   limited   10.11–10.14
      use, as to manner of   10.13, 10.14,
         10.19
   manner of use   10.13, 10.14
   non-exclusive   10.8, 10.9
   quality control   10.15–10.17
   proprietor in breach   10.8
   quality control   10.15–10.17
      carrying out   10.16
      need for   10.15
      standards   10.17
   registration of   4.14, 10.7, 10.10,
      10.18
      delay, effect of   10.10
      systems worldwide for   14.5
   sole   10.8, 10.9

Licence – (*contd.*)
    statutory   10.3 *et seq*
    subcontract, as   10.4
    terms   10.15–10.17, 10.18
    territorial limitations   10.12, 10.20
    types   10.8
    use in relation to proprietor's own goods
        10.4
    use of mark under, colour, size etc
        10.13, 10.14
Licensee   10.7–10.10
    see also Licence
    breach of contract by   10.6
    choice of   10.7
    control of use by, need for   10.1
    infringement action by   7.2, 10.8,
        10.9
        challenging   8.9
        joinder of proprietor   10.9
    infringement action by proprietor
        10.9
    infringement by   10.6
    interlocutory relief   10.9
    registration of interest   9.2, 10.10,
        10.18
    rights of   3.24
Licensor   6.6
Limitation period
    infringement action, for   8.11
    statutory delivery up, for   7.44
Limits to protection   4.1 *et seq*
    extrinsic   4.1, 4.11–4.15, *see also*
        Territorial limits
    intrinsic   4.1, 4.2–4.7
    territorial   4.1, 4.8–4.10, *see also*
        Jurisdictional limits
Limits to registration   5.24
Local right   8.11
Lurpak   12.7, 12.8

Madrid Arrangement   14.7,
        14.10–14.16
    advantages of   14.16
    applicants for registration under
        14.10, 14.11
    'country of origin', definition
        14.10
    application
        filing of   14.11

    language for   14.11
    shopping around for easiest State
        14.10
    base registration   14.10, 14.11
        independence from   14.13,
            14.14
        invalidation of, effect   14.13
    'central attack'   14.13
    international bureau   14.11
    members   14.10
    Register   14.11
    registration of marks under   14.10,
        14.12–14.14
        designated countries   14.15
        period of and renewal   14.14
        refusal, period for   14.12
Madrid Protocol   14.17–14.20
    advantages of   14.19, 14.20
    applications   14.17
        basis for   14.17
        conversion into national applications
            14.17
        language for   14.17
    catering for full examination systems
        14.16
    ratification of   14.18, 14.19
    registration
        duration and renewals   14.17
        refusal of   14.17
Malicious falsehood   3.20, 3.21
    infringement action combined with
        7.38
    malice, meaning of   3.21
    protection of earlier unregistered mark
        by   5.37
Manufacturer   1.8
Mareva injunction   7.41
Mark
    see also Sign
    definition   2.2
    identical, *see* Identical mark
    registration, *see* Registration of mark
    similar, *see* Similar mark
Market survey   5.13, 5.14, 7.23
Marketing
    see also Advertising
    evidence of manner of   5.16
Marques Internationales, Les, publication in
        14.11
Merged registration   5.22

Middleman   1.8
Misdescriptive word   2.30
Misrepresentation, *see* Passing off action
Misuse   6.2
  correction of   6.14
Model numbers   5.17
Monogram   2.25
Monopoly
  trade mark as form of   4.13, *see also*
    Competition
Morality, sign offending   2.35, 5.19, 9.7,
  9.8
  subsequent to registration   9.8
Multiple use   12.1, *see also* Certification
  mark; Collective mark; Licence
Musical notes   2.21
  see also Sound
  jingle   2.4

Name
  see also Company name
  business and company, use of
    1.21–1.24
  geographical   1.25, *see also*
    Geographical origin
  own   3.18, 4.7, 8.11
    company   8.11
  passing off action   3.9
National Consumer Council   1.16
National flag
  restraining use of   2.34, 7.39
Netherlands   4.10, *see also* European
  Community
Nice classification   1.17, 1.19, 5.2
Non-commercial use   1.35
Non-distinctive sign   2.22–2.34
  conflicting with other mark   2.32,
    2.33
  deceptive information as to origin
    2.32–2.34
  descriptive ab initio   2.26
    acquiring distinction through use
      2.26, 2.27, 5.11
    'covert and skilful allusion'   2.28
    foreign word(s)   2.27, 2.29
    quasi-descriptive   2.29
    referring to distinctive feature of
      goods   2.27

distinctive sign becoming descriptive
  2.31
generic   1.7, 2.31
incapable of conveying information
  2.24, 2.25
  acquiring distinction through use
    2.24, 5.11
misdescriptive   2.30
two- and three-letter combinations
  2.25
Non-trade mark use   1.36, 1.37, 4.6,
  7.16, 7.17
  defence to infringement, as   8.11
Non-use   1.15, 6.3, 6.9
  ground for removal from register
    9.12, 9.13
    lack of demand, and   9.13
    marketing constraint, and   9.13
    not genuine commercial use   9.12
    out of use for five year period
      9.12
    proper reasons for   9.13
    resuming use   9.12
Northern Ireland   7.43
Numerals   2.2, 2.25
  passing off action   3.9

OAPI   14.7
OPTICS   2.19
Objection to registration, countering
  5.9–5.27, 5.28
  amendment of application   5.20
  concurrent user, acquiescence to
    5.25, 8.11
  conditions   5.23
  disclaimer   5.23
  division of application   5.22
  earlier registration invoked
    5.17–5.20
  evidence   5.9, 5.10, 5.11–5.16
    marketing, use, etc, of   5.16
    use, of   5.11–5.15
  hearing   5.9, 5.40
  limited registration   5.24
  market survey   5.13, 5.14, 7.23
  mistake of fact or law   5.10
  specification of goods/services,
    amendment to   5.21
Obliteration of mark   7.42

Obscenity laws, offending   2.35
Offences, *see* Criminal offences
Offensive marks   2.35, 5.19, 9.7–9.8
Office for Harmonisation in the Internal
     Market   13.5, 13.7–13.11, *see also*
     Community trade mark
Opposition   5.40
Oral use   7.33
Origin   1.1, 1.11, 1.12, 1.13
   certification of, *see* Certification mark
   change in place or country of
     manufacture, effect   1.28
   collective mark, *see* Collective mark
   common source, as   1.26
   deceptive information as to   2.32
   geographical   1.25, 1.32, *see also*
     Geographical origin
   guarantee of   1.25, 1.26
   link with proprietor, nature of   1.26
   meaning   1.25
Own-brand goods   1.8

Packaging   2.2, 2.8–2.13, 7.33, 7.34
   appearance as trade mark, passing off
     cases   2.11, 2.12
   labels etc, on, printer's liability for
     infringement   7.34, 7.35
   registration, graphic representation for
     2.20
   repackaging bans   13.21
Parallel imports   8.11
Parallel rights   4.10
Paris Convention   14.8, 14.9
   see also International matters; World
     Intellectual Property Organisation
   agreements open to members   14.9,
     14.10–14.20
   collective mark, and   12.5, 11.21
   headquarters of   14.8
   priority date in UK, and application
     under   5.3
   well-known mark, and   12.6, 12.25,
     see also Well-known mark
Patent Office   5.1
   see also Registration of mark
   hearing at   5.9
Partnership
   assignment, transmission of   11.15,
     11.16

   liability of partners for infringement
     7.53
Passing off action   1.17, 1.22, 3.5–3.19
   acquiescence   3.19
   advertiser's use of another's mark
     1.30
   certification mark users, by   12.4
   cessation of business, after   3.12
   'classical trinity' analysis   3.8
   commercial activities, need for   4.2
   comparative advertising, for   7.13
   concurrent right to use mark   3.18,
     4.5
   confusion   3.5, 3.6, 3.14
   damage   3.6–3.8,
     3.15–3.17
   deceit   3.6
   defences   3.18, 3.19
   development from tort of deceit   3.5
   elements of   3.6, 3.7
   estoppel   3.19
   get-up   3.9
   goodwill, damage to   3.6–3.8,
     3.15–3.17
     customer base in UK, need for
     3.11
   infringement action combined with
     7.38
   injunction   3.18, 3.19
   misrepresentation   3.6–3.8, 3.13, 3.14
     actionable   3.14
     confusion of consumer   3.14
     goods emanating from plaintiff
     3.13
     types of, Table   3.13
   own name, use of   3.18
   packaging, and   2.11
   professional or other organisation, by
     3.12
   reputation   3.9–3.12
     damage to   3.15–3.17
     group   3.10
     localised   3.11
Penguin practice   5.21
'Person aggrieved', removal from Register
   by   9.1
Personal property
   registered mark, as   1.30, 3.24, 11.4
Photograph, for registration application
   2.20
Place of manufacture, *see* Origin

Prize or award   12.8
Privilege   3.28
Priority
  assignment of right of   11.21
  Community trade mark   13.8
  date   5.3, 11.21
Professional, etc, organisation
  passing off action by   3.12, 4.2
Prohibited goods   7.45
Promotion   1.30, *see also* Advertising
Proprietor
  actions possible by   7.38, 7.39
  exclusive rights   7.3–7.12
    old law   7.3–7.5, 7.9, 7.10
    use of mark or closely resembling
      mark   7.9
  goods identified as those of   7.36,
    7.37, 8.11
  licensing, and   10.4
  infringement actionable by   7.2, 10.9,
    see also Infringement
  joint   11.17, 11.18
  licensing by, *see* Licence; Licensee
  surrender of registration   5.27, 9.2,
    9.18, 9.20
  well-known mark, of, *see* Well-known
    mark
Public policy   2.35, 5.19, 9.7, 9.8
  mark becoming invalid because of
    9.8
Publicity
  function of mark, as, *see* Advertising
  registered mark, of, *see* Register;
    Registration of mark
Purpose
  word descriptive of   2.26

Quality
  certification mark, signifying   12.8
  change in, and validity of mark   1.28,
    1.29
  collective mark, and   12.1
  customer perception of mark, and
    1.27
  function of mark   1.11–1.13,
    1.27–1.28
    protection of, by registration   1.29
  licence, of goods and services under
    10.15–10.17

  control, person to carry out   10.16
  standards of   10.17
  word descriptive of   2.26

Radio   2.4, 2.17
Records
  use of registered mark, of   6.5
Red Cross
  sign suggesting connection with   2.34
Register
  computerised   2.19
  division into parts, abolition of   5.45
  error in, rectification application
    9.19
  European Community   13.9
  falsification of, offence   7.52
  form of   2.19
  history of   3.2
  new, transfer to   5.46
  removal from   5.44, 6.2, 9.1, *see also*
    Invalidity, declaration of;
    Revocation
  restoration   5.44
  search of, *see* Search of Register
Registered trade mark agent, use of term
  3.29, *see also* Agent
Registration
  assignment, of   11.13
  licence, of   4.14, 10.7, 10.10, 10.18
    delay, effect of   10.10
  mark, of, *see* Registration of mark
Registration of mark   1.15, 1.17–1.20,
  3.23–3.25, 5.1 *et seq*
  advantages of
    customers and others, for   3.25
    plaintiff, for   3.23, 3.24
  appeal against refusal   5.42
  application   5.1–5.6
    abandoned, treated as   5.5
    acceptance   5.40
    amendment of mark during   5.20,
      12.7
    assignment of   11.3
    bad faith, made in   5.9, 9.10
    co-pending   5.37
    defective   5.5
    division or splitting of   5.22
    examination of, systems providing for
      14.3, 14.16

Registration of mark – (*contd.*)
  application – (*contd.*)
    form for   5.1
    merger of   5.22
    nature of   11.3
    pending, transitional provisions
      5.47
    procedure   5.8
    void   5.5
  bar to   2.26, 6.12, *see also* Non-
    distinctive sign, and 'prohibition'
    below
  cancellation   9.1–9.20, 14.3, 14.5, *see*
    also Invalidity, declaration of;
    Revocation
  certification mark   1.32
  chemical formula, by   2.20
  classification method   1.17, 1.19, 5.2
  collective mark   1.33
  Community trade mark, interaction
    with registration of   13.8
  compound mark   2.14, 5.23
  concurrent user
    both registered   8.11
    where is   5.25
  consent, when needed   5.4
  criteria   5.1–5.6
  date   5.6
  deposit systems   14.3
  development of mark   1.10, 6.3
  distinctive, capability of being, and
    2.22–2.34
  drawing, photograph, or unfolded 'net',
    for   2.20
  earlier mark, conflict with   2.33,
    5.28–5.39
    date at which assessed   5.34
    duration of earlier mark   5.36
    examples   5.38
    meaning of 'earlier trade mark'
      5.35
    other rights protected   5.37
    reputation, unfair advantage of
      5.34
    unregistered earlier mark   5.37
  effect of   11.2, 11.4
  entering on register   2.19
  European Community, harmonisation
    of procedure in   13.4
  evidence   5.9–5.16, 5.40

  examination   14.2, 14.3, 14.16
  extension of range of goods or services
    5.18
  false representation of   7.52
  fee   5.1
  filing date   5.6
  first-to-file or first-to-use methods
    14.2
    change for UK under 1994 Act
      14.2
  forms   5.1, 5.40, 5.49
  graphic representation, *see* Graphic
    representation, need for
  hearing   5.9, *see also* Objection to
    registration, countering
  history of   3.2
  identical mark
    absolute objection   5.28
    relative objection   5.27, 7.18
  infringement proceedings   3.26, *see*
    also Infringement
  joint names, in   11.17, 11.18
  limited   5.24
  merger of   5.22
  need for   1.22
  object of   1.12
  objections   5.9, 5.28, 5.40
    extrinsic   5.9, 5.28
    inherent in mark   5.9
    relative   5.27–5.38, 7.18
    see also Objection to registration,
      countering
  opposition to   5.40, 5.41, 14.4
    counter-statement by applicant
      5.40
    evidence   5.40
    form for   5.40
  period of   5.44, 5.46
  priority   5.3
    assignment of right of   11.21
    Community trade mark, and   13.8
  process   1.8, 5.7, 5.8
  prohibition   2.8–2.13, 5.1, 5.28
    absolute   5.9, 5.28
    'exclusively'   2.13
    voluntary disclaimer, use of   2.13
    see also Objection to registration,
      countering
  proprietary nature of registered mark
    1.30, 3.24, 11.4

publication   14.4
refusal, *see* 'bar' and 'prohibition' above
relative grounds for objection
    5.27–5.38, 7.18
removal from   5.44, 6.2, 9.1–9.4, *see
    also* Invalidity, declaration of;
    Revocation
renewal   5.44
    failure, as means of surrender   9.3 ·
    period for   9.3
    systems for, worldwide   14.5
repellant, acting as   3.24
restoration   9.20
revocation, *see* Revocation
search, *see* Search of Register
services, of, *see* Services
similar mark   5.28
    already registered by applicant
        5.17
    confusion, test of   5.28, 5.29
    same description   5.30, 5.31
    services and goods, confusion
        between   5.32, 5.33
sound, of   2.20, 2.21
specification amendment   5.21
stay of Registry proceedings   5.43
surrender, *see* Surrender of mark
systems of, worldwide   14.1 *et seq, see
    also* Community trade mark;
    International matters
    classification   14.2
    elements of   14.4
use of mark   4.3, 6.2, *see also*
    Exploitation of registered mark by
    use; Use of mark
UK system   14.2, 14.3, 14.16
variants   5.17
Registry
    consumer protection, and   2.33
    creation of general   3.2
    district office in Manchester   3.3
Remedies   7.2, 7.40–7.45, *see also*
    Infringement; Injunction
Removal from Register   5.44, 6.2,
    9.1–9.4, *see also* Invalidity, declaration
    of; Revocation
Removal of mark   7.42
Renewal of registration   5.44
    failure, as means of surrender   9.3
    period for   9.3

Representation, graphic, for registration
    2.20, 5.1
    need for   2.1, 2.4, 2.19, 5.1
Reputation   3.9
    see also Passing off action
    earlier mark with, and refusal to register
        5.34
    infringement of mark having
        7.27–7.30, *see also* Infringement
Restoration of mark   9.20
Restraint of trade   4.11–4.15
    common law doctrine   4.13
    Europe, in   4.12, 13.20–13.25, *see also*
        Competition law
    licences, and   4.14, 4.15
    registration of agreements   4.14
Restrictive Trade Practices Court,
    reference to   4.15
Retail service mark   1.18, 1.23, *see also*
    Services
Retailer   1.8
    group of   1.32
Revocation   1.15, 4.3, 5.27, 9.5,
    9.12–9.17
    appeal   9.19
    application for, in addition to invalidity
        application   9.12
    certification mark, additional grounds
        12.16
    counter-statement   9.19
    effect of   9.5, 9.20
    forms for   9.19
    grounds for   6.2, 9.12–9.17
        deceptive use   9.17
        distinctive nature, and   9.16
        generic, mark becoming   9.15
        misleading public   9.17
        non-use   9.12, 9.13, *see also*
            Non-use
        use on some goods only   9.14
    hearing, rules   9.19
    partial   9.14
    procedure   9.19
Royal Arms   5.4
Royal Family
    sign suggesting connection with   2.34

Scent
    see also Smell

Scent – (*contd.*)
　registration of　2.4, 2.20
Scotland　3.24, 3.26, 7.1, 7.43
　forfeiture order　7.51
　registered mark, nature of　11.4
Search of register
　Community trade mark application, on
　　13.9
　need for　2.37, 3.24, 3.25
　Registry staff, by　2.33, 5.8, 5.34,
　　14.4
Second-hand goods　8.11
Sensory use　2.2, 7.33
Service, address for　5.1
Services
　classes of　1.17, 5.2
　complaint on　1.8
　registration of mark for　1.17–1.20,
　　2.2, 3.3
　　certification mark　1.32
　　introduction of　1.17
　　similar to existing mark　5.28–5.33
　　systems for　14.5
Settlement　8.13
Shape　2.2, 2.4, 2.7
　infringing use of　7.33
　passing off action　3.9
　prohibition on registration　2.8–2.13
　　giving substantial value to goods
　　　2.10–2.13, 2.15
　　necessary to obtain a technical result
　　　2.9
　　resulting from goods themselves
　　　2.8
　registration, graphic representation for
　　2.20
Sheffield Register　3.2
Sign　2.1, 2.8
　see also Name; Numerals; Words, etc
　non-distinctive, *see* Non-distinctive sign
　when acting as a mark　1.37
Similar mark
　infringement by use of　7.19, 7.22
　invalidity declaration for　9.11
　registration of mark, and　5.28
　　already registered by applicant
　　　5.17
　　confusion, test of　5.28, 5.29
　　same description　5.30, 5.31

　services and goods, confusion
　　between　5.32, 5.33
Similarity of product, need for　4.4
Slander of goods　3.20
Slogan　2.18
Smell　2.3, 2.4, 2.15
　registration of　2.20
Solicitor
　trade mark work　3.29
Sound　2.2, 2.3, 2.4, 2.15
　broadcasting, *see* Radio
　non-distinctive　2.24
　registration of　2.20, 2.21
Spain　13.3, 13.5
　Community trade mark registration,
　　default State　13.15
　ratification of Madrid Protocol
　　14.18
　Spanish Community Trade Mark Court
　　13.12
Spare parts　8.11
Specification
　amendment to　5.21
Stationery
　printer's liability for infringement
　　7.34, 7.35
Statutes, *see* Legislation
Stay of Registry proceedings　5.43
Stilton　12.7
Subliminal advertising　2.5
Suggestive mark　2.36
Suitability of mark　2.6
　advertising medium, for　2.17
Supplier
　asking for name of, whether threat
　　8.7
Surrender of registration　5.27, 9.2,
　　9.18
　date for　9.20
　form for　9.18
　partial　9.18
　procedure for　9.18
Survey evidence　5.13, 5.14, 7.23
Symbol for (registered) trade mark, use of
　　6.14

TRIMS　2.19

TRIPS agreement   12.28, 12.29,
    14.21
  Dunkel draft   14.21
  European Union and UK conformity
    with   14.21
Tactile mark   2.4, *see also* Shape
  registration of   2.20
Taste   2.3, 2.4, 2.15
  registration of   2.20
Teletext   2.17
Television   2.17
Term of registration   5.44
Territorial limits   4.1, 4.8–4.10
  assignment, in   11.8
  control of movement by mark's
    proprietor   4.12
  licence agreement, in   10.12
Textile marks   3.3
Threat of proceedings for infringement
    3.25, 8.3–8.8
  notification of registration   8.7, 8.8
  remedy   8.3
  when action not available   8.5
Time of production or rendering
    services
  descriptive word or phrase   2.26
Torts   3.20, 3.21, 3.23
  see also Passing off action
Trade
  definition   4.3
  'in course of'   4.2, 4.3, 7.6
  interference with   3.23
  organisation not involved in, *see*
    Professional, etc, organisation
Trade association, *see* Association
    (organisation)
Trade connection   1.4–1.7, 1.26
Trade description, false   5.37
  certification mark   12.18
Trade dress, *see* Get-up
Trade mark agent, *see* Agent
Trade mark attorney, use of term   3.28
Trade libel   3.20
Trader   1.8
  plaintiff and defendant both are   4.4
Trading standards officer, powers   7.49
Trafficking   10.5
Transfer   11.8
  see also Assignment
  Community trade mark, of   13.14
Transitional provisions   5.45–5.49, 7.3

assignment, on   11.23
conversion of application to new Act
    5.47, 5.48
infringement, on   7.54, 7.55
non-infringing use prior to
    commencement, defence   8.11
Translation   5.7, 14.6
  languages for Community trade mark
    13.7, 13.17
Transmission   1.30, 11.8, 11.14, 11.15
  certification mark, of   12.13
  form for   11.15
Typeface, use of different   6.14

Undertaking   4.3, 12.19
  transfer of, effect on Community trade
    mark   13.14
Unfair advantage, taking   7.29, 7.36,
    7.36
  criminal offence, as   7.46
Unfair competition   3.22, *see also*
    Competition
United States of America   14.2, 14.18
Unjustified threats of infringement
    proceedings   3.25, 8.3
Unlawful interference with trade   3.23
Unregistered mark
  assignment of   11.1, 11.5, 11.9
  protection of   3.2, 3.6, 5.37, *see also*
    Passing off action
Uruguay round of GATT   14.21, 14.22
Use of mark
  see also Exploitation of registered mark
    by use; Functions of mark
  commercial transaction, in   1.1, 1.8,
    1.9, 1.11
    when trade mark use   1.23
  comparison, for, *see* Comparative
    advertising
  deceptive, *see* Deceptive use of mark
  definition   2.2
  evidence of   5.11–5.15
  'genuine commercial'   6.9, 9.12
  infringing use   6.7, 7.1 *et seq*, *see also*
    Infringement
  meaning   6.7
  misuse, *see* Misuse
  multiple   12.1, *see also* Certification
    mark; Collective mark; Licence
  non-commercial   1.35

Use of mark – *(contd.)*
   non-trade mark use   1.36, 1.37, 4.6
      defence to infringement   8.11
      infringement, when is   1.37, 7.16
   non-use   1.15, 6.3, 6.9, 9.12
   sensory   2.2, 7.33
   significance of proper use   6.2
   registered mark   6.1 *et seq*
      exploitation by use   6.1–6.14, *see
         also* Exploitation of registered
         mark by use
      proprietor's rights, *see* Proprietor
      use as registered, need for   6.3
   registration, and   4.3, 6.2
   restricted   2.35

Value
   word descriptive of   2.26
Variants   5.17
Video cassette
   trade mark encoded electronically
      6.7

Well-known mark   1.32, 1.34, 7.31,
      7.32, 12.6, 12.23–12.31
   acquiescence to use   12.27
   bad faith, used in   12.25
   cancellation   12.25
   definition   12.27, 12.31
   degrees of awareness, and   12.31
   'earlier trade mark', as   5.35

non-similar goods and services, use on
      12.28
   Paris Union, and   12.6, 12.25
   protection of   12.25, 12.28
   registration   12.29
      defensive, abandonment of   12.30
   rights of owner   12.27
White Paper, Reform of Trade Mark Law
      1.2, 2.3, 2.22, 7.27, 10.1
   advertisement requirements for
      assignment   11.7
Wholesaler   1.8
Will, disposal of mark by   1.30, 11.8,
      11.14
WIPO, *see* World Intellectual Property
      Organisation
Wool-mark   1.32
Words   2.2, 2.20
   see also Non-distinctive sign
   comparison of, test for confusion
      5.28, 5.29
   foreign, *see* Foreign word, use of
   passing off action   3.9
World Intellectual Property Organisation
      1.19, 7.2
   administration of Paris Convention
      14.8
   arbitration centre   14.22
   relationship with World Trade
      Organisation   14.22
   Trademark Law Treaty   13.4, 14.1
World Trade Organisation   14.22